# THE
# BONFIRE

# THE
# BONFIRE

## THE SIEGE AND BURNING
## OF ATLANTA

### MARC WORTMAN

PUBLICAFFAIRS
*New York*

Published in the United States by PublicAffairs™,
a member of the Perseus Books Group.

PublicAffairs books are available at special discounts for bulk purchases in the U.S. by corporations, institutions, and other organizations. For more information, please contact the Special Markets Department at the Perseus Books Group, 2300 Chestnut Street, Suite 200, Philadelphia, PA 19103, call (800) 810-4145, ext. 5000, or e-mail special.markets@perseusbooks.com.

Designed by Pauline Brown
Text set in 11-point Caslon

Library of Congress Cataloging-in-Publication Data

Wortman, Marc (Marc Josef)
    The bonfire : the siege and burning of Atlanta / Marc Wortman.—1st ed.
        p.  cm.
    Includes bibliographical references and index.
        ISBN 978-1-58648-482-8 (hardcover : alk. paper) 1. Atlanta Campaign, 1864. 2. Atlanta (Ga.)—History, Military—19th century. 3. Sieges—Georgia—Atlanta—History—19th century. 4. Fires—Georgia—Atlanta—History—19th century. 5. Atlanta (Ga.)—Social conditions—19th century. 6. Civil-military relations—Georgia—Atlanta—History—19th century. 7. City and town life—Georgia—Atlanta—History—19th century. 8. United States—History—Civil War, 1861– 1865—Social aspects. I. Title.
    E476.7.W67 2009
    973.7'36—dc22

                                                                    2009021108

First Edition

10 9 8 7 6 5 4 3 2 1

FOR JODI, REBECCA,
AND CHARLIE

*Haven't you heard, though,*

*About the ships where war has found them out*

*At sea, about the towns where war has come*

*Through opening clouds at night with droning speed*

*Further o'erhead than all but stars and angels,—*

*And children in the ships and in the towns?*

*Haven't you heard what we have lived to learn?*

*Nothing so new—something we had forgotten:*

War is for everyone, for children too.

*I wasn't going to tell you and I mustn't.*

*The best way is to come uphill with me*

*And have our fire and laugh and be afraid.*

      —ROBERT FROST, "THE BONFIRE"

# CONTENTS

CONTENTS

## V: THE THIEF IN THE GLOAMING

## VI: WAR IS CRUELTY, AND YOU CANNOT REFINE IT

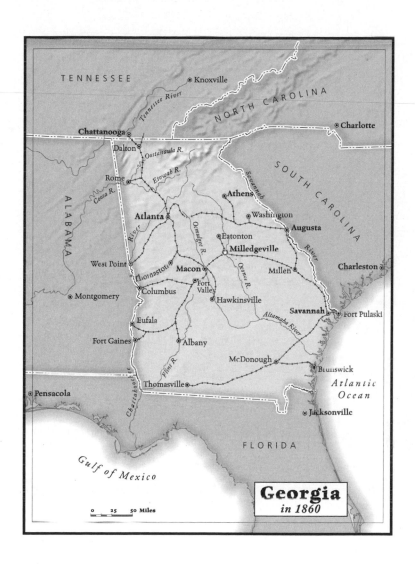

**Georgia**
*in 1860*

0 25 50 Miles

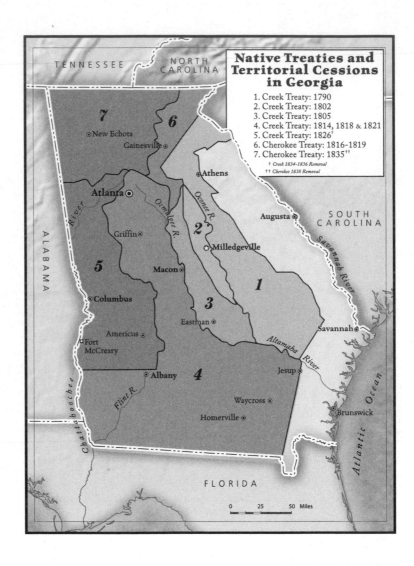

Native Treaties and Territorial Cessions in Georgia

1. Creek Treaty: 1790
2. Creek Treaty: 1802
3. Creek Treaty: 1805
4. Creek Treaty: 1814, 1818 & 1821
5. Creek Treaty: 1826[†]
6. Cherokee Treaty: 1816-1819
7. Cherokee Treaty: 1835[††]

† *Creek 1834–1836 Removal*
†† *Cherokee 1838 Removal*

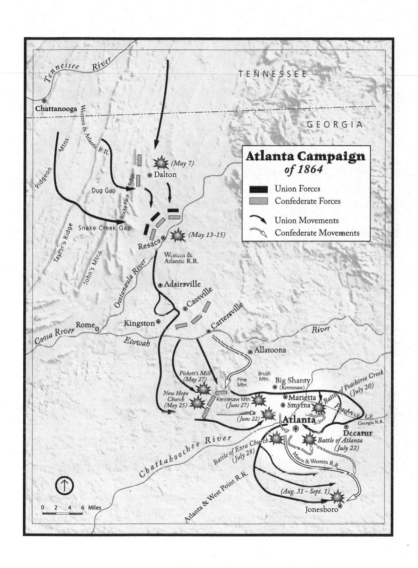

Tennessee River

TENNESSEE

Chattanooga

GEORGIA

Western & Atlantic R.R.

Pidgeon Mtns.

Taylr's Ridge

John's Mtns.

Dug Gap

Rocky Face Ridge

(May 7)

Dalton

Snake Creek Gap

Resaca

(May 13–15)

**Atlanta Campaign**
*of 1864*

Union Forces
Confederate Forces
Union Movements
Confederate Movements

Oostanaula River

Western &
Atlantic R.R.

Adairsville

Cassville

Consa River

Rome

Kingston

Cartersville

River

Etowah

Allatoona

Pickett's Mill
(May 27)

Pine
Mtn.

Brush
Mtn.

Big Shanty
(Kennesaw)

Battle of Peachtree Creek
(July 20)

New Hope
Church
(May 25)

Kennesaw Mtn.
(June 27)

Marietta

Smyrna

Peachtree

Cr.

(June 22)

**Atlanta**

Georgia R.R.

**Decatur**

Battle of Atlanta
(July 22)

Chattahoochee River

Battle of Ezra Church
(July 28)

Macon & Western R.R.

Atlanta & West Point R.R.

(Aug. 31 – Sept. 1)

Jonesboro

0  2  4  6 Miles

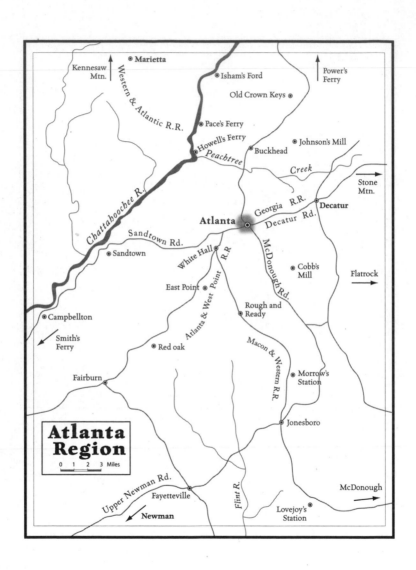

## Atlanta Defenses

0   ½   1 Mile

Chattahoochee R.

Buckhead

Howell's Ferry

Howell's Mills

Peachtree Cr.

S. Fork Peachtree Cr.

Battle of Peach Tree Cr.
(July 20, 1864)

Collier Mill

Mt. Zion Church

Western & Atlantic R.R.

Shoal Cr.

Peachtree St.

Jones Mill

Proctors Cr.

Clear Cr.

Bethel Church

Fort
Hood

Lewis Mill

Battle of Ezra Church
(July 28, 1864)

Marietta St.

Decatur

Cliffton

Ezra
Church

Atlanta

Georgia R.R.

Five Points

Decatur St.

Sugar Cr.

Whitehall St.

Battle of Atlanta
(July 22, 1864)

Utoy Cr.

White Hall

McDonough Rd.

Heron Mill

Atlanta & West Point R.R.
Macon & Western R.R.

Harper

Entrenchment Cr.

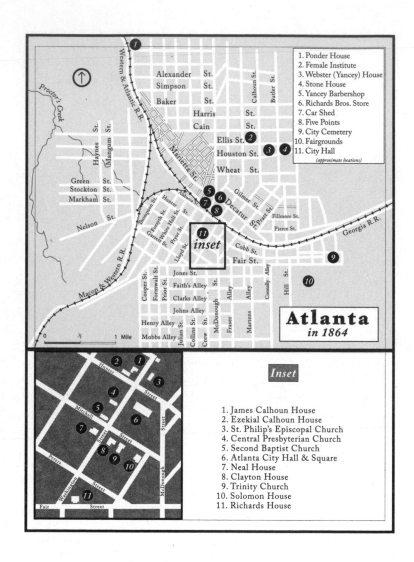

Atlanta
*in 1864*

1. Ponder House
2. Female Institute
3. Webster (Yancey) House
4. Stone House
5. Yancey Barbershop
6. Richards Bros. Store
7. Car Shed
8. Five Points
9. City Cemetery
10. Fairgrounds
11. City Hall
*(approximate locations)*

Inset

1. James Calhoun House
2. Ezekial Calhoun House
3. St. Philip's Episcopal Church
4. Central Presbyterian Church
5. Second Baptist Church
6. Atlanta City Hall & Square
7. Neal House
8. Clayton House
9. Trinity Church
10. Solomon House
11. Richards House

0    ½    1 Mile

# INTRODUCTION

CIVIL WAR ATLANTA has been wreathed in legends. Made into the poignant epitome of the defeated South, Atlanta as portrayed was filled with tragic defeated Southern heroes with nary a single solitary sympathizer for the Union or for Lincoln. The city's black inhabitants appear as passive spectators in a war fought in part over their freedom. Then, there are what may be the two most famous quotations associated with the entire Civil War, both supposedly spoken in Atlanta. Both of them were invented. "Frankly, my dear, I don't give a damn," Rhett Butler's line of seventy years ago, still ranks as the most memorable ever uttered on the screen. The other is credited to Gen. William Tecumseh Sherman as he put the torch to Atlanta 145 years ago: "War is hell." In fact, he probably never said these words, and if he did, he certainly didn't while in Atlanta. The story of Atlanta is more than misplaced one-liners or the saturated colors of melodrama.

Sherman did write something far more cold-eyed and to the point when the mayor of the Lower South's most important Confederate city appealed to the Union army commander to take pity on his already destitute and battered citizens and rescind his order expelling them from their homes. Sherman answered him, "War is cruelty, and you cannot refine it." End the war, and the cruelty would end. We have sanitized modern war in ways that allow us to ignore what Sherman knew. We forget his words time and again at our peril.

The cruelty the Union armies inflicted upon the Gate City, along with Ulysses S. Grant's attempt to batter down the defenses of Richmond, became the great object of worldwide attention throughout

1

the summer of 1864. However, that cruelty, too, has become mythologized. Sherman was charged with torching Atlanta, conducting a war without restraint upon civilians. His "statesmanship" by military means has since been used as a justification for the modern practice of total war. In fact, he is unjustly charged with being solely responsible for the city's devastation. Two monumental bonfires engulfed Atlanta, the first set off by its defenders, the second by its invaders. The people of the United States and the would-be Confederacy played with fire and ignited a conflagration they could not control. Once the nation went to war with itself, "you might as well appeal to the thunderstorm as against these terrible hardships," Sherman insisted.

War is cruelty. Its bloodshed and destruction—the "hard hand of war," as Sherman really did call it—struck Atlanta with a greater ferocity than it has any American city in history. This is the story of how Atlanta and its people came to be in the direct line of the whirlwind, what one of the besieged city's Confederate defenders called "a grand holocaust of death."

## I

# FRONTIER

AND ALL SWAY FORWARD on the dangerous flood
Of history, that never sleeps or dies,
And, held one moment, burns the hand.
—W. H. AUDEN, "XXX"

# CHAPTER 1

# FLAGS

THEY STIRRED EARLY. Climbing out of their cellars and bomb-proofs, the sheltering people looked up as if surprised to see the sun return. As if a sign of the world's sudden transformation, the sun they gazed up at looked different from those that had come before; it pulsed blood red, suffusing the dense, smoky sky with an unearthly crimson glow. Cinder and ash peppered the late-summer air.

A reeking sulfurous stew that stung the eyes had already settled over the town, filling the railroad cuts, hollows, and streets. Its tendrils wavered along the hillsides and ravines and sifted through the blackened skeletons of what once were houses and factories, railcars and machine shops. It was the silence, though, that shocked people most. Three predawn hours of gut-rattling, earsplitting, and window-shattering explosions and gunfire made the previous night feel like the announcement that the Apocalypse had finally come. But the infernal noise had ended shortly before the morning's light tipped into the eyes of those hunkered down within the earth.

Slowly, tentatively, they stepped out into the dawn. Here and there, heads poked above the ground, one by one like mushroom tops. White and black, all filthy and stricken, the bone-weary women, children, and old men, straggling soldiers and rearguard cavalry began making their way tentatively toward the center of Atlanta. It was the morning of September 2, 1864.

"I HAVE NEVER SEEN the city more quiet," said Thomas Kile. The Atlanta shopkeeper and fireman watched the people begin to gather at the Five Points. He and his fellow fire company members had watched helplessly through the night as the exploding bonfire set off by the fleeing Confederate army flattened the Georgia Railroad's roundhouse, obliterating five locomotives and an eighty-one-car-long line of munitions-packed freight wagons, together with the parallel quarter mile of trackside brick depots and scores of neighboring homes. Yankee and rebel soldiers and officers more than twenty miles away watched the glow on the horizon from the ensuing firestorm; thousands of Atlantan refugees in Macon nearly eighty-five miles away heard the thunder of the explosions. A big chunk of their city was simply gone. Not even a crow flapped over the smoldering ruins.

At least while they were under fire, the people had known where the enemy was and understood his intentions clearly. But suddenly they were suspended between two great armies, one a closing fist, massive and unyielding in its grip on the city's throat, the other a rapier, bent and broken, yet still lethal, lashing out desperately from point to point to bloody the invader's death grip enough to make him yield.

Gen. William Tecumseh Sherman hunched with his 85,000-man Union army somewhere in woods and fields out past the seven miles of surrounding earthworks, waiting to conclude their violent task. "Whether . . . inside Atlanta or not," proclaimed the commander of the southern U.S. Army, the largest and most ferocious fighting force ever assembled other than commanding general Ulysses S. Grant's own Army of the Potomac, "it will be a used-up community when we are done with it." He had yet to capture his great prize, but he was right. "The hard hand of war," in his apt metaphor, had indeed smashed up Atlanta, squeezing and crushing it with greater fury than any ever unleashed on an American city before.

Knowing nothing of their fate except the news brought into town on the rushing waves of opposing rumors and smuggled newspapers, the city's survivors proceeded to the dead center of a vast continental storm. Two days before, word had gone out of a great Confederate victory on the city's outskirts; the previous night, nearly the entire corps left within the city marched away. Would the small remaining cavalry force make a final stand? Would their Yankee foes, in their lust for Southern blood, loot, and women, charge into the city, leveling everything and killing everyone in their path?

The people of Atlanta were perfectly alone, though the eyes of both American nations, the United and the Confederate States, indeed the whole world, watched closely as their final fate played out. President Abraham Lincoln in the Washington Executive Mansion and his Richmond counterpart, Jefferson Davis, hovered near their telegraph operators, waiting for word. They understood, too, that their fate, no less than that of the people of Atlanta, depended on the siege's outcome. They watched for the greatest urban fight in American history and the climatic battle of the war to reach an end.

"NO MOB," KILE SAID of the people searching each other out after the cataclysmic night. "All appeared to be quiet and decent and no disorder, whatever."

By ten that morning, five hundred people stood in clutches and individually about the Five Points, the city's central square where the great thoroughfares of Peachtree, Decatur, Marietta, Whitehall, and Cherokee streets met and where the four rail lines converged, making Atlanta the one, crucial city of the lower South. The battered brick, stone, and wood walls of the buildings that lined the square, businesses bursting with commercial energy until just days before the Yankees arrived on the city's outskirts, now threatened to topple. The vaulting roof of the car shed across the square, terminus for the trains that even a few days before still moved through town at all hours of the day and night and powered a small frontier crossroads into the center of the world's attention, covered a vacant silence.

The hoof clatter of Mayor James Montgomery Calhoun's horse rattled the emptiness. He carried a white flag from a pole behind him. He was soon joined by eight other men who circled their mounts at the corner of Marietta and Peachtree streets.

One turned to Calhoun. "Shall we go armed?" the man asked. He brandished four six-shooters.

Calhoun's thick chin beard had gone snow white, and exhaustion had eaten up his melancholy and narrow face. The mayor looked older than his fifty-three years. He rose up in his saddle. No guns, he insisted. "Our white flag will be our best protection," he said.

He had taken another step to protect the party, clearer in its way than any flag of surrender in this would-be Southern nation. Calhoun was cousin to John Caldwell Calhoun. The U.S. senator, two-time vice president, and would-be American president from South Carolina, dead now nearly fifteen years, had set the stage for the rebellion with his famously unbending promotion of the states' right to set their own course within the Union. Now his far younger cousin, mayor of the Gate City of the South, the indispensable railroad hub of the Confederacy, had done what would have been unimaginable even the day before. He asked Bob Yancey to ride out with them to meet the Yankee army.

Yancey, too, claimed kinship to a once nationally powerful politician, also a U.S. senator and presidential aspirant. Gone almost as long as Calhoun, Daniel Webster, the Cast-Iron Man's Puritan nemesis from Massachusetts, formed with him two of the three corners—together with Kentucky's "Great Compromiser," Henry Clay—of a triangle of heroic political orators, the "Great Triumvirate." They had dominated the now-failed civic debate for most of the first half of the century over just what type of nation America should be—or if it would continue to be one nation at all.

Yancey's possible blood ties to the "Defender of the Constitution and the Union," buried more than a thousand miles away in the North, would not, however, deflect a single jumpy, trigger-happy Northern marksman's bullet from the riders' heads. What mattered was Yancey's skin color. It was black. Yancey was a slave. Though by rights neither man nor citizen, Yancey would ride out together with a group of the Citadel of the Confederacy's leading white citizens, slaveholders among them. He would meet their city's besiegers as the other men's equal, perhaps their savior, on a short journey to determine Atlanta's fate.

THEY RODE WARILY ALONG, Calhoun leading the way northwest out the Marietta Road. They guided the nervous horses through the scattered bricks, shell fragments, and downed trees, past the many shattered houses and charred outbuildings along the dusty clay road running parallel with the Western & Atlantic Railroad cut. Cantering up a steady incline toward the city's perimeter, they reached the suburban fringes of town, where they emerged from the shade of the trees hanging over the road into the barren, sun-raked, fought-over land. Barely a tree and few structures of any kind remained standing for as far as the eye could see. Here they passed the wreckage of the once graceful Ponder family estate, twenty-five hilltop acres of boxwood gardens and orchards where the residents caught the cooling breezes and enjoyed the view from an observation deck atop the stout yet stately plastered stone mansion. The house's windows made for ideal sharpshooter's nests. Yankee artillery had blasted away ceaselessly at the house until it seemed a miracle that the remains continued to stand at all.

Just in front of the Ponder house, the massive earthworks ran past like a thick, livid scar demarcating the edge of their island city. The horses stepped around the obstacles and beyond the sandbagged trenches, through the palisades and tangle of tree branches and trunks. Here and there a spiked canon stood mute and useless. They entered the half mile of denuded killing ground that for nearly two months had spanned the distance between the warring armies.

Tens of thousands of young men who had never heard of Atlanta before had come from farms, towns, and cities across the land. They came willing to kill or die for possession of the city. The humps of hastily dug graves and bleaching bones showed where many of them had done just that. The bloated and blackened corpses of dogs and horses brought down alongside their masters lay willy-nilly in grotesque poses where they, too, had come to violent ends on the shell-plowed slopes. The fouled air smelled of death combined with the rotting debris and human and animal waste left behind by the thousands who, until the day before, had lived for six weeks within the trenches. Calhoun's party covered their faces against the evil stench and waved away the clouds of bluebottle flies. The nickering horses tossed their heads and tails against the swarms. No birds called. Even the vultures had long ago fled.

Leaving the ruins of Atlanta behind them, the men simply did not know what lay beyond the city's bristling frontier. Calhoun glanced back at the beloved hometown he had worked so hard to preserve from such a reckoning.

# CHAPTER 2

# VIRGINIANS

JAMES CALHOUN TURNED FIFTEEN just about the time his father, known as Farmer Billy to one and all, died in 1827. His death left a whiskerless boy as the oldest male on a farm that could barely support his family. Their red-dirt plot of cotton fields and grassy pastures lay near the Savannah River, in the Upstate South Carolina county of Abbeville. The Calhoun farm was one of many smaller ones that had been sliced out of a series of four far larger land grants made to the four Scotch-Irish Calhoun brothers, James's grandfather and great-uncles, in Colonial days. They had carved out what became a growing community of family farms known as the Calhoun Settlement from the rolling wilderness hills and fens cut here and there by ancient Indian trails along South Carolina's border with her sister colony, Georgia. Several Calhoun Settlement farmers enjoyed a good deal of success over the decades and managed to expand their landholdings, purchase slaves to plant and harvest the cotton, and, with the profits, send their sons off the farm for an education.

By the time Farmer Billy passed on, though, a glut of Upstate cotton had depressed the market and its growers' profits. The federal Tariff of 1824, which raised import duties to 33.3 percent, brought retaliation against American exports that further undercut the local farmers and depressed the entire South's economy. The region's farmers shared the blame for weighing the region down. The once dark loam underfoot, a creamy black matter able to nurture virtually anything planted within it when the Calhoun brothers arrived, had gone stale and dusty through overfarming. The used-up earth ran now like red sand between a man's fingers and could no longer sustain the kind of intensive cash crop farming that had once enriched the Calhoun families and others in the settlement. For a young man like James, left to work the inhospitable land, a farmer's future pressed on his heart like the canvas bags of low-value cotton hanging off the shoulders of the slaves in the fields. The life of a backcountry planter held little allure for him in any case.

Less than two years later, his mother, Rebecca, followed her husband to the grave. That set James free. He determined to act on his conviction that something better awaited him out there, off the farm. He would go west into the Georgia frontier.

BUT IF JAMES HOPED to find a new and better life than he had so far led on the family farm, he knew the path toward his future also carried him back to a harsher past, a time of terrible tragedy indelibly etched in the memory of every Calhoun. The family's pioneering history placed them at the heart of conflicts between white settlers and native tribes, whose country the whites had long sought to claim.

FOR GOING-ON THREE CENTURIES nearly unbroken, European settlers in the American Southeast and one or more of the region's many Indian tribes had been at each other's throats. The violence between white and red started at the very beginning, when the Spaniard Hernando de Soto first explored the region for the queen of Spain in the early 1540s, passing through what would one day be Georgia and South Carolina. His conquistador army laid waste to numerous Indian villages, some dating back more than a thousand years. The arrival of the English brought waves of new emigrants, who quickly plunged inland, hungry for land to farm away from the teeming coastal cities, and established lowland plantations.

While the Spanish, French, and British vied for control of the New World, native tribes entered into a series of shifting alliances with the white nations. Despite the occasional conflicts over the upcountry land between the newcomers and the native Cherokee, Indian and white traders out of Charleston carried on a lucrative fur trade. Following their deeply rutted trading roads, settlers arrived to homestead on Indian hunting and fishing grounds under the protection of the British garrison at nearby Fort Augusta in Georgia. It was not far from there, in February 1756, that the earliest Calhouns arrived. James, William, Ezekiel, and Patrick Calhoun, four brothers still speaking in the brogue of their native Donegal County, Ireland, moved from the Old Dominion, where they had been farmers and road builders, to more than a thousand well-drained acres of loam, loosely rooted cane towering up to twenty feet high, and tangles of pea vines, which brother Patrick had surveyed for them along the western bank of Long Cane Creek. That tributary fed the Little River and from there flowed to the broad Savannah River running between South Carolina and Georgia to the ocean.

The brothers brought the large extended Calhoun clan with them, including a sister, their young wives, multitudinous children, and their seventy-two-year-old mother, Catherine. This would be the last in her life's long series of perilous journeys. Born in Scotland, she had been driven to Ireland as part of a forced migration by the British Crown to establish a Protestant presence within the belligerent Catholic land. From that unhappy place, she crossed the Atlantic to farm a tract in Pennsylvania before uprooting for Virginia. Now, she hoped to find a permanent home awaiting her in this rich, fertile Southern land.

The Calhouns and other Virginians coming into the Carolina and Georgia piedmont frontier came to Long Cane not just for its fertile wilderness. They came for peace. The area seemed a safe haven from the violence pressing in on their former home. The war between the French and English raging in Ohio, western Pennsylvania, and elsewhere in the upper colonies put all Northern frontier settlements at risk of sudden, brutal attack—by French armies and by their Indian allies. Every mile they jostled about in their wagons bouncing southwards, they believed, would carry them farther away from war and deeper into safety.

They were wrong. War followed hard on their heels. These Virginians could not have chosen a worse moment to accept the promise of the Southern frontier.

The French and Indian conflict with the English and their own native proxy armies followed the Calhoun party southward. As a sideshow to the far greater global war, later known as the Seven Years' War, between the English and French nations and their European allies, the ongoing collision between the natives and the new settlers in traditional Cherokee hunting grounds—as local a skirmish as could be imagined—played right into the needs of the European world powers and the vanity of a petty territorial ruler.

THE RICH UNDULATING LAND that the Calhouns rode into along Long Cane Creek lay within the canebrake that gave the region its name. By the time they had constructed their new log houses and cleared enough acreage to begin producing crops, friction flared into the threat of violence between British and Cherokee warriors—formerly allies against the French. Minor skirmishes raised fears of full-scale conflict. South Carolina's royal governor, William Henry Lyttelton, anticipated the worst, a Cherokee alliance with France. He was also a pompous martinet keen for military glory. He sent his troops out to make a preemptive strike on the natives. The heavily armed infantry torched several Cherokee villages in the up-country. When the Redcoats marched out, nothing living remained in their wake. Native rage at the attacks sparked the very alliance with the French Lyttelton had feared.

The Indians retaliated, attacking isolated frontier settlements and murdering their residents, often leaving the bodies horribly mutilated and sometimes stealing away women and children. The royal governor's infantry forces answered barbarity in kind, sweeping through more native villages. With atrocities mounting on both sides, settlers in the Abbeville district lived in constant fear, kept armed guards posted, and demanded that the royal forces protect them.

ALMOST PRECISELY FOUR YEARS after the first Calhoun families arrived, the alarm rang out from farm to farm through the settlement. Cherokee in war paint were seen crossing the Savannah River. On February 1, 1760, the settlement families collected their valuables and set off in fright in a train of heavily laden wagons south on the old Cherokee trading road for the safety of the fortified village of Augusta, Georgia: 110 settlement family members, mainly women and children, rode and walked alongside the wagons under the watchful guard of forty musket-toting militiamen from Fort Augusta.

Just a few hours after the wagon train embarked, its wheels bogged down in the cane-shrouded mud lane. The men stowed their muskets and put their shoulders to freeing the wagons bellied into the muck.

The traveling settlers should not have been surprised when the attack came—but they were. They had no chance to repel it. One hundred whooping, war-painted Cherokee horsemen swooped in on the crowd of men, women, and many children milling about the wagons. The warriors swung their sharpened tomahawks and fired their English-made muskets.

The militiamen who didn't fall in the first volley ran for their weapons, but few reached them before warriors were swinging axes and slashing knives in their midst. The whites ran screaming in terror into the surrounding canebrake and forest. The raiding party chased down women fleeing with their children. In half an hour, the blood-letting was over.

When it ended, twenty-three of the Long Cane settlers lay dead in the muddy road—some versions of the story say as many as fifty—women and children in the main, "most inhumanely butchered," reported Charleston's *South Carolina Gazette* based on eyewitness accounts a few days later. Not only were there the dead; the Cherokee men spirited seventeen women and children away with them. Before their escape, the native raiders plundered and incinerated the wagons and set the surrounding canebrake on fire to flush out those who had cached themselves within the reedy fastness.

WILLIAM CALHOUN, FUTURE GRANDFATHER of the wandering James, eventually reached the safety of Augusta. A few days later, he returned to the Long Cane attack site. He found the scalped remains of his mother, the Calhoun matriarch Catherine. She lay dead along with her mutilated son James and James's wife. William searched the surrounding woods, fearing more losses, and his horror was not ended. Not only had the Indians brutally murdered his family members, but two of his own daughters and a niece, Rebecca, were among the missing. He finally found her, but there was no trace of his own girls, though the searchers came across large numbers of children wandering in shock through the canebrake, "some of them terribly cut with tomahawks and left for dead, and others scalp'd, yet alive."

Not having found his daughters on his first return to the massacre site, two weeks later he joined with a militia company to track the missing and seek revenge for the massacre. The Cherokee, though, found the search party first. In the ensuing fight, a musket ball tore through William's hand. He was more fortunate than the regiment's leader, Ulric Tobler. The Indians scalped him and "left a Hatchet sticking in his Neck on which were three old Notches and three newly cut." So it was that the Calhouns first spilled their blood contesting the land of Georgia.

—◦—

15

THE LONG CANE ATTACK SEEMED to spend the native and white fury in South Carolina. Lyttelton's failure to contain the violence and his self-aggrandizing tactics soon brought him reassignment. With his departure and the end of the French and Indian War, the British reached an accord in 1763 with the Cherokee and other Indian nations. The Crown's negotiators laid the groundwork for several years of peace by discouraging further Colonial incursions beyond the Appalachians, a council of several Indian tribes having ceded all claim to the fertile piedmont region of the Carolinas and Georgia in return for native control of the land beyond the Ogeechee River. The Calhouns and the other up-country settlers enjoyed a period of relative tranquility with their native neighbors.

Although the fight for the Calhoun Settlement died away, the surviving Calhouns did not forget that terrifying day's violence or the many other tragedies that befell their kinfolk in their confrontation with the Indians. One of the surviving brothers, Patrick, placed a stone marker to memorialize the Long Cane massacre. Generations of Calhoun children and grandchildren were almost certainly directed to pay their respects there.

They and others passing by on their journey west toward the next frontier saw its blunt inscription: "In memory of Mrs. Catherine Calhoun aged 76 years who with 22 others was here murdered by the Indians the first of Feb 1760." For the generations who came to know the story of the terrible human price paid for the conquest of the land, the words would gnaw like an aching hunger, a goad to greater conquest and a boundless hole in their gut.


THOUGH LASTING JUST A few short years, the resolution of the Indian-English boundary dispute enabled thousands more settlers to flood the region. The frontier families took advantage of the peace to build out their farms and expand their crops, first mainly tobacco to go with their subsistence needs. The surviving Calhoun brothers gradually built thriving farms for which they acquired slaves—Patrick eventually owned thirty-one. That left them with relatively moderate wealth compared to the large coastal plantation owners, whose slaves numbered in the hundreds, but they were still among the richest in the up-country. The advent of Eli Whitney's cotton gin in the early 1800s suddenly made it possible to grow the more valuable cash crop beyond the coastal plains. Piedmont farming became far more profitable. Northern and English mills took as much cotton as they could produce. More and more farmers acquired slaves, and many of the Virginians soon enjoyed luxuries formerly available only to the great planters they once worked for—including fortune-building steps like sending their most promising sons off the land for their educations.

Liberty from some of the daily toil of farm life brought by cotton profits and slaves also permitted another family tradition to commence, public service. John C. Calhoun's father, Patrick, was the first of the family to serve in the Colonial legislature. When the colonies rebelled against the British, he, like most frontiersmen of the age, sided with the rebellion. Independence offered the swelling populace the likeliest way to further its advance into the frontier. For the colonists, the prospect of independence meant new land for settlement and access to the lucrative fur trade, now governed by a Crown monopoly. The wealthy Tory planters of the coast shared the royal governor's opposition to further incursions into the frontier, which could only disrupt the valuable fur trade and create more Indian troubles for the island empire, which already had many far-flung problems on its hands.

Patrick won a seat in the newly formed Provincial Congress in 1775. In the next and glorious year of 1776, he became a member of the freshly independent state's first general assembly. He would be re-elected continuously until his death in 1796, by which time he was known as "the patriarch of the upper country" and widely revered as South Carolina's most powerful legislator—that is, until his son's incomparable rise to political power.


JOHN C. CALHOUN, PATRICK'S AMBITIOUS son, had not been much older than James was when he left the Calhoun Settlement for Yale College in New Haven. After graduating, he had continued on to law school in Litchfield, Connecticut, and from there, the spellbinding orator and ingenious political philosopher began his meteoric rise to the very pinnacle of national power, where he helped rule an entire nation feeling its way to the greatness of its land's promise. The teenaged James barely recalled his few meetings in the settlement with his forty-seven-year-old cousin, who was now the nation's seventh vice president, the first born in the United States and not in a colony under British rule.

He was also the lower South's preeminent spokesman and, many believed, the man destined to become the nation's next president. He was one political leader whose words in defense of the lower states'

17

minority in Washington had the power to break the fragile union in two—or keep it from splitting asunder. A nationalist, but one who believed that protecting sectional rights was the only way to keep the union of the states intact, he had emerged as the philosophical voice for the individual states' ultimate power to nullify federal laws they considered unconstitutional. A state had a veto power that, he declared, enabled its confederation with the others into a national whole. In particular, his present fame as a so-called nullifier rested on his opposition to what he called the "Tariff of Abominations," enacted the previous year, 1828.

That bill designed by a Northern and Western (when the West still reached only to the banks of the Mississippi River) majority in Congress to protect their emerging industries' manufactured goods had raised duties on raw materials to fully 50 percent. The tariff threatened already hard-hit Southern planters, dependent on fields of cotton and their millions of slaves, with ruin. It also raised the specter of Northern abolitionists' using the protectionist levers of federal power to undermine the South's "peculiar institution," its centuries-long heritage of eternal human bondage based on race, the muscle and backbone of its agrarian economy.

As vice president under President Andrew Jackson, the populist centralizer of national power, Calhoun anonymously penned a pamphlet urging his home state to refuse to collect the import duties, defining what he saw as a first principle of the Union in the rights of any state to veto a law its own constitutional convention deemed unconstitutional. He even went so far as to suggest that states might consider seceding from the young union should a congressional majority unfairly impose its will to overreach constitutional limits on its authority. "The despotism founded on combined geographical interest," Calhoun wrote to Virginia's senator Littleton Walker Tazewell, "admits of but one effectual remedy, a veto on the part of the local interest, or under our system, on the part of the states." This, he implied, applied equally to any attempt to legislate against Southerners' right to own slaves, bring their slaves wherever they chose within their country, and protect their property from flight outside slaveholding territory to lay claim to freedom. He argued that only if constitutional authority rested with the individual state could a congressional majority be held in check and kept from enacting legislation that amounted to an unhaltable overreaching of the limits placed upon its power. Calhoun had laid the grounds for the South's challenge to the authority of the federal government to limit the South's economic behavior, including slaveholding.

The nullifiers' threat to battle the tariff placed economic issues at the center of the table. Southern fears of Northern dominance and the growing abolitionist movement threatened to turn the table over. Calhoun declared prophetically that his fellow South Carolinians were ready to fight to the death to keep the tariff from being collected. "Death," he avowed, "is not the greatest calamity: there are others still more terrible to the free and brave, and among them may be placed the loss of liberty and honor. There are thousands of her brave sons who, if need be, are prepared cheerfully to lay down their lives in defence of the State and the great principles of constitutional liberty for which she is contending." Though he aligned himself with the most radical elements of the South, he privately believed that without a veto right for the states, the Union would inevitably break apart. He viewed himself as a defender of the American democratic experiment, even as many so-called "fire-eaters" in the South hoped, and prepared themselves, for its dissolution.

President Andrew Jackson did not distinguish by faction. He also personally despised Calhoun. They had common Southern origins and shared party affiliation, a similar racist ideology, and slaveholder status, but Jackson prided himself on being the common man in the White House. He believed in the common man's equality within a popular democracy. Calhoun, the plantation owner, saw little in the common man he liked; he belonged to a Jeffersonian elite fulfilling its duty to govern the general rabble.

In the face of the nullifiers, Jackson mounted a military force and muttered a threat to "hang every leader . . . of that infatuated people," his own vice president included, for treason. At a Washington Jefferson Day dinner on April 13, 1830, designed to bring the Democrats' fractious and increasingly embittered pro- and antitariff factions together under a shared set of principals, Calhoun made clear their differences. "The Union, *next to our liberty, the most dear*," he declared in a riposte to Jackson's attempt to preserve the party—and the Party— around his toast's thematic proclamation, "Our Union, *it must be preserved*." Little wonder that two years on, Calhoun became the first man to resign the vice presidency. Another 140 years would pass before a second vice president resigned.

THE TEENAGED JAMES KNEW little at the time about such momentous matters tearing at his nation. He worried more about the source of his next meal. He would one day come to take many of the same political stances as his famous cousin, but for now he mainly shared the family's high forehead, framed in his case by chestnut hair—though he combed his over rather than back like the senator's scarecrow mane—along with unearthly high cheekbones and a thin-lipped mouth. Not as strikingly handsome as John C. Calhoun, whose entrance into a room as a young man turned all heads, James also lacked his cousin's most prominent physical feature, enormous, globular eyes that engaged whatever they spied with a piercing stare and flashed in the heat of congressional debate like hot coals in the night.

In any case, James looked not to John C. but to his eldest brother, Ezekiel Noble Calhoun, as the model of what a sensible young man with an education might accomplish. Twelve years James's senior, Ezekiel had left the Calhoun Settlement behind in better times to earn a medical degree in Philadelphia, then returned South to set up what was now a flourishing medical practice more than one hundred miles inland at Decatur, Georgia, a small village 135 miles west of the South Carolina border but still the most important settlement in that state's white northwestern frontier. The people of the sparsely settled region turned to Ezekiel as their most capable physician, known for his patent medicines' exceptional healing powers—and potent alcohol content.

ONCE JAMES HAD TURNED the farm and its slaves over to his sisters, he rode west, alone on horseback with just the clothes on his back. Along the way, he stopped overnight with a cousin, Joseph, before continuing the next morning with ten borrowed dollars in his pocket.

If the past he rode away from had left him penniless, he traveled toward golden prospects—literally. Gold—glistening metal, long storied, and able to make a man rich overnight—had been discovered the year before in the mountainous north of Georgia. This year, 1829, America's first great gold rush sent an estimated 35,000 prospectors pouring into the land in a matter of months. In their frenzy to get rich, the men—some, like James, looking to escape their hard-times backcountry farms, many more arriving in hopes of owning property for the first time—paid no heed to the existing claims to the land they prospected on. Why should they? The Cherokee owned most of it, and Indian tribes living within Georgia's borders had few rights to legal protection from the white government and scant recourse for fending off the prospectors' invasion of the lower Appalachian reaches.

Recognizing the reality on the ground, the Georgia government made clear, too, that it no longer respected treaties, signed in some cases nearly four decades before, giving the Cherokee Nation sovereignty over the mountainous northwestern triangle of the state, including the lower Blue Ridge foothills where prospectors panned the first bits of gold. The great Indian fighter Andrew Jackson had declared during his first days in office his intention to rid the Southeast of its native population once and for all. The federal government, which in the past had intervened on behalf of the Indians to fend off illicit white incursions, offered little hope for protection any longer. Among the men who owned one of the most productive mines was Jackson's own vice president, James's powerful cousin, John Caldwell Calhoun.

Even without the gold fever, though, the great, fast-opening West tugged at James's and thousands of other young Americans' hearts like a magnet. The very air they breathed and water they drank drew them further and further inland. "To move was in the blood of everyone," recalled the son of one pioneering family that pulled up stakes from a farm not far from the Calhoun Settlement in the same year as James Calhoun to plunge deep into Georgia. Another Abbeville neighbor, whose family traveled from there west and then again to move still further into the Georgia frontier, remembered how he was "reared to a belief and faith in the pleasure of frequent change of country." The vastness of America, the opportunity that vastness represented, and these new Americans' ever-present need to move on, to search for a better, or simply a new, life over the horizon, drew these Southern pioneers like a great calling.

The Indians contemptuously termed the flinty men, often illiterate and sometimes belligerently racist, as well as the rest of the white pioneers moving into their former Georgia lands from Virginia and out from the Carolina piedmont, "Virginians." The Cherokee and their sometime enemies, the Creek, hunted the land neighboring the frontier trading roads over which wagon trainloads of Virginians bounced by the hundreds every day. Well-off whites, including wealthy plantation owners and cotton and slave merchants, also sneered at the peripatetic and typically impoverished pioneers passing through on the move west, derisively calling them "crackers."

Indifferent to the scorn, the Virginians, or crackers, arrived by the hundreds and even thousands day after day. During the first four decades of the nineteenth century, Georgia's white population exploded, growing by nearly fourfold, from 162,000 to 691,000. They would fill the beckoning promise of Georgia's vast interior emptiness—an emptiness to all, that is, except its indigenous inhabitants.

JAMES UNDERSTOOD THAT HIS own life's journey would carry him westward out the winding roads beyond the sun-baked fields, boggy canebrake, and pine and hardwood stands of the Calhoun Settlement, but the destiny he saw for himself was unlike that of most other Virginians. At the end of his westward road, he would not be panning for gold or otherwise sweating beneath a hot sun. He understood that life in the young republic could offer other paths to opportunity for an ambitious American boy. The career of John C. Calhoun had proved that a man's mind, not just his brawn, could win him great standing and fortune in the young nation.

# CHAPTER 3

# REMOVAL

A FTER SEVERAL DAYS OF RIDING, James Calhoun arrived broke, achy, and tired in Decatur, the most important white town near the Chattahoochee River, the new border with the Indian nations. His brother Ezekiel, with his large family—eventually incorporating ten children, not counting two others who died—welcomed him. Ezekiel rejoiced at his coming. Moreover, he was pleased to discover he liked his much younger brother, with his pleasant disposition and eager manner. He saw in him the best of the Upstate farming community they had grown up in. Practical and resourceful, industrious and scrupulously honest, the teenager was comfortable in his own skin, combative when warranted, yet sober when necessary. Though his parents had valued education, they had had little means left for his formal education by the time he reached school age. However bright James was, he could read and write only haltingly; he would need more education to succeed. Still, his brother recognized in him a forthrightness, native intelligence, and ability to win the trust of those around him, even among Ezekiel's circle of the leading citizens of Decatur. He was a young man who merited nurturing.

Ezekiel sent his brother to David Kiddoo's small academy in town. There James acquired the rudiments of a classical education. The notables of Decatur soon saw his qualities. Hines Holt, a local judge and political leader, watched the young man in a debate competition. Holt was so impressed by his carefully prepared argument and convincing delivery that he invited James to apprentice in his law firm's office. In 1832, James was admitted to the bar, passing, said the presiding judge, "a fine examination, indeed." For James, the first, all-important step in realizing a long-suppressed hope had come to pass. He had never dared to tell anyone that his life's secret dream had been to become an attorney.

LAW QUICKLY BECAME THE backbone of his life. All else formed up around it. That same year, he met Emma Eliza Dabney on a visit with her brother, a fellow Decatur attorney with whom Calhoun partnered for a period. Emma was a belle, the daughter of a Jasper County settler who had prospered such that he was now a plantation owner with extensive land- and slaveholdings. James and Emma married. Seven children would follow over the coming decade and a half.

James realized beyond his imaginings the ambitions for a better life he had harbored back at the Calhoun Settlement. He almost immediately developed a thriving legal practice, winning a reputation as the most effective collections attorney in that part of the state. He also made his mark as a trial attorney and became known for untheatrical but persuasive oral arguments before the bar. As an attorney and a friend, he gained a reputation for honesty and integrity. "There were no concealments, disguises or two-faces about him," recalled a later neighbor. Explaining his success, the same man said that, though "he exhibited no flash of genius," Calhoun possessed above all "sober common sense. He took a view of a subject and fully grasped it, and so presented it to gain the conquest in the hour of contention."

He was also "social, kind and mild in disposition" as well as "a gifted speaker," remarked another family friend. Cautious good sense and popularity among the region's leading citizens soon led many to call upon him to gain his views on the day's political questions. As he traveled for the court circuit, he also built a widening circle of admirers.

And he made money, plenty of money. Successful attorneys at the time could earn more than $20,000 a year. From the percentage of the payments he collected for his clients, Calhoun made even more. Soon, he owned a large Decatur house and purchased the first of what would eventually be several plantations, locally and in the state's southern cotton belt. He also acquired slaves, families of whom would eventually amount to fifty bondsmen working his farms and serving his family at home. Slaves betokened prestige since a skilled and healthy one cost as much as $1,500 at a time when arable cotton land could cost as little as $2 an acre.

To his many household servants and field hands, his son Patrick would later insist, "he was a kind master, and resembled but little the characters of slave owners as portrayed in *Uncle Tom's Cabin*." Of course, no former slave owner's descendents would say otherwise. Undoubtedly, James, like most large-scale slave owners, engaged in the trade of men, women, and children without regard for its impact on the individuals and their families. A quarter of all slave families were separated by sales—husbands from wives, children from parents. James would seem to have found the idyll that eluded the Calhoun settlers. But peace had not yet come to Georgia. The Southeast's Indian "problem" that had so plagued the Calhoun Virginians from the time of their migration into the up-country frontier remained unresolved. The natives' destiny continued to influence James Calhoun's own destiny, even as tragedy fell, forever, on the Indians.


DECATUR SAT JUST BELOW what had once been a shifting line between the Cherokee tribal land to the north and the vast southern territory where their once-fierce former rivals, the Creek, or Muskogee tribe, had ranged over millennia. Despite the 1829 gold rush, the Cherokee enjoyed a measure of isolation and a chance to develop a successful tribal economy within their greatly reduced, mountainous northwestern Georgia nation. The Creek hadn't been so fortunate. Their lands abutting those of their Seminole cousins in Florida were composed of black, rich soil, fertile and ideal for King Cotton. Whites coveted the chance to build new plantations and spread their settlements swiftly over the natives' traditional land.

The fiery Andrew Jackson had earlier crushed the Red Stick tribe at the Battle of Horseshoe Bend, forcing them and U.S.-allied Lower Creek tribes to agree to the Treaty of Fort Jackson. Its terms ceded fourteen million of their acres to white settlement—all Creek southern Georgia territory and most of what shortly formed the state of Alabama. The once fierce and feared natives moved from their former towns and hunting range to a rump of Georgia land along the Chattahoochee River and a larger tract in the Alabama hill country west of the river. (Some Creek also descended into Florida to live with the Seminoles.)

The 1814 Fort Jackson treaty made Georgia's opening to white settlement all but complete—except for the northwestern corner still in Cherokee hands. The U.S. Army manned a chain of forts running from a site near Decatur southwest to Columbus 110 miles away on the middle far western border of the state and on down toward the Florida swamplands to protect rapidly filling settlements along the Chattahoochee.

Following the humiliation of the Treaty of Fort Jackson, the Creek Tribal Council declared that any chief who made further territorial concessions to the white government, at any price, acted without his people's support and faced execution. That didn't stop William McIntosh, a chief of the Lower Creek tribe, though a half-caste, with an Indian mother and a white trader father. Educated in white schools, McIntosh readily sided with U.S. military ambitions in leading a large Lower Creek force against the Red Sticks at Horseshoe Bend. He also happened to be cousin to the governor of Georgia, who would employ almost any means to rid the state of its last Indians. McIntosh shared the belief common among sympathetic whites that the only viable course for his people's survival was accommodation to white demands. A decade after Fort Jackson had seemed to settle the matter, he brokered a new treaty with representatives of President James Monroe's secretary of war, John C. Calhoun. (Calhoun was not only active in Southern Indian affairs but also formulated policy for exiling the Old Northwest's battered and reduced tribal remnants from north of the Ohio River to the trans-Mississippi West's northern Indian Territory.)

The deal they reached provided the natives a newly designated home in the vast arid spaces beyond the Mississippi River in the Oklahoma Territory. Concluded in 1826, the Treaty of Indian Springs ceded all but a last strip of Creek land in Georgia and Alabama along the Chattahoochee for white settlement and, at $2 an acre plus the promise of federal assistance in resettling in the West, enriched McIntosh personally.

When John Quincy Adams took office, with Calhoun as vice president, the Massachusetts patrician son of a Founding Father president was more sympathetic to the Indians' plight and even threatened to use military force to keep white surveyors off Creek land. However, he needed Southern support and soon dropped his opposition to the unequal treaty. The final Treaty of Washington sweetened the deal but ceded nearly all the Creek land. Despite the Creek Council's strong opposition, McIntosh signed the treaty, which was promptly ratified by the U.S. government. McIntosh pocketed $40,000.

During a triumphal return tour through the United States at about the same time, the Marquis de Lafayette, the Revolutionary War hero from France, visited Georgia and, while traveling through the frontier region, paid a visit to some white-educated Creek tribesmen. When Lafayette asked about the McIntosh treaty with the federal government, one Creek man gestured toward his knife. "McIntosh," he spat out the name, "has sold the land of his fathers, and sacrificed us all to his avarice."

McIntosh never had much time to enjoy his gains. He soon paid the price for his actions. Not long after Lafayette's visit, fellow tribesmen surrounded McIntosh's house, where they carried out the council's edict, slashing and stabbing him and three compatriots to death.

MCINTOSH WAS GONE, but the Creeks' agony had really just begun—though it would soon be over, for Georgia and Alabama were ready to gobble up every last morsel of their once great nation. A further deal forced upon the tribe required those members who wished to remain in the East to take private ownership of specific plots of land surveyed by the government, which drew up property lines and issued deeds to tribesmen. Most of the new deed holders could not read their papers. Never having owned private property before, few grasped the significance of the title papers they had pocketed. They proved easy marks for swindlers, who fleeced many of the natives out of their deeds in return for a pittance, often after getting the deed holders drunk. The Indians complained but had no right to recourse through the white judicial system.

The Creek were quickly reduced to an ever-more constricted homeland filling rapidly with white settlers. In many cases, desperate Creeks were left homeless. Impoverished and facing starvation, small groups crossed beyond tribal boundaries into settled Georgia to hunt on white-owned land. They also occasionally raided farms and stole cattle. Local whites thought little of killing Indians suspected of thieving or even those just found walking through their unfenced property. With tensions building, the federal government urged the last remaining Indians to move west to the new national home designated for them in Oklahoma—or face a worse fate if they remained.

On March 23, 1829, Jackson, referring to himself as "your Father," addressed the Creek chiefs and their allies in a message both conciliatory and grim. He noted their endless conflict with their white neighbors, their refusal, in his view, to adapt to white society, and their consequent dire condition: "Where you now are, you and my white children are too near to each other to live in harmony and peace. Your game is destroyed, and many of your people will not work and till the earth." But, he reminded the Indians, they had an alternative. "Beyond the great River Mississippi," he told them, "where a part of your nation has gone, your Father has provided a country large enough for all of you, and he advises you to remove to it." To end further conflict, he promised "a fair price" in return and that "there your white brothers will not trouble you; they will have no claim to the land, and you can live upon it, you and all your children, as long as the grass grows or the water runs, in peace and plenty."

In answer, Creek chief Speckled Snake pointed to Old Hickory's and other previous presidents' addresses to the Indians. He proclaimed,

> I have heard a great many talks from our great father, and they all began and ended the same. Brothers! When he made us a talk on a former occasion, he said, "Get a little farther. Go beyond the Oconee and the Ocmulgee. There is a pleasant country." He also said, "It will be yours forever." Now he says, "The land you live on is not yours. Go beyond the Mississippi. There is game. There you may remain while the grass grows or the water runs." Brothers! Will not our great father come there also?

Jackson did not wait for the natives to choose their course. He rammed the Indian Removal Act through Congress in 1830, authorizing land and money in return for migration by the remaining Indians of the Southeast. Even the legendary frontiersman Davy Crockett, now a Tennessee congressman, who had fought the Red Stick with Jackson at Horseshoe Bend, declared himself, in response to what he termed "a wicked, unjust measure," more willing to be "honestly and politically damned than hypocritically immortalized." Crockett broke with his former field commander over the act. He paid the price for opposing the immensely popular legislation by losing his congressional seat in the next election.

By contrast, Jackson's vice president at the start of his first term, John C. Calhoun, had abandoned his ties with Adams and the National Republicans, precursors to the Whigs, to run on Old Hickory's triumphant Democratic ticket. He now loudly endorsed the relocation measure. Its passage sounded the death knell for the natives' and their white supporters' hope of staving off final federal action against them.

In the winter of 1834, a first group of 634 Creek Indians departed voluntarily for the West. The exodus proved a disaster when private contractors, paid out of Indian reparation funds, failed to deliver on the government's promised aid. Unprepared for the cold they encountered along the trail and lacking food, scores of Indians froze to death. Many more perished from starvation and sickness. By the time the wanderers reached Oklahoma, 161 had died.

WORD CAME EAST ABOUT this early group's horrific experiences. This did little to encourage the remaining tribe members, no matter how destitute, to follow them. Most were disinclined to move, sharing Speckled Snake's bitterness about the trail of broken promises. The Creek ignored Jackson's warnings and Georgia's and Alabama's governors' increasingly vocal and threatening insistence that they go sooner rather than later. Over the next few seasons, clashes between the Creek and white settlers intensified and grew more violent. To the south, settlers faced worse Indian troubles. Along the vast Florida peninsula, sparsely populated settlements lived in terror of depredations by Seminoles. That nation had a long warring tradition. It had also become a haven for runaway slaves, who lived freely among the natives. White pressure to hand over the blacks living among them incensed the Seminoles. Rather than acceptance of the government's paltry removal terms, which dictated they relocate among the Creek in the West, resistance grew.

In December 1835, Seminoles ambushed two companies of U.S. Army troops near present day Ocala, killing more than one hundred soldiers. Just three from the companies survived the fight. With the rallying cry of vengeance for "Dade's Massacre," a viciously murderous war exploded in Florida. It would prove the longest in American history until the Vietnam War 130 years later.

The army's inability to quell the Florida violence swiftly sparked fears all along the Chattahoochee River that the Seminoles' Creek brethren would be inspired to rise up there. Rumors flew that a warmaking alliance was in the offing between the Seminole and the Creek. U.S. Army and militia troops patrolled the swampy, largely unpopulated space between the tribes to keep them from linking up. But those efforts could not stave off continuing Creek depredations. A second, and this time final, war erupted between white Americans and Alabama and Georgia Creeks in 1836.

Starting in early May, ragtag bands of Creeks in war paint began attacking homesteads and murdering settlers. Local estimates claimed the uprising warriors totaled more than a thousand men, though the number was likely much lower. On May 15, the conflagration became open insurrection when a Creek band, said to have numbered three hundred or more, infiltrated Roanoke, a small settlement town on the east bank of the Chattahoochee River about thirty miles south of Columbus, while its residents slept. The raiders shot and hacked to death at least a dozen townspeople and slaves in their beds, scalped several, and torched the town. Native warriors later attacked two troop transport steamers plying the Chattahoochee, leaving numerous crewmembers and passengers dead.

Word flew about the river towns and farms of "men, women and children murdered in every direction." Terrified families abandoned their homes and fled for protection within the stockade fort at Columbus. Some 2,400 refugees streamed into town, living in camps, lean-tos, and churches.

U.S. ARMY TROOPS UNDER Gen. Winfield Scott already had their hands full dealing with the Seminole uprising in the Florida swamps. Georgia called for federal support, and General Scott, dismissed from Florida for his failure to quell the violence there, moved to Columbus to take charge of what had become a second front in a regional Indian insurrection. Shortly after the burning of Roanoke, Gov. William Schley sent out a statewide call for volunteers to suppress the insurgency. Georgia had a long history of assembling citizen self-defense forces, and men from across the state joined hastily formed militia companies. Most men came from nearby towns, but counties as far off as the South Carolina border contributed companies.

Though living at a comfortable remove from the troubles, the Calhoun brothers in Decatur responded, as had their forebears, to the call to battle the Indians. In Decatur, Ezekiel Calhoun formed the region's first militia regiment, the mounted DeKalb County Light Infantry consisting of seventy-four men. Under a new company flag, he led them through a cheering crowd down the Chattahoochee. The DeKalb militia joined the flood that soon amounted to nearly 4,800 Georgians and others—including some from as far off as New York, along with more than 1,100 Creeks who sided against their fellow tribesmen—who came riding into Columbus and neighboring forts to join up with about 1,100 regular army troops in the region. In addition, 4,300 Alabamans joined the effort.

Not long after watching his older brother lead his men away to war, James set aside his budding law practice and bid his young wife and infant children goodbye. He joined a second DeKalb cavalry formation. Calhoun's fellow militiamen elected him captain. In late June

1836, he rode at the head of a company of irregulars to Columbus and entered the midst of the last fitful violence of the Creek War.


THE ARRIVAL OF THE hastily assembled militia companies in Columbus drew army surgeon Jacob Motte up short—and gave him little confidence in their fighting ability. Sent here from his home in Charleston, he watched company after company come into town. "They presented a glorious array of dirks, pistols, and bowie-knives, with no scarcity of dirt," he observed of the motley militiamen parading along the streets of Columbus. "It seemed as if every ragamuffin of Georgia, deeming himself an invincible warrior, had enlisted under the standard of Mars, which many from their conduct must have mistaken for the standard of Bacchus, as they observed the articles of the latter god with much greater reverence."

Poorly armed and likely hungover like the others, both Calhoun brothers' companies mustered into the army in Columbus with the Battalion Georgia Cavalry, commanded by its flamboyant major, Julius Caesar Alford. "The Old War Horse of Troup" was a States' Rights Whig leader in Troup County. In the following year, he would go to Congress, where he scared the daylights out of other representatives on the House floor when he let out an Indian war whoop in defiant answer to a Northern representative's condemnation of white actions against the Creek.

It wasn't long before things took on a more serious cast, and the DeKalb cavalrymen were called into action. At the end of June, following an Indian raid on riverside plantations in Stewart County downriver from Columbus, Alford's ninety-eight-man force was quickly dispatched to reinforce nearby Fort McCreary. The Fort Mc-Creary blockhouse and stockade commanded a hilltop overlooking the war-blasted countryside. The militia and army men stationed there could peer out over the flats along the Chattahoochee River a mile away and miles beyond into the Alabama Creek hill country. Lookouts and scouts watched from there for Indian incursions into Georgia.

Most major clashes with the Creek in Georgia had occurred around the fort, including the war's most important battle, on June 9, across William Shepherd's plantation's fields and swamps. The several score soldiers and civilians killed in that and other fights lay buried along the crest of the Fort McCreary hill. The bones of the many more Indians killed in the fighting lay unburied, bleaching in the sun.

Surgeon Motte marched through the region shortly before the Calhoun regiment arrived. He saw "nothing but a continued series of black heaps of ashes" where settlers had once made their homes.

By early July, though, the last Indian combatants, starving and short on ammunition, began turning themselves in. The fighting appeared over, and Governor Schley declared the need for the militia at an end. Thereafter, James Calhoun and others held over on army duty spent their time arresting Creek stragglers and preventing the few bands remaining in Georgia from returning across the river or fleeing into Florida. Toward the end of the month, Major Alford was called back from Fort McCreary to Columbus. He turned to James Calhoun, younger than many officers on hand, and placed him in command of the company composed mostly of his DeKalb County neighbors.

On the morning of July 24, a scout reported spying evidence of Creek bands making their way across a swamp through the same plantations natives had attacked earlier. Calhoun assembled eighty men from his command and led them out in pursuit of the enemy. In scouring the swamp, they found a fresh trail heading in the direction of the village of Lumpkin. The troops followed the Creek trail on foot, leading their horses through the boot-sucking, mosquito-infested bog. It was not long before they came upon a thirty-member Indian party, naked and painted, which distinguished the unfriendly tribesmen from their government-aligned kinsmen. A hot skirmish ensued.

Calhoun's men killed seven Indians. The rest of the band broke in headlong flight down the trail. The DeKalb company gave chase, pursuing the retreating natives through the swamp and into a hammock. Suddenly, the Creek combatants halted and turned around on their pursuers. The militiamen drew up in a line and prepared to fire on them, but at the same time gunfire burst from the surrounding brush, raking Calhoun's line. They had been lured into an ambush. The militiamen discovered they were completely flanked by what some estimated to be more than two hundred Creek warriors. Several whites fell.

Calhoun's men returned fire, but in their rush to chase after the escaping natives, they had carried too few cartridges and balls. Their little firepower soon spent, they fell back. As they did, Calhoun returned to retrieve his horse, which he had left in the clearing when the fighting commenced. The Creek concentrated their gunfire on him, making mounting too dangerous. "Affording the Indians a fair opportunity to cut him down," reported one of his men, he ignored the balls whistling around him. Fortunately, the Indians were poor shots. He took the horse's reins and led the terrified animal back to the shelter of the brush before retreating with the rest of his troops.

His superiors praised his bravery, but five DeKalb County men had been shot dead in the day's fighting. Several others had fallen wounded. A Columbus newspaper proclaimed that, had they not run short of ammunition, "the DeKalb boys would never have turned their backs upon their enemy, although they may have outnumbered them three to one." That bravado—and the reality of an inadequately prepared military force flushed with the fever of war and inebriated with equal measures of high spirits and liquid spirits rushing headlong into battle—would recur in the South's future. Next time, however, battling Southerners would encounter an enemy far better prepared to meet them on the battlefield.

The hungry and outmanned Indians had little but their oft-practiced guerilla tactics and desperation to bring to the battlefield. Over the next few days, Fort McCreary troops returned in force to the Stewart County fields and swamps. The major general in command of U.S. forces in Columbus ordered them to flush out the "fugitive" Creek. "The Indians must not escape," he declared. Few did.

THE LAST CREEK HOLDOUTS soon turned themselves in or were killed. By the end of August, white forces had ended all Creek resistance in Georgia. Operations to search out remaining tribesmen in Alabama continued until early the following year, when not a single Creek remained to fight in Georgia or Alabama.

The next spring, the army rounded up thousands of Creek families, including many whose men had fought together with U.S. Army forces, and drove them into concentration camps before moving them west. Even then, some resisted to the end. According to army surgeon Motte, rather than be taken alive, Creek men and women would often poison or drown their children before slitting their own throats. "With them their country was life, and without the former the latter was valueless," he commented.

A series of water and overland transports took the natives to Oklahoma. Many never made it. At least one steamer overloaded with chained Indian prisoners sank, drowning 311 Creek men, women, and children.

Few government-guaranteed resources for food or shelter ever materialized for those who reached the Indian Territory. In 1832, 21,792 Creeks had lived in Georgia and Alabama. Twenty years after the Second Creek War and the natives' removal beyond the Mississippi River, the tribe had not recovered from the devastation. Just 13,573 Creeks remained alive in Oklahoma—though back east, a few Creeks had disappeared among the Seminoles to fight on in the Florida swamps, while whites enslaved others captured during the fighting.

ALTHOUGH THE BATTLE WENT badly for Calhoun's forces, he showed himself cool in command and brave under fire. A superior officer described the stand by the outnumbered militiamen as "one of the best battles fought during the campaign." Calhoun would never forget his trial by fire or the violence and its consequences. He counted that day among the two "proudest" events of his life. The next would not come for another thirty years—this time in a far greater war, one fought against his own countrymen.

James Calhoun returned home from the Creek War to a hero's welcome. The Indian problem was nearly resolved with the removal of the Creeks. The Creeks' ancient foe, the Cherokee, watched the doings in the state's southern tier with trepidation. Georgia and its Alabama neighbor could embark on settlement and development unhindered by a foreign civilization in their midst.

For James Calhoun, this marked another turning point in his life too. Vigorous, thirty-five years old, increasingly wealthy and respected, and now emblazoned with military title and honors, he was ready to embark on the next stage of his career—in a boundless, sunny, southern land emptied of all but the last of its aboriginal inhabitants.

# CHAPTER 4

# SHERMAN IN THE SWAMP

JAMES CALHOUN AND HIS Georgia militiamen were not alone in learning new military skills in the Indian Wars. Although the South's frontier demarcated by the receding native presence had moved across the Mississippi to the vast western reaches of the continent, and almost everywhere the land once populated by Indians was opened to white settlement, there remained one glaring—and to the United States galling—exception: Florida. There the story was different. The Seminoles fought a running guerilla battle within the labyrinth of mangrove swamps, saw-grass glades, pine barrens, and hammocks. They refused to capitulate. The war between white and red, though, was a seasonal affair. Only a fool would willingly fight the enemy as well as the heat, humidity, and malarial mosquitoes in the summer months. Fighting by the calendar worked in the Indians' favor. After harvesting their summer crop and tending to their cattle in the peninsula's remote interior reaches, they returned in small bands each winter to raid settlers' homes and attack army patrols before melting away into the impenetrable greenery.

For years, white civilians, terrified to remain in their homes, lived within the shield of a chain of army forts, often while receiving federal subsistence payments. After summers spent lounging in the palmetto shade, fishing the lagoons, and hunting the glades, army companies garrisoned in the forts embarked each fall down the trails left by the Indians through the dense, razor-edged saw grass. There they braved possible ambush—and alligators—at every turn.

The heat and humidity of Florida's unmapped wetlands was the chief enemy American soldiers and officers faced. Poorly acclimated, they were miserable and frequently fell ill. Disease was the soldier's deadliest foe. More than 1,200 soldiers died of disease, mostly malaria and yellow fever, while Seminole ambushers killed 328 more, along with 55 militiamen.

With a force that numbered between 4,000 and 9,000, the army enjoyed at least a four-to-one numerical advantage over its Seminole opposition, growing to as much as a twenty-to-one advantage—higher yet when the home guard was included. Native and allied black warriors were estimated to total just 2,000 at their peak, their number declining over the course of the war to little more than one hundred. The army's failure to stomp out the resistance despite such overwhelming odds drove the old, but still fiery, ex–Indian fighter Andrew Jackson to a spitting fury. He railed at a military performance he proclaimed "disgraceful . . . to the American character."

Unable to answer the Indians' guerilla tactics or even understand their baffling diplomatic maneuvers—which seemed to veer without explanation between acceptance of surrender terms and renewed attacks—several of the nation's most famously heroic officers from previous wars had seen their careers sullied or destroyed, including Generals Winfield Scott, Thomas Jesup, Alexander Macomb, and Zachary Taylor. Year after year, the army's next new leader announced that the war's end was near. Winter after winter, the "beaten" Seminoles swept back, plundering and killing settlers and ambushing troops.

A ditty chanted by troops captured their sense of the futility:

Ever since the creation
By the best calculation
The Florida war has been raging . . .
And yet, 'tis not an endless war
As facts will plainly show
Having been "ended" forty times
In twenty months or so.

With the war approaching its fifth anniversary and seemingly no end in sight, a young second lieutenant fresh out of West Point must have wondered what the devil he was getting himself into as he stood in a whaleboat being pulled through the tossing green surf breaking across the haulover at the bar of the Indian River Inlet in October 1840.

Traveling down the Atlantic seaboard to the country's far corner, the nineteen-year-old William Tecumseh Sherman knew he was entering "into a new world." His first posting to an Indian war made his unusual middle name, given to him by his father for the Shawnee Indian chief who had battled the American settlers in his native Ohio, more apt than ever. After being rowed across the three-mile-wide lagoon fronting Fort Pierce, he stepped ashore as the sun set into the silhouetted palmettos and saw grass that extended as far as the eye could see. The home of Companies A and F of the Third Artillery served as the eastern anchor for a line of bases running from Tampa Bay across the peninsula. Fort Pierce looked nothing like those that "Cump," as he was called by academy classmates, had studied on the banks of the Hudson River. It looked more like an indigenous fishing village than a refuge for hardened soldiers fighting a war.

Three rows of colorful, raised log houses thatched with Palmetto leaves, tropical tree houses perched over the sandbar on stilts, served as officer quarters. Bunkhouses open to the breezes off the lagoon housed the men. Bird feathers, animal pelts, rattlesnake skins, and shark jaws and teeth decorated the structures. A stockade fence not sturdy enough to stop anything more aggressive than an encroaching alligator demarcated the inland intervals between the houses. Horses, chickens, cawing crows, "a full-blood Indian pony," and a fawn wandered and fluttered about the parade ground. Large green turtles languished in cages in the lagoon where they were being fattened for butchering.

The bayonet-straight Cump was described by an officer, who encountered him for the first time there on the banks of the lagoon, as "thin and spare, but healthy, loquacious, active, and communicative to an extraordinary degree." He found the red-headed young man with the sharply observant eyes "as bright as the burning bush." Intense, hardworking, and smart, he had left his mark at West Point, he felt, as much for demerits earned for indifference to the academy's rules and regulations as for academic prowess. But the young officer quickly adapted to his new surroundings, fitting in well among the rest of the regular army men who'd already spent their summer baking under the blazing sun. "The fragrance of the air, the abundance of game and fish, and just enough adventure, gave life a relish," he recalled. Amid the palmettos, slash pine, and mangroves, he soon longed for "those splendid Ohio orchards of apples and peaches," but he savored oysters by the bushel and turtle meat at the officer's mess table. Fishing was presently the fort's principle business. He waded into the clear warm water, learning from a local character "of some note," Ashlock, "the best fisherman I ever saw," to spear shark along the bar, troll for red fish, and net turtles. With crows, hens, and rabbits wandering in and out of his room, he admitted that it wasn't clear whether it "was the abode of man or beast."


A MONTH AFTER CUMP'S arrival, however, the refreshment of cooler days brought the return of the winter campaign in earnest. The Fort Pierce troops started "hunting up and securing" bands of Seminoles they encountered in their patrols, mostly by boat through the chains of lagoons, ranging north some two hundred miles and south about fifty to the Jupiter Inlet, and even down to Lake Worth and the Everglades. The soldier's life in the field pleased Sherman. He relished "threading through the intricate mazes of the Everglades in canvas, wading through the endless swamps carrying our 'five days rations, to last ten,' piling up the bushes to make a bed above the water—testing the comparative merits of alligator & crow stands."

On one occasion, company soldiers struck upon fifty Indians camped near the Indian River Inlet haulover, shooting down several and capturing many others. One of the soldiers who claimed to have "dispatched" three Indians brought a scalp back to the fort as a trophy.

Sherman saw little good in the native enemy, who succeeded in staving off his demise only through "cunning and perfidy." Still, he could admire captured Indians as "noble looking" and appreciated their stoic acceptance of their miserable fates at the government's hands. He was also impressed by their ability to endure pain, including an Indian girl who survived a shot in the back that exited through her cheek.

He did not have even such grudging compliments to offer the "cursed militia," with whom he dealt during the campaign. "Good for nothing" and a "pack of rascals," he complained, they "never rendered a particle of service but when called upon to act have either disgraced themselves and the regulars with whom they have acted or else."

While Sherman never shot an Indian and complained that the effort resulting in "picking up here and there a family" was "absurd" to call a "war," the hunt for Seminoles was a good training ground, he contended, because "the Indian is most likely to be our chief enemy in times to come." While his assessment would not prove true until decades later, the experience of fighting the Indians did help shape his outlook on more conventional war making. He gained a sense of what it took to win against an enemy fighting over its own ground—and what was wrong with a war being waged on the enemy's terms. While in Florida, he studied geography and geology in his spare time, believing that knowledge of terrain was part and parcel of a winning strategy and that inadequate mapping and scouting badly undermined the army's efforts to ferret out the Seminoles.

He also learned to distrust anything less than an enemy's complete capitulation. The young lieutenant saw how easily the natives, fighting over their own turf, could utilize subterfuge to continue their resistance even when they seemed beaten. Every time the government negotiated with a few of the Indians for their removal, when the time came for them to surrender, he complained, "None present themselves." The government responded by sending in the army to round them up, but in too few numbers, and, not surprisingly, "they all get massacred." In the farce acted out time and again throughout the Southeast, a larger force followed upon the first, but the enemy was now positioned to choose the place of battle, resulting in "a few hundred killed," at which point "the Indians retreat, scatter, and are safe," to repeat the process "ad infinitum." A fighting force, he reasoned, should not relinquish the signal advantage by letting its enemy choose the field of battle.

The exasperating, slow-motion war was a withering disaster for a great army, top to bottom. Sherman was sympathetic to the failures of the Florida commanders, who quickly found themselves stuck in figurative swamps that added to their woes in the real swamps. Little wonder few good men lasted when, he lamented, "the best officer is selected to direct the affairs of the army—comes to Florida, exposes himself, does all he can, gets abused by all, more than likely breaks down his constitution, and is glad enough to get out of the scrape." He expected to fight on until the war ended, though, he lamented, "when that will be God only knows." He feared that he might die of old age chasing Indians through the steamy green Florida maze.

INSTEAD OF GETTING TIED up in the drip-drip-drip of a hit-and-run war against an enemy able to sustain such combat indefinitely, he longed for "something decisive." Sherman wanted the government to launch "a war of extermination . . . the most certain and economical method" for winning against an enemy that fought over its own ground and refused to capitulate, though so obviously overmatched.

While it was too late for a total peninsular war, he did witness how effective a well-organized campaign ruthlessly aimed at the enemy's morale—his shelter and stomach—could prove. Col. William Jenkins Worth took command of Florida that winter. His aide-de-camp described the now standard dilemma that the new army chief faced in battling the Seminoles:

> Every hammock and swamp was to them a citadel, to which and from which they could retreat with wonderful facility. Regardless of food or the climate, time or distance, they moved from one part of the country to the other, in parties of five and ten; while the soldier, dependent upon supplies, and sinking under the tropical sun, could only hear of his foe by depredations committed in the section of the country over which he *scouted* the day before.

Worth would need to come up with a new strategy and the ability to move his men with the same swift mobility as his enemy if he wanted to end Seminole resistance for good. His determination finally succeeded.

In May 1841, at a time when the war would normally have begun to wind down and the Indians to retreat to their interior crop and pastures, Worth renewed the attack. He arranged his forces in a bayoneted net extending from the Gulf of Mexico to the Atlantic, designating companies to destroy whatever Indian stores, herds, and crops under cultivation they found. He also sent small mobile detachments of twenty men into the swamps to eliminate Indian refuges. The smoke from the many fires they set wafted on the humid air. He intended to starve the last Seminoles out, leaving them nowhere to hide and driving them straight into the army's guns.

LIEUTENANT SHERMAN PARTICIPATED in one of the most significant results of Worth's comprehensively enveloping strategy and ruthlessly aggressive tactics. That summer, the normally blasé Fort Pierce lookouts spied a band of Indians approaching the stockade wall. Calling up to the alarmed soldiers, they announced that Coacoochee, Chief Wild Cat, leader of one of the most violent and elusive remaining Seminole parties, was ready to surrender. Wary of a trick, the post commander sent Sherman to lead a squadron to follow the Indians into the swamps to bring Coacoochee back to Fort Pierce.

When Cump met the native chieftain in a hammock almost ten miles from the fort, the white officer refused to dismount when invited. He also made sure to secure Coacoochee's warriors' weapons. After taking a leisurely bath and the time to dress ceremonially, which included donning a bloodstained shirt clearly taken off a dead white man, Coacoochee and a few of his men went willingly under Sherman's escort. Once in the fort, he offered to surrender upwards of 150 of his followers in return for provisions. However, he demanded thirty days to ready his people. The fort's commanding officer accepted the deal.

Throughout the month, Coacoochee and several in his band freely roamed in and out of the fort, eating base food and drinking commissary whiskey. Finally, the fort's commander understood that the delay would continue indefinitely; the Indians had no intention of surrendering. He invited Coacoochee and another chief to his quarters for a council. Once there, the two were clapped in irons while Sherman and others seized as many Indians in and around the fort as they could.

The rest of Coacoochee's people fled inland, but his capture broke their resistance. Even the most intransigent among them turned themselves in and soon found themselves back with Coacoochee beyond the Mississippi.

The fitful violence would last another year, but in August 1842, Worth reached an agreement with the last Seminoles in Florida—301 in all, including 112 warriors—to establish a reservation for them in southern Florida. Sherman later admitted that "it was a great pity to remove the Seminoles at all," since the swamps of Florida proved to be less valuable land and more fittingly reserved to create a homeland for all the southeastern tribes. But that was hindsight. The Second Seminole War was over.

During his time in Florida, Sherman's regiment, he boasted to his foster brother, "had caught more Indians and destroyed more property in a fair method than the rest of the army." And the endless war finally came to an end.

Sherman left Florida having gleaned valuable lessons about the shortcomings of what he had learned in the West Point classroom. The kind of Napoleonic line-of-march battleground parades waged between two opposing professional armies colliding in open fields often did not apply in the American frontier. Topography, natural history, waterways, even trees and other vegetation had to figure into an army's deployment. Conventional Napoleonic tactics against an enemy fighting close to the ground and not reliant on a supply line resulted only in waste of the conventional army's men, money, and materiel. Such warfare tipped the balance strongly in favor of the force fighting over its homeland and placed the army dependent on supply lines at a grave disadvantage. Other ways of fighting would be needed.

To fight an Indian war, the army would need to think, if not fight, like Indians, with unorthodox methods that sometimes breached accepted rules of war. In such a fight, war was not simply a question of killing more of the enemy; it required psychological calculations as well. A different strategy and mind set were necessary in a war in which victory depended on sapping an enemy's will to fight by destroying the base of his strength—his family, home, and larder. Entire populations would need to be uprooted. In such a conflict, cold-hearted ruthlessness was Sherman's key to victory.

THE SECOND SEMINOLE WAR was over, but its hangover lingered. In February 1844, now twenty-four years old and still a lieutenant, Sherman was detailed to the army's inspector general to investigate compensation claims for equipment and horses lost in the war filed by Georgia militia who had mustered for the fight. After several months in Charleston and Savannah, he found himself in Marietta, Georgia, a small, well-to-do resort town in the shadow of a blue-gray pine- and oak-cloaked hump rising out of a northwestern Georgia upland plain called Kennesaw Mountain. His keen sense of irony—and dislike for civilians and home guards—got a heavy workout during the six weeks he spent taking depositions, "cross question[ing] and pump[ing] the claimants to see whether the old horse (killed in Florida) is not still at work in his corn field at home." His investigations led him to witness "many a rich scene and . . . unfolded some pretty pieces of rascality for an honest and religious people."

While there, Sherman spent his free time riding "repeatedly" over the nearby mountain. From its summit, he appreciated its preeminent place within a chain of three humps in the spreading up-country plateau. He could also overlook the railroad survey and construction work underway on the new Western & Atlantic (W&A) Railroad. The state-owned rail line was moving out from its southern terminus, a settlement formerly known rudely as just "Terminus" and recently redesignated "Marthasville," on the far side of the wide brown Chattahoochee River about twenty miles to the southeast. It was a densely forested spot, yet one where John C. Calhoun would say in the following year that geography dictated any railroads connecting the Mississippi River valley and the southern Atlantic coast "must necessarily unite." Cherokee and Creek tribes had warred over that site, believing it was the sacred center of their universe. The first stretch of W&A track, now eight years in the building, was already complete through Marietta. It would continue from there to snake its way north to the banks of the Tennessee River opposite Chattanooga. From there, the hope was that railroad would bring western produce and other products from as far away as St. Louis. Other lines were also now being planned that would intersect at Marthasville to carry those goods the rest of the way to the big port cities of Charleston and Savannah.

Marthasville in 1844 didn't amount to much. It had no streets, though four dirt through roads converged there near the W&A's zero marker, and there were about a dozen or so log houses (some offering saloon service), a general store, and a grocery, plus a sawmill busily churning out railroad ties. Two hotels were set to open to guests in the coming year. Until then, fewer than one hundred people called Marthasville home. The town wasn't even on the map, but its ambitions were already telling. A move was afoot to rename it "Atlanta," a coined word emblematic of its reach toward an oceanic future.

IN MARCH, CURIOUS TO SEE more of what he called Georgia's "wild Cherokee country," Sherman took a long horseback ride and camping trip through the northwestern corner of the state where the Indians had lived until six years earlier, visiting the mysterious Indian mounds at Etowah and the surrounding vine-tangled pine-forest wilderness. Riding along the unfinished W&A grade, he employed his time pursuing his military engineer's passion for geography, making a "topographical sketch of the ground" around the rugged Allatoona Pass. He could not yet know it, but his visit to the region would prove of "infinite use" when he returned to the same spot twenty years later.

The accumulated learning of his early army years spent chasing Indians through the swamps in Florida and then touring through Georgia would later seem "providential." When he returned to war against an enemy fighting, as had the Indians, over its own homeland, he found that "every bit of knowledge then acquired [was] returned tenfold."

# CHAPTER 5

# ANOTHER PASSAGE

EIGHT YEARS BEFORE William Tecumseh Sherman's first entry into the Southeast, sometime in 1832 around the time that the twenty-one-year-old James Calhoun had begun to realize the lifelong dream that had impelled him to ride across Georgia's warred-over western Indian frontier, another young man departed on a daring passage of his own. Though his journey was far shorter, really no more than a fifteen-minute walk along a muddy boulevard frantic with carriage traffic, he nonetheless crossed a vast and potentially dangerous gulf. Race, too, demarcated this frontier.

At age twelve, Bob Gadsby, as he was then called, was probably already noticeably handsome, with what were said to be alert, dark eyes topped by a broad forehead. He ventured out a rear door of the National Hotel, where he lived with his mother and her many other children in Washington, D.C. Considered the nation's capital's pre-eminent inn, Gadsby's, as it was known in deference to its locally famous English owner John Gadsby, was a five-story limestone-and-brick structure that shouldered Pennsylvania Avenue for nearly a block and stretched even further up Sixth Street. Congressmen, military officers, foreign ministers, and other dignitaries arrived nonstop at its elegant portico to take up temporary residence, enjoy drinks in its saloon, or join the celebrations in its ballrooms while in town. In its lobby, cigar-chomping men assigned to curry favor in support of their patrons' government interests would buttonhole the powerful men who passed by.

As Bob hurried up the sidewalk, he likely prided himself on the natty, brocaded hotel-staff uniform he wore. He walked with a youngster's quickstep from the National up Pennsylvania Avenue to Capitol Hill, making sure to step aside and tip his hat to other pedestrians. Reaching the Capitol, he leaped up the broad marble staircase until slowed by the great East Portico doors to the Temple of the Republic.

Once beneath the soaring rotunda, he would have slowed his pace, while he crossed the stone-and-tile floor to the Senate chamber doors.

There, he encountered a Senate page, Isaac Bassett, who, at age thirteen, was just a year older than the boy who stood before him. The younger boy asked the older if he might see Senator Daniel Webster, who was at his desk inside the chamber.

Isaac's reaction to Bob's sudden presence went unrecorded, but surely the teenage page boy, who had the powerful senator from Massachusetts to thank for his post, was shocked at the young man's temerity. Nobody approached the senator without some trepidation. Webster would have it no other way. The fifty-year-old statesman could appear frighteningly austere and imperious. He looked like the Puritans of old from whom he was descended, able to pierce a man's heart with his very eyes and ready to smite all sinners who dared cross his path. He redoubled his priestly aura by always dressing in a black suit. Tall and black-haired, with a narrow raptor's beak of a nose, he looked down on those around him, figuratively and literally, with dark eyes that burned "almost superhuman," Bassett later recounted, from under his "precipice of brows." If his appearance was not enough to intimidate his senatorial peers, let alone the boys, his "majestic" voice surely would be. It resounded from his monstrous chest with a force that shook even "the earth underground." He used his basso profundo to turn his famously forceful eloquence to its greatest effect on the Senate floor—and in his frequent rages. Little wonder that his legions of admirers called him "the Godlike Daniel." People who reviled him, numbering nearly as many, spoke rather of "Black Dan."

But what had to make Isaac's eyes open wide was that the boy who came knocking on the Senate chamber doors mustered the courage to ask to see "his *father*." According to a later description, Bob's resemblance to the handsome Webster was "striking," but Bob was black, and not figuratively like Senator Webster. Though light-colored, young Gadsby was a slave at the National, where he lived and worked with his mother and siblings, who were among the thirty-nine bondsmen owned by the glad-handing innkeeper, barkeep, and sometime slave trader.

AFTER THIS VISIT, Bob almost certainly never mentioned his paternal origins again outside the most limited company until decades later. He had good reason to keep quiet about the matter. If the boy's paternity claim were true, the slave was walking proof of a crime—interbreeding of the races—a serious legal matter even in the senator's abolition-minded home state. It was also a moral abomination in the eyes of nearly all Americans. Any public declaration of the existence of Senator Webster's black son would surely have destroyed his career. His self-proclaimed son faced a more serious danger. If he dared to make such a scandalous claim in public again, he would in all probability face a grave threat to his life or at least his station in life.

Whatever danger Bob ran, the slave boy braved the senator's "black look" to spend time with him that day. And Webster did not rebuff the boy at the Senate Chamber door. He must in fact have welcomed the presumptuous lad, for after Bob's first visit, Bassett, who soon became Senate doorkeeper, would often bump into him when he "freekently came up to the Senate Chamber to see Senator Webster."

THE GODLIKE DANIEL WEBSTER was a colossus of the nation, exalted Concord, Massachusetts's transcendentalist philosopher and essayist Ralph Waldo Emerson, "the representation of the American Continent." For Emerson, here in the flesh was "the completest man. Nature had not in our days, or not since Napoleon, cut out such a masterpiece." What captured Emerson and the nation were his sometimes flowery, always spellbinding speeches. The "Demosthenes of America" swept away his audiences, often speaking hours at a time. Emerson, one of the age's most popular orators himself, credited Webster with raising the nation's political discourse "out of rant and out of declamation to history and good sense." Webster's famous defense of the national union in his reply to Senator Robert Young Hayne during congressional debate over the nullification principle two years earlier—when he declared the national government to be "made for the people, made by the people, and answerable to the people"—would echo even more famously as his words were picked up down the years. Abraham Lincoln studied his reply to Hayne and called it "the grandest specimen of American oratory." Webster would run for president three times, three times failing. He also served as secretary of state and, as the age's leading Constitutional attorney, argued many influential cases before the Supreme Court.

Revered by so many in the young republic, the Godlike Daniel was nonetheless a dark pearl. Beneath that lustrous black surface hid a hollow—some would call it rotten—core. Few who spent time with him away from public view could deny the man's disturbing personal failings. But few outside his Washington circle knew anything of them. Even though newspapers of the day stood almost as one in never publishing stories about Black Dan, hot-breathed rumors engulfed him like the Foggy Bottom humidity. There was no doubt about Webster's insatiable appetite for money and his persistent, accompanying indebtedness—and willingness to take loans he never intended to repay from many who could call upon him for Capitol Hill favors. Widely known, too, was his heavy drinking, which would damage his liver and contribute to his death.

As a bachelor following his first wife's death, then after his remarriage when alone, he welcomed women, high born and low, into his Washington chambers. His lack of sexual restraint was infamous in the nation's capital. James Henry Hammond, a fire-eating South Carolina congressman, governor, and U.S. senator, lamented in a diary entry of December 9, 1846, his own ungovernable adulterous and even incestuous desires, including "more than two years continuously" in which his sister's four daughters, ages thirteen to eighteen, "permit[ed] my hands to stray unchecked over every part of them." He sought to excuse his lecherous ways, though, by noting that throughout history powerful men have succumbed to sexual temptation. In the same entry, he wrote that in "our present day and nation the very greatest men that have lived have been addicted to loose indulgences with women. . . . Among us now Webster . . . [is] notorious for it." Prominent New York attorney and diarist George Templeton Strong more temperately described Webster as "slightly heathenish in private life."

Rumors of womanizing—and interracial couplings—accompanied him his whole career. But not for almost another twenty years after the "colored boy" came to see "his *father*" would a muckraking female journalist, Jane Grey Swisshelm, seek to pin down Black Dan with the scurrilous charge that he kept "colored women" as mistresses and had fathered numerous mixed-race children. Swisshelm, the first woman to report from the Senate Press Gallery, had her reasons for using her pen to take down one of the most powerful men in America. She held staunchly abolitionist views. Like many in her political wing, she was outraged by Webster's turncoat support for the Compromise of 1850, which balanced slaveholding and nonslaveholding territories and included the Fugitive Slave Law, which forced Northerners to turn escaped slaves in to the authorities for return to their owners or face criminal prosecution. To the compromising Webster, this suspended the Union's rush to civil war—and he hoped raised his chances for the presidency. For the law's opponents, his compromise with what they viewed as an unmitigated evil was at one with the taint governing the rest of his life. A frequent contributor to Horace Greeley's leading *New York Tribune*, Swisshelm caught a "moral stench" arising from Webster's reputation and hoped to identify its source and bring him down.

She reported, "His mistresses are generally, if not always, colored women—some of them big black wenches as ugly and vulgar as himself." She asserted that he had fathered "a family of eight mulattoes" living in Washington and "bearing the image and superscription of the great New England statesman, who paid the rent and grocery bills of their mother as regularly as he did those of his wife." Swisshelm lost her *Tribune* job for publishing the stories.

In fact, Webster's own career would falter badly due to his support for the Compromise. Though Webster's colleagues later falsely accused Swisshelm of having "killed" him—he died two years later—the accusation regarding "colored women" did not stick. But growing up, Bob always knew who his real father was.

IT IS POSSIBLE THAT Webster urged Bob's owner to sell Bob away from the nation's capital to squelch just such rumors. That is not known. Bob would later recount that his mother, Charlotte Goodbrick, was "a mulatto of rare beauty," purchased by John Gadsby, owner of the National, from a Fredericksburg, Virginia, man. Webster eventually bought Charlotte from John Gadsby to serve in his own household. Before his death, the senator granted freedom to her along with the rest of his slaves.

Bob was not so fortunate.

John Gadsby was one of the wealthiest men in Washington and, though described by the French minister to the United States as "an old wretch who made a fortune in the slave trade," also among its most sociable. He and his third wife lived in what may have been the city's stateliest and best-situated private home, Decatur House, built originally by the naval war hero Stephen Decatur on Lafayette Square behind the White House. Washington society flocked there to attend the couple's frequent parties. Their house and the large adjoining slave quarters added to it by Gadsby stood across the street from Daniel Webster's own residence. Gadsby's seventeen house slaves likely trafficked back and forth between there and the National.

During his time at the National, Bob mastered cooking, barbering, and a few other trades. He may even have cut the bright red hair of a jumpy sixteen-year-old who, in 1836, stopped at Gadsby's for a night at the start of his first visit to Washington, D.C., while traveling from his home in Ohio to take up his appointment at the U.S. Military Academy at West Point. William Tecumseh Sherman would return to town frequently in later years. He went from the National Hotel to the boardinghouse where his foster father, Ohio senator Thomas Ewing, resided.

At the National, Bob probably also learned to win the hotel clientele's trust, developing qualities that enabled him to move around comfortably within an alien and often hostile white society. Gadsby thought enough of Bob's abilities that he gave the valuable bondsman, then about age twenty, to his son William for his personal use. That wouldn't last long. The "rash, hot headed" William Gadsby didn't have his father's gifts for turning his sociability to profit. Instead, he drank and gambled heavily. Losing badly in a high-stakes card game in Richmond, William doubled down, betting his manservant Bob against another player's $1,500 in gold. Bob was soon on his way into a new and strange life.

THE GAMBLER WHO WON this human betting pot needed money more than slaves, for shortly after winning him, he sold Bob off. This passage took Webster's urbane slave son deep into the Lower South and the heart of the South Carolina cotton Black Belt, where he was quickly sold again. In 1840, the powerful and wealthy planter Robert Cunningham bought him for his Rosemont Plantation, a thriving 2,100-acre estate outside the Upstate South Carolina town of Greenville, in the original Abbeville District, not far from the Calhoun Settlement. Bob became the latest addition to Cunningham's holdings of well over 100 bondsmen—peaking at more than 150 slaves at one point. For someone like Bob, who had grown up in the midst of the capital city's hubbub, life on an Upstate plantation, with its cotton fields stretching to the horizon and long rows of creaky slave cabins, must have felt like a descent into a dangerously self-enclosed and turgid land. Nonetheless, he managed to thrive.

FOR THE NEXT SIX YEARS, he likely lived on Rosemont Plantation as Cunningham's son John's personal servant. That led to the next fateful step in his life's journey. John was first cousin to, and close friends with, Benjamin Cudworth Yancey Jr., the occasionally hotheaded son of another prominent South Carolina landowner and legislator. Ben's first years of life were spent on a plantation near Rosemont, but after his father's early death and his mother's remarriage to a Northern minister, he went to Upstate New York for prep school and then Yale Law School. When he returned to Greenville, he practiced law and helped his uncle with the management of Rosemont. There, he and his cousin's slave, who was close to him in age and probably enjoyed sharing tales with him about life outside the South, developed a mutual respect and what amounted to a loyalty, if not a friendship, that would endure. Each would come to the other's aid in times of dire need.

Shortly after the Second Creek War, the lure of the newly available western lands drew Ben and his even more impulsive and violent brother, William Lowndes Yancey, to try to raise their fortunes in Alabama. There Ben acquired a large estate along the Coosa River. He soon added to his landholdings and began moving among large Alabama; Athens, Georgia; and Greenville properties. Together with his brother W. L., he launched and edited an Alabama newspaper. Both brothers acquired numerous slaves. As their personal fortunes grew, they also followed their late father in entering the thicket of Southern politics and ended up strong supporters of the Calhoun faction of the Democratic Party. Ben was elected to the South Carolina legislature for several terms and also to the Alabama state senate, where he served as its president for a term.

W. L. in particular became an ardent states' rights advocate, emerging as one of the South's most vocal and fiercest fire-eaters. He openly declared himself ready to go to war in defense of Southern slaveholders' rights. He won a seat from Alabama to the U.S. House of Representatives, where he was closely allied with the most radical of the Calhounite faction. He drafted what was known as the Alabama Platform calling for radical resistance to what were viewed as the antislavery portions of the Compromise of 1850. When he spoke his political mind, he made sure his words stung, and following his very first speech in Congress, a personally affronted Whig representative, Thomas Clingman, challenged him to a duel. Neither man was injured in the exchange of pistol fire. Both avoided criminal charges and congressional censure.

ALTHOUGH WILLIAM WROTE OF his beloved younger brother Ben, he "is said to be a little more staid in temperament than I am, tho I think a chip of [*sic*] the old block!" Ben was less intent on battling for Southern and personal honor than on getting rich. His Greenville and Alabama law practices thrived, as did his cotton plantations and other investments. In 1846, the Cunninghams' twenty-six-year-old slave Bob, now married, asked Yancey to purchase him together with his wife. Yancey hesitated. He had scores of slaves already, nearly eighty on his Alabama plantation alone, but he appreciated Bob's many talents, describing him as "a very intelligent and accomplished house servant." He noted his skill in the kitchen with meats and pastries, as well as his "fine" way with preserves and pickling, and that he was "a good barber." He finally consented to buy the costly slave couple he didn't really need—on one condition. Evidently, Bob had contracted William Gadsby's fondness for gambling, or he turned to games of chance for easy money. He had a good mind for numbers and probably won more hands than he lost. Yancey would agree to buy the slave couple only if Bob would give up his "card playing." Bob accepted.

Yancey quickly came to think even more highly of his new servant, who proved, according to his fifth owner, "truthful, sober, affectionate, honest. . . . He was a faithful servant, much attached to me, my wife and children." Yancey's confidence in Bob grew to the point where he gave him a position of authority within his large, oft-moving household, having Bob "training up under him several young favorite negroes." Guests were frequent and the demands of the family lifestyle complex. Yancey testified, "I would have trusted him with anything."

Bob responded well to the faith his owner placed in him, but the mutual respect between master and slave could not mask the reality of their relationship. Yancey may have felt a paternalistic fondness toward Bob, but he viewed his slaves and their families with little more concern than he did any other costly, productively useful property he owned. There's no evidence that Yancey or his overseer physically mistreated slaves, but chattel was chattel. When one of his brother's bondsmen grew "sullen and rebellious," William told Ben, "I shipped him without a minute's warning to New Orleans to be sold." No doubt Ben would have done the same.

# CHAPTER 6

# THE COMPROMISE

J AMES CALHOUN'S NEW-WON stature as a result of his valor and heroic leadership in the Creek War during the summer of 1836 helped launch a political career. The following summer, he received a virtually "unanimous" vote, sending him as Decatur's representative to the state's general assembly in Milledgeville, the current capital. He returned for two more terms; then, after a period focused on growing his legal practice, a state senate seat followed from DeKalb County and, later on, from Fulton County. In the brick Gothic Revival capitol halls and chambers, he proved adept at both backroom political maneuvering and public administration. A recognized authority on the intricacies of the state's tangled, multitier legal system, his legislative work helped codify property rights. That enabled investors to acquire rights-of-way needed to plan the railroad lines that would open Georgia's interior to development.

Above all a "good government" legislator, he strived to consolidate the rule of law along civilization's frontier, a chaotic region where the lynch mob's rope—or an accused man's vanishing into the wilderness— too frequently marked the final resolution of criminal cases. Civil disputes were often still resolved by duels. As a member of a celebrated Senate Judiciary Committee, his leadership helped close the door on vigilante justice—at least for accused white citizens. An entirely separate legal code determined a black person's fate when such cases reached a court. The state assembly passed numerous reforms that James Calhoun coauthored to modernize the legal system, most importantly streamlining the judicial process from indictment through state supreme court appeals. •

For many frontier Georgians, judicial matters, tort law, civil procedure, and legal statutes seemed arcane or, worse, out-and-out intrusions into their lives, but Calhoun understood the practical benefits his fellow citizens would enjoy from his outwardly bureaucratic efforts at reform. As late as 1858, one of his clients accused of murder was nearly pulled out of his jail cell by an angry mob intent on lynching the prisoner. Unarmed, Calhoun stopped them at the calaboose door with his sober arguments in favor of letting justice take its course. Though frontier-style punishment still occurred, for the state's growing urban centers, codified laws and efficient, powerful courts meant more than safer streets and a way to settle arguments without resorting to violence. For the first time, towns hired sheriffs and deputies to enforce the law and ensure fair trade practices. They elected judges and juries to bring felons to justice.

The establishment of a modern legal system encouraged civil society to develop. Merchants and banks, tradesmen, builders, and investors of all kinds, even the small farmers bringing crops to market, could trust increasingly that whatever financial risk they ran and whatever reward they aspired to depended not on a gun but business conditions.

Calhoun seemed destined for great things. In a land where a man bore his family name like a shield of honor, he possessed a Southern one that would have amounted to royal lineage on another continent. Despite this "honorable parentage," recalled one who knew him, "he claimed nothing from them." He need not. The name echoed through the government chambers. He counted as legislative and personal friends among the most influential men in the state, including Alexander Stephens, Robert Toombs, and Howell Cobb, politicians with national renown who would rise from Milledgeville to Washington, where they would serve as powerful congressmen, senators, and cabinet members in several administrations. Calhoun seemed to be on course for a similar ascent to high national office.

DURING HIS FIRST TERM in office, Calhoun dealt with the brutal business of purging the last sovereign Indian nation from within Georgia's borders. The gold discovered within Cherokee country made it too valuable to be left to the Cherokee. An 1832 Georgia State–sponsored land lottery law had raffled off the entire Cherokee territory to whites. The Cherokee were legally barred from participating in a chance to win back their own farms and towns.

The state and federal governments moved to lay the groundwork for the tribe's final removal to its designated land in the far West. Once again, the white governments turned to native leaders who were not empowered to negotiate on the tribe's behalf. With the Creek and Seminole wars as a backdrop, in 1836 a dissident Cherokee group led by Major Ridge agreed to terms for the peaceful, compensated departure of all remaining tribe members in the region. Nearly all 20,000 tribe members protested against the agreement, but congressional ratification of the Treaty of New Echota gave the natives a two-year deadline to complete their move to the trans-Mississippi West.

By the beginning of 1838 though, only about 2,000 tribe members had complied. Force would be needed for the rest. Would it lead to another bloody Indian war? Gov. G. R. Gilmer dispatched Rep. James Calhoun to survey conditions in the Cherokee territory. Calhoun traveled along the course of the new railroad line the state government was building, the Western & Atlantic, its bed presently being cut and graded directly through Cherokee land.

Reporting back to the governor on February 20, Calhoun was worried by what he *didn't* see. He found relations between white and native residents remarkably calm. He had encountered none of the tensions that had presaged the outbreak of the Creek War. He noted many Cherokee men on the work crews building the new railroad. The natives, he reported, "make very good hands at work," and their work teams were "making considerable progress."

The peaceful progress raised the hair on the back of his neck. Whites showed no fear of what might happen. Those living and working in the northwestern corner of the state "do not apprehend that there will be any hostilities." He found, "They seem to be pretty generally, so far as I could ascertain, of opinion that the Indians would leave without doing any mischief of consequence." He feared they were being naïve about the consequences of the pending, long-rumored removal of their neighbors and coworkers.

Despite the region's calm and the native's quiescence, he predicted another Indian war was in the offing. He wrote to the governor, "I am afraid that the people in the Cherokee Country have too much confidence in the Indians. . . . They should bear in mind the condition of the white citizens in the Creek nation at the time of the breaking out of hostilities there. If hostilities should break out there, the same results would be experienced that were in the Creek Country"—that is, insurrection, property destruction, civilian panic, bloodshed, and large-scale warfare.

The government, determined to prevent another drawn-out conflict like that in Florida, moved swiftly, stealthily, and with overwhelming strength. Unprepared or too depleted and defeated to resist, the Cherokee never fired a single shot in defiance when their last day in Georgia arrived.

A WARM MAY 24, 1838, marked the final sunrise on 12,000 years of Indian civilization in Georgia. The state of Georgia took official possession of Cherokee County, the last sovereign native nation within its borders. Under Gen. Winfield Scott, 7,000 troops descended upon an estimated 16,000 Cherokee. Uniformed soldiers, hurling insults and firing their rifles to terrorize and cow the population, swept through the small towns, isolated farms within the pine forests, riverside mills, and scattered dwellings. Men, women, and children were seized where they were found. There would be no opportunity to raise an alarm, let alone organize resistance. (In North Carolina, where a similar removal was underway, some Cherokees fled into the remote areas of the Appalachian Mountains and lived on there to gain a tribal reservation in later years.) The troops forced the Cherokee people at bayonet point into awaiting stockade-enclosed fields.

A soldier participating in the removal described what he saw:

> Women were dragged from their homes by soldiers whose language they could not understand. Children were often separated from their parents and driven into the stockades with the sky for a blanket and the earth for a pillow. And often the old and infirm were prodded with bayonets to hasten them to the stockades. In one home death had come during the night, a little sad faced child had died and was lying on a bear-skin couch and some women were preparing the little body for burial. All were arrested and driven out leaving the child in the cabin. I don't know who buried the body.

As they were marched by the soldiers into the concentration camps, the Cherokees could look back to their former homes being torched and looted by whites who followed in the army's wake. A hardened war veteran from Georgia declared the Cherokee roundup to be "the cruelest work I ever knew."

In less than two weeks, all the Cherokee homes and villages stood empty or destroyed. White squatters moved immediately into the better remaining structures. By June 3, the soldiers' work in Georgia was done. Over the next five months, troops herded the 16,000 Cherokee people some six hundred miles west across the Mississippi River to Oklahoma. At least 4,000 died of starvation, cold, and disease along what came to be known as the Trail of Tears.

Not an Indian soul remained within Georgia's borders as a speed bump to slow the Empire State of the South's development.

For James Calhoun, the final capture of the state's western frontier marked an auspicious moment to live within and represent Georgia's wilderness upland, perhaps not unlike what his forebears experienced when finally rid of their dangerous native neighbors eight decades ago. Senator John C. Calhoun, who had followed his young cousin's rise with interest and familial pride, reached out from his U.S. Capitol office in Washington, where he was now the South's greatest voice, writing a letter to commend James, though "still young," for "the formidable start you have made." He was confident that "you may accomplish all you desire."

His belief in the young man's political promise was to prove unfounded. James Calhoun would never scale the heights his apparent and oft-touted gifts indicated. As he strove for higher office, he faltered again and again. The aspiring political leader knew exactly what held him back: the national controversies that swept local politics aside.

In that same 1839 letter, the "Cast-Iron Man" warned his up-and coming cousin that he should not expect an easy time of it in the rough-and-tumble politics of the age. He confessed, "My political course has, indeed, been one of great difficulty; as any public man's must be, who honestly performs his duty, without regard to personal consequences."

Honestly performing his duty came easily enough for James Calhoun, but unlike the senator, he would pay a price for his sense of duty that would keep him pinned down in his home district. Twice in succession he ran for a congressional seat, and twice he lost. (A third, much later effort at a race for the House of Representatives proved equally futile.) He had little chance, despite his many assets and personal popularity.

James Calhoun, like a large percentage of the antebellum nation's men of wealth and high standing, from the South and North, was a political Whig. He was an avowed supporter of popular causes including sectional rights and the nation's self-proclaimed Manifest Destiny to conquer the continent. However, unlike Senator Calhoun in Washington, he would not move from his Whig alignment to side with his home district's dominant political organization, the Democratic Party, because, above all else, he believed in the need for effective governance in the ripening republic. The need was especially evident in his frontier home, where the population had doubled, then doubled again, while raw local institutions failed to keep pace. The frontier was an anarchic place, lacking the foundations of civil order necessary to build a thriving American civilization. James Calhoun went to Milledgeville—and he hoped beyond—to create the conditions that would boost the region's opportunity and affluence.

Good government, though, mattered little to the large majority of voters, many of them newly arrived in western Georgia. Most settlers rolling into the region in fact resented government, whether in Milledgeville or the dimly perceived federal government 650 miles and several weeks' travel away in Washington, D.C. Government legislators were thought by many to erect legal structures that more often than not acted as an imposition on their freedom to pursue their individual interests. Government meant tariffs on goods, laws against the taking of native land, high and mighty bankers with their notes and interest, militia drafts, schools and sheriffs, state roads and lands, and debt, duties, and taxes to pay for them. Mostly, it meant a publicly supported official's interference in the conduct of their lives. In the South, yeoman farmers toiling to make their small piece of red dirt feed their family formed the largest bloc of voters, and to their eyes the Whig Party had come to represent all those dominant people and institutions the men once known as Virginians resented most: banks and corporations, city dwellers, Yankees and Puritans—abolitionists all—plus the plantation owners, the bloated self-styled squires who looked down on the crackers. The frontiersmen despised those who dared tell them where they could settle and what laws would govern their lives and property. Little wonder that in Calhoun's almost entirely rural DeKalb County district, Jacksonian Democrats outnumbered Whigs by nearly two to one.

Calhoun's personal popularity, keen legal mind, and in-state legislative effectiveness overcame the odds, winning him local races despite his party's deep minority status. Those assets were not enough to overcome the Democratic candidates' enormous majority among voters, though, when it came to the races for U.S. Congress.

Senator John Calhoun tacitly appealed to his talented cousin to consider switching parties if he hoped to climb the political ladder. Party meant little to the elder Calhoun, an outlook shared by most men of an earlier political generation. He had already made several canny moves from his early days. Why should his young cousin not climb his way up via the most convenient ladder?

IN EARLY 1846, U.S. Senator Calhoun sent James a copy of his already widely circulated speech calling for a compromise—eventually passed—to avoid going to war with Britain over the disputed northern boundary of the vast Oregon Territory in the Northwest. America was in the process of sealing its continentwide hold on the land, its Manifest Destiny. The position Calhoun staked out pitted him against Jacksonian president James K. Polk's administration, as well as against the public's enormous support for annexation well beyond the forty-ninth-parallel compromise he favored—as the Democratic slogan went, it would be "Fifty-four-forty, or fight." His views even placed him against his own party in Congress. He seemed to have set a course for himself at odds with his own political future.

James could sympathize well with the challenge the senior Calhoun faced in Washington. He wrote back a long, introspective letter discussing his own dilemma over principles that placed his still young, yet already stumbling, political career in jeopardy.

James found himself in hearty agreement with the senator's views. He applauded his cousin's actions at the time. "I was one of the first nul[l]ifiers in Georgia though then very young," James proclaimed and added, almost apologetically, "and eaven [sic] now I scarcely know of any great question but upon which I agree with you entirely." This put him directly at odds with his own Whigs.

He stopped himself, though, and asked the obvious question that had to be on his cousin's mind: "Then you will say I agree with the Democratic Party upon most all of the great questions of the day. Why are you a Whig?" He understood that on the most defining issue of what it meant to be an American, indeed of the continued life of the nation, he parted ways with his cousin's party and the South's now dominant political organization. It had to be an agonizing choice, for, with that, he blasted to pieces whatever hopes he may have held for winning national office from Georgia.

Remarkably, James's party allegiance was driven not by grand ideological ideas like federal power, the creation or dissolution of a national bank, states' rights, western expansion, or even the unspoken Southern fundamental of slavery's future. He split from the Democrats over what seemed a less than consequential matter: good government and who would best be able to bring it to the young nation. He was a practical man, but for him practicality harbored a deep philosophical core. "I think the successful administration of the laws of the government of more importance, than a fiew, eaven great questions," he insisted. The value of government—what defined a democratic nation—was found in its practical success in executing the laws of the land, its ability to serve its citizens fairly and efficiently. Good government would sustain the explosively fast-growing American nation better than resolution of the great questions that threatened even now to split it in two. Building and maintaining law and order was government's preeminent role. That enabled all else, including peaceful debate and potential resolution of the "great questions."

James Calhoun displayed no uncertainty about his loyalties: "I do believe, the Whigs, have been the best dispensers of the laws of the government both State & national, & feel very sure it has been so in Georgia."

He was confident that if he were a Democrat, his advance to higher office would be smoothed and more than likely assured. The local Democratic Party, which "has ever treated me with great kindness" and helped him "very warmly" in his legal practice, made abundantly clear the future they planned for him if only he jumped. Still, he could not do it. As a result of his political principles, he lamented, "it has been a great misfortune to me to dif[f]er with the Democratic Party. Could I have acted with that party, & done justice to my honest opinions—I do not doubt but that I might have been elevated to respectable offices."


THE YOUNGER CALHOUN'S moderate views were largely out of step with most of his neighbors', but his ability to work behind the scenes helped put the brakes on what appeared at the time to be an unavoidable national train wreck. Still, he needed to break with the Southern States' Rights political faction for good to do so, even as its leader John C. Calhoun used the little remaining energy left to him in his last, dying days to fight a compromise that his cousin James had worked so hard to see enacted.

Extension of the nation from coast to coast brought to a head the question of the place of slavery, protected in the original thirteen states by the Constitution but now abolished throughout the nation's northern tier. White expansion throughout the Southeast, largely complete within that corner of the nation, continued westward. Mexico's Texas territory was the natural next step—with only the weak Mexican government standing in the United States' way. American settlers and disenchanted Mexicans in Texas first declared their independence in 1836. In 1845, Polk offered to purchase Texas outright, but Mexico refused. Despite Mexican opposition, Polk went ahead and formally annexed Texas with statehood, as a slave state, in March. By the following spring, Mexico and the United States were caught up in a bloody war. A greatly disproportionate number of Southerners joined the U.S. Army as it fought its way south into Mexico City. Mexico acceded to the victorious America's peace terms in 1848, granting the United States all of its territory north of the Rio Grande. The United States at last reached from sea to sea.

The new territory promised almost boundless opportunity—especially after gold was discovered in California in 1849. But acquisition of the new territories brought the suppressed question of slavery, in the form of slaveholders' rights, to a head. Most Northerners wished to exclude slavery entirely from the new territories. "Free soil and free men," they cried. A Northern majority in Congress appeared ready to do just that. The potential to carve several additional free states out of the western territory cast a dangerous shadow over the South. Fire-eater James Henry Hammond of South Carolina expressed Southern fears that the North, with an expanded free-state majority, would "ride over us rough shod. . . . Our only safety is in *equality* of POWER. If we do not act now, we deliberately consign our children, not our posterity, but our *children* to the flames."

The gnawing question of America's national identity exploded. Literal fistfights broke out on the floor of the Capitol in Washington. Threats of worse violence abounded. Many fire-eating Southerners declared themselves openly ready to go to war for their freedom from an increasingly tyrannical Northern majority. Even Senator Calhoun was shocked by what he saw among his Southern colleagues in Congress, who rose up "more determined and bold than I ever saw them. Many avow themselves disunionists, and a still greater number admit, that there is little hope of any remedy short of it."

Disunionists considered this the moment and the cause they had long sought for a national split. From his Alabama power base,

William Lowndes Yancey urged the South to "teach the North, that when we speak brave words, we will follow them, if needs be, by brave acts." He told his followers that if the people in the North were not ready "to respect our rights, we will promptly dissolve all political connection with them." Many in the Lower South cheered such fiery words. Ever hopeful of preserving the Union through a unified Southern polity, John Calhoun battled the Free Soilers, as well as Yancey, Hammond, and others ready to secede.

Back in Georgia, the issue was as hot as anywhere in the country. The *Georgia Telegraph* called for "secession . . . resistance, open unqualified resistance." Tempers flared; violence struck home. On a fall day in 1848, then Whig congressman and Unionist Alexander Stephens bumped into Judge Francis H. Cone, a state supreme court justice and lead voice of opposition to any compromise with the Free Soilers, on the steps of Atlanta's Thompson Hotel, one of several new inns built in the booming upstart railroad town. Bad blood already existed between the two men. The foolhardy, ninety-pound Stephens berated the two-hundred-pound Cone, who lashed out with a knife, slicing Little Alec multiple times, nearly severing his hand, and stabbing him deeply and almost mortally near the heart. Stephens barely survived. His hand was permanently mangled. Cone pled guilty to attempted murder and got off with an $800 fine.

ALTHOUGH STEPHENS WAS laid up for months, a force committed to reaching a solution to the crisis arose among his fellow Southern Whigs in concert with some of their Northern party brethren and more moderate Democrats. Record high cotton prices, which raised concerns about the economic debacle a true sectional split would bring, aided the desire to reach a compromise. As close as James Calhoun was to his cousin the senator on most political questions—and as personally devoted as he was—his moderate outlook gave him no doubt that he sided with those working to preserve the Union.

In Washington, moderate voices bid desperately to stave off secession. In September 1850, Congress enacted a legislative series, known collectively as the Compromise, put forth in the Senate by Kentucky's Great Compromiser, Henry Clay, revised by a young Stephen Douglas of Illinois, and supported by a coalition including Massachusetts's Daniel Webster. The acts postponed the question of slavery in the new territories until they had applied for statehood, granted California statehood as a free state, banned the slave trade in

Washington, D.C., and, as recompense for the electoral imbalance in favor of the North, promulgated the Fugitive Slave Law. That engendered a system for capturing and repatriating runaway slaves and set criminal penalties for those harboring them. For slaveholders, this was the prime element enabling them to support the Compromise, and for abolitionists, it was the most repugnant. Vociferously opposed by an increasingly consumptive John Calhoun and even more vituperative fire-eaters and abolitionists, the Compromise nonetheless passed.

Its passage put the fire-eaters on the defensive throughout the Upper South and Northern border states, deflecting calls there for a sectional split back to a national debate about the best ways to resolve differences between the sections. Things were different in the Lower South, where the debate raged on. As cast by Calhoun, Hammond, Yancey, and others, the Compromise could only be viewed as a defeat of Southern interests, presaging far worse defeats to come. Calls went out for resistance, even the taking up of arms. South Carolina, above all, was ready to secede. If it did, Alabama would follow, and likely Georgia after that. Surely other Southern states would in turn.

WITH THE NATIONAL UNION at stake, the thirty-nine-year-old James Calhoun played an unsung but important role in gaining his state's support for the Compromise. In late 1850, he was elected as a delegate to the state convention convened on December 10 to consider Georgia's response to the Compromise. The die was cast ahead of time because he, like most of the popularly chosen men sent to Milledgeville, was an avowed Unionist. He formed part of a persuasive block at the convention that included Howell Cobb, the Georgia Democrat and Speaker of the House of Representatives who had steered the legislation through Congress; a now largely recovered Stephens; and fellow Whig congressman Robert Toombs. As part of a thirty-three-member committee, Calhoun helped draft and, following a tumultuous debate, push through the convention's final resolutions. Together they came to be known as the Georgia Platform.

The platform declared the state's fealty to the Union and urged "preservation of our much loved Union," but only upon the condition that the compromise laws of 1850 remained in force. Above all, read the final resolution, continuation of the Union "depends" on enforcement of the Fugitive Slave Law. The convention in its platform presented a defense at once of slavery, state sovereignty, and the compact between the states and the national government in the formation of the Union. "Southerners," proclaimed Cobb, "have a natural right to revolution [should their inalienable property rights be violated] but not a constitutional right of secession." He would come to disavow those words, but for now he joined Calhoun and the other convention leaders in crisscrossing the state to win support for the Georgia Platform.

Though the Compromise seemed only a stopgap measure to hold together two fundamentally misaligned sections of the nation, the Georgia Platform proved a triumph for all wishing to keep the Union whole. Col. John Milledge of Augusta gushed as the convention's Unionist outcome checked the drive toward secession, "The eyes of the world were upon [Georgia], but calm and inflexible, she came forth in the midst of unparalleled excitement, holding in her hands the destiny of this Empire. . . . Her voice was for peace and the Union. *She joined it in 1776 and she saved it in 1850.*" Georgia's leadership in supporting the Compromise quickly brought its more resistant neighbor states into line and assured its popular acceptance. Radical disunionists had been defanged—for the moment.

NEAR DEATH, Senator John Calhoun saw the Compromise as a loose bandage over a massive, bleeding wound. He was convinced the Union could not hold under its terms. In the last days of his life, he prophesied the coming cataclysm with uncanny accuracy. "I fix its probable occurrence within twelve years or three presidential terms," he told Virginia senator James M. Mason. "You and others of your age will probably live to see it; I shall not. The mode by which it will be done is not so clear; it may be brought about in a manner that no one now foresees. But the probability is, it will explode in a presidential election." He died less than two weeks later, on March 31, 1850.

JAMES CALHOUN, having worked diligently to ensure Southern acceptance of the Compromise that Senator Calhoun died while fighting against, moved, like many Southern Whigs, from his rapidly dissolving party to the newly created Constitutional Union Party, which, as the name indicated, placed loyalty to the United States as laid out in the Constitution above any sectional feelings. He rose within the party's ranks, which included many former Whigs, Northern and Southern. Loyal to his region, his country, and his party, he won election to the state senate in 1851 as part of an electoral wave in support of the Compromise that swept through much of the South. Loyalty to town and district, though, was another matter.

Within a year, he uprooted his family and law practice and moved, in 1852, from the small but refined village of Decatur to Atlanta, the new railroad stop growing up fast within the pine-forested hills and gullies a few short miles to the west. His brother Ezekiel moved his medical practice and home there as well.

Where once there had been only log cabins, a new city was sprouting. Two more rail lines, one from Macon and another from Augusta, followed the Western & Atlantic down from Chattanooga to the new upland mercantile hub. Though many respectable people still refused to move in among the roughhewn laborers who had come for the jobs building the new rail lines through the land the Cherokee once called home, the clear-sighted attorney and politician could see where Georgia's future lay. Here, he would finally win "respectable" office, and the South would build its Gate City.

## II

# GATE CITY

REVOLUTION THUS RAN ITS COURSE from city to city, and the places which it arrived at last, from having heard what had been done before, carried to a still greater excess the refinement of their inventions, as manifested in the cunning of their enterprises and the atrocity of their reprisals. Words had to change their ordinary meaning and to take that which was now given them. Reckless audacity came to be considered the courage of a loyal ally; prudent hesitation, specious cowardice; moderation was held to be a cloak for unmanliness; ability to see all sides of a question, inaptness to act on any. Frantic violence became the attribute of manliness; cautious plotting, a justifiable means of self-defence.

—THUCYDIDES, *THE HISTORY OF THE PELOPONNESIAN WAR* III:82,
TRANS. RICHARD CRAWLEY

# CHAPTER 7

# THE CORNERSTONE

MANY PEOPLE REMAINED SKEPTICAL about the value of the railroads penetrating the remote up-country Georgia. Even James Calhoun reportedly had his doubts. An acre of land in Terminus could still be had for fifty cents. With comparatively few miles of track in the South and not enough people or goods to ride over the existing lines, the Western & Atlantic seemed a state-financed railroad to nowhere. Calhoun supposedly insisted, "The terminus of that railroad will never be any more than an eating house." Fellow DeKalb County representative Chapman Powell was said to have retorted, "True, and one day you will see a time when it will eat up Decatur."

Calhoun would come to eat his words, apocryphal or not. Only a dozen families, less than two hundred people, lived in the renamed Marthasville when the first W&A train rolled into town in 1845, but things changed quickly, and the tiny settlement never looked back. It shortly outstripped the older Decatur and Marietta to the north. Although Calhoun's Decatur neighbors vowed to build a wall between their aristocratic village and the upstart rising in the forest crossroads to the west, within five years of that first train's arrival, Atlanta, as the crossroads with metropolitan ambitions was ultimately rechristened, had captured three-fourths of Decatur's population.

Drawn by railroad jobs and the money the trains brought to town, new residents moved in daily. "It was said that no one was ever born in Atlanta," wrote Lucy Hull Baldwin, an Atlanta diarist, "but everyone moved there from somewhere else." They came from all over the

South and even included a smattering of Yankees and foreigners in search of opportunity. At first, most came from the up-country neighborhood, James and Ezekiel Calhoun among them. Acknowledging the new reality, in December 1852 the two brothers moved their families into big brick houses they built on Washington Street, a short walk from where the hulking car shed would soon be built and across the tracks from the burgeoning Five Points central business district. The family houses stood directly across the street from Saint Philip's Episcopal Church; it was a few steps further to the Central Presbyterian Church, and not far beyond stood the Second Baptist and the Trinity Methodist churches, houses of worship that rarely saw the brothers. Like everyone in the town center, they lived close enough to the railroad tracks that soot from trains passing on the Macon & Western line grayed hanging laundry. Bells, whistles, and the clickety-clack of the cars over the rails provided a rhythmic accompaniment to their lives night and day. A fire engine house was stationed across Washington Street to deal with the frequent blazes ignited by sparks flicked out by the passing trains. The town's three fire companies could do little once fires ignited in any case. Several times, whole streets of trackside houses went up in flames. The city council finally required all downtown structures to be built of fireproof brick or stone.

James's eldest son, William Lowndes Calhoun, grew into adulthood in the Atlanta house. Lowndes, as he was known, recalled the elegance of his father's home with its "very large rooms . . . handsomely finished and decorated." It was a lively place. His father's sociability and good nature drew frequent guests, including many leading political figures of the day. "Within its walls, true Southern hospitality of the old time ever prevailed," Lowndes said. His father also entertained guests on a large plantation he purchased just outside the incorporated town limits. The property was about a mile beyond the newly surveyed City Cemetery, later renamed Oakland Cemetery, and stood close enough to his house and office that he spent many peaceful afternoons there, returning home before sunset.

If Calhoun was boundlessly hospitable at home, he was all business at work. His relocated law practice grew with the city. To his great pride, Lowndes apprenticed with his firm starting in 1853, at age sixteen. When court was in session, father and son walked together almost daily from the family's house around the corner to the new two-story, brick, hundred-foot-long City Hall and County Courthouse. An oversize version of a classic Southern village courthouse, it was topped by a cupola and overlooked a large public square where it served as the city's most important civic structure and meeting place. It was a place Calhoun would soon come to know intimately.

In 1854 the last of the four new railroad lines linked up at Atlanta's central Union Station, a new car shed with a massive vaulted roof perched on heavy brick piers where passengers exchanged trains among the four lines across four parallel platforms. Goods and people now reached the city swiftly from nearly all points of the compass. From nearly a thousand miles away, the *New York Times* noted that in passing through Atlanta, travelers could now make an unbroken rail journey from New York City almost to New Orleans in less than four days. The tracks across the country, the paper enthused, "are social ties—nationalizing powers—bonds of love and peace. Every mile of them is a new argument for union."

Whatever railroads symbolized for the nation's political future, the locomotives in and out of Atlanta drove startling growth. On most days, close to fifty passenger and freight trains chugged in and out of the center of town, carrying thousands of people and vast amounts of freight with them. The 171-mile run from Augusta took ten hours and forty-five minutes and cost $5.50; for $5 more a passenger could continue on for the nine-hour and fifteen-minute connection over 138 miles to Chattanooga (eleven and a half hours by night), a journey that formerly required five or more uncomfortable days by mule-drawn wagon in fair weather and twice that or longer in snow, ice, or rain.

Frequent derailments, car fires, and delays to let opposite-running trains pass through were the norm. But comfort mattered less than the railroads' speed and dependable, low-cost transport of goods for sale, warehousing, and distribution. New residents, new businesses, iron mills and foundries, and fast construction followed the trains into Atlanta like the dense smoke trailing from their stacks. Just five years after the first train chugged into town, the population had grown more than twelvefold, to 2,572 residents. Five years after that, the population had more than doubled again. The city continued to add about another thousand residents a year after that, making it by far the fastest growing in the state. Soon it trailed only Savannah and Augusta in size. Although still far smaller than New Orleans, Charleston, and Richmond, by 1860 the tiny up-country frontier village, not even shown on the map fifteen years before, stood among the fifteen largest urban centers in the South.

Nobody anticipated Atlanta's stupendous growth, so nobody planned for it. A tradition of haphazard development took hold. New streets paralleled the railroad tracks, causing through roads that had once been Indian paths and cross streets to intersect at odd angles. Businesses, houses and their garden plots, warehouses, and foundries were built willy-nilly along the same roads, often bumping up against railroad tracks. Traffic tie-ups became all too regular. So did accidents, as wagon drivers and pedestrians rushed across the tracks ahead of the trains, sometimes paying a tragic price for their impatience.

What lay beneath the wagon wheels—mud—also slowed traffic. The red-clay streets were affairs of mud in the rain and deeply rutted and potted when dry. Walking or even driving through town could prove slow torture. Kate Massey, who grew up in Atlanta, remembered how, after it rained, the streets and sidewalks, paved with stone only in the central downtown, turned into thick, gluey mud. "We had intimate relations with it," she recalled. "Pedestrians waded through it; vehicles mired in it. It was very intrusive, very sticky, and very red."

The constant construction and poor street drainage added other dangers. In the same year that the Calhoun families moved to town and three years before the first gas lamps illuminated downtown streets at night, Atlanta's *Daily Intelligencer* newspaper warned visitors straying out of the center of town not "to walk [the] street[s] unless the moon shines particularly bright, or unless you can hang on the coattail of some friendly guide." The pedestrian unfamiliar with his surroundings would "probably find [him]self . . . at the bottom of a pit" and also risked toppling into "deep trenches dug out for cellars." Little wonder that a New York travel writer journeying throughout the South in 1856 described the overgrown and disorganized town as "the most unattractive place" he had seen on his entire tour.

Barnyard animals grazed freely, sparking complaints from "greatly annoyed" neighbors about other neighbors' failure to stable "cows lying around their gates and lots." Others bemoaned the similarly boorish behavior of the out-of-town visitors on stopovers for train connections or markets. Farmers bringing produce for sale bedded down in wagon yards. Any who sought entertainment, sin, or both found plentiful offerings while staying in town. Even in 1860, when the city was much calmed from its early frontier-settlement days, a census of white residents' occupations found twenty-three barkeepers, nine professional gamblers, and forty-nine admitted prostitutes. Bearbaiting and cockfighting, one saloon or grog shop after another, brothels on Line Street, outdoor gaming at card tables along Fair Street, public hangings, and other popular amusements drew rollicking crowds. Further out Fair Street, bettors gathered at the fair grounds racetrack for horse-racing sessions. Audiences at the new eight-hundred-seat Athenaeum stage in the Five Points reveled in appearances by the famed midget General Tom Thumb, accompanied by a giant, a bearded lady and a whiskered nine-year-old boy, and concerts by the likes of the savant black pianist Blind Tom. A local semiprofessional acting troop, the Atlanta Amateurs, performed there to rowdy and often drunk audiences.

The Athenaeum filled the upper floors of a large building, with a grain depot and sometime slave auction mart occupying the first floor. The structure stood directly across the railroad tracks from the Atlanta Hotel. A planter who had come to town to sell his harvest and purchase more slaves with his earnings could spend a comfortable overnight at the hotel, belly up to its bar to enjoy fresh oysters brought in daily from Savannah, stroll over to catch a show at the Athenaeum, and perhaps gamble, drink, and indulge in the town's other blue offerings, before catching an outbound train home. For the more family minded, parents in summertime could take their children to enjoy ice cream at a parlor on the outskirts of downtown on Peachtree Street, next to a sixty-foot-high, horse- or slave-powered version of the Ferris wheel fully fifty years before the Chicago's World's Fair made it a universally popular amusement park ride.

The genteel and high-minded found little outside church to comfort them. "A rougher village I never saw," one circuit judge said of early Atlanta. For a small town, Atlanta managed to engender a large and colorful underworld. Prostitution, thievery, brawls, gunfights, and even murder were common, especially in the parts of town known as Snake Nation on the southwestern side of town along Peters Street, where the bodies of murder victims were frequently tossed, and Murrell's Row, on Decatur Street not far from the car shed. Those who wanted to civilize frontier Atlanta sought to bring order to its streets. A semiofficial organization known as the Rowdy Party liked things the way they were. The two sides battled for control of the town. With no sheriff, jail, or local court until after 1850, criminal gangs had the upper hand.

When the mayor convened a special court and threatened a Rowdy with imprisonment in Decatur, the accused's incensed and drunken brethren rolled a War of 1812–era cannon across the street from the town office, at the time on the second floor of the mayor's dry goods store, and blasted a wad of grass, rocks, and mud through the window. That was the last straw. A committee of brave and well-armed citizens surrounded a house where the Rowdies gathered. The posse captured the gang's leaders, threw them into a makeshift calaboose, and scattered their followers into the surrounding wilds. Not long after, the shanties and shacks that filled Snake Nation went up in flames.

NOBODY CAME TO ATLANTA to appreciate its beauty or gracious citizenry in any case. From Charleston to New Orleans, most other Southern towns moved to the rhythms of the planting and harvest seasons. Planters formed their elites, and long-standing aristocratic families dominated social, business, and political life. But in the fast-rising commercial crossroads of Atlanta, people came for business. Their major crop was cash, cash grown through trading and railroad services. Money knew no season, no past, only what it could grow into tomorrow. Young, industrious, and increasingly rich, Atlantans harvested bales of it at all times of the year. The freight cars ferried Black Belt corn and cotton; western grain, bacon, and produce; Virginia and Carolina tobacco; Louisiana salt and sugar; coastal rice, oysters, and fish; Tennessee coal; Appalachian iron, copper, and other minerals; and Northern and European textiles and manufactured products. The town also became the regional foodstuffs market as yeoman farmers from the surrounding countryside rolled in with their wagonloads.

Trade in all those goods kept the streets and shops crowded, market stalls lively, salesmen barking, the freight depots jammed. A reporter for the *Daily Intelligencer* observed, "Passing along Whitehall Street [an important commercial street] this morning, we thought of Broadway, New York, and her wholesale trade." Others boasted that their town was "wonderfully New Yorkish in its notions." Few elsewhere in the South would have welcomed the comparison; to Atlanta's "Georgia Yankees," it was flattery. They were Yankee only in their business-first outlook. Although a number of Atlanta's leading citizens had immigrated from the North, the makeup of its white population differed little from other Georgia towns. Southern-born natives comprised more than 90 percent of the city's populace.

Even the haughtiest outsider had to admire the town's surge to success and the wealth its industrious citizens acquired and displayed. One visitor from Athens exaggerated only somewhat when he marveled at its "thousands of fine, substantial and costly houses"; another from Augusta agreed that "no city in the South has ever made such rapid and astonishing strides in all avenues of progress."

Atlanta was an instant city, one modern in character and mores, unlike anything the South had known. An Atlanta mayor at the close of the 1850s freely admitted that "rough and unpolished [the town] may be . . . [but it is on its way] to becoming a bright and glittering jewel in the diadem of Southern cities." In a nod to the source of its swift journey to prominence, the city's new seal was emblazoned with a steaming locomotive. Atlanta's doors were flung wide open to all who rode in. At a spring 1857 banquet in Charleston, William Ezzard, mayor of Atlanta, was toasted with a salute to his increasingly important city on the move: "The Gate City: The only tribute she levies is the affection and gratitude of those who partake of her unbounded hospitality."

HER HOSPITALITY WAS SKIN DEEP. Atlantans shared white Southerners' deeply ingrained and fiercely defended racist support for the South's peculiar institution, slavery, even though slaves were a luxury that few Atlantans wanted or needed. Georgia had more slaves and slaveholders than any state in the Lower South, second only to Virginia in the South as a whole, with a slave population by 1860 of more than 462,000, or 44 percent of the state's total residents. That belied a heavy imbalance among different regions. African-descended slaves formed around two-thirds of the population in the coastal area and more than half of all people living in the Black Belt, the fertile strip of dark cotton-producing soil running from the South Carolina to the Alabama borders through the lower piedmont. Things differed markedly in the up-country, particularly in Atlanta, where the black portion of the population, slave and free, never amounted to more than 25 percent of residents. In 1860, Atlanta's population consisted of 7,751 whites, 1,917 slaves, and just 23 freemen. Fewer than 1 in 20 white Atlantans—373 in all—owned slaves. Elsewhere, the number of slaves a man held determined his stature and wealth. In Atlanta, only 44 slaveholders bothered to possess 10 or more bondsmen; just 15 possessed 20 or more.

The bondsmen who lived in town worked mainly as household domestics and servants—women predominated in the local slave population. Male slaves here stood out because the vast majority worked in nonagricultural settings. They labored in small factories and artisanal shops or in construction. Many had blacksmithing, coach-making, cobbling, and other skills that their masters could hire out; other bondsmen joined railroad and building crews or helped as hospital orderlies. Increasingly, as the need for labor grew, owners allowed their slaves to keep a few cents of the payment as an incentive for hard work or for extra hours of employment they contracted for on their own.

In working outside the plantation economy and far from the farm fields, Atlanta's slaves represented a tiny fraction of the South's overall black population, perhaps fewer than 5 percent. Atlanta's urban bondsmen worked alongside whites, sometimes even in competition with whites. They heard city talk, those able to read newspapers, and they shared what they learned, creating an information network beyond that of isolated rural slaves. They cared deeply about the tumultuous national events that revolved around their slave status.

These people, neither fully slave nor entirely free, came to form a unique class of Atlanta residents who lived precariously between the society of their white masters and perpetual enslavement.

Thus it was that Bob Yancey came to grow rich.


LAWYER, POLITICIAN, AND PLANTATION owner Ben Yancey, like other men of affairs in the Lower South, watched Atlanta's explosive growth. With tristate business interests and family ties, he noted its central location, convenient transportation network, plentiful markets, and brimming shops. He finally decided to move his family in 1856, purchasing a large mansion in the most fashionable residential downtown neighborhood on Washington Street, one house below the square in front of City Hall. No sooner had the Yanceys arrived than they packed up again. James Buchanan, a Northern Democrat who supported slaveholders' rights as fully as any Southerner and courted favor in the South, had won the presidency. He passed over Ben's powerful brother, W. L., for a cabinet post he longed for. As a sop to the influential Alabaman's electoral base, Buchanan appointed W. L.'s brother, Ben, commissioner to the Argentine Confederation.

Ben's household was shaken up by the move. Slavery had been abolished in Argentina three years before, and Ben risked the valuable Bob's flight if he brought him to Buenos Aires. So, he would have to leave Bob behind. Atlanta offered Ben a way to turn his multitalented bondsman into an interest-bearing asset. Ben provided Bob the necessary papers, for blacks could not legally own a business, plus the start-up capital needed "to rent a shop and go to public barbering— and trading." In return, Bob would pay his owner a hefty premium, $150 a year. At about the same moment when Ben's brother, W. L., declared in a commencement address to the 1857 graduates of the University of Alabama, "Owing to the existence of African slavery in the South, the laws of labor were fixed—permanent—under perfect control," his brother enabled his slave Bob to open his first barber shop in Atlanta. "I gave him practical freedom and the means of making and using money," admitted Ben years later.

For a black man in nineteenth-century America, barbering was one of the rare ways to make a good income. Few whites cut hair. Bob Yancey's shop on Marietta Street flourished. The barber's chair provided him with a venue where his skills and personal qualities, including his comfort working closely with whites, paid off handsomely. Clients poured in, and soon he had two shops and employed seven barbers. He and his wife moved into a four-room house he built on land he purchased on Houston Street on a Northside rise just inside the town limits overlooking the downtown. They lived harmoniously alongside several prominent white families, including prosperous slaveholders such as James Calhoun's former law partner, Amherst Stone, and his wife, Cyrena, as well as Jared Whittaker, influential Southern Rights publisher of the city's leading *Daily Intelligencer* newspaper. Unlike his white neighbors, though, Yancey could not walk downtown to enjoy the town's festive nightlife without a pass and needed to entrust his property deed to Ben Yancey; slaves could not legally own real estate. Notwithstanding the strictures, within a couple years he boasted, perhaps with some merit, "No man in the place stood higher than I did, although I was a colored man."

He never made, so he claimed, less than $100 a day—phenomenal riches for a man of any color at the time. Most astonishing, he made that much even on days when few customers needed a shave or hair cut. Barbering was a good business for sure, but what enriched Bob Yancey, as he came to be known during the time Ben owned him, were his side businesses. He bought and sold goods, including fish, fruit, and chickens, through his shops. Boxes of costly tobacco and cigars moved steadily through his store.

Mostly, though, Yancey, who could not write and probably could not read, had a gift for doubling his dollar. He had "a good financier's mind and money," recalled Ben Yancey—plus a market. He carried on the suspect trade handled so often by repressed groups throughout history: high-interest usury. With its steady stream of railroad travelers, tradesmen, and farmers come for the markets, Atlanta routinely ignored laws against gambling, prostitution, and drunkenness. All those vices required ready cash. Bob Yancey had it. He loaned out money at what Ben Yancey termed an "enormous" monthly interest rate to "white gamblers."

As an experienced card player himself, he knew his clientele's weaknesses and strengths. It could be a dangerous business, attracting unsavory sorts. A seventeen-year-old ended an argument with a twelve-year-old "about a foolish bet" in Yancey's shop by shooting the boy, "inflicting a dangerous if not mortal wound." Money from loan-sharking came back to Yancey "fast." When the exchange of currency became a life-or-death matter for people passing through Atlanta, Yancey's money-handling skills would prove more valuable still. It was work only a black man in his unique position could do. He managed to save the astounding sum of $16,000 over the next few years. A slave became one of Atlanta's wealthier men.

As EXCEPTIONAL AS YANCEY'S practical freedom and business success seem, he was not unique among the city's slave residents. Joshua Badger, descended from early Massachusetts Bay Colony settlers, worked as a dentist and grew wealthy enough to own a substantial Decatur plantation. There, he fathered several children, some with his wife, plus two sons, Roderick and his half-brother, Robert, born of two different slave mothers serving in his household. Rare among white men who fathered children with their female slaves, the senior Badger freely acknowledged his sons. That did not change the fact that two of his children were born slaves to him.

Living on the family property as family property, Roderick and Robert deeply resented an enslavement that their white siblings did not know. While still a boy, Robert escaped at least three times, only to be captured and returned each time. When Joshua Badger begged his son to remain at home and asked why he fled his father's love and protection, Robert answered, "Because I want to be free." His father could do little for him in any case: Even a son required a formal writ of manumission from the Georgia General Assembly, something the legislature was increasingly reluctant to grant.

The static world of Decatur plantation and village life offered the Badger brothers nothing but slavery. Joshua educated his slave sons, teaching them dentistry. Joshua took a risk. Since 1833, anyone caught teaching a slave or freeman to read or write faced a fine and possible imprisonment.

Joshua Badger sent his boys off with their education, dentistry skills, and tools. In 1856, Roderick and his wife moved to Atlanta, where he began to practice the trade. Although they went as "free people of color," they were officially regarded as slaves. Roderick set up a dentistry practice as perhaps the first dentist of African descent in the Lower South. Most of his clients were white. Like his acquaintance Bob Yancey, Roderick Badger soon began to make and save money that would enable him to lead a life beyond the imagining of most Southern slaves—and prepare him for the day when the freedom he and his brother wanted so dearly might come.

THREE YEARS AFTER YANCEY and Badger came to Atlanta, a white man, Ephraim Ponder, saw in this emerging black entrepreneurial class and the growing industrial economy a pathway to a comfortable retirement together with his beautiful wife, Ellen. The forty-eight-year-old Ponder and his fourteen-years-younger wife lived in Thomasville, a small cotton town fragrant with pine on the state's southern border above Tallahassee. One of the southern Georgia Black Belt's wealthiest men, Ponder had grown rich trading slaves in Virginia during the mid-1850s, frequently in association with his brother, William Ponder, a Thomasville plantation owner. While in Virginia, Ephraim apprenticed many of the slaves he purchased in a variety of artisanal skills, making of them expert carriage makers, cobblers, blacksmiths, metalworkers, carpenters, masons, and other types of craftsmen. The skills greatly increased their market value, and Ponder owned around sixty slaves.

After Ponder settled back in Thomasville and married Ellen, he was finished with buying and selling slaves for a living. His son described him as "a kind and generous man" toward his bondsmen, though the lynching of a Thomasville neighbor's slave in 1855 for disobedience was a stark reminder to any rebellious bondsman of the potential consequences, should he consider testing the limits of any master's kindness and generosity. At some "future" point, his son later contended, Ponder wanted to free his slaves, but for now, he angrily resented "the intolerant bigotry of New England hypocrites" from whom his own father had bought the family's first slaves and whose abolitionist sons now railed against the very institution their forefathers had created. Until that day when he might grant his slaves their freedom, Ponder decided to turn his costly slave property into a profitable labor force. Their skill sets represented a potentially large and steady stream of income for him and his wife. But to capitalize on them, he would need to move to a place where their industrial skills were in demand. The swift growing City of Atlanta offered all the Ponders needed.

They prepared to live a gracious country life on the outskirts of the town while enjoying its expanding urban advantages. They purchased one hundred acres, for $1,460, out the tree-shaded Marietta Road, a mile and a half from the hubbub surrounding the car shed. The Western & Atlantic trains clattered by in a cut down the hill from their house, but boxwood hedges and orchards they planted sheltered the view. The attractive, sloping woods and fields were topped by a hill where they constructed one of Atlanta's most imposing estates. They modeled their new home on their former house in Thomasville. Sitting foursquare at the crest of the hill on a large lawn, the house had massively solid stone walls with a thick impasto of whitewashed plaster. The Ponders attached a brick kitchen—a rarity in the period when kitchens were normally kept far removed from the main house for fear of fire. From a rooftop observatory, they enjoyed the fresh breeze and panoramic views over orchards, clipped geometric boxwood, topiary bushes, and parterre beds, far into the surrounding countryside and down towards the center of town. Their slaves could take in work in three large industrial workshops on the property and lived in a neighboring row of slave cabins. Ponder foresaw in Atlanta a comfortable retirement, likely more enriching than anything possible for even a large Black Belt plantation owner.

NOT SO FOR FESTUS FLIPPER, the Ponders' most trusted bondsman; the prospect of the Atlanta move drove him to despair. He faced a likely permanent separation from his wife, Isabella, and their three-year-old son, Henry. Mother and child belonged to a Thomasville neighbor, Rev. Reuben Luckey. He ran a prominent local Methodist academy, and neither he nor the Ponders were willing to put up the purchase price to keep the Flipper family together. Flipper's wife and son would have to remain behind. It was a tragically common fate for slave families. Flipper refused to remain separated from his wife and son.

He worked his way through the web of laws designed to keep blacks from advancing beyond their day-to-day dependence on their owners. He labored past the daily hours required of him, selling his services on nights and Sundays. He accumulated enough money to buy Isabella and Henry from Reverend Luckey. The Ponders agreed to accept two more slaves onto their estate. They would repay Festus at some point when "convenient."

Flipper likely spent more than $1,000 for his wife and child to remain slaves, but the family could now dwell together at the Ponders' new Atlanta home. "The joy of the wife can be conceived," their son, Henry, later wrote, "—it cannot be expressed."

THE FLIPPERS MOVED WITH their owners to Atlanta. Once there, Flipper and the other skilled slaves were free to contract their own time. Ponder would have nothing to do with their business other than to provide them with necessary permits and travel passes and to collect his "rent." They became independent businessmen of sorts, in most respects little different from any white man selling his time and skills. But they turned over all they made to their owner, keeping any extra time or bonus earned. When in search of work, each morning bondsmen from the Ponder property would walk downtown to what was long known as "Hungry Corner," where slaves available for hire would gather to meet those looking for labor.

The Ponder slaves "acquired and accumulated wealth." According to Henry Flipper, who grew up on the property, they "lived happily," lacking "but two other things to make them like other human beings, viz., absolute freedom and education." Atlanta was not yet ready for that momentous step—far from it. Still, amidst slavery's unbending constraints, Atlanta's black population was laying true freedom's foundations. A black man could not at that point hope to buy his freedom in Atlanta, but he could earn some of freedom's blessings.

MANY ATLANTANS RECOGNIZED THE contradictions underlying their slaveholding society. Hired slaves gave whites who could not afford their own bondsmen access to slave labor, but it also provided the rented slave with leverage that came from having an absentee owner and a temporary master whose interests were often in conflict. The bondsman could exploit the situation to gain exceptional benefits never available to him in his normal conditions. Some open-minded whites, as well of course as those who benefited from being able to hire out a slave, supported the new freedom; others rebelled, seeing it as an "evil" undermining the permanent indenture of slave to master. Not surprisingly, large numbers of white Atlantans also resented the competition they faced from black men like Yancey, Badger, and Flipper. They bristled at the partial freedom these putative slaves enjoyed in their midst. The town's own government seemed unwilling to enforce laws restricting the slaves' activity. An 1855 Fulton County grand jury pleaded with the "proper authorities of the City of Atlanta to rigidly enforce the law against all persons who allow slaves to hire their own time, and prevent the continual trading of such slaves and free persons of color in the city." In 1858, two hundred white "regular citizen mechanics" protested to the Atlanta City Council and petitioned for protection from "negro mechanics whose masters reside in other places" who were underbidding them. Not long after, resentment aimed specifically at Roderick Badger and his successful dentistry practice boiled to the surface. On July 15, 1859, white dentists petitioned the city council, bemoaning the fact "that your honorable body tolerates a negro dentist, in our midst, and in justice to ourselves and the community it ought to be abated." The protestors appealed "for justice." The city council did not respond. In 1861, another protest to the town fathers against Badger again failed to elicit any restrictions on him. Badger's largely white clientele kept him in business, but pressure mounted to rein in the growing underground black economy.

On April 13, 1860, the city council added more restrictions on the business activities of black residents or other people of color coming to town, forbidding "any slave or free person of color from buying or selling or offering to buy or sell any liquor, eggs, chickens, or fish or any other article . . . in the corporate limits of Atlanta." But the business-minded city dwellers were a practical lot, more attuned to price than purveyor. The order was widely ignored.

Probably in a direct response to the many Ponder slaves competing with white workmen, the toothless city council made still another attempt to control the hiring of slaves in the first days of 1861, noting that "the employment of Negro Mechanics" whose owners lived outside town "operates very injurious . . . upon the interest of Citizen Mechanics." The council resolved to impose a $100 annual tax on the Negro mechanics. A week later, the council backed down and tabled the ordinance.

THIS QUASIFREEDOM BLACK RESIDENTS enjoyed could not be mistaken for real freedom. White citizens made sure that blacks understood that their marginal status could at any moment be stamped out.

Race laws designed to keep blacks in their place and to prevent any rebellious acts governed their lives. They could not legally smoke a pipe, walk with a cane, or leave their master's house or slave quarters after dark. They needed their owner's written permission to carry tools or drive a carriage. Given the different nature of slave life outside the plantation economy, where an overseer's whip and citizen patrols, or paddyrollers, doled out summary judgment and punishment, the city itself took measures to ensure obedience. One of the first ordinances passed by the city council directed the marshal to "fix . . . rings and poles on the calaboose for the convenience of whipping nigras."

Blacks could never let down their guard. The consequences might prove severe. For instance, if a white person carried a lighted candle or torch into a barn, he might be fined up to $50. A "slave, free person of color or Indian" faced thirty-nine lashes and fifty for abuse of the gas fixtures and streetlamps first installed in 1855.

White citizens also hoped to keep the region's rare free persons of color from ever entering town. The city council passed an ordinance requiring that "all free persons of color, coming within the limits of Atlanta, to live . . . pay to the clerk of the council two-hundred dollars." Failing to pay the exorbitant fee entailed a far higher price: jail and reenslavement until the offender had worked off the $200—plus repayment for food and lodging while in the calaboose. If nobody came forward to hire the offending freeman's time, he could be sold forthwith back into slavery. In the face of such a risk, freemen stayed well clear of Atlanta.

Any freemen who needed reminding of what slavery felt like could look in any of the slave yards scattered about town. At 8 Whitehall Street, between a cigar maker's and a lamp-oil dealer's storefronts, Crawford, Frazer & Company did a brisk business as the city's leading slave dealer among its nine "negro traders." Slaves sat chained to benches lining the Crawford, Frazer display room. A city resident recalled seeing prospective buyers walking through the room and examining the rows of men, women, and children before making "their selections just as they would have a horse or mule at a stockyard."

DESPITE THE PRESSURES AND the increasingly vitriolic white resistance, an interdependent interracial community developed. This lent Atlanta a largely unique status in the Lower South. At a time when the vast majority of Southern blacks dwelled in rural isolation with little personal contact with whites, yet depended upon them for virtually everything, a vibrant African community, supported in part by the increasing wealth and independence of men like Badger, Flipper, and Yancey, grew up alongside, and often freely intermingled with, Atlanta's burgeoning white bourgeoisie. For fortunate and skilled black Atlantans, unprecedented opportunities arose within the interstices of white society for them to better their lives, even as Atlanta clamped down officially on their liberties and chained and whipped the rule breakers.

Churches played an increasingly important role. Whites and blacks came together on Sundays most typically in the same downtown houses of worship. White men and women sat in the Baptist and Methodist church pews, while blacks filled the galleries overhead or attended services after the whites departed. Legally, blacks could not congregate in public places without a white observer on hand for fear that such meetings might stir up trouble. This was true for religious worship as well. Nonetheless, with Atlanta's churches' slave galleries overflowing, religious whites encouraged formation of black congregations.

The first black church opened in the 1850s, though services, even if led by a black preacher, always included a white pastor or marshal on hand. Henry Wright, a slave hand from a Decatur plantation who eventually found his way to Atlanta, attended Sunday services in a white church as his master required. Once the white pastor finished preaching to his white congregants, he turned to the black audience at the back or in the balcony. "His sermon usually ran," recalled Wright, "'Obey your master and your mistress and the Lord would love you.'" Black preachers were "instructed" not to stray from that message. Their words apparently carried little conviction and less effect. "None of the slaves believed in the sermons," said Wright, "but they pretended to do so."

## ⌖ CHAPTER 8 ⌖

# EARTHQUAKE

JAMES CALHOUN'S UNIONIST POLITICS seemed out of step with wider Southern sentiment, but he found a welcome in his new Atlanta home. He emerged as a local civic leader. His law practice grew with the growing city. Among his many activities to better the growing community, he served as a trustee in the founding of a new Atlanta medical college in 1854—a precursor to Emory University's School of Medicine.

THE CONFLICTING PARTS that made up the Compromise of 1850 quickly became brittle. The terms were scarcely able to hold the fragile, fragmenting nation together. The one-time triumph for conservative Unionists like Calhoun's Georgia alliance had proved short-lived. All over the country, North and South, radical figures increasingly dominated the debate. There was little margin for bipartisanship. Most Whigs became either Northern or Southern Democrats or, if committed to halting slavery's spread, joined the new Republican Party. In Georgia, the party realignments drove the Whig Party largely out of existence. Former Whigs Robert Toombs and Alexander Stephens, with whom Calhoun had once warmly served in the state's legislature, now held higher office in Washington, where they, especially Toombs, moved sharply into the Southern States' Rights fold. Union Democrats like Howell Cobb kept the Union in their party allegiance only so long as the party was prepared to defend the Slave Power, as Northerners called the Southern slavocracy.

Any Georgian committed to holding the Union together found keeping his footing on the shifting middle ground increasingly difficult. Calhoun held fast to his principled support for the national union and its constitutional underpinnings, joining men—most of them much older than he—who were willing to reach across the sectional divide. But after the Senate's compromise, the Whig leadership, Henry Clay and Daniel Webster, died in 1852, two years after John C. Calhoun, whose concept of a national confederation of states enabled by a defense of minority rights died with him. Nationally influential voices for the preservation of the Union were literally falling silent.

Democratic senator Stephen Douglas of Illinois drafted the Kansas-Nebraska Act in 1854, partially to open the territories beyond Missouri to railroad builders, but also to secure a future Southern electoral base for a presidential run. The act repealed a compromise ban dating from 1820 on slavery north of 36° 30 in the old Louisiana Purchase lands—a resounding victory for Southern Democrats, particularly for Speaker of the House of Representatives Alexander Stephens, who engineered its final passage. The 1854 act permitted slavery in the territories until they became states, at which point their residents could vote by plebiscite whether they wished to enter the Union as a free or slave state. Once slavery was established as an accepted institution outside the South, it seemed any check on its growth would be undone. Kansas became the focus of debate and the locus of confrontation between Free Soilers and Slave Power advocates, who vied for control of the territories—and thus future control of national electoral politics.

The new situation became a line in the prairies that the South was ready to fight for. Both houses of the Georgia legislature voted unanimously "that opposition to the principles of the Nebraska bill, in relation to the subject of slavery, is regarded by the people of Georgia as hostility to the rights of the South." As such, any who opposed the principle of free movement of property, including human chattel, anywhere the American flag flew stood, in the minds of large and increasing numbers of Southerners, for the destruction of the Slave Power.

On the ground in Kansas, angry, determined, and increasingly violent men confronted one another. Few slaves in fact ever reached the plains, but Free Soil and Slave Power ideologues created separate and competing legislatures. "Border ruffians" adhering to each would-be governing body attacked each other, sometimes with guns. Outside agitators streamed in. Bearded like an ancient prophet, John Brown, an abolitionist minister and farmer with roots in Connecticut and Ohio, saw an opportunity in Kansas to spark a wider war he hoped to carry out against slavery. He traveled to Kansas, where his sons were Free Soil homesteaders who now felt threatened by slaveholding neighbors. After a Northern church-based campaign of speeches, Brown came well funded and armed.

The South would not be outdone in its readiness to meet slavery's opponents. The sons and daughters of the Virginians, too, were on the move toward the frontier again, motivated this time not just by economic opportunity. Large parties of Southerners bent on home-steading in the territories and tipping the new states-to-be in favor of slavery passed through Atlanta, reported the *Intelligencer*, "almost daily" after passage of the new law. Mass meetings in town raised funds in their support. An Atlantan group called Emigrants for Kansas Territory organized to send local residents to colonize the plains for the South. The newspaper editorialized, "We doubt not the[ir] success . . . in the new territory, while the cause of the South will have in them true and efficient friends." It was not long before open guerilla warfare broke out in Bleeding Kansas and men on both sides lay dead.

SOMEHOW, WHILE THE SOUTH'S most powerful leaders rattled sabers and demanded respect for Southern rights, Calhoun still commanded his neighbors' support. A new county, Fulton, encompassing the en-tirety of Atlanta and weighted heavily to its residents, was carved out of the more rural and heavily Democratic DeKalb County in 1853. Despite the ever-heavier push of national affairs against his old Whig views, Calhoun won the race to become the new district's first state senator in 1855. He was reelected in each of the next two years as well. Ever the pragmatist, Calhoun worked in Milledgeville in the area he knew best, winning wide praise for his judicial-reform efforts. He also agitated on Atlanta's behalf to have the state capitol moved to the city—to no avail. But the effort put the rest of Georgia on notice that the upstart up-country town had mighty ambitions.

Outside Atlanta, a rising tide of radicalism threatened to swamp such good-government, business-first approaches. With the 1856 elections on the horizon, the Southern Whig Party's splintering sent its former members scrambling into various other emerging and still-born political organizations, none with even close to the regional or national clout of the Southern Democrats under its radicalized and more powerful leaders, like Cobb in Georgia, W. L. Yancey in Alabama, and Jefferson Davis in Mississippi. Calhoun and other Southern Unionists joined in supporting Millard Fillmore as a third-party American Party candidate.

In the North, many old Whig Party members gradually coalesced into the newly formed Republican Party, which, along with support for industry-minded infrastructure and tariff policies, sought to halt the spread of slavery. The Republicans' first presidential candidate was the famed western explorer John C. Frémont, now a slavery-loathing senator from California. The Democrat candidate was James Buchanan, a Pennsylvanian whose major political virtue was having been out of the country as minister to the Court of St. James in London, thus missing the entire Kansas uproar. Sympathetic to the slaveholders, he captured the South and enough Northern electoral votes to win the presidency. Fillmore could win only Maryland. Frémont handily captured the upper Northern states. The voting patterns made clear, though, that a Republican candidate who took another large Northern state such as Pennsylvania or Illinois could be president.

Two years later, in the closely watched off-year senatorial race in Illinois, Stephen Douglas defeated a little known Republican vying for his Senate seat in a hard-fought contest. Abraham Lincoln was a lanky small-town lawyer and former single-term Whig congressman given to humorously sardonic pronouncements that masked powerful ambition and a keen political intelligence. Douglas's opponent told large audiences during a series of nationally discussed public debates that, though "I, as well as Judge Douglas, am in favor of the race to which I belong having the superior position . . . there is no reason in the world why the negro is not entitled to all the natural rights enunciated in the Declaration of Independence. . . . I hold that he is as much entitled to these as the white man." More importantly for the Union, argued Lincoln, the divisiveness brought on by a nation contending over the further spread of slavery was a political hobble laming the country. Extension of "an apple of discord and an element of division in the house" would likely cause it to fall.

Lincoln favored effective compromises that would halt slavery's nationalization, closing off its spread beyond the slave states and placing it back "in the course of ultimate extinction." Such an outcome might take "one hundred years," but "it would be going out of existence in the way best for both the black and the white races." Ultraist Slave Power leaders viewed this "Black Republican," more widely regarded as a moderate Whig, as little different from the most ardent abolitionist. Whether the abolition Lincoln advocated came sooner or later, he threatened "the cornerstone" of Southern life and national power. The two views were irreconcilable.

IN RESPONSE TO THE THREAT, GEORGIA, like most slaveholding states, further knotted its already tight restraints on blacks. In December 1859, the state legislature passed a comprehensive package of laws designed to end any hopes blacks might have entertained of winning their freedom or, if free, relaxing within the safety of their liberty. Among its new statutes, the legislature closed the remaining loopholes prohibiting freeing of slaves by restricting dying owners stricken with deathbed guilt from releasing their human chattel from bondage through statements made in extremis. The newly promulgated laws also created a vaguely defined illegal-vagrancy status for free blacks apprehended "wandering or strolling about, or leading an idle, immoral or profligate course of life." That gave any court leeway to sell offenders, scooped up on an afternoon stroll or caught drinking, into slavery for two years for a first offense. A second conviction led to permanent reenslavement.

The possibility that racial unrest sparked by Northern abolitionist politics might engulf Georgia sent shivers through Atlanta. The shivers became pandemic when news broke of John Brown's return east and bungled October 19 attempt to instigate a slave revolt with a dramatic raid on the Harper's Ferry arsenal. Rumors of threatened or imagined black insurrections, more often than not based on unfounded reports of abolitionist provocateurs come south, ricocheted through the region. Just days after the calendar turned to 1860, the *Daily Intelligencer*, an influential Democratic Party organ, reported the arrest in Knoxville, Tennessee, of "an Abolitionist in the shape of *a traveling dealer in fruit trees*" (their emphasis). The editor, Jared I. Whitaker, had political ambitions in the city, and his newspaper, according to another Southern editor, enjoyed "tremendous sway . . . over the political arrangements of this State." He and his readers were "no advocates of mob law . . . unless the case be an extreme one," but they recommended taking firm steps "for such gentry," when identified, such as, "notify them to leave at once, and on their failure to do so, arrest and *whip publicly*."

The swift condemnation and hanging of John Brown and his small band of Harper's Ferry insurrectionists in early December 1859 had done little to allay Slave Power fears. Volatile Atlantans would no longer stand for affronts to their rights. Touchiness quickly became trigger happiness. Gunfire broke out at a New Year's Eve ball in a downtown hotel in answer to "someone giving expression to Abolition sentiments," the *Intelligencer* reported. Whitaker approvingly suggested, "Gentlemen of the Abolition *cloth*" learn from the incident. They should "well be chary of expressing such opinions and sympathies, for it is a noted fact that our climate invariably becomes unhealthy to such." Another disturbance broke out at a public celebration shortly after New Year's Day when a dry goods store clerk named D. S. Newcomb toasted the late John Brown, "stating," reported the *Intelligencer*, "that he should not have been hung." When the owner of the store was informed about his clerk's "conduct savoring of Abolition," he "gave him his walking papers." Newcomb fled town, "although," the newspaper archly pointed out, "delegations of citizens would have been glad to pay him their respects could they have discovered him. . . . The sooner he treads Northern soil the better it will be for him."

High tensions wound higher still as the November 1860 general election date neared. Dissenters were driven out of town, and blacks were often attacked. Barn fires were credited as the work of abolitionist arsonists or blacks. Vigilante committees rounded up and brutalized unwary slaves and freemen, who in desperation "confessed" to their evil acts or intentions. Lynchings and even burnings at the stake terrorized an already cowed populace.

Even the remote Georgia up-country, where relatively few slaves lived, reacted in panic to possible slave-revolt plots being hatched. Much as happened during the Indian removal wars, men went out on patrol duty at night, while women and children huddled together in windless rooms, recalled Sallie Clayton, then a Kingston schoolgirl. "There was very little sleeping and we gladly hailed the morning" after those nights spent listening for the murderous black men stalking whites to massacre. Despite having armed protection along, she and other children out on a nighttime ride "crouched in the bottom of the carriage like frightened hares." Many up-country parents moved their families to Atlanta, where they believed they'd be safer. Clayton's family soon moved into a large house on Mitchell Street, directly across from the open square in front of City Hall, next door to Ben Yancey's mansion on Washington Street.

Rumors of black insurrection could not be doused that summer. Finally, whites struck first. Word went out that on the night of August 25, dozens of black men in cahoots with a white abolitionist intended to burn down Dalton, a rail depot town on the Western & Atlantic line in the rough terrain of the northwestern corner of the old Cherokee country. The insurrectionists allegedly hoped to "accomplish all they could in the work of destruction" by night and then to take to the rails the next day, capturing a train and beginning a town-by-town rampage until they reached Marietta to "pursue the work of killing and burning." After that, "thence as far on the road as they were successful." That meant Atlanta. Shortly after sunset, a citizen force gathered near Dalton and then swept through several slave and freemen's quarters nearby, capturing thirty-six black men. One white man was taken and lynched.

The railroads that brought prosperity to the region took on a different, grimmer cast. Those tracks of prosperity could also carry a different and dangerous cargo, violent men bent on destroying Atlanta. White citizens all along the Western & Atlantic armed themselves, took to patrolling streets, and challenged all who dared move about at night.

In Atlanta, Whitaker got a popular hearing when he urged ending any freedom for blacks, which undermined public security and corrupted the slave population. He opined,

> Free negroes . . . go to and fro without any one to look after them specially—live by thieving—are almost invariably lazy and indolent, and are continually corrupting the slave population. We should be glad to see free negroism totally abolished, and we think the next Legislature cannot do a better thing than pass a general law compelling them to choose the alternative of leaving the State or being sold into slavery. Every negro in Georgia should have a master; it will be better for the community and infinitely better for the negro himself.

Even as Atlanta's black population lived in unprecedented freedom, many white neighbors shared his view that just as dogs should not roam free, their chains should bind them forever.

ATLANTA'S WILLINGNESS TO LOOK the other way while its black population lived in quasifreedom, at the same time that it was tightening the bonds of slavery, led to a singular publication event in the history of the Slave Power. Harrison Berry, a forty-four-year-old Covington slave hiring his time as a shoemaker, apparently in Atlanta, authored an extraordinary pamphlet in 1860, titled "Slavery and Abolitionism as Viewed by a Georgia Slave." With his owner's support, the forty-six-page diatribe was printed in Atlanta the following winter. It is the only known published writing about slavery by a slave still in bondage.

Berry had received what he called "some knowledge of an education" as a child on a Black Belt plantation where he worked as a field hand. Sold three times and thwarted in his efforts to purchase his freedom from his master, and probably deeply embittered, he became convinced that whites anywhere would never tolerate blacks other than as their inferiors. "The colored man," he wrote, "is but the tool North and the servant South." Northern whites used blacks indifferently to their ends; Southern whites openly enslaved them. Berry saw little that either side offered him except oppression. He addressed his pamphlet to those he labeled "the fanatical Abolitionists, who call themselves Republicans." He derided their activities, which, he insisted, only made the slave's life worse. The sole thing blacks, in slavery or freedom, might hope for from whites was an oppression less brutal. When the Black Republicans agitated the slavery question, "slaves," lamented Berry, "are much worse treated."

To demonstrate the abolitionists' poisonous effects, Berry created an imaginary dialogue between two slaveholders after one has spied a slave reading newspaper reports of the "proceedings of that Convention of the Abolitionists," then communicating his gleanings to the owner's other slaves that "they would not be Slaves much longer, for the Abolition party intended to set them all free." The first master gave his bondsman "two hundred lashes," and then both "whipped every one" of their slaves to convince them that their condition would never change. The political climate in the South, made toxic by Northern politicians, contended Berry, drove Southern whites to greater brutality, not fairness, toward their human property. "You [abolitionists] are absolutely the worst enemy the Slave has ever had." Their work for slave liberation was driving their slaveholding enemies to worsening repression of the slaves. "Even now," he reported, "the oppression is commenced, but where it will end God only knows."

Making vividly clear what form white reaction would take should Republicans ever come to national power, he laid out a vision of hell for people of color. He wrote,

I see gibbets all over the Slaveholding States with negroes stretched upon them like slaughtered hogs, and pens of light-wood on fire! Methinks I hear their screams—I can see them upon their knees, begging, for God's sake, to have mercy! I can see them chained together . . . and shot down like wild beasts. These are but shadows of what would have been done, had John [Brown] succeeded.

Berry feared that an impending Republican victory would "put mana-cles on every Slave South of Mason & Dixon's line," and lead to worse, much worse.

THE AUGURIES FOR JAMES CALHOUN, too, were dire: The fateful year 1860 started off ominously in February when Emma, his wife of twenty-eight years, the mother of his seven children, died. While he grieved, he also worried. In the following months, John C. Calhoun's deathbed prediction about the fate of the Union following a divisive presidential election came true. The forces that had so long threatened to split America faced off over the race for the presidency and its probable outcome. James Calhoun, his nation on the line, traveled out of the Lower South for the first time in his life in a desperate bid to help save the union he held so dear. The opposing sides, though, were moving swiftly to the extremes, leaving men who clung to the center, like Calhoun, gasping for political oxygen.

The die was cast after nearly all Southern delegates bolted from the National Democracy convention. At the party's April platform-drafting meeting in Charleston, South Carolina, W. L. Yancey penned a separate Southern position paper, supported by Howell Cobb, Robert Toombs, and most other leading Georgia Democrats. The Yanceyites insisted that their party commit itself to congressional protection for slavery in the territories—and, with Southern expansionists eying Cuba, Haiti, and even Mexico, in any future American lands. The Northern delegates, led by Stephen Douglas's backers, held a nominating majority, but the Yancey men controlled the Charleston meeting. They wanted to destroy the Douglasites' hold on the party. "Ours are the institutions which are at stake; ours is the property that is to be destroyed; ours is the honor at stake," intoned Yancey in demanding federal protection for slaveholder rights anywhere within the growing nation as a condition for his followers' support for Douglas. The

Douglasites resented Southern intransigence, on the grounds that it would serve only to drive Northern voters away. When they rejected the Yancey men's demands, the Southern Democrats walked out.

With the Southern wing out of the National Democracy Party, a split Democratic vote in the November election was assured, almost certainly paving the way for Republican victory. Yancey and his followers took heart. Before he left Charleston, a huge crowd gathered in the port city's moonlit courthouse square to hear his farewell speech. A deafening three cheers went up for "an Independent Southern Republic," followed by Yancey's declaration that "perhaps even now, the pen of the historian is nibbed to write the story of a new revolution."

Northern Democrats put forward Douglas as their candidate, with former Georgia governor Herschel Johnson, a Calhounite Unionist, as his running mate; the Southern Democrats came together in a separate convention to back Buchanan's vice president, Kentucky's John Breckinridge. Not tightly bound to the Southern Rights faction before his nomination, Breckinridge warmly endorsed Yancey's platform, moving the press and public to link his candidacy closely with the Yanceyite ultraists. Larger crowds turned out to hear Yancey at his campaign stops on behalf of Breckinridge than for the party nominee himself. The fearless Yancey did not hesitate to campaign anywhere, even in New York City and other Northern locales, where he faced angry National Democracy audiences, yet, ever the duelist, still lashed out at Douglas, "that arch-enemy of true Democracy," and declared that only the election of Breckinridge would "keep the [federal government's] hands off of us and let the Constitution work its own way!" to save the Union.

In Atlanta, the Breckinridge Yanceyite men were proclaiming a victory that would enshrine Southern rights while at the same time using the campaign to build a local base in the South's fastest-growing city in support of separation from the Union, should it come to that. They exuded a confidence in the city's future, whatever happened. Even as the *Intelligencer* urged a crackdown on dissenting voices and tighter control of free blacks and hired slaves in town, its pages crowed about Atlanta's miraculous progress. The instant city could not be contained. "Springing, as it were, spontaneously out of a wilderness, she proudly rears her head and *demands* audience of her sister cities." Atlanta's strides were unprecedented in such a short span of time. "The quiet path once trod by the stalwart form of the red man, is now the busy street; the woods that once knew no sound save that of the whoop of the savage, is now familiar with the shrill whistle of the engine. . . . All branches of business are prospering; and we are emphatically going ahead." Atlanta was cocky enough to stand up to any challenge.

That economic engine armed Atlanta with trade weapons it could fire at its Northern enemies. A letter writer in the *Intelligencer* declared the time had come to "strike, merchants of Georgia, at the black Republican and Abolition trade of the North! Repudiate it, give it no countenance, no quarter; reject it, spurn it, and spit upon it." Merchants who continued to trade in the "black" merchandise faced barely veiled threats. A few days later, a gathering of many city merchants drew up resolutions for cutting off trade with Northern merchants known to be in favor of abolition and to form a mercantile association open only to those ready to declare their fealty to the Southern Rights cause.

Not to be outdone, the *Intelligencer's* leading daily rival, the *Southern Confederacy*, under its ferocious editor, James P. Hambleton, published what it called the "Black and White List" of New York businesses. The editor demanded merchants boycott the "black list" entities until they "make an affidavit that they are neither Black Republicans, Abolitionists, Free-Soilers, or have never been enemies to the institution of Slavery and the rights of the South in any shape or form whatever." Reporting on the list, the *New York Times* responded tartly that all operating under "the Atlanta ban" need only "abjure all that is to be abjured, and avow all that is to be avowed, and they will have no further trouble in disposing of their silks and muslins. The streets of Atlanta will once more rustle with constitutional crinoline; the drummers of New York will once more shake hands with the buyers of Georgia; and the names of the faithful will shine as the stars in glory upon the new-washed pages of the *Index Expurgatorius.*"

The South was confident that its economic power would persuade the North not to risk the consequences of a Douglas or Lincoln victory. The sectional split that would ensue would deprive the North of supposedly indispensable Southern commodities—sugar, rice, tobacco, and above all cotton—its economy depended on for trading, shipping, and manufacturing. Yancey's arguments were widely repeated: If the South were forced to secede, it would come out on top. A united South acted from a position of strength. "We are independent of the world," Yancey boasted. Any foes would quickly be forced to capitulate, but it would never come to that, he claimed. "We have the great peace-maker, King Cotton, within our midst," clothing the world. Whitaker in the pages of his newspaper followed the Yanceyite argument to conclude similarly, "Dissolution of the Union would involve the North in commercial ruin, from which we see no means of her recovering. The South would be very much inconvenienced by dissolution, for a time at least, but the fearful effect, the national disaster, the permanent bankruptcy, would be to the North." As such, support for Breckinridge would work to the advantage of those who hoped to see minority Southern rights permanently enshrined within the nation. Or, as Yancey more vividly laid out the issue, "Unless these people, therefore, want to go naked, and show their nakedness, they had better come and solicit the support of our cotton planters."

TOGETHER WITH MANY OLD Whig Unionists, James Calhoun watched the city hotheads with deepening unease. He doubted their argument and questioned the legality of secession talk. A slaveholder and cotton planter, yet he remained a "Union man . . . in favor of peace all the time." This position put even the most respected of Atlanta men at risk. Still, he spoke out against those driving a wedge between the national sections—and local political factions. His friend Joshua Hill, whom he had known since their Abbeville childhood, now a Georgia piedmont congressman, voiced his and other former Whigs' fears in Washington when he wrote, "the Union . . . cannot be preserved in my honest opinion, unless these ultra opinions are surrendered upon the altar of our country." Hill and Calhoun would try to build that political altar. They joined others out of both the South and North, a small group of figuratively old men—many of them literally old as well, Calhoun being one of the younger at forty-eight— whose Whig memory encompassed a time when country stood above party and personal interest. Calhoun made the three-day train journey to Baltimore in the first week of May 1860, where he served as vice president of a convention calling together former Whigs and oppositionists of all stripes into the Constitutional Union Party. The delegates wished to turn back the clock by choosing a presidential ticket that stood for nothing except its opposition to the sectional ideologies cannibalizing the nation. (They also secretly hoped their candidate might prevent any more radical candidate from gaining an electoral majority and force the election back on Congress, where a compromise president might be more likely to emerge.)

In Baltimore the convention delegates pointedly made no effort to draft a real platform, declaring, "Platforms adopted by the partisan Conventions of the country have had the effect to mislead and deceive the people, and at the same time to widen the political divisions of the country, by the creation and encouragement of geographical and sectional parties." Instead, the men on hand pledged "to recognize no political principle other than *the Constitution . . . the Union . . . and the Enforcement of the Laws.*"

Mocked by Georgia newspaper editorials as "shifting, halting, ambiguous, Delphic," the party without an ideology nominated a white-haired Whig ticket—both men were born before 1800 and remembered well the spirit of the young Republic—with Tennessee senator and slaveholder John Bell at its head and former Harvard University president and classics scholar, famed orator, and Cotton Whig, Massachusetts senator Edward Everett as his running mate. One Kentucky newspaper derided as quaintly nostalgic the Constitutional Unionists' call for the nation to leap off the trains rushing headlong down the same track toward each other by launching a "party which shall ignore the slavery question. That issue must be met and settled." National politics assured that indeed it would be.

THE CONSTITUTIONAL UNION'S Baltimore convention took place a week before the Republicans met in Chicago to nominate Abraham Lincoln. A man from the Old Northwest whose humble origins gave him some of Andrew Jackson's common man's appeal, his dislike of slavery, yet his willingness to countenance its continuance on constitutional grounds within its existing slave state boundaries, lent him an air of moderation appealing to Union-leaning border-state residents. He also was unlikely to control Congress, and the Supreme Court was stacked heavily in Southern Rightists' favor. His hands would be tied. Little matter, Southern Democrats and even many Constitutional Unionists declared that a Black Republican victory would tear the Union apart. "Let the consequences be what they may," warned a Georgia secessionist editor, "whether the Potomac is crimsoned in human gore, and Pennsylvania Avenue is paved ten fathoms deep with mangled bodies . . . the South will never submit to such humiliation and degradation as the inauguration of Abraham Lincoln."

With November's election just days away, the *New York Times* reprinted a warning from Hambleton in the *Southern Confederacy*:

"The Southern masses, almost to a man, regard the simple election of Lincoln as an 'overt act,' and *it is the solemn determination of the eight cotton states to secede immediately on his election* . . . and we tell our Northern brethren that the South is dreadfully in earnest for once." But there had been many previous calls stretching back to the Nullification Crisis and beyond to drive the Northern wolves from the Southern henhouse. Few Northerners, Lincoln included, took the latest threats seriously.

The electioneering infused Atlanta. Yancey campaigned widely for Breckinridge, including a stop in Atlanta with his brother, Ben, now back from Buenos Aires. More than 1,200 people turned out to hear W. L. speak in front of City Hall. They responded, as they did throughout the South, with the "wildest enthusiasm." A few days later, he warned another gathering that if the Republicans won, Southerners would be no better than slaves to Northern masters. They "intend to make us hewers of wood and drawers of water," he proclaimed. Before that would happen, though, his land would, he vowed, fight. Southern patriots would "take the banner of liberty and plant it on the mountains of [Virginia], and there we will entrench ourselves as a body of freemen."

Not long after Yancey's stop in town, on October 30, one week before Election Day, the Northern Democrats' candidate, Stephen Douglas, held a campaign rally in Atlanta. He, too, was introduced to a roiling crowd. While a twenty-one-gun salute welcomed the Illinois senator, the enormous gathering threatened to turn violent when Douglas repeated a warning he had made at other stops that "secession doctrine is revolution."

As the leader of the local committee in support of the Breckinridge Southern Democratic ticket, *Intelligencer* editor Whitaker submitted a questionnaire to Douglas designed to undermine any claim he had on wavering Southern voters. He asked whether, "upon the election of Abraham Lincoln," each state had "the sovereign right to decide to withdraw," and "what shall be sufficient cause for a withdrawal from the Union?" If the Southern states did secede, would he support the federal government in "coercing" them back into the Union—and would he regard their citizens "as rebels and traitors" to be punished? Douglas didn't answer, but he had already made clear that, as he had just told a North Carolina crowd, he would "hang every man higher than Haman who would attempt . . . to break up the Union by resistance to its laws."

The Breckinridge supporters let voters know where they stood in the event of a Lincoln victory. "States' Rights men of Georgia," they asked, "will you sustain the abominable Federal government? Are freemen of the South slaves of the Federal government? Are you to be punished as rebels and traitors, when acting under the sanction and mandate of our own State?"

Those questions needed no reply, but in answer, the next day eighty-five men took up the mantle of the Revolutionary War, declaring themselves a minuteman association. A few days later, they passed a series of resolutions proclaiming their readiness to take on the United States—a new war for independence—should the Black Republican win. The resolutions concluded with a vow "to unite our people as a band of brothers in resistance to Northern aggression, and in defense of ourselves, our property and our firesides." Ben Yancey, who had released his slave Bob to hire his time and live virtually as a free man in a city readying itself to go to war over their eternal master-slave relationship, called for approval of the resolution, "not as a partisan addressing partisans, but as a patriot addressing patriots."

UNLIKE THE MINUTEMEN WHO published their views and their resolve to fight, if it came to that, a self-styled Union Association met "very privately often at night," according to Amherst Stone, a member of the group. The men, totaling more than twenty but with a core of fifteen or fewer, moved their meetings from place to place among their offices and homes, entering and exiting two or three at a time to remain as inconspicuous as possible. Stone said, the "confidential friends" sought "to sympathize with each other all we could" and to promote the cooperationist cause. A local attorney and well-off property owner, Stone had moved from Vermont to Georgia in search of opportunity before finally settling with his Vermont-born wife, Cyrena, in Atlanta in 1850. With their growing savings, they built a comfortable home with quarters for their six slaves and two white servants on a hill overlooking the downtown. The property was sold to them by their neighbor, the *Intelligencer*'s Southern Rights publisher, Jared Whitaker. Both the Stones' and the Whitakers' houses were within sight of Bob Yancey and his wife's small home. All knew their prominent black neighbors well.

The Unionist circle was almost an alternative, if clandestine, chamber of commerce, uniting some of the town's wealthiest and most respected businessmen. Among its adherents were William Markham, mayor of Atlanta a few years earlier and co-owner of the Atlanta Iron Rolling Mill, second in the South only to Richmond's massive Tredegar Iron Works; foundry owner James Dunning; Nedom Angier, a city councilman, physician, and real estate developer; Michael Myers, coproprietor of the city's largest dry goods store with twelve clerks in his employ; and Julius Hayden, president of the Atlanta Gaslight Company, which illuminated the downtown with coal gas, and owner of a thriving construction and brick manufacturing firm. These men had also come south from New England, grown rich in Atlanta, and, no matter their political outlook in the current crisis, acquired numerous slaves. While many were Northern transplants, several in the group did come from the South, including real estate magnate and banker Alfred Austell, perhaps Atlanta's wealthiest citizen, and his fellow Tennessean, local schoolmaster Alexander Wilson.

Not surprisingly, there were no black men on hand, though Markham knew Bob Yancey, among other leading blacks in the city, was "heart and soul a Union man." They could not possibly attend Union circle meetings, which would have served to confirm the abolitionist paranoia. Had Yancey wished to attend the nighttime gatherings, he would have needed a permit from his owner, the fiercely secessionist Ben Yancey, to move about after curfew in any case.

There's no evidence that James Calhoun attended the Union circle's meetings, but he was the city's foremost defender of cooperation with the incoming national administration and counted many of the Union Association's members among his longest-standing business associates and closest friends. He almost certainly knew of their clandestine gatherings and very likely joined in from time to time. Amherst Stone was his former law partner, and both men, along with several others in the group, were part of the syndicate behind the much-ballyhooed Georgia Air Line railroad, chartered by the state in 1857 to run through to Charlotte, North Carolina, connecting on to Virginia. Although the first shovel of dirt in the line's construction had been turned earlier in the year, work was now suspended following the fiscal collapse set off by secession fears. Most of the men meeting that summer were also former Whigs, and certainly all supported Calhoun in his campaign on behalf of the oft-belittled Constitutional Union ticket of Bell and Everett.

Few in the group were willing to go public with their opposition to those calling for a secessionist reaction should Breckinridge lose, as appeared likely. However, another Tennessean in the group, James

Stewart, a prosperous flour miller, published a letter in the *Intelligencer* in the early days of summer with an apocalyptic warning should "the low mutterings of disunion fire give vent to the pent up flames." Those who spoke of secession needed "to complete the sum of horrors which must inevitably result from the consummation of your frenzied schemes." He urged readers to envision the undoing of Southern civilization that would follow. "Clip the telegraph wires," he wrote, "pull up your iron rails—stop the transportation of our mails—compel non-intercourse between the North and South—involve our now peaceful inhabitants in civil war—close up our workshops and factories—abandon our plantations and farms—neglect the education of our children, and let famine and pestilence ensue." In the political firestorm, such dire predictions appeared as another attempt to undermine Southern unity and were quickly discounted.

The mounting political crisis had also turned economic. A local Unionist newspaper aligned with Fillmore's former American Party and now Calhoun's Constitutional Unionists, the *National American* noted that "the bare prospect" of disunion and consequent disruption of trade had crushed the price of cotton on the Atlanta market. More importantly, worried bankers no longer accepted bills of exchange for cotton, the South's major credit source, sending the rest of the economy based on King Cotton into a tailspin. Adding to consumer woes were unprecedented jumps in basic food prices caused by fears about a cutoff of access to the big northwestern producers of grain and bacon. All this anxiety arrived before a shot was fired.

The *National American*'s editors soberly reminded readers that "disunion is civil war." If the secessionists carried the day, the prospects for Atlanta, together with the whole South, could not be bleaker: "*All who are in favor of civil war, starvation, ruin, desolation, robbery, arson, murder, and the utter destruction of the South, should go for disunion if Lincoln is elected.*" War, the *American* jabbed its finger at the ultraists, would impoverish Southern society, leading to anarchy and crime.

In the heat of the polarized election season, few voters in the Lower South were in any mood to heed such Cassandras. Except in Atlanta. Bucking the tide, many Atlantans stepped back to take a second look at what lay ahead.


THE ELECTION'S OUTCOME IN GEORGIA, the South, and the nation as a whole was never in real doubt. Breckinridge won handily in Georgia, as he did throughout the entire Lower South, capturing nearly 49 percent of the state's ballots, followed by Bell's 40 percent, and Douglas's 11 percent—though that did give a Georgia majority to the Unionist candidates. In a heavily Democratic region that favored Breckinridge by as much as 70 percent in some nearby counties, Atlanta continued its contrarian ways, choosing Bell over Breckinridge. Bell received 1,070 votes, Douglas, 345, and Breckinridge the secessionist, 835. Combining the votes for Bell with those for Douglas, voters here demonstrated a decided readiness to compromise for the sake of the Union.

Lincoln was not on the ballot anywhere in the Lower South. He failed to win a single slave-state electoral vote, but with slightly less than 40 percent of the national votes cast, he nonetheless won the election. "With the election of the Black Republican Lincoln," harangued the city's *Daily Intelligencer*, "the irrepressible conflict is upon us."


IF A LAND ALREADY STRAINING to its utmost to thwart abolitionist sentiment could become further aroused, Georgia did. Lincoln's election sparked a racial backlash unlike any seen before. Gov. Joseph E. Brown owned few slaves and was regarded as an up-country Unionist, but he held deeply racist views about the need to keep black "inferiors" enslaved. Now, he sounded the alarm about the impending threat to the white man's place. On November 7, he addressed the legislature on its opening in Milledgeville just hours before the expected election results were confirmed. He warned that once the Republican administration took office, a "hungry swarm of abolition emissaries" would arrive to "eat out our substance, insult us with their arrogance, corrupt our slaves, and engender discontent among them; while they flood the country with inflammatory abolition documents, and do all in their power, to create . . . a war of extermination between the white and the black races." As he spoke, rumors flared of a slave insurrection in the nearby countryside, lending credibility to his inflammatory words.

Mobs in several communities responded by attacking blacks and Northern whites of whatever stripe. The gibbeting of blacks the pamphleteering slave Berry warned against had begun. "The Anarchy [I] predicted . . . some eight months before the election," he wrote, "stating that the election of a sectional man to the Presidency would inevitably bring about the state of things which stands before us in a monstrous form at the present time, may be conceded to me as a good guesser, at least." Little imagination was needed to predict that worse lay ahead.

The state legislature responded to the "threat" of a race war by rushing to "disarm" would-be black insurrectionists. Laws reaching back before American independence barred blacks from owning horses, carrying firearms, being employed by druggists, or purchasing poisons. Georgia legislators reinforced the bans in December, adding penalties against whites caught furnishing weapons or poison to blacks. Locally, in towns and the countryside, vigilante committees formed to patrol roads and check in on slave quarters.

Portions of Atlanta society went on alert. In early December, the minutemen, now numbering nearly two hundred and campaigning openly for secession, designated twenty-one members as a Committee of Safety. Without the city's official permission—with Mayor William Ezzard a founding member of the association, it was a given—the minutemen's special committee took on the authority to summon before it "all suspected characters, with power to rid the community of such when they should be proved to be hostile and dangerous to the rights and interests of the city or the state."

After the election, Calhoun and other Unionists despaired. They urged acceptance of the results but resistance to any attempt by the federal government to restrain slave property rights. Instead, they tried to revive the words of the Georgia Platform behind the Compromise of 1850. It was futile. They could no more hold back the gathering popular forces pushing for disunion than an ancient tree can resist a hurricane. "All Union men here were held in reproach," Calhoun said. As if physically poisoned by the political miasma engulfing his beloved city, he fell "dangerously sick" with typhoid fever. Nonetheless, the Union Association and others put him up to represent Fulton County in opposition to secession ordinances a state convention, called by the legislature for mid-January, would consider. He ran together with his friend and protégé George W. Adair, a former lawyer and train conductor turned successful real estate developer. Calhoun and Adair still stood for compromise, though their position left them "very unpleasantly situated," said Calhoun. With the vigilance committee poking into their loyalty, it now became "dangerous for Union men to express themselves publicly," he added. The cooperationist men faced off against a secessionist slate pledged to stand united for "war in every way in which it was defined or definable" if the incoming president should try to force the state back into the Union.

The Unionists' chances largely evaporated after news reached Atlanta of South Carolina's epochal December 20 vote to secede. Jubilant minutemen blasted a fifteen-gun salute to the first state to proclaim its withdrawal from the Union at sunrise two days later, marking the start of a daylong celebration. They fired off one hundred more guns in the afternoon in front of a huge throng come from far and wide to hear fiery speeches, including one by Howell Cobb, who had just resigned as the lame-duck president James Buchanan's secretary of the treasury. That night a torchlight procession wound its way through Atlanta, gathering strength as it went, until stopping with thousands on hand downtown to burn Lincoln in effigy. The sound of gunfire rang through the chill night air. The U.S. flag came down, and a state flag flew in its place over Atlanta and the rest of Georgia.

Lincoln's inauguration was still three months off, but secession was increasingly a foregone conclusion. Ever optimistic about an independent Southern nation's future, the *Intelligencer* made a Christmas Day promise that independence would come without "the shedding of a single drop of blood." On New Year's Day, its ultraist sister newspaper in Augusta, the *Daily Constitutionalist*, urged its readers to vote their hopes for secession: "If you would hush this quadrennial struggle which convulses the land every Presidential election, and still political discord, and give peace and quiet to our disturbed land, go on! look not back! for daylight will now be sooner seen before than behind."

Not everyone believed such rosy forecasts. On the night of December 31, rather than celebrate the New Year or his recent remarriage, Calhoun, still only "partially recovered," addressed a public gathering. "Ardently attached" to the United States, he made what he called "the best argument I could to induce the people not to dissolve the Union." In somber tones, he asked listeners to recognize that "the Constitution of the United States had not been violated" by Lincoln's election. The South had "no sufficient cause of war, or secession." In the white heat of the secessionists' call to arms, his dispassionate words melted away into the last night of the year.

ATLANTA LIVED NOW WITH its feet in the raging river of rebellion. The current swept the people away. Their own and their Virginian forebears' successful settling, shaping, and exploiting of the landscape and human chattel bolstered their hopes for a still better future through the radical step of secession; they were an independent-minded people creating an independent nation of independent states. They had a model in mind in their grandparents' and great-grandparents' fight against their British overlords. This would be the *second* American Revolution.

On a miserable rainy January 2, the pro-secession slate crushed Calhoun's by an almost two-to-one margin. His sometime business associate Whitaker had worked hard in person and in the *Daily Intelligencer* pages for the stunning outcome. He trumpeted, "There is, perhaps, no place in Georgia where the result looked more doubtful a month ago." Statewide, the secession delegates won a bare majority, with about 44,000 votes for immediate secessionists to some 42,000 favoring cooperationists. The vote was so close that Governor Brown wouldn't publish the final tally for several months and, even then, claimed a much wider majority in favor of secession. On that historic day, Brown ordered Georgia militiamen to seize Savannah harbor's Fort Pulaski, a currently empty federal garrison. On January 19, the convention delegates gathered in Milledgeville, where they needed little time to vote 166 to 130 for secession. Georgia left the Union.

LITTLE INTERESTED IN LIFE beyond his family and his religious and business activities, bookseller and paper goods merchant Samuel P. Richards could not help but notice the booming guns, peeling bells, and exploding fireworks echoing throughout the city. With family and business connections above and below the Mason-Dixon Line and in England, his homeland, he had followed his brother Jabez from New York City to Georgia. They sold Bibles and religious tracts, stationery, greeting cards, and sheet music out of a traveling buckboard until they set enough money aside to open their first Book, Music, and Fancy Store in Macon in 1848, where Samuel remained for thirteen years. "Jabe" made the move to Atlanta first, opening a second Richards Bros. store on Decatur Street. Samuel would not follow him there until 1861. Once in Atlanta, after crowding in with his brother's family, he built a four-room, two-story stone house near his brother's on Washington Street at the Fair Street corner on the edge of the fashionable Southside residential district. They found a ready welcome for their wares in the flourishing town.

Samuel Richards turned thirty-seven in early 1861, sharing his birthday celebrations with those for the swiftly advancing secession movement. He seemed years older. With just a smattering of gray in his dark hair and beard, he rarely relaxed his severe churchman's demeanor. Devout to a fault, "there was no figure more familiar than his" at the Second Baptist Church, a few minutes' walk up Washington Street to where it fronted City Hall Square. He volunteered as the church's deacon and clerk and could be found there on his knees twice a day. He also sang bass at choir practice in the evenings and at Sunday services.

His sole worldly diversion, other than harmonizing with amateur singing groups, together with tens of thousands of other eager readers, was to devour the latest Charles Dickens novel as soon as the most recent installment reached his shop. At times, he seemed to step out of one of those pages—and not as one of the more likeable characters. Like the sanctimonious and blustery Mr. Bumble, the church beadle of *Oliver Twist*, he seemed "always angry and cross" and quick to "correction and discipline" with his own and others' children, recalled a woman who was an "everyday intimate" of the Richards household as a child. Mischievous local boys shared "tales of his ogreish behavior" and, out of spite, "plagued him to death" by taunting his cow, picking fruit from his trees, and plucking flowers out of his carefully tended garden. He never lost the habit, gained from his long days as an itinerant back-roads peddler, of selling at the greatest profit and accounting for every penny in his household and shop. He won few friends with his abstemious and sometimes cutthroat business tactics. Increasingly well-to-do, he nonetheless welcomed only paying boarders into his home, renting even to relatives. He was, recalled his granddaughter's dearest childhood friend, "the absolute antithesis of the old Southern type." Little matter, for he felt right at home in his store alongside the two hundred other shopkeepers in the town's bustling Five Points commercial center.

In an age when politics was the all-consuming topic of conversation, Richards rarely concerned himself with the day's controversies—except as they interfered with sales. Now, with "people . . . too much engrossed in political matters to think of buying books," politics did matter to him. He feared that the national crisis sparked by the election would force the brothers to shut their doors. "Disunion . . . will prove ruinous to *our* business," he moaned. "No business doing, no money coming in and nothing heard but 'Secession,' 'Secession,' until I am tired and sick of the word." He blamed the belligerent secessionists in town for his business falloff. He scorned the rabble-rousers as "*professional* men and young *squirts* who have but little or nothing to lose in any event, or *politicians* who aspire to office in a Southern Confederacy."

The die now cast for Southern separation and independence, though, he knew which way the wind was blowing. At present, he rented two household slaves, but even as he taught biblical injunctions against covetousness, he observed his neighbors' fine liveries and their large landholdings and many slave hands outside town. He aspired to all the wealth the South offered, and here that equated with ownership of land and slaves. He watched minutemen parading past his storefront and heard the local Mercantile Association call for a boycott of the Northern dealers whose wholesale goods he retailed. He ordered larger shipments on credit. He agreed that the time had come to "form a Southern Republic, a '*White* Man's Republic' . . . and leave niggerism and 'free dirt' proclivities to the North, and the Abolitionists upon whom surely the curse of a just God must rest for *they have destroyed our Country*."

He set sail on the rising secessionist tide. A dire letter from his brother William, a minister in New York, did not dissuade him. William warned him that "the [secession] measures we are taking [are] suicidal in the extreme as well as unjust," but that same evening he rehearsed "a Southern Marseilles Hymn" that his choir would sing at a public demonstration called by the minutemen to celebrate slave-state independence. Who among those walking past the lamp-lighted church's open doors could hear the rousing chorus of rich voices echoing out and continue to question the grandeur of the South's future as a new, independent land? If Richards could not yet "sympathize" with the radicals' enthusiasm for what lay ahead, he now accepted that secession had become "a stern necessity for us in the present crisis." Failing to take this final step toward state sovereignty would give "aid and comfort to the Abolitionists in their fell designs of making war upon the South."

IN THE HEAT OF THE SECESSION CAMPAIGN, the necessity for a breakup of the United States and the bright prospects for a united South seemed certain. The future lay through the unifying, daring, and forward-looking choice of secession, contended Atlanta print opinion leaders like Whitaker and Hambleton.

A small number of men, including many in a position to know, spoke out against such excessive optimism. William Tecumseh Sherman, who had come to love the South during his army years in Florida, South Carolina, and Georgia, burst into tears when he learned about South Carolina's vote to secede. He recognized immediately that secession meant war. He told his closest Southern friend, David French Boyd, that he would have to fight "against your people, whom I love best."

Cump had left the army in 1853 after his military career reached an apparent dead end. He was not much good at other professions either, failing first as a San Francisco banker and railroad investor and then as a territorial lawyer. In 1859, he accepted a job as the first superintendent of the Louisiana State Seminary of Learning and Military Academy in Pineville. Now, Sherman paced about and sputtered with tears of rage, while Boyd, a fellow faculty member, listened in. "You don't know what you are doing," he bellowed. "I know there can be no such thing [as peaceable secession]. . . . This country will be drenched in blood. God only knows where it will end. . . . [The people of the North] are a peaceable people but an earnest people, and they will fight, too." He predicted disaster for the South.

> You are rushing into war with one of the most powerful, ingeniously mechanical, and determined people on Earth—right at your doors. You are bound to fail. Only in your spirit and determination are you prepared for war. In all else you are totally unprepared, with a bad cause to start with. At first you will make headway, but as your limited resources begin to fail, shut out from the markets of Europe as you will be, your cause will begin to wane. If your people will but stop and think, they must see in the end that you will surely fail.

Less than a month later, the governor of the seceding state of Louisiana sent arms seized by the state militia from the U.S. arsenal in nearby Baton Rouge to Sherman at the Pineville academy. He refused to accept the munitions, resigning his post instead. He departed for St. Louis, not knowing when he might return south again.

AS IF THE VERY GROUND beneath the Southeast was trying to signal the splitting of the nation in two, on a cloudless day following Georgia's secession vote, the earth literally cracked. A minor earthquake lasting ten seconds rattled Atlanta and its surroundings. Such seismic events typically shook the region once every twenty years. The superstitious might have viewed the temblor's timing as a warning sign; secession's ardent backers claimed just the opposite. The absence of damage was an auspicious omen that the fracturing of the Union into two nations would shake things up while causing little harm. Jared Whitaker in the *Daily Intelligencer* thought it prophetic. "May not its coming and passing away so easily," his newspaper related, "with the clear and bright sky, be symbolical of the present political convulsion in the country, which in the South will pass away so easily, leaving the spotless sky behind."

Just to be clear, he added, "So far as civil war is concerned, we have no fears of that in Atlanta."

# CHAPTER 9

# NEVER! NEVER!! NEVER!!!

WITH THE STARS AND STRIPES no longer flying over Atlanta, the city voted for town officers two days before the Milledgeville secession convention. Some still hoped the city might return to being a moderate bastion against the rising radicals, but it was not to be. The agenda-setting secessionists now held the stage and would fight to stay there. James Calhoun's older brother, Ezekiel, the physician, militia captain in the Creek War, and one of the region's earliest white settlers, ran for mayor. Even finding a soapbox from which to speak his mind was difficult. "Every Union man was muzzled," said the Unionist builder Julius Hayden. The white-haired physician had doctored a goodly number of the town voters at one time or another, but, like other Unionists, "could not express any opinion at all unless he expressed it in favor of secession." Opponents questioned Calhoun's manliness and readiness to stand up to the Black Republicans, labeling him and several city council candidates "submissionists." They withdrew in protest two days before the vote. *Intelligencer* publisher Jared Whitaker, who had beaten the drum for secession, was no moderate, but he was in fact less radical than his opponent, a former mayor, William Ezzard. Whitaker won the office he had long had his eyes on.

Confederate Atlanta now assumed the cause of nation building with the same boosterish fervor it brought to its own rise. Mississippi senator Jefferson Davis, named president of the Confederate States of America, resigned his Washington seat and traveled to the government's temporary capital in Montgomery, Alabama. Once there, the triumphant overlord of the rebel government, William Lowndes Yancey, introduced his man to the cheering crowd turned out to greet him, declaring in the words that would become the best remembered of his life, "The man and the hour have met!" During Davis's journey south, on February 16, two days before his own inauguration and two weeks before Abraham Lincoln's inauguration in Washington, he stopped over for a night in Atlanta. Militia units paraded and fired volleys in his honor. Five thousand people gathered to hear him speak outside the Trout House hotel. Meeting in his room, city leaders urged him to build the new government's capital in Atlanta. They touted the city's healthy air, central location, unmatched rail access, seven hotels, and abundance of fresh seafood, meat, and vegetables, "including," wryly boasted the *Gate City Guardian* newspaper, "goobers, an indispensable article for a Southern Legislator." The *Southern Confederacy* newspaper proclaimed its hometown would gladly serve, being "*par excellence* the most suitable point within the limits of the Southern Confederacy for the locating of the Capitol and other public buildings." Rising in the distance, Stone Mountain contained more than enough granite "to construct the public buildings of a thousand Southern Confederacies."

SOON AFTER THE DAVIS VISIT, the city dispatched a trio to Montgomery to promote those same advantages to the new government's assembly. The chosen men were Mayor Jared Whitaker and former mayor William Ezzard, both widely known secessionists, and one prominent former opponent, James Calhoun. Whatever his resistance to secession and fears about the future, Calhoun felt bound to the course the South had determined upon for its future. His heritage, family, wealth, social standing, personal ties, and loyalties made this *his* land. He was a *Calhoun*. Moreover, much of his personal wealth was tied up in his more than fifty slaves. He "sympathized with the cause of the South." The vote had been taken, the state had seceded, and now, he believed, "it was my duty to go with the South."

Choosing a course of continued resistance would place the proud former legislator outside the constitutional bounds set by the new government in Montgomery. The Southern legislature quickly passed laws "defining treason," he said, "to obey [to] which every citizen was bound at the peril of life, liberty, and property."

The peril became quickly apparent. Under a headline reading, "Loyalty to Government the Duty of Every Good Citizen," James P. Hambleton's *Southern Confederacy* recognized that some might question where their duty lay, and "regardless of the authority of this Government, and their obligation to support it, have turned their longing eyes towards the Black Republican fleshpots of Lincoln, Greeley [the influential Republican *New York Tribune*'s editor] & Co." The newspaper condemned all Union partisans and urged that they "be summarily dealt with as traitors. There should not be among us any man who is so base, and treasonous . . . [as to] recognize the authority or laws of the United States as extending over us." The new government should wield its power to exile or punish any who undermined the rule of its law.

"REGULATORS OR INVESTIGATING COMMITTEES," an extension of the minutemen's Committee of Safety, applied other, more direct means to bring former Unionists in line. They went from house to house, meeting with known Unionists. After the encounters, most dropped their public opposition to the new order. Hayden trembled as he watched the committees do their work. "Every Union man they could find who expressed Union sentiments was ordered to leave the State and a good many were whipped or lynched," he said. Some still resisted. A local committee rode up to Harrison Baswell at work in his farmyard outside his house on the rich bottomlands he worked along the Chattahoochee River just outside Atlanta. The men demanded he support the Confederate cause and join a military company they were forming. If he did not, right then they would string him up as "a traitor and Tory to his country." Baswell retreated into his house and came back out, pointing his shotgun at them. "Gentleman," he said, leveling his gun, "I ain't got but one time to die, and before I will go off with you, and fight against the Union, I will die in my own yard." The men turned out of his property, but he hid out after that. When he discovered his son J. T., not yet sixteen, had joined the Confederate army, his nephew recalled Baswell spitting out angrily that he would have shot his son rather than "see him go off like he did to fight against the Union."

Inside the Atlanta town borders, secession leaders had subtler means of silencing opposition to the new national government's authority. Outspoken Union supporter James Stewart could no longer get his views published in local newspapers. He did find a Nashville newspaper willing to print a letter in which he declared, "I may be coerced to obey but will never acknowledge the government *de facto* of the seceding States." He was unwilling to recognize the legitimacy of Confederate authority, but he called for peaceful resolution of the sectional dispute. He hoped "the incoming [Lincoln] administration will not countenance or recommend war upon the erring people of the South." He roundly criticized the seceding states' seizure of U.S. arsenals as "stupendous farce," yet urged moderation, calling for the defeat of the radicals, North and South, through ballots and not bombs. The *Intelligencer* ignored his pleas for peace and reprinted the Nashville article for its readers as an example "bristling with rank treason." The editor fulminated, "We cannot live with incendiaries and traitors in our midst," and then, invoking an ancient city ultimately destroyed from within, urged the swift expunging of such men. "If the Greek horse is among us, let us cast him into the sea." The newspaper would not let the matter rest. A few days later, it branded Stewart as "dangerous" and decreed that "all such men as this Stewart is must leave this community 'peaceably if they may, forcibly if we must.'"

Finally, two afternoons later, *Intelligencer* publisher and now city mayor Whitaker, acting "at the invitation of a highly respectable Committee of [unidentified] gentlemen," called privately on Stewart. Stewart emerged clearly shaken by what Whitaker told him. He now contended that his words were "misapprehended." In a public statement printed in the *Intelligencer*, he swore his loyalty to the new government and vowed to "support with all my power any war measure necessary to resist coercion, by the Federal Government, or the invasion, by any other power, against the Confederate States of America." He never published another word challenging secession or questioning the legal authority of the Confederate government. Not long after that, his flour mill won a rich contract to produce hardtack for the Confederate army.

IN LIGHT OF SUCH FORCED CONVERSIONS, Calhoun and nearly all of his many Atlanta neighbors who had once spoken out for, or at least voted in favor of, cooperation and compromise threw their lots in with the Confederate cause. The editors of the *Southern Confederacy* likely had Calhoun in mind when the paper admitted "that many of our best citizens were opposed to secession." Such men, in the heat of the crisis, "were honest, and we have not the slightest word to say against or fault to find with them on this account." The newspaper welcomed their newfound readiness to accept the revolution, praising each former opponent who had "since manifested his patriotism and fidelity to his country, by yielding a cordial and cheerful obedience and support to its policy."

Such generosity toward former oppositionists had its limits, however. "We do think it is the *bounden duty* of every good citizen to defend his country in every measure she may adopt," the editors averred, "or leave it at once. It is wrong and wicked to remain among us, opposing our government, and stirring up strife and dissensions among our people, in opposition to the established order of things; and no good man will be guilty of it." Those who remained in Atlanta should now declare and show their loyalty or leave—or face other, more serious consequences.

IN THE SPIRIT OF REVOLUTIONARY patriotism infecting the city, there were practically endless opportunities for Atlanta residents to demonstrate their zeal for the new order. The city's rail hub location made it a frequent layover point for government and military officials and troops in the newly forming rebel army traveling among the seceding states. On March 12, the new Confederacy's vice president, Alexander Stephens, spoke to several thousand people outside the Atlanta Hotel. Little Alec had dropped his long-standing opposition to secession, even competing with fellow Georgians Howell Cobb and Robert Toombs for the Confederate presidency. He could hardly have failed to catch the irony of where he now stood and looked out over a sea of beaming faces. On these same steps, thirteen years earlier, he had run into Judge Francis Cone, who had refused to retract his "traitor" charge against Stephens, then in the unequal ensuing fight, nearly stabbed him to death. Now, Stephens—"his withered hands in gloves much too large—a face like a mummy—except the bright black eyes—and when on the stand . . . look[ing] like a little boy"—stood one rung below the top of the new Southern national government.

His words to the crowd have not survived, but he probably rehearsed the argument he would famously deliver in Savannah less than two weeks later, his widely reprinted and much discussed "Cornerstone Speech" on the basis for the new Southern republic. In that speech he insisted that responsibility for the collapse of the national union rested with those who did not accept "that slavery—

subordination to the superior race—is [the negro's] natural and normal condition. This, our new government, is the first, in the history of the world, based upon this great physical, philosophical, and moral truth." The Confederacy's "cornerstone," he intoned, "rests upon the great truth that the negro is not equal to the white man." Those in the North who clung to ideas of equality

> with a zeal above knowledge, we justly denominate fanatics. All fanaticism springs from an aberration of the mind—from a defect in reasoning. It is a species of insanity. One of the most striking characteristics of insanity, in many instances, is forming correct conclusions from fancied or erroneous premises; so with the anti-slavery fanatics. Their conclusions are right if their premises were. They assume that the negro is equal, and hence conclude that he is entitled to equal privileges and rights with the white man. If their premises were correct, their conclusions would be logical and just—but their premise being wrong, their whole argument fails. . . . They were attempting to make things equal which the Creator had made unequal.

The new nation's people had much work ahead of them. With state militias moving against federal arsenals and military facilities, Alexander Stephens told his Atlanta listeners to expect the surrender of Charleston Harbor's Fort Sumter any day now. He assured his audience that war was not in the offing but urged them to secure the peace by preparing to fight.

Georgia was ahead of him. As well as federal Fort Pulaski, Georgia militiamen also seized some ships from New York docked in Savannah Harbor, holding them hostage until shipments of arms ordered from New York factories before the secession vote were released. Georgia forces grabbed the Augusta arsenal as well.

The two standing Atlanta militia companies, the Gate City Guards and Atlanta Grays, were the first to muster for the new Confederate and state armies. Other units formed swiftly, often sponsored by wealthy citizens who took captaincies or made sure their sons were elected officers. With bounties and the inducement of colorful and dashing uniforms for those who could afford them, hundreds of privates joined the Safe Guards, the Free Trade Rifles, and ten other new companies that came together before the year ended—along with cadet corps and home defense guards made up of those too young or too old to enlist. Six of Atlanta's volunteer fire companies transformed themselves into military organizations that spring. In June, Ben Yancey formed up the Fulton Dragoons, a cavalry company, which joined the Georgia Legion, whose officers included Thomas R. R. Cobb, Howell's younger brother, and former Atlanta mayor Luther Glenn, who was married to the Cobbs' sister. The following November, when Cobb the cadet took a seat in the Confederate Congress for a period, he placed Major Yancey in command of his famous legion already winning battlefield fame in Virginia as part of the Army of Northern Virginia.

Although Fulton County had long resisted the cry for secession, with Atlanta at its center, its citizens provided the largest number of volunteer companies of any county in the state in this first call to arms, together with 150 enlistees in the regular army. By the following October, more than a thousand Atlanta men had joined forty Georgia regiments leaving for the battlefields. By the end of the war, Fulton County had provided the Confederacy with 2,660 soldiers.

Like the militia of earlier wars, the citizen soldiers assembled into motley bands, making up in spirit for what they lacked in professional training. Soon they gained a measure of discipline and order. The tread of marching boots in the streets now competed with the sound of clattering train cars. Parks and squares were turned into drill grounds. Fife and drum bands filled the air with martial music. Despite the seizure of federal arsenals and forts, the city and state had few munitions to offer or spare; men marched with their personal revolvers and bowie knives or shouldered shotguns and old muskets left from the Mexican-American War and the Indian Wars. Those without long guns even carried fence posts instead. Officers rode their own horses. Crowds of women and men too young or too old to serve gathered to cheer the parades on. An Atlanta mother beamed with pride as her young son, enthused by the passing lines of men, assembled the family slaves together into a company and marched them about the house yard.

The city turned out its pockets and purses in support of the incipient military buildup. Wealthy citizens donated cash, valuables, and household items to benefit the new companies. The Atlanta Amateurs dramatic group held regular fund-raising performances at the Athenaeum. Many evenings, men's voices from political meetings rang out from City Hall where town ladies also came together in adjoining rooms to form support societies, sewing regimental flags, uniforms, and socks for the new companies. When Sarah Huff's father and uncle prepared to join Yancey's Fulton Dragoons, entering Cobb's

Legion, her "weeping" mother and aunt "began basting and fitting the uniforms." After they were uniformed, Ben Yancey's men started off on the road to Virginia. It would be four years before the Huff women would see them again. Soon, they and other women formed associations to make bandages for the wounded.

AMONG MANY TOWN FAMILIES busied with making their sons and husbands at least look like soldiers were John and Mary Jane Neal. Their eldest two sons, Andrew Jackson, or A. J., Neal and older brother James, were among those who mustered at the earliest call. James, became captain of an Atlanta company known as the Jackson Guard, also known as the Irish Volunteers for its large contingent of Irish-born volunteers, which was quickly detached as part of the Nineteenth Georgia Infantry to the new Confederate army in Virginia. The twenty-four-year-old A. J., an attorney, had only recently opened his first office in the swampy inland Florida town of Micanopy. When the state seceded, he promptly enlisted. He was now a mounted lieutenant with the Marion Light Artillery in its first encampment near Pensacola. The rebel troops there were preparing to move against the large federal garrison on an island across the harbor. First, though, the company needed to uniform its men. A. J. wrote to ask his father to search out merchants in Atlanta able to supply "uniforms, swords, sashes, shoes, clothing, etc.," everything to outfit the battalion. In a few days his company's Captain Powell would arrive in Atlanta with "plenty of money" in hand. A. J. Neal knew it would be impossible to find enough "cadet gray" cloth uniforms, but with the need to fight still uncertain, he assured his father that "flannel shirts and cheap pants" would do.

The Neal family had moved just the year before from its large plantation in Zebulon, in Pike County, south of Atlanta, into its new house, a block down Washington Street from Calhoun's place. The Neals lived at the corner of Mitchell in a brick Greek temple of a mansion admired as perhaps the grandest in-town house yet built in Atlanta. It had two-story white Corinthian columns supporting a pediment roof extending over the length of a front porch from which the parents, their three girls, and another son still at home cheered on the men marching past or drilling in the shady square in front of the City Hall and Fulton County Courthouse. With guests such as the Calhouns or the Claytons, who lived on the opposite corner of Mitchell Street and whose young daughters and sons were playmates of the younger Neal children, at their table, the Neals shared their sons' letters from the developing front.

For now, the family anxiously awaited the arrival of Captain Powell, who would carry word about "how affairs stand . . . and what are the prospects of war." The lively dinner table companions enjoyed the bountiful provender from their farms, never imagining that the violence of what would surely be a short-lived war, if it came to that, could directly impinge on them. The same things that made Atlanta so attractive to them and increasing numbers of new residents, though, would one day bring the leader of the enemy forces to eat at the very same table they presently shared.


LARGE CROWDS ROUTINELY gathered to watch newly commissioned regimental officers receive their new command's flags at elaborate patriotic ceremonies in which a young local beauty committed the flag to the regiment's designated color bearer and called upon him "to guard it with his life." At the ceremony for the Confederate volunteers, the Athenaeum's eight hundred seats were jammed as Ben Yancey's daughter presented a flag she had sewn for the departing company. As she transferred the colors to the regiment's protection, the loud rhythmic bass voice of the receiving sergeant resounded through the hall with his promise that "Never! Never!! Never!!!" would he "allow its folds to trail in the dust." The house went wild, refusing to quiet until the orchestra launched into a rousing martial tune.

On hand for this and many other patriotic displays, sixteen-year-old Sallie Clayton watched and shared in the events that had transformed her adopted hometown into a military camp. "Everything seemed to be preparing for active service," she recalled, "and on all sides the cockade was visible." She and her more than two hundred fellow students from the Atlanta Female Institute now drilled and trained for elaborate ceremonies to honor their male neighbors forming up to defend their new nation. While the city had as yet no public schools—despite the urging of many leading citizens that some alternative be found for the many poor children running unattended in the streets—the Female Institute opened its doors in 1860 to those daughters of families able to afford the $36 half-year's tuition. Sallie walked nearly a mile each way—four times daily, counting her return home for lunch—to and from the brick and stone building on Ellis Street near Houston, overlooking the city. The Female Institute's dome atop what came to be known as College Hill was visible from nearly any vantage point in town. Though the walk left Sallie and her younger sister and constant playmate Gussie weary, "and it was never known at what moment a cow would dispute the passage of a street with us," they loved sharing in morning religious services in the buildingwide first-floor chapel, followed by Latin, French, oratory, reading and arithmetic recitations, calisthenics, dancing, and music in the upper-floor classrooms. She felt, "No building in the place could have been the scene of more joy and happiness."

Through the open windows on College Hill, the students could hear the shunting trains and crowds jamming the car shed, where company after company from up-country towns piled out of cars to reassemble in the neighboring open field of trees, mud, and grass known as City Park "amidst stirring martial music and firing of cannon." Local women were always on hand to greet the young men, "all recognizing," shared Clayton, "in every soldier a father, husband, brother or son and all were anxious to aid each one of them in some way." The chaos and emotion around the station sometimes proved dangerous. After many hours packed together on trains—even the car roofs were filled—spirited young soldiers in the making leaped from cars slowing into the car shed and began firing their revolvers into the arching ceiling, stampeding the throng of panicked well-wishers on hand to welcome them.

Neighboring streets also filled with wagon trains and long lines of uniformed men moving through. Walking home one afternoon, a demure Sallie needed to cross Marietta Street as one company after another filed past. As she waited at first patiently, "the opportunity for a little fun . . . more than they could resist," the soldiers began taunting her, calling her their "personal property" in words that put a "crimson hue" into her cheeks. Unable to get across the street, she was forced to walk the entire length of the long marching columns of men, accompanied by "shouts and laughter" the whole way. Only "with the utmost difficulty" did the blushing young woman keep a "dignified pace" before finally reaching her door.

While in town, the soldiers camped in the new Confederate barracks built on Peachtree Street toward the outskirts of Atlanta near the spot where townspeople used to ride the early version of the Ferris wheel and eat ice cream on hot summer nights. On April 1, 1861, "the greatest gathering that was ever witnessed in this city took place" to salute the seventy-five Gate City Guards under its captain, former mayor William Ezzard, debarking along with companies from the Cherokee County towns of Ringgold and Cartersville to join with A. J. Neal's and the many other regiments assembling in Pensacola for the assault planned on the resisting federal garrison there. Cheering onlookers filled the balconies and windows, even the rooftops, of the Trout House, the Atlanta Hotel, the Athenaeum, and other neighboring buildings and depots, even straining to see from the tops of rail cars parked in the yard. "Every available space was crammed with living masses," reported the *Southern Confederacy.*

The entire Atlanta Female Institute student body lined up along the Atlanta Hotel facing the file of soldiers. Each young lady dressed in white carried a small version of the new "Stars and Bars" Confederate States flag in her gloved hand. The carefully rehearsed line of girls moved across the street and handed a flag to each soldier opposite. Inscribed on the back of the flags, turned over by the doe-eyed girls for the young men in their fresh uniforms, were the loin-stirring words, "From the Young Ladies of the Atlanta Female Institute. None but the brave deserve the fair." As it pulled out whistling, the thirteen-car train holding the flag-waving men bound for the army was accompanied by "the booming of cannon and the cheering and shouting of the unnumbered throng, and waving handkerchiefs by the ladies from the windows and balconies contiguous." Each departing soldier felt the warmth of a pretty girl's hand linger in his own as the train carried him off to the front.


DESPITE THE PREDICTIONS THAT not a shot would be fired to win Southern independence, Lincoln made clear that the Union was indissoluble—and war came. South Carolina forces opened fire on Fort Sumter outside Charleston on April 12, 1861. Lincoln had a tiny 16,000-man army at his disposal and a small navy. The South, with its state militias, enjoyed an actual manpower advantage over the Union when the first shots rang out. On April 14, the Confederate flag rose over Fort Sumter. A day later, Lincoln called for 75,000 militiamen for ninety days' service to suppress the insurrection "too powerful to be suppressed by the ordinary course of judicial proceedings."

Atlanta's streets erupted in what were now becoming routinely boisterous and pyrotechnic displays of support for the Confederate attack. Two days after the bombardment of Fort Sumter, a "citizens committee" threatened to visit all Northern merchants to insist they hang Confederate flags over their stores. If they refused, they would "be accommodated to a coat of tar and feathers."

The town's high society enjoyed more refined displays of patriotic ardor indoors. Sallie Clayton and other students of the Female Institute held a floral pageant beginning with the raising of the American flag, at which the young women on stage tossed floral "bombs," bringing the Stars and Stripes to the floor, followed by a bouquet bombardment of a floral model of Fort Sumter. The performance shook "the house with stamping feet and . . . wild shoutings and cheers," according to a witness.

With many of Atlanta's leading citizens on hand for the pageant, the school's founding trustee, Amherst Stone, and his wife, Cyrena, were almost certainly in the audience. Even more than her Union-leaning husband, Cyrena was troubled by slavery and deeply opposed secession. A local writer and essayist of some note, she fought against the radicals' ascendance as she could, pseudonymously with her pen. Probably reflecting on the girls' floral desecration of the American flag, writing as "Holly," Cyrena lamented in the city's "lively evening paper," the *Commonwealth*, the dying of "our country, so long the boast of every one proud to call himself American!" She dreaded what might lie ahead. "The ['late United States'] fair corse [*sic*] still 'lies in State,'" she declaimed, "for it is yet unknown whether her burial should be as her baptism—in the crimson life-blood of thousands— or whether they shall wrap around her . . . the Stars and Stripes that have waved so long over our Washington's grave—as fitting drapery for the death-sleep of the fairest, the noblest Republic upon which ever shined the Sun." In the privacy of home, she hoped for a better outcome, "nerv[ing] ourselves against despair, and believ[ing] yet, that this Strife between Truth & Treason must soon end—triumphantly for Truth."

On a "beautiful spring day," the second after Samuel Richards learned of the taking of Fort Sumter, the book merchant went to church, where his inspired choir "made a greater display than our church has ever before seen or heard in the musical line." His objections to secessionists vanished. He sang out boldly for the new Southern republic's rise. In spite of his spiritual exaltation, he could not help feeling "sad to think that our country is actually at war brother against brother." The war of brother against brother was, in his case, more than just a phrase. Samuel Richards decried "our traitor brother," William, who had gone north to preach, and now "his sympathies and his hopes are with the despotic government that is doing their utmost to destroy us and make slaves of freemen." At this point, he wrote, "I pity him for his blindness and infatuations." His anger at William built as the gathering violence played out on the coasts and in Virginia. "Our family hitherto has been united in feeling and affection if not in bodily presence, but now we are widely separated indeed and have nothing in common." He claimed to have formerly been "a strong Union man" as the two sides drew apart with the approach of the election, "but now it has got to have a stinking savor since I have seen what measures are taken in order to *save* [the Union]."

A week later, he announced he would muster with the Silver Grays, Macon's new home guard battalion composed of men "whose locks are turning gray with age, as *myself*," but with all arms already consigned to other companies, the militia company shortly disbanded. His longtime clerk Asa Sherwood, though, departed for Virginia to join the army.

With gunfire and death came venom and ambition for conquest. On April 24, 1861, Atlanta mayor Whitaker addressed a public letter to Mechanic Fire Company No. 2 accepting their offer to serve voluntarily as a home guard militia for the city. He assured them, "We will teach Mr. Lincoln and his cohorts before this war is over that the South never surrenders, and that the people of the South will never be satisfied until the Capitol at Washington is rescued and our flag raised upon it; and the Confederate States acknowledged to be free and independent of all nations." The city council soon seconded his sentiments, with a resolution denouncing "one Abraham Lincoln of certain nonslaveholding States of the late old United States having announced its determined policy to subjugate the Slave States." The council members asserted that "the people of the Slaves States are *determined never* to be subjugated by such *demons* as long as there is an arm to raise and a God to rule and to sustain the cause of the Confederate States of America."

THE HOPE THAT THE WAR wouldn't last long derived from the smallness of both professional armies. Some believed the Union would let the Confederacy go in a negotiated divorce. The *Southern Confederacy* called for military restraint, declaring a readiness for a quick end to the conflict. "Justice," a columnist temperately admonished, "does not require, and no one desires to wage an offensive war against our enemies. We all want peace as soon as it can be obtained on honorable terms; therefore, every indication of it is hailed with pleasure." The newspaper suspected that the Yankee people could not "fail to discover the utter hopelessness and futility of prosecuting this war" and would soon abandon the fight or vote out their warmongering rulers.

While hailing peace rumors, the editors warned "our people" against being "lured from their place of safety on account of it. Don't, for a moment, slack your zeal—no matter what may transpire, until peace is not only proclaimed, but *established*. Continue to organize, equip and send out your companies."

Just to make sure that nobody doubted the sincerity of their support for the Southern nation, the editors urged the Confederate Congress to anticipate peace by "pass[ing] such laws as will prevent too great an influx of Yankees among us after the war. We are now cut off from them—we hope forever."

The violence needed to sever the ties of union became clear soon enough. Not long after the *Southern Confederacy* published its recommended peace terms, the first full-scale clash of Confederate and Union armies took place at Bull Run, near Manassas Junction, Virginia. The Confederate forces routed the Yankee army within a short ride of Washington, D.C. The electricity of the telegraphed news crackled through the South. Still in Macon, Samuel Richards, who had no doubt that "our cause is a just one in His sight," now shared the "universal" rejoicing in "the direct interference of God, for our force was not half as great in point of numbers as theirs." When word of the rebel army's "complete triumph" reached A. J. Neal's camp, he listened as the news traveled from campfire to campfire and "regiment after regiment took up the shout and hurrahed for Jefferson Davis and the Southern Confederacy." He exclaimed to his mother, "I have never seen anything to equal the enthusiasm created." He envied the Georgia companies who had "covered themselves with glory" at Manassas and shared the widely embraced view that this "most decisive victory ever achieved . . . ought to put to an end this wicked and unholy war."

But word also soon reached Atlanta that sixteen of its citizens had fallen. The victory heartened the town, but the first shipment of coffins arriving at the car shed, followed by funerals and mourners' clothes, brought home the full measure of what lay ahead.

# CHAPTER 10

# SPECULATION

ATLANTA WAS THE NEW Confederate nation's turntable. The re-bellious South had fewer than half as many miles of railroad track as the North, but a third of all lines traversing the Lower South, and just about all the 1,400 miles of track within Georgia, met up in the car shed. For thousands of soldiers, soon to be tens of thousands, and their equipment riding the rails from the Lower South to practically any front in the slowly developing continentwide civil war—Virginia, Tennessee, the Mississippi Valley and beyond, the Gulf or Atlantic coasts—the fastest route ran through Atlanta. The iron rails that gave birth to Atlanta also set the town's factories and industrial workshops on a wartime fast track. The South had less than 20 percent of the Union's industrial capacity. Atlanta's industrial base had been created to service railroad needs and now offered a ready foundation for Southern military manufacturing. President Jefferson Davis's military advisors urged him to move swiftly to put "the whole population and the whole production . . . on a war footing, where every institution is made auxiliary to war." No place in the South was more prepared to benefit from a policy of total militarization.

Atlanta had long resisted secession, and few rejoiced at the prospect of civil war, but once it came, the city's citizens rode a warhorse, and many thought they had picked a winner. Even before the first shots were fired, the Gate City offered up all it could to meet its new land's military needs—and to boost the city into its next, explosive phase of growth. The *Daily Intelligencer* could soon boast with some merit, "Atlanta . . . is destined to be a great manufacturing city." In their exuberant pursuit of that destiny, few in Atlanta suspected they might also be pursuing their own destruction.

"PERPETUAL MOTION DOES EXIST in this city, whose seal might well be a mammoth child directing a locomotive at full speed," exclaimed an awed journalist on a visit from Columbia, South Carolina. Industrial fumes and the rhythmic clanging of ironworkers' hammer blows blended with locomotive smoke and chugging engines as a steady and mounting flow of rich Georgia State and Confederate army contracts kept trackside factory forges blazing and machinery in motion: Winship's Foundry and Machine Shop produced desperately needed freight cars and railroad supplies, along with bolts and plating for armoring ships; the Stewart and Austin flour mill produced hardtack troops came to curse; James McPherson's match factory sold products to both army and civilians; numerous saddle and harness makers produced goods under government contract; Hunnicut and Bellingrath filled orders for alcohol, vinegar, and spirits of niter; High, Lewis, and Company distilled close to 80,000 gallons of liquor for the Confederate army annually; the Empire Manufacturing Company produced railroad cars and bar iron; a percussion cap factory opened in the first year of the war; W. F. Herring and Company and Lauishe and Purtrell Company turned out uniforms, knapsacks, and other cloth goods; gunsmiths milled and rifled gun barrels; the Peck and Day planing mill produced rifles and, without enough machinery and skilled mechanics to meet firearm requisitions, also contracted for 10,000 ten-foot-long medieval pikes; the foundries of Solomon and Withers Company forged brass and iron implements and "C.S.A." belt buckles, spurs, and horse tack; the Confederate Iron and Brass Foundry also specialized in military accoutrements; and second only to the Tredegar Works in Richmond, the Atlanta, later the Confederate, Rolling Mill produced cannon, rails, and armor plate, including iron sheathing used on the *Merrimac* and other ironclads. The Atlanta Sword Manufactory turned out 170 finished swords for Confederate officers per week.

The Confederate army, too, set up its own operations in Atlanta. The general of the western Army of Tennessee, Braxton Bragg moved his Quartermaster Department's headquarters here. In February 1862, he transferred the threatened Nashville arsenal to the buffered safety of Atlanta. Soon, thirteen separate shops were in production in scattered buildings, including a machine works, arsenal, and tannery. Munitions laboratories went up at the old fair grounds racetrack, where many of the nearly 5,500 yellow-skinned arsenal men and women—more than the entire town's population less than a decade earlier—hunched over benches, packing percussion caps and artillery and small-arms ammunition, as many as 25,000 rounds and 150 artillery shells per day by August 1862, eventually churning out 23 million musket and pistol caps and 4.1 million rounds of small-arms ammunition. The Army of Tennessee's Quartermaster Department employed a small army of some 3,000 "needle women," or seamstresses, most hauling home heavy bolts of flannel to sew into jackets, pants, and shirts. One hundred cobblers in a government shoe factory turned out as many as five hundred pairs of boots a day on those rare days when enough leather could be secured.

In the wartime frenzy, houses and barns became workrooms and factories, making it "impossible to detail at this time the numerous establishments for manufacturing purposes in Atlanta," noted the visitor from Columbia. "They are daily increasing." At her Marietta Street home, a young Sarah Huff watched in astonishment not only as the men in her life departed but as "the wheels of industry, the spinning wheel, the reel and the winding blades moved swiftly in my mother's wartime household," as they, too, began producing clothing, tents, blankets, and uniforms. Much like everywhere in town, "decided changes . . . [took] place very early in the war," and her neighborhood filled with workers and their machines. "Right there in sight of us," her industrious Scots neighbors built "a factory [that became] . . . the most extensive button factory in the south." She and her friends looked through the doorway in awe at the "wonderful sight" of powerful cutting machines banging out thousands of cow-bone buttons for soldiers' uniforms.

AN UP-COUNTRY TOWN not to be found on a map fifteen years earlier soon became the South's second most important war materiel production center, after Richmond itself, where Jefferson Davis moved the Confederacy's capital in May 1861 as a direct affront to nearby Washington, D.C. To many minds, given Atlanta's location in the heart of the rebellious states, its importance exceeded even the capital city's. Few people in the North or among Union military officials had heard of Atlanta before the outbreak of the rebellion, but most soon recognized that "the Citadel of the Confederacy" lay nestled beyond the fastness of the lower Alleghany ridges and hills. On distant battle-fields, Union soldiers began to make mental note of the "Atlanta" stamped on captured Confederate wagons, artillery pieces, and ammunition boxes—calling cards from the Gate City. The Yankees would remember the name of the town as they marched south.

To HELP KEEP ATLANTA'S Confederate engine and hub of war making on track, Mayor Jared Whitaker resigned his office in late November 1861 to become commissary general for the Georgia State army, setting up his headquarters downtown. City councilman Thomas Lowe filled in for Whitaker for the month and a half before the next election. With nearly all hope for a brief war dashed and the conflict assuming an all-consuming gravity and awesome violence, in January the electorate jettisoned political ideology and turned to a steadying and moderating hand to guide the town. James Calhoun remained perhaps the best-known Atlanta citizen *opposed* to secession. Moreover, he had never turned his back on friends or professional associates who had remained avowed Unionists and, in some cases, been harassed and even attacked as traitors. His own politics, though, were now in alignment with the needs of his regional home. Said his son Patrick Henry, his father still "thought that our differences should be settled peaceably, and not by war." But the war had come, and though his father would later contend that he, too, had remained a Unionist all along, his youngest son insisted, "There was no better Confederate than he."

In running for City Hall, he benefited from swiftly changed voter demographics. Many of the men eligible to cast ballots, including many of the most militant secessionists, had already departed for military service. The electorate left in town comprised primarily older and wealthier men more likely to favor the fifty-year-old Calhoun's good government and pragmatic brand of politics. He won the election, handily defeating T. L. Thomas by 530 to 256 votes for his first one-year term in office.

In stepping into his City Hall office, Calhoun faced a burgeoning and unprecedented set of challenges, perhaps more daunting than those faced by any American mayor ever, to govern his still-young municipality. All that expanded and new industry brought jobs. Jobs and the Union army nibbling sharply at the slave states' frontiers brought new people to town in droves. The population doubled in a year to fill the needs of the factories and shops. Refugees and wounded soldiers arrived by the thousands. A backwoods railroad transfer stop and regional market town instantly became a substantial small city, the fourth largest in the Lower South, after only New Orleans, Charleston, and Mobile. While most towns diminished in the face of Yankee threats, Atlanta just grew and grew.

Those who knew Atlanta best found it practically unrecognizable from prewar days. Observed one frequent longtime visitor a little over a year after the war began, "The car shed was there, the people were there. . . . The faces I had usually met were no longer visible, but strange people in strange costumes met me at every corner." Another visitor watched as "all day long and even during night, it is 'clang, clang, clang,' as the cars arrive or depart—filled to their utmost capacity with the crowd of floating population going somewhere, or returning from that direction." This mounting tide of opportunity and need overwhelmed every aspect of town services. Thrust into its leadership, Calhoun worked to keep Atlanta functioning, believing that City Hall should do all it could to ameliorate conditions. He was soon forced to manage the city with little help from the city council as more than half its members shortly resigned to enter military service.

At home, his life was merely an extension of his day's labors. Calhoun's law partner and son, William Lowndes, watched the heavy traffic of men passing through their Washington Street house. He would shortly depart for the army, but while still living in his father's house, Lowndes recalled "scarcely a day or night that it was not visited either by confederate officers, civil officers or citizens, and many times wounded and sick soldiers were cared for therein."

ALL THOSE OLDER, wealthier Atlanta citizens, refugees arriving daily, skilled railroad mechanics and others exempted from military service, needle women with their meager earnings, thousands of convalescing soldiers well enough to walk around, and troops in transit or on leave carried more or less cash with them. They made ready customers for the Five Points' profit-sniffing merchants. The shopkeepers of White-hall, Alabama, and Peachtree streets, too, saw war as a chance to expand their businesses like never before. With Northern manufactures no longer to be had, shopkeepers needed to extend their reach to find goods to sell this vast new clientele. Atlanta, along with the rest of the South, would have to shrug off any lingering provincialism to become an international city. The local chamber of commerce traveled far beyond the South, dispatching representatives across the Atlantic to find new trading partners, and forwarded weekly editions of local newspapers to European manufacturing cities with ads for local importers.

In the early fall of 1861, the chamber addressed a boosterish circular to its London counterpart in which the pint-size city's merchants audaciously proclaimed their hometown, symbolically "located upon a granite or primary formation at a high elevation" and standing at "the geographical centre of the new Confederacy," now rivaled New York City. The Gate City opened its doors wide to new trading partners, while, declared the chamber, the great Northern metropolis and trading hub was "from various causes already becoming inoperative." Blithely ignoring the federal naval blockade of the entire southern seaboard, Atlanta merchants invited English producers to ship their goods without fear or tariff. "Our whole coast is thus open to the commerce of the world."

When the *New York Times'* editors read the Atlanta pamphlet, they sneered at "the ridiculous cockerel circular of a Chamber of Commerce of a little wooden village in Georgia." But the Gate City put potential business partners on notice that it "want[ed] the freest possible trade with all the world."

Atlanta aimed to become a world trading hub for the new Confederacy, and wealthy Atlantans wanted to profit from that overseas trade. Leading city merchant partners Sidney Root and John Beach secured Atlanta's largest interest in the trade by establishing a large fleet of ships and a port warehouse in Charleston. Beach moved to England, where he set up a prominent import-export office in Liverpool. Soon the Root & Beach firm had as many as twenty-one steamers running at any one time. Besides their warehouse in Charleston, Root & Beach had eleven in Atlanta. Other Atlantans envied their enormous profits. "Almost everybody who had any money was anxious to go into a blockade company," recalled Amherst Stone, who would soon leave the city and his wife, Cyrena, behind in hopes of acquiring a ship to bring "considerable cotton" out for trade. Scheming to put his northern contacts to use, he collected tens of thousands of dollars from business associates to finance a move north, where he hoped to win official permission to bring cotton to the Union. He quickly found himself locked up in a prison in the New York Harbor.

Root & Beach ships got through the blockade often enough, and as a result of ships eluding the blockade, by the summer of 1862, the

*Southern Confederacy* reported, as much from aspiration as fact, "our own city is getting to be full of English goods." Traders overseas appeared eager to expand their entry into the Southern market. Before secession, most trade passed through Northern ports before making its way south. "Soon," crowed the *Confederacy*, "we shall have plenty of English goods here, which have not been polluted by the touch of Yankee fingers, and which have not greased their palms in passing through; but they will have come direct to us from England." The present "sufferings, inconveniences and privations" boded well for the future of an independent and self-sufficient Southern republic. "The blockade and the high price for goods have accomplished, and will accomplish, more for us to introduce and establish direct trade than twenty years of diplomacy."

IN THE EARLY MONTHS of the war, the *New York Times* could still disparage "the great centropolitan Atlanta," which it dared "Mr. Bull" to find on the map "if the stupid chartographer has not left it out." But by the end of the second year of fighting, the *Times* needed to acknowledge a new center of gravity in the rebellious states. The newspaper reported,

> Atlanta is really the heart of the Southern States and therefore the most vital point in the so-called Confederate States. [The region's towns] manufacture one-third of the horseshoes, guns and munitions of war made in the South. The machinery for the production of small arms has been taken to Atlanta, which place has extensive foundries. . . . Besides it is a flourishing city, an important railway centre, and extensive depot for Confederate commissary stores. Atlanta to the South, is Chicago to the Northwest, and its occupation by the soldiers of the Union would be virtually snapping the backbone of the rebellion.

Yankee boots marching on distant battlefields remained far from the Confederacy's industrial and commercial heart, but strategic planners considered it a future target.

THE CONFEDERATE SUPERINTENDENT of armories, Lt. Col. James Henry Burton, was drawn to Atlanta, or so he thought when he came looking to secure a site to build his massive new armory for

131

manufacturing Enfield model rifles in the summer of 1862. He was dismayed by the reception he received. The land was "so broken and rolling" that finding even "an acre of perfectly level ground" proved nearly impossible. He finally chose the old racetrack as the best spot, next to the fair grounds where the arsenal's munitions laboratory buildings were going up. The property's absentee owner was renting the site for the labs. He was willing to sell land for the new armory outright to Burton and the Confederacy, but, as a journalist noted, "the value of property [was] advancing with railroad velocity." The land's owner knew the value would only increase with time. He asked $15,000 for fewer than fifty acres, at least a twentyfold markup over the prewar rate for land outside the city limits.

Burton might have negotiated further but ultimately felt rebuffed by "the prevailing feeling of the people of this place generally towards the Govt." Atlanta, he discerned, was in the Confederacy but not entirely of the Confederacy. City council officials delegated to assist him met his offer to build one of the largest industrial enterprises—and one most vital to Confederate military success—with "indifference." He angrily concluded, "Speculation in real estate seems to be the sole object in view by the citizens of this place." Business was booming.

Fortunately, other, less prosperous inland Georgia towns were more than happy to take what Atlanta spurned. Macon's town fathers offered him "a free gift" of "an ideally suited" thirty-acre tract of land. "The citizens of Macon are most anxious for the location of the Armory at that place . . . whilst quite the contrary seems to be the prevailing sentiment *here*." Burton chose Macon. "Now," he scolded his hosts, "here is a good opportunity of accomplishing, *without cost*, what it seems I cannot accomplish at this place at any cost." He saw little chance for Atlanta to become "a thriving place" in the new nation without a change of heart. He could only shake his head. "I am disappointed in Atlanta," he wrote the Confederate chief of ordnance in Richmond.

OTHER VISITORS TO ATLANTA may have shared Burton's discomfort with the town's money-first attitudes, but few shared his predictions for its future. A Tennessee reporter surveyed the Five Points not long after Burton gladly left for Macon. He observed many of the same traits Burton did but from a different perspective. War had not changed the town; Atlanta had merely become more of what it had always been. The Tennessee journalist reported,

I strolled up the streets, and there was the same hurly-burly confusion of business-men as heretofore. Everybody wanted money—everybody made money. The Jew and the Gentile were found whispering together for a bargain. The milliner declared that 'this cannot be bought elsewhere for less than such a price.' The auctioneer from the stand was astonished as usual that his crowd would not bid more for this article, as the stores would charge double what they were bidding. Brokers had gold and bills scattered profusely upon their counters, ready to give you as clean a shave as any one of the many barbers that line the principal streets. . . . The engines whistled, cars were shifted hither and thither, and people passed the crossing as usual without being run over. I concluded that Atlanta, in point of business, was unchangeable, and that she has felt the shock of war less than any of her sister cities.

By contrast, many other Southern cities and towns withered. On a stopover in the Black Belt market town of Americus a few months later on, book and paper goods seller Samuel Richards found the once thriving Sumter County seat "*dried up*, the stores nearly all closed and most of the men gone to the war or somewhere else."

Prior to the war's advent, Richards had fretted in his languishing hometown of Macon. Even the prospect of the massive new armory's construction gave him little cause for optimism. Meanwhile, his brother Jabez had all he could do to handle customers at their Atlanta store. Those in Samuel Richards's Macon circle who knew Atlanta were "much pleased with it," he noted; the city was "no doubt a more healthy and salubrious place than Macon." It was also a healthier place to do business in those days. With "our stocks . . . decreasing and the prospect of supply very unpromising," Samuel Richards finally packed up the Macon store and closed up his house on the first day of October 1861. He crowded his wife and three children, including a new baby, and all their possessions into two rooms in his brother's small place off Washington Street.

It was an auspicious moment for him to move on. The Confederate Congress had just confiscated all Northern goods and debt. The $5,000 the brothers owed Northern wholesalers for purchases on credit "will never reach the hands of those to whom we owe it." Among his creditors was his "fanatical" and "renegade" older brother William, gone north in location and outlook. He, too, would have to lose out. Shrugged Richards, "We shall have to treat our brother

William as we do other 'alien enemies.'" In fact, he lamented, "What I most regret in his case is that he *is* an alien enemy."

Once in Atlanta, Richards found that business *was* good, very good indeed. On the last day of 1861, he noted that the brothers' stock was "getting low in quantity but pretty high in price!" With paper goods growing scarce—and families corresponding more than ever with their far-flung soldiers—Richards wished only that their stores carried exclusively difficult-to-source "paper and envelopes. We could make a small fortune out of it." Less than a year after Samuel Richards's arrival, the brothers' "profits [continued to be] splendid." Though some sales did not exactly enrich them—for instance, "for *books* in general we only get *double* former prices"—others brought astronomical gains. "Some of our profits are enormous truly," he recorded when well settled in Atlanta. "Today Jabez sold a bill of pens & holders for $28 which cost originally 75¢!"

Before long, "money," he celebrated, "comes in so fast that we hardly know how to dispose of it to advantage." With their business earnings and the thousands of dollars they saved when the rebel government wiped out their debts to Northern creditors, the Richards brothers joined the investor class in town. They bought several building plots and houses within and just beyond the city limits. They diversified, backing a shoemaking shop, putting a couple thousand dollars into Amherst Stone's ill-fated blockade-running scheme and a thousand more into the Confederate Insurance Company, briefly operating a grocery store until shortages caused them to sell out, and acquiring a religious-tract printing house. Jabez also bought several bondsmen for household servants and to work a farm he purchased outside town.

Finally, Samuel, now an ardent secessionist who "rejoiced[ed] to hear that our invading cruel foes are being destroyed," achieved a long-standing milestone of his own: He "committed the unpardonable sin of the Abolitionists in buying a negro." For the past two years, he could afford only to hire the time of Ellen, a slave girl "13 years old, healthy and ugly," whom the family brought with them from Macon. With his newfound wealth, he drove a hard bargain before concluding a deal with her former Macon owner, buying her for $1,225, "$275 less than [he] priced her at three months ago," Samuel gloated. He was satisfied he had purchased "a pretty good girl," but he ignored the "good whipping" he had lately given her after catching her using his wife's "toilet articles." It wasn't the first time he had beaten her; nor was it the last. A few months later, he took a lash to her again, this time for a spool of thread missing from his wife's drawer "and other misdemeanors." Despite such transgressions, he believed her to be worth nearly double what he had paid, and expecting "when we come to a successful end to this war that negroes will command very high prices," he purchased another entire slave family.

THE MONTH BEFORE ELLEN became a chattel member of the Richards household, his infant daughter Alice got terribly sick. The benefits of Atlanta's "salubrious" climate proved short-lived. The city's small-town sanitation system struggled to support its swelling citizenry as well as the people passing through by the tens of thousands. Privies overflowed; people relieved themselves in open toilets; army horses hauling supplies and men added to the fouled water supplies. Mayor Calhoun's court began issuing fines for owners of privies the Board of Health deemed in an "unfit condition," and the city council hired laborers to "put in healthy condition all privies used by the Authority of the Confederate States of America." The city government sold lime for privy use at cost to residents, though the supply was so limited that there wasn't enough to blunt the stench or contain the swarms of flies.

A physician diagnosed Alice with *cholera infantum*, a catch-all term for a childhood gastrointestinal disorder accompanied by fever, but she likely had typhoid fever, a diarrheal disease, increasingly common among warring troops and in overcrowded urban areas, spread through feces-polluted drinking water. The child lingered for a painful week before the disease wasted her away. "Distressed and troubled," Richards found, "one thing however gave me some comfort." He was desperate to avoid being called up for military service. A local printing shop was on the verge of hiring him, giving him one of the few jobs the Confederate government considered crucial enough to "exempt me from conscription."

He recorded shortly before the first anniversary of his move to Atlanta, "Our sales continue good and our profits also good." But he also admitted, "I would willingly go back to old trade and moderate profits if we could only have peace and independence. We live now in a state of feverish excitement and disgust that *gain* cannot render bearable or desirable."

AT LEAST RICHARDS HAD his gains. Many citizens had only the "feverish excitement and disgust." The porous and wavering boundary between loyal and rebellious states and the enduring need for Southern cotton in the North encouraged extensive quasilegal trade via Memphis and other Mississippi River cities until mid-1862. Finally, due to hardening army and governmental outlooks about commerce between the warring sides, coupled with Yankee military successes in the West, nearly all shipments of western crops into the South were cut off. The lack of rolling stock and the government demand for the rail lines also sharply curtailed food reaching Atlanta. Less than a year after the taking of Fort Sumter, shipments into the city of flour, hogs, sheep, and corn had declined between 30 and 80 percent from what they had been in 1860—while the population had more than doubled.

In addition, the Confederate army began seizing farmers' harvests for the military. The Richmond government passed an impressment statute, requiring farmers to turn over to the government 10 percent of everything they raised, from livestock and grain to vegetables, tobacco, and cotton. Impressment agents, accompanied by armed soldiers, confiscated their 10 percent levy and very often took anything else they wanted. When the woman of the Atlanta Hospital Association tried to sell sugar to finance an "invalid ladies" home, the Confederate army impressed the sugar. The roving government officials—and bandits masquerading as Confederate authorities—commandeered farm wagons traveling to Atlanta, with promissory notes for future payment in return. With the army impressing civilian property and thieves ready to make off with anything not tied down, Atlantans started hiding their most valuable items, even going so far as to bring their horses and buggies up the steps and into the house. When the Army of Tennessee ran desperately short of shoes, leaving much of the army to march barefoot in the frozen hills, General Bragg seized every boot in town not being worn. Citizens howled at the confiscations by "high officials who set the example of lawlessness by appropriating what did not belong to them," in the words of a *Southern Confederacy* correspondent.

Afraid of further confiscations, farmers squirreled away their harvests in bulging granaries and corncribs and stayed clear of the roads and Atlanta's markets. Mayor Calhoun wrote to Confederate president Davis about the legality of such seizures and to what extent the city could expect to face continued impressments. Davis replied that the practices were indeed legal. He offered to investigate unauthorized seizures—to no effect.

WITH BASICS IN SHORT SUPPLY, inflation spiraled out of control. By December 1862, the wholesale price index in the South had increased seven times above that of the heady days of spring 1861. Contributing to the inflationary spiral, the counterfeiting of so-called shinplasters—illegal currency issued by private corporations and individuals after silver change disappeared from circulation—and Confederate dollars was rampant. Numerous deals fell apart after currency and notes proved worthless paper. Jabez Richards discovered that $1,000 in cash he'd put up in partial payment for a slave were counterfeit, forcing him to fight against returning the slave to the previous owner. The Fulton County Superior Court tried 136 counterfeiters in a single year. Few issuing false notes were ever apprehended. In the summer of 1862, the *Southern Confederacy* reported that illegal shinplasters were "as thick as the frogs and lice of Egypt."

The Richmond government added fuel to the inflationary fire by printing government paper as quickly as its presses could operate, without any backing except a promise to redeem it at face value two years after the war. Prices stepped up and up, reaching a 12 percent per month rate of increase by the end of 1861. A bag of salt costing $2 before the war went for $60 in the fall of 1862. Goods were "changing hands," reported the *Southern Confederacy* in early 1863, but only "at big figures that are unquotable." Soon a street laborer could earn $2.50 a day, the pay for a skilled laborer before the war, but that was still a starvation wage. Eventually, inflation soared to ninety-two times prewar prices, the highest rate in American history.

Cyrena Stone recorded prices from her account book "for the amusement of future generations." They would remain the highest ever paid for such goods. A pound of pepper cost $10; a ham, $54; four pounds of butter, $40; fifty pounds of coffee, $500; a Merino (wool) dress, $400; "a green silk 'love of a bonnet,' with pansies & plums $150." She concluded, "No purse is large enough to hold all the 'needful' that is *needed* to make more than one purchase."

The once thriving newspapers began to look threadbare themselves. Merchants found little cause to promote the goods they had for sale, other than tobacco, corn whiskey, and slaves. A few ads boasted of the arrival of European goods by blockade runners via Nassau. Numerous ads called for the apprehension of runaway slaves and army deserters—all described and named. Long lists of the wounded filled columns, as did lists of those who had distinguished themselves in battle. Some notices detailed captured slaves brought to jail and waiting for their owners to pick them up. The occasional house or land was offered for sale. Many more ads solicited housing. Owners needing cash put up household items for sale, especially pianos. Publishers themselves were forced to scramble to find sufficient newsprint and ink for their runs, eventually resorting to printing issues on half sheets and even wallpaper.

POVERTY STRUCK WOMEN, whose men were gone to war, hardest. Gaunt mothers dressed in burlap came to Cyrena Stone's Houston Street door everyday, seeking sewing or begging for food. One evening three barefoot women came by, their husbands having long since departed for war, all now left destitute. Stone recorded, "They said their rich neighbors persuaded their husbands to volunteer in the first war [*sic*], promising that their families should never suffer. But the promise was forgotten, & the little sewing they could get, hardly kept them alive." Each woman beseeched her aid with "the same cry—'How *can* I get bread for my children!'" Another mother of five children stopped at her house on her two-mile walk to the Army of Tennessee's Quartermaster Department to take home government sewing, at the going rate of $1 for a pair of pants, $1.50 for a coat, and 50 cents for shirts. According to Stone, she at least did not have far to go for the work. "Many a woman walks eight or ten miles to town to get sewing." This woman "was so delighted" to show her sympathetic friend the new pair of shoes "she had been sewing for months to get." The well-to-do secret Yankee Stone did not suffer so, but she wondered, "Is it any marvel that crime and prostitution are so common?"

Newspapers published advice on ways a woman like Cyrena Stone could make do without her past luxuries. These included recipes for brewing coffee out of beets or sweet potatoes—"those who give it a fair trial will be unwilling to go back even to the best Java." To the fashion-minded lady, the *Southern Confederacy* suggested, "You can cut up your last fall dresses, and out of the skirts make the children nice new dresses; and, rather than miss doing a good thing, you can wear some of them yourself this fall and winter. You can 'take in' your hoops (to suit the hard times—shorten sail in this storm) and save several yards in making a new dress for yourself. There are a thousand little plans which a thrifty house-wife can adopt to save money, and look well too."

ATLANTA'S FAST-GROWING and transient population, exceptional access to goods through its superior transportation network, and wealth from manufacturing made conditions ripe for a speculative economy. Its individualistic, get-ahead commercial spirit drove men to seek quick profits—sometimes at the expense of neighbor and nation. "Atlanta," complained John Steele, who took over from Jared Whitaker as editor, in the *Intelligencer*, "is now made headquarters for itinerant speculators in gold, bank notes, Confederate currency, *meat* and *bread*." An Alabama soldier's wife, Mrs. Wellborn, watched storekeepers stash inventory under counters "to get it out of reach of the city authorities" to be sold later at a higher price. Such practices demoralized people who could ill afford the higher prices and led Steele to proclaim, "These men are greater enemies to the Southern cause than the foe in the field."

Many in Atlanta resented the traders they branded as speculators. Those who drew some of the sharpest rebukes were erstwhile slaves. One of the most enterprising traders in the city came from the sixty skilled bondsmen on the Ephraim Ponder estate on the outskirts of town. All of the Ponders' slaves were more or less free to contract out their labor. Several took advantage to pursue opportunities denied to nearly all other slaves. A few saved up enough to become traders. Little held them back after their master left his wife, Ellen, alone on their big estate. Fourteen years her husband's junior, Ellen had long been admired as "beautiful, accomplished, and wealthy." Ephraim was devoted to her and trusted her enough that "in consideration for the great love and affection he bore," he placed his entire estate, including his slaves worth an estimated $45,000, in trust for her. He came to regret his generosity.

Not long after the couple moved to their new Atlanta home, scandal rocked the household. Others had long whispered about his wife's "dissolute" ways and frequent adulterous liaisons, but Ephraim did not learn of them until 1861. Ellen, he declared in his divorce deposition, had been cheating on him at least since 1854. He accused her of being unable to refrain from "illegitimate pleasures," drunkenness, abusive language, and the "utmost disrespect," even threatening him with a gun.

While the shocking divorce proceedings dragged on, Ephraim, "brokenhearted," left Ellen to live alone at their beautiful Atlanta dream estate and returned to Thomasville. Alone in her house, the chatelaine's "only thought or care was to remember when [her slaves'] wages became due and then to receive it," recalled her most trusted slave, Festus Flipper's young son Henry, who grew up in the teeming Ponder slave quarters. After the master's departure, Henry recalled his childhood in the midst of slavery being "virtually free." With no white overseer on the estate, he and the other young children even began to receive reading lessons from another slave on the property.

Henry's cobbler father and the other men and women living on the estate hired out their time in town. One Ponder slave, Prince Ponder, a wainwright by training, tried to ply his craft, but the local white mechanics resented the competition and would not let him practice his trade. He saw other opportunities in the war for a black man. Although subject to harassment by the patrollers, he had his mistress's written permission to travel and trade "anywhere" in Georgia. With some savings, he took the risk of buying and selling "on anything there was any money in." He made some money, speculated in gold as Confederate money lost its value, and with the profits bought more items to sell. Soon he had enough to rent a house in Atlanta, which he used as a warehouse, and opened a grocery store where he sold corn, rye, hops, flour, bacon, whisky, tobacco, boot leather, and "anything else," he said, "on which I could make any money." He moved his wife and children to a farm outside of town belonging to his friend, the wealthy Unionist builder Julius Hayden. He even lent money to Hayden at times.

The underground economy open to anyone daring enough, even a slave, proved astoundingly lucrative in a time of scarcity. Though he may have exaggerated his success in accumulating money, Prince Ponder claimed he "often" took in $5,000 to $6,000 in a single day. He estimated that while still a slave, he earned a total of $100,000 in inflated Confederate currency and had as much as $50,000 tucked away at any one time. Inflated money or not, he was as wealthy as some of the richest men in town. He purchased a pair of mules, two horses, a buggy, and a wagon. He had cows, hogs, and poultry. Each month, he made his way back to the Ponder place to turn over a few dollars to Mrs. Ponder. In return for his freedom to hire out his time, he at first paid her $40 per month. As the war continued, his rent coming back to her eventually reached $100 monthly. She had no idea how much money he was making for himself.

Prince Ponder invested some of his money in gold, likely purchased from his friend and fellow slave-entrepreneur Bob Yancey. In his barbershop and out of his Houston Street house, Yancey, too, traded in anything he could move at a profit. He continued to loan money to gamblers but also bought Yankee dollars and bits of gold, often purchasing them from Union prisoners he met when he went into hospitals or when they were in transit through Atlanta on their way to the Andersonville Prison. The army guards paid little attention to him, a barber and slave, while he shaved Yankee prisoners. That gave him time to dicker over the price of greenbacks, the Yankee paper currency; the Union men in turn hoped to use Confederate dollars to escape. Yancey then went into the Confederate barracks where he shaved rebel soldiers' beards and exchanged Confederate money in return for prized Northern currency.

Yancey showed the Unionist industrialist William Markham two thousand-dollar bills he'd purchased from Yankee prisoners for $8,000 in Confederate money. He turned around and sold those U.S. dollars at a rate reaching three hundred Confederate dollars to one greenback, "though," noted a Confederate deputy provost marshal who had tried to stop him, "it was a dangerous thing for a man to do." The Confederate Congress made dealing in greenbacks a crime punishable by up to three years in jail and a $20,000 fine. Few thought of the possibility that blacks could be among the most prosperous of the moneychangers, and the law did not provide additional penalties for slaves or other blacks caught dealing in greenbacks. According to one local white businessman, Yancey was "about one of the biggest traders we had here," white or black.

Atlanta seemed unable to contain the growing population of slaves in town who lived in a state bordering upon freedom. John Steele of the *Intelligencer* was no friend of the mayor, John Calhoun, and accused him of ignoring laws governing slave labor and conduct. In a long list of shortcomings he hoped to see corrected during the Calhoun administration, Steele editorialized,

> The next thing desired is to stop this habit of negroes hiring their time and making contracts with white men for the performance of work and charging the most exorbitant prices they can think of. Such conduct is against the laws of the State and should be severely punished. It is absolutely shameful to see the liberties that negroes are taking in this city. . . . If the negro slaves of this city are to be allowed their own way and to continue in the same course they have been hitherto pursuing, we shall very soon have the same abolition curse that caused this war, started in the State. Slaves should be treated as such and not allowed the rights and privileges of white men, and we shall insist that if any

responsible white man gives information of any violation of the laws respecting slaves that Mr. Calhoun will listen to the charge and promptly investigate it, without thinking such an act on his part a disgrace to his magisterial dignity. He was put there to do it and he has a right to attend to it.

THE MAYOR AND OTHER ATLANTA officials tried without success to rein in speculators of all colors. They had few tools at their disposal. The DeKalb County grand jury, which in addition to its judicial role acted as a kind of citizen's council, blamed "the unnatural and implacable war waged against us by the North" for "the scarcity of money and the enormous high price of the necessaries of life." But the "enemies without" were "enhanced by enemies within." The jury sent a message calling upon the state legislature to apply its powers against "those capitalists who are using their means to speculate and reap immense profits upon the necessaries of life." The Georgia General Assembly quickly criminalized speculation, but the laws were easily circumvented and rarely enforced.

With resentment building against Atlantans "riding in their four-thousand-dollar carriages, dressed in thousand-dollar silks and two-thousand-dollar cloaks, and at night attending the theatre or joining in the dance[s]," simmering anger at speculators inevitably boiled over into violence. An Atlanta woman racing through town in a buggy ran over what she thought to be a soldier. She pulled up in horror and turned back to look at the prostrate man. When she recognized him as an "extortioner," she whipped her horse on, "regretting that her buggy wheels had not run over his neck."

Food thefts were rampant in Atlanta. Cows and chickens, even vegetables and fruit, disappeared from family plots. Whitaker reported burglars struck his Commissary Department's food warehouses so often, they had depleted his inventory—mostly of bacon—to almost nothing. Police did not bother to investigate robberies of private gardens and livestock, as well as of household goods and tools, so many were reported. Citizens stopped bothering the city marshals with their troubles.

In a notorious incident that made headlines even in the North, a dozen or so women barged into a Whitehall Street store on a late winter mid-afternoon in 1863. "A tall lady on whose countenance rested care and determination," according to newspaper reports, asked the clerk the price for bacon. He answered $1.10 per pound. The

woman told him she and the others were wives and daughters of soldiers. They could not afford that price and wanted the government
price for bacon. The grocer refused. At that, she drew "from her
bosom a long navy repeater, and at the same time ordered the others
in the crowd to help themselves to what they liked." The women
walked away with nearly $200 worth of bacon.

Many people in town stood up for the "mob of ladies." The *Intelligencer*'s portly, fire-eating editor, John Steele, intoned that the
"scene moved the sympathies of his soul." But in a follow-up to the incident, his leading daily rival's editor, the now hardnosed Confederate
G.W. Adair, was not so sympathetic in the pages of the *Southern Confederacy*. He insisted that these were no starving wives and daughters
of soldiers but greedy exploiters of public sympathy for personal gain.
"The tall female with determination in her eye, and who had elicited
so much sympathy as the 'boss' of the seizing crowd, is the wife of a
shoe-maker in this city who had not been to the army and is receiving
very high wages for his labor, and in comfortable circumstances." The
identities of the ladies involved were never fully resolved. Perhaps for
fear of arousing further public ire, none of the women was arrested.
The *Confederacy* urged any truly hungry women thinking of following their example to "let their wants be known—if they will go to the
Clerk of the Council and register their names and place of residence
their wants will be supplied."

Despite such claims about the ready availability of charitable and
public assistance, Calhoun's city government in fact could do precious
little to meet the citizens' needs. At $4,062.67 in 1862, the city bud-
get for relief for the poor was the third largest item behind city
salaries and street and bridge repairs. In the next year, relief for soldiers and aid to the poor had become the city's single largest expendi-
ture, at $16,200 for the year. But with inflation jumping manyfold
faster and the number of indigent people increasing daily, that
amount was nowhere near enough. Calhoun's government did what it
could to alleviate the spreading misery. "In view of the *almost* impossibility of procuring the necessaries of life, food & fuel," the city council
set up a committee chaired by the mayor "to devise a plan by which
such articles shall be furnished at their cost when distributed." Calhoun tried, with rare success, to jaw merchants into holding their
prices down or even donating or selling at cost basic foodstuffs. One
grocer donated 1,000 pounds of rice to the needy to much acclaim;
salt donations were made to stem the cries of "salt famine." The *Intelligencer*'s John Steele called on City Hall to open Atlanta's treasury "to

purchase large supplies of fuel to be held for the use of those who will be unable to pay the high prices for fuel demanded." With the winter of 1863 approaching, the mayor persuaded the railroads to carry firewood from the countryside free of charge to distribute to the poor. Only a few sticks ever made it to the cold hearths of the needy.

1760 Long Cane Creek Massacre Stone
at the South Carolina site where
Indians attacked Calhoun settlers

Senator John C. Calhoun, the
voice of Southern states' rights

Senator Daniel Webster,
"the Godlike Daniel" or "Black Dan"

Atlanta Mayor James M. Calhoun,
cousin of John C. Calhoun

FULTON COUNTY JAIL         CITY HALL  SOLOMON RES·     CREW RES·   TRINITY CHURCH     NEAL RES·
G·A·R·R·  ENGINE HOUSE 2  ST·PHILIP'S CH·          CEN'L PRESB·CH·  2ᵈ BAPTIST CH·
ROUND HOUSE  WASHINGTON HALL  CITY PARK                 IMMACULATE CONCEPTION C
LOYD ST·                     CAR  SHED              M·&W·
    MASONIC HALL  TROUT HOUSE             ATLANTA HOTEL
PRYOR ST·                        ATHENÆUM       FIVE  POINTS
            PEACHTREE ST·                   BRIDGE (BROAD) ST·

Historical artist Wilbur G. Kurtz's bird's eye view rendering of Atlanta in 1864 prior to the siege

# ATLANTA IN 1864

CONCERT HALL    INTELLIGENCER OFFICE                    CITY MARKET
S' STORE    GEN· MARCUS WRIGHT'S HDQRS          CALABOOSE    ENGINE HOUSE
        TALLULAH FIRE CO·                           BRIDGE
            ST· LUKE'S CH·                  WADLEY (FORSYTH) ST· ·MARIETTA S

JACK'S BAKERY: C·S·A·

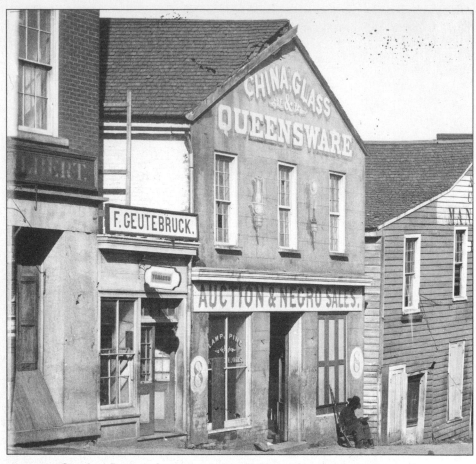

Crawford, Frazer & Co. slave market on Whitehall Street where buyers made "their selections just as they would have a horse or mule at a stockyard"

Looking north on Washington Street: the Neal family home at the corner of Mitchell Street, where General Sherman made his headquarters, the Second Baptist Church beyond, and the Calhoun house in the distance

Train rolling into the car shed, Peachtree to Whitehall Street crossing visible

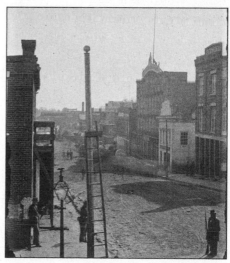

Downtown Alabama Street from the corner
of Whitehall, near the Five Points

Bookseller and diarist Samuel P. Richards ran a
thriving store with his brother on Decatur Street

Plantation owner and
politician Benjamin C. Yancey

Mayor and *Intelligencer* owner
Jared I. Whitaker

*Southern Confederacy* owner
George W. Adair

*Intelligencer* newspaper offices on Whitehall Street,
over liquor store and next to railroad tracks

Atlanta City Hall and Fulton County Courthouse with
2nd Massachusetts Infantry camp in City Hall Square

Sarah "Sallie"
Conley
Clayton

Clayton family house on Mitchell Street

Colonel George W. Lee,
Atlanta provost marshal

Captain and future
Mayor William Lowndes Calhoun
and wife Mary Jane Oliver

# CHAPTER 11

# STREET
# THEATER

CONTENDING WITH RISING CRIME dominated James Calhoun's
days at City Hall. As the city's chief elected official, he not only
headed the city government but also served as judge of the Mayor's
Court, doling out justice in petty criminal cases. The court's docket
exploded, more than doubling to 427 cases of disorderly conduct, illegal liquor sales, prostitution, slave-code violations, and misdemeanors
within his first year in office. Trying to contain the disorder, Calhoun
doubled his police force, but it still numbered just twenty-eight and
could do little to curb offenders. Serious criminal cases increased
even more quickly than those reaching the Mayor's Court. In 1863,
the city experienced a fourfold rise in larceny cases tried before the
Superior Court of Fulton County; attempted murders doubled and
arson tripled, while there were six trials for "fornication" when no such
cases had been tried in the two prior years. Convictions for bigamy
and adultery rose sharply.

Atlanta was spinning out of control, and drunk soldiers were responsible for much of the trouble. Calhoun shared his neighbors' desperation to get drinking in town under control. He pleaded with the
government in Richmond to find a constitutional means to keep liquor
out of soldiers' hands. "I hope & believe," he wrote Confederate secretary of war George W. Randolph, "there is some legal way in which
the retail of spirits can be prohibited at such a time, in such a place,
as this."

The Confederate army soon realized the scale of the problem and tried to take control of cities considered militarily vital "to preserve the efficiency of the army and to maintain its discipline" at a time when "civil administration is everywhere relaxed, and has lost much of its energy." On May 1, 1862, Gen. Braxton Bragg made Atlanta a military post. The War Department turned to Col. George Washington Lee to serve as provost marshal for the city. Lee, a son of the city, quickly set out to take control of *his* streets. Taking control for Lee, though, did not necessarily mean enforcing the law. The co-owner of a Decatur Street bar, the Senate Saloon, seemed to have trouble at times deciding which side of the law he was on. Lee's background was shady: Though the charges may have been unfounded, he had been forced to resign his commission in the Confederate army after it was said he stole from his men, and General Bragg described him as "a man without education or character."

When Lee came back home, though, Jared Whitaker ignored his friend's troubles with Confederate higher-ups. The pages of the *Intelligencer* wrote glowingly about the "gallant Georgian," now on "furlough," who had "made a considerable reputation during his service." The then mayor's newspaper went so far as to pronounce the disgraced Lee "a great favorite" of General Bragg's.

PROVOST MARSHAL LEE QUICKLY conscripted his own private army. With most able-bodied men of military age now serving in the regular army, he enlisted a ragtag force of 683 men consisting mainly of unemployed teenagers too young for formal military service and paid substitutes. They took it upon themselves to enforce order in the city, check up on suspicious characters, and ensure citizen loyalty. They were posted as guards around town, in the car shed, and at depots full of valuables. Just as often, particularly as inflationary prices for goods spiraled upwards, Lee's gang of, in the main, ruffians and hoodlums used their official powers to steal for themselves and to harass those who opposed them, frequently with clubs and fists.

In mid-May 1862, Lee took the unprecedented step of issuing a general order requiring all soldiers—and soon all citizens—to carry passes at all times, forbidding the sale of alcohol to soldiers, placing a strict nighttime curfew on blacks, and threatening to toss drunk and disorderly troops into the brig. He summarily established his own drumhead court, ignoring habeas corpus rights, to arrest and jail suspected traitors. His men filled the army prison barracks. The city had become, Lee wrote to the secretary of war in Richmond, "a point of rendezvous for traitors-swindlers-extortioners-and counterfeiters," with an especially insidious "predominant element" in its population of foreigners, Northern immigrants, and other transients, of suspect loyalty. His force would "untiringly . . . watch, direct and consign to suitable punishment these miscreants."

Lee's actions often overstepped the line and infringed on the powers of the civil authorities. To ease strained relations with Calhoun, he "earnestly invite[d] the aid and cooperation of His Honor, the Mayor . . . in preserving good order and sobriety in the city." The town was now, considered the thriving paper goods merchant Samuel Richards, "under Martial Law." He carried his pass with him constantly "to prevent our being taken up at night and put in limbo." Lee's provost guard began shuttering offending barrooms, seizing whisky barrels off wagons, and taking axes to them in the streets.

General Bragg in his Chattanooga headquarters formally declared martial law in Atlanta and its surroundings in August 1862, but he did not empower Lee. Instead, Bragg sent Mayor Calhoun a letter appointing him "civil governor" with the city council members as his "officers." He urged close cooperation with Lee's military authorities. Calhoun was stunned. He had no idea what his new title meant, what duties it entailed, or what additional powers he now exercised. In reality, the man who had always believed in the rule of law and constitutional doctrine was outraged by what he considered a grave and unconstitutional abuse of power. He wrote to his friend in the Confederate Congress, Georgia senator Benjamin Hill, to protest the fact that he could invoke martial law as the city's governor. Hill passed his letter along to Confederate vice president Alexander Stephens.

Stephens wrote a public letter back to Calhoun. "I am not at all surprised," he wrote, "at you being at a loss to know what your powers and duties are in your new position, and your inability to find anything in any written code of laws to enlighten you upon them. The truth is your office is unknown to the law. General Bragg had no more authority for appointing you civil governor of Atlanta than I had; and I had, or have, no more authority than any street walker in your city."

Stephens did not stop there. He assured Calhoun that as long as "we live under a Constitution . . . there is no such thing as martial law." As such, Bragg's act and naming of Calhoun as civil governor was "simply a nullity. You, by virtue of it, possess no rightful authority, and can exercise none." Stephens recognized that a principal reason for imposing martial law was to keep soldiers from drinking while in

Atlanta. But only an act of the Confederate Congress could prohibit liquor sales. "Until this is done," he declared, "no one has any authority to punish in such cases; and anyone who undertakes to do it is a trespasser and a violator of the law." He added particularly harsh words for military men who sought to impose their authority over civilians. He clearly had General Bragg and Provost Marshal Lee in mind when he intoned, "Neither generals nor provost marshals have any power to make, alter, or modify laws, either military or civil; nor can they declare what shall be crimes, either military or civil, or establish any tribunal to punish what they may so declare." Even in the midst of war, Atlanta remained a city of laws.

By early September, opposition to the arbitrary decree reached the point where the Confederate War Department felt compelled to reverse Bragg's act and issued instructions forbidding military officers from again declaring martial law without express authority from the president. Calhoun and the city councilmen returned to enforcing the civil law. John Steele's *Intelligencer* overlooked Calhoun's objections to the whole affair and archly proclaimed, "'Governor Calhoun' is therefore defunct in our city as well as his corps of aides-de-camp by whom he is surrounded, and we trust that General Bragg will make no more appointments of like character, which confer only temporary titles, and give the distinguished recipients nothing to do."

FOR HIS PART, Lee ignored the public controversy and the government's repudiation of his power in Atlanta's city affairs. His armed henchmen kept the barrooms closed. However, dry men encountered little trouble wetting their whistle. A year after Lee's order closing the bars, the *Intelligencer* reported, "We do not know where the liquor comes from, but there is evidently a large quantity of it sold in this town, from the number of drunken men we have seen upon the streets, in the hotels, and at the theatre." For those who wanted their whisky by the glass, raucous "dramshops" opened up like night peepers to draw off the shut-out drinkers from Atlanta. Not long after Lee's men lost their martial law powers, it became known that "thirsty members" of Lee's own militia force used their authority and guns "to force themselves on the train" to Marietta, where they enjoyed no jurisdiction, "when all other expedients to get drink here have failed."

The issue came to a head when four provost guardsmen bullied their way onto a crowded night train to Marietta. They went on a binge that ended only when the quartet got into a barroom brawl.

When the fight started to go against them, the young men pulled their pistols and began "shooting at the crowd in the most reckless manner." After shooting up the place, the four fled into the darkness. On the floor lay two wounded men and a dead soldier, "a fine looking, noble young man, of good family and standing," killed by a "ball [that] entered his face near the mouth and passed out at the back of his head."

WITH SALOONS CLOSED, some of Atlanta's raucous street theater moved indoors nightly to the Athenaeum. Performances by traveling musicians and acting troops and the local Shakespearean dramatic company filled the eight-hundred-seat auditorium with crowds of townspeople eager for relief from their daily cares. Local residents often sat next to young men who, reeking of whisky, heckled the performers and called out to the young women in the crowd. Complaints flooded Calhoun's office about "boys and disorderly soldiers . . . smoking . . . and drinking liquor . . . making use of language not at all fit for . . . hearing" in the hall. City residents and respectable "ladies of Atlanta [were] kept away by the rude conduct of a few men in the habit of visiting it." Calhoun placed a police officer in the hall, but, finally, unable to quell the mobs, the mayor refused to renew the Athenaeum's license and forced it to close.

John H. Steele at first railed in the pages of the *Intelligencer* against Calhoun's "usurpation of power." Though Steele had asked Calhoun "to issue an order regulating the theatre," he now accused the mayor of seizing dictatorial power. "The people of Atlanta are not under an absolute city government," he wrote. "The Mayor is but their servant, and must abide by the laws framed by them, and given to him for the purpose of enforcement."

Calhoun defended himself. He disingenuously claimed to have closed the theater not to stop the misbehavior of the few rowdy young men but because the dark days of war were no time for frothy public entertainments. "As our country was involved in a civil war, and as it needed all the recourses [*sic*] of men and means," he insisted, "this was no time for fun and frolic." Calhoun also made note of the strong opposition to him voiced continuously in the *Intelligencer*, leaving him damned if he did act and if he didn't. Steele responded tartly, "The assertion of the Mayor that we have always been opposed to him, is in the main, correct, the reason for which is, that we have been unable to find any action on Mr. Calhoun's part that we could approve."

Calhoun sarcastically noted that the paper "seem[ed] to be the special champion of the theatre." The *Intelligencer's* condemnation of his closure of the theatre, he asserted, had more to do with money than concern over any possible abuse of his authority, because "such companies . . . are generally full of money, and may pay liberally for advertisements."

With the December 1863 election approaching, Steele sneered back, "Of one thing we feel certain, that unless the duties of the Mayor are performed in a more efficient manner than they have been heretofore, we might as well abolish the office and save so much salary from the city treasury." However, without crediting Calhoun, the paper noted the reopening of the Athenaeum a little more than two weeks after its closing. "Ladies can now attend with perfect safety, as no noise or unruly behavior will be tolerated."

The tranquility didn't last. A few months later, the Athenaeum was closed for good. Its stage was converted into a slave auction house.


As quickly as Atlanta was growing and industrializing, it was rapidly slipping back into its frontier ways of unpunished crime and vigilante justice. Mayor Calhoun, who had previously fought lynch mob justice in town, resorted to appointing a twenty-five-member Vigilance Committee to bolster the police. The *Intelligencer* suggested that the city give out shotguns to law-abiding citizens for self-defense—to protect themselves not against any impending threat of Yankee invasion but from criminals lurking in dark corners of town.

Finally, an enraged mob grabbed two men accused of pilfering from guest rooms at the Trout House hotel. The crowd shaved, tarred, and feathered the woeful pair before parading them through the downtown streets with signs pasted to their backs declaring "Trout House Thieves."


A week before the 1863 elections, the *Intelligencer* used the chaos in Atlanta to attack Calhoun's mayoralty:

> Will our very *efficient* and worthy Mayor look over the municipal laws, and see whether he has the power to close the barrooms or not?—Mayor Calhoun is very anxious to *close theatres*, when he has not got one shadow of authority for so doing, but (so it appears to us) does not think it any harm for liquor to be

sold to the soldiers, and for them to be marching intoxicated over the town, making an uproar and disturbing the peace, while our *very efficient and law keeping* police are looking on with a complaisant smile on their venerable countenances. We request the voters of Atlanta to make a small note of the above for reference on election day.

The voters ignored Steele. In spite of the turmoil and violence in his city's streets, Calhoun easily won reelection, not even bothering to campaign. After Calhoun's victory, the *Intelligencer* sourly suggested that the popular mayor had used the police to "go electioneering for their favorite candidate."

Law enforcement in a time of war, abrupt social change, and increasing economic privation proved a never-ending task for a police force underresourced and dependent on the very young, the invalid, and the very old. It was, in short, doomed. Even the supposed law enforcers were a source of the problem. Before the war started, G. Whitfield Anderson had served as the first lieutenant of the town police. He quickly joined the army and fought until badly wounded in the carnage at Antietam (Sharpsburg) in September 1862. Furloughed, he came home to recuperate. Though not fully recovered, he wanted his old job back. But when Anderson left for the war, Thomas Shivers had taken over his post. The fifty-six-year-old Shivers was a former stagecoach driver who had lived in the town since its Terminus days and served during that rowdy time for a term as elected town marshal. With Anderson the war hero wanting his old job back, in early 1863 the city council put the question up for a vote. The members split evenly over who should be deputy marshal. Mayor Calhoun had to cast the deciding ballot. He chose Shivers. An enraged Anderson cursed them all and stormed out of the council room.

On a Saturday night not long after that, the last day of January, Anderson and Shivers happened to be drinking in the same saloon. The pair, one a lawman, the other wanting his job, exchanged more angry words. Shivers drew his pistol and slammed it down on Anderson's head, before hurling a bottle at him as a coup de grâce. Groggy and unarmed, still nursing battle wounds, Anderson got up from the floor bleeding from the head. He backed out of the saloon, warning Shivers that their business wasn't finished. Monday afternoon, two days later, Anderson came looking for the deputy marshal. The two would-be lawmen walked from opposite ends of a busy Whitehall Street until they faced each other in front of Muhlenbrink's

Saloon between the north- and west-bound railroad lines and Alabama Street. The usual big crowds moved through the car shed down the tracks.

Anderson, his head now bandaged to go with his lingering Sharpsburg wounds, declared, "I am now fixed up. Are you ready?" The men pulled their guns. After the smoke cleared, a crowd gathered around Shivers's perforated, lifeless body in the street. He was the first police officer killed in Atlanta history.

Two months later, a grand jury charged Anderson with murder. His case came to trial not long after that. A Fulton County Superior Court jury agreed with his self-defense claim and acquitted him. Freed, Anderson became an Atlanta police officer and deputy sheriff of Fulton County to boot.

## III

# CLAMOROUS TOWN

O YOU WHO WERE FULL OF TUMULT,
You clamorous town,
You city so exultant?
Your slain are not the slain of the sword
Nor the dead of battle.

— ISAIAH 22:2

# CHAPTER 12

# THE DEAD HOUSE

T HE CONFEDERATE ARMED FORCES made up for their amateurism and comparative lack of firepower with spunk, martial spirit, and a clever and knowledgeable leadership corps drawn from resigned U.S. Army officers and graduates of the seven military colleges in the slave states. Northern states had only one such institution to draw upon. Better-equipped and -supplied, more professional, and backed by a sounder dollar, the Union military nonetheless seemed unable to get out of its own way. Since the rout at Manassas, the demoralized federal army was far from an aroused lion and looked more like a paper tiger. Frustrated by the lack of progress against the rebels, Abraham Lincoln changed commanders of the Union army three times and of the Army of the Potomac, his most visible command, five times within the first two years of war. A wary, if pleased, Samuel Richards, surveying the year 1861, was roundly satisfied with his decision to relocate to Atlanta and felt bold enough to declare, "We know not what another year may bring forth but of one thing I am certain, that is that *the Union* will not be restored!"

But the Army of the Potomac was not the only Union army. Elsewhere, the Union had made significant advances. They commanded the coast and pressed on the major ports of the arterial rivers. The war for Southern independence ate men up, and the enrollment terms for many state and Confederate soldiers who had joined in the first days of the rebellion were drawing to a close, while casualties and sickness mounted. More than 700,000 men had already enlisted in the Union army. Additional Southern troops were desperately needed. The Confederate Congress and Georgia's governor appealed for volunteers—and, for the first time, threatened to begin drafting eligible men. Whereas Atlanta's husbands and sons had rushed to join at the first call, they now failed to respond at all. An army recruitment officer, his hard-earned battle scars apparent, trolled the Five Points "asking for volunteers," but in five weeks not a single new man joined up. According to one disheartened observer, "Hundreds of our citizens who are physically able to bear arms . . . pass him every day on the streets, and seem to have no interest in his efforts." In an early February letter to the *Southern Confederacy*, "Stonewall," as he signed his complaint, beseeched, "What is the matter with the men of Atlanta?" He pointed out the grand ambitions of a city that "aspires to be the seat of Government of the Confederate States, and the heart of the Nation in all respects for all time to come."

He harkened to the months ahead when winter camps broke and fighting would resume in Kentucky, perhaps even spreading into neighboring Tennessee. "The enemy will be upon us in the spring; and if our army is beaten, of what value will be the gains which many of the people of Atlanta are laying up in store—many of them ill-gotten, by extortionate speculation upon the necessities of the Government and the poor of the country?" He issued "a general 'fall in to ranks.'"

The enemy did not wait for spring. At the very moment Stonewall issued his public plea for Atlantans to stop loading their wallets and begin loading their rifles, Yankee forces invaded neighboring Tennessee. On February 6, 27,000 soldiers and marines under the combined command of the bibulous Midwestern Brig. Gen. Ulysses S. Grant and the teetotaling Connecticut Yankee navy commodore Andrew H. Foote stormed Fort Henry, northern portal to the Tennessee River. Its capture opened the river to federal navy gunboats all the way to Alabama and exposed Fort Donelson, a brief march across a narrow isthmus to the Cumberland River, to Grant's army. Offering "no terms except unconditional and immediate surrender," Grant took 12,000 prisoners there on February 16. Thinly spread Confederate forces could not hold the weakly defended Nashville. They evacuated the city, its hospitals, and its arsenal before the Army of the Ohio marched in unopposed on February 23. It was the first capital city of a Southern state to fall to the Union army, and it would not be long before Memphis and then New Orleans fell, leaving Vicksburg as the last major Confederate bulwark holding the Yankees back from turning the Mississippi River into a north-south federal highway straight through the Confederacy.

WITH THE UNION ARMY advancing deeper into Tennessee, the need for city defenses first became apparent in spring 1862 when a group of twenty-two federal soldiers dressed as civilians under the direction of a murky spy and contraband dealer, James J. Andrews, captured a Western & Atlantic Railroad train at Big Shanty (today's Kennesaw) less than thirty miles above Atlanta and rode it back toward Union lines near Chattanooga, hoping to destroy the single-track rail line behind them. This would have cut off the main supply line from Atlanta to Confederate forces in the southwest corner of Tennessee at Chattanooga. From there, few defenders stood in the way of a Union army on the march over the 130 miles to Atlanta. Thanks to a sharp-eyed conductor who chased down the train while alerting soldiers, the Andrews raid failed, and all of the raiders were captured. Still, the incident signaled that the war was extending its reach toward Atlanta.

The *Southern Confederacy* described the raid as "the deepest laid scheme, and on the grandest scale, that ever emanated from the brains of any number of Yankees combined. . . . The mind and heart sink back appalled at the bare contemplation of the consequences which would have followed the success of this one act. We doubt if the victory of Manassas or Corinth were worth as much to us as the frustration of this grand *coup d'etat*."

Eventually, the captured men were brought to Atlanta, where they were tried as spies; eight of them, including Andrews, were hanged on a public street and their bodies tossed into a shallow grave. The city was shaken. So were some of the hundreds who watched. Sallie Clayton's eight- and ten-year old younger brothers witnessed the hangings and saw two of the ropes break under the men's weight, requiring that the half-hung pair be strung up again. Their teen sister recalled the hanging of the "bridge burners" as "the first thing that happened in our midst to give us a realization of the sad things of war." Atlantans' assurance of their immunity to the war's violence was no longer so easily sustained.

Instead of unshakeable confidence, the city's residents began to experience wild mood swings as inaccurate and exaggerated news, good and bad, of the war found its way unevenly to the city. Samuel Richards recorded that following the grim war news from western Tennessee, "Our citizens are desponding and think we are done for."

He felt glummer yet when walking through the car shed a few days later he saw three boxes containing soldiers' remains being unloaded from a train. But some months later, despite having been pushed out of Kentucky, A. J. Neal wrote his sister Emma in Atlanta from his artillery brigade's camp outside Knoxville in Middle Tennessee that, despite all the doomsayers, for his part, he saw "nothing to cause despondency" and urged her "not [to] grow despondent at home or think it possible for the South to be subjugated." It was, he wrote, "nonsense" to think an army of so many men defending their own homes could "ever be conquered." He and his men were ready to keep fighting on until the South was burned over, should it come to that, leaving the Yankees nothing but ash and ruins for their pain. "Rather than affiliate with the North again I hope our rivers and branches may run with blood and that when subjugated the victory may be," he wrote, paraphrasing Shakespeare, "As cities won by fire / So won, so lost."

NEAL GOT HIS WISH by April. Under the leadership of Grant and a now battle-ready William Tecumseh Sherman, the Union victory at the Battle of Shiloh (Pittsburgh Landing) on the shores of the Tennessee River in southwestern Tennessee in the first week of April 1862 opened up northern Mississippi to invasion at an unprecedented cost. The two armies together sustained nearly 24,000 casualties in just two days. Neal's and other soldiers' battle cry of "Death Before Dishonor" resonated at home. George W. Adair's *Southern Confederacy* took up the rebel yell and called out,

> Arouse, ye men of the South! Rush to the field of battle! Sink down in your own blood and hail it as a joyful and happy deliverance, in preference to submission to the heartless abolition Yankees. Let your battle cry be, 'Victory or Death!' Far better would it be for the Atlantic Ocean with one swell surge to rise up and sweep us and all we have into the Pacific than for the infernal hell-hounds who wage this wicked war on us to triumph. Let any cruelties, any torments, any death that earth can inflict come upon us in preference to the triumph of the Yankees!

Still living in his father's house, William Lowndes Calhoun heard the call. While refugees from Nashville were just beginning to flood the car shed, the twenty-four-year-old attorney and son of the mayor led in organizing the first new infantry company from the city since the summer. Named the Calhoun Guards in honor of his father, who likely funded it, the company elected the mayor's son as its first lieutenant. Eventually he became captain of the Guards, which was designated Company K, Forty-second Georgia Infantry. In the first months of his term, he rode away from the battlefields, detached by the army to run a prison camp in Madison, Georgia. After mustering out at the end of his enlistment, though, he quickly reenlisted in his company in time to join the party at Chickasaw Bluffs line above Vicksburg. He would see plenty of action this time.


IN DEPARTING FOR THE SERVICE, Lowndes had already heard plenty of tales about the fighting going on far from Atlanta. Not long before he left, his cousin, Ezekiel's son, Edward Calhoun and Edward's foster brother, Robert Clingan, their enlistment year expired, returned home from Virginia. Both were far thinner after a year on short rations than when they set out. "The idol of the household," Edward regaled the family with tales, in his nephew's breathless words, of "thrilling experiences when on the red fields of carnage, his hair-breadth escapes when so nearly captured, the many ghastly sights he saw; and the acts of bravery and cowardice displayed by men when engaged in battle."·

The heroism they'd shown, though, had more to do with braving the elements than contending with enemy fire. The Gate City Guards had fought briefly with Gen. Braxton Bragg's army at Pensacola before being ordered to northwestern Virginia, where, less than a week before the great victory at Manassas, they were caught up in the first heavy land battle of the war at Laurel Hill. Edward Calhoun, Clingan, and the other Gate City guardsmen were among hundreds of men who broke and fled across a branch of the Cheat River, where they found themselves cut off from the main body of retreating Confederates and their supply wagons. To rejoin their army, they sought a path to the safety of the Valley of Virginia. Demoralized, hungry, without enough clothes or blankets, the men climbed and hiked across the Allegheny ridges and descended into the vast western Virginia wilderness forests, where they became completely lost. After wandering without food for four days, drenched, cold, and exhausted, many men grew sick and some deranged, scores falling by the wayside. Finally, a local hunter chanced upon the wandering troops and led them down the valley to safety. Thirteen men out of the Gate City

Guards died; many others were left too debilitated to continue serving. Edward, Robert, and the other survivors still fit for service rejoined the regrouping army in Richmond, serving under Robert E. Lee and Stonewall Jackson.

After barely a month at home, though, Edward and Robert felt encouraged and fit enough to return to the fight. This time, these Calhoun men joined Ben Yancey's replenishing Fulton Dragoons cavalry. Young Pickens Calhoun's time to serve had arrived. Edward's younger brother was now old enough that his deeply distressed father could not keep him from joining the others. Ezekiel "vigorously protested." Pickens told him that should he stay home now, he would fare worse than anything he might face in the army. He "would rather fill an honorable soldier's grave than be branded as a coward." The three brothers in arms left with their new company for Virginia to join Gen. Wade Hampton's already legendary Legion. The Legion would eventually fight in virtually all the major engagements in the Northeast, including the Wilderness and at Antietam (Sharpsburg), Gettysburg, and the siege of Petersburg. Those who lived long enough would finally close out the war at Appomattox.

The physician Edward was placed in charge of a regimental ambulance. By September 1862, he found himself in the middle of the horrendous slaughter at Antietam, driving his ambulance wagon to pick up wounded soldiers in the field when the Union line charged. Rifle and cannon fire flew about him. An exploding shell tore away the wagon's canvas top as he started back for his own lines. The howling wave of Yankee soldiers, stopping only to shoot, overtook him. He and his wagonload of wounded were taken prisoner and led into the Union line. In the lashing tidal sweep of the battle, though, the Confederates regrouped and charged back into the Union line. In the ensuing chaos, Edward saw his chance and drove his careening wagon back through the battling men, black smoke, whistling balls, and exploding shells, reaching safety "without even receiving a scratch."

DISEASE WAS KILLING EVEN more fighting men than shot and shell. Thousands of men in filthy encampments fell ill with typhoid, dysentery, and smallpox. With his trained eye, Edward noticed that Pickens Calhoun was starting to look weary and flushed; he could see that his little brother was sick and told him to take a furlough, but Pickens refused. Over the next few days of riding, his grey eyes dimmed, his cheeks hollowed out, and his long and already slender frame grew skeletal. Finally, Pickens could ride no further. Edward helped carry him to a nearby house, where a mother and daughter took him in. Edward returned a few days later to find Pickens had died.

A few months after Pickens's death, his foster brother, Robert Clingan, was sent out on a courier mission on horseback while a battle raged. Just as he approached the officer for whom the message was intended, an artillery shell exploded nearby, ripping into the officer and knocking him from his saddle. Clingan jumped to his side and carried him behind the shelter of a tree. As Clingan stood, a Yankee sharpshooter put a minié ball through his forehead.


FIGHTING AND ILLNESS RAVAGED both armies. Unimaginably huge numbers of sick and wounded soldiers needed care and respite away from the front. With hot fighting raging west, south, north, and along the seaboard, Atlanta offered a refuge not just for manufacturing but also for wounded and sick soldiers. The long trains of empty freight cars running into town to pick up war munitions offered ideal transport. Atlanta's vaunted "pure waters, salubrious air, and delightful climate" were still good enough that a month after James Calhoun took office for his first term in January 1862, the *Southern Confederacy* reported, "These great blessings which Heaven has favored us with, are about to be put to practical use in a line not heretofore attempted. The Medical Director of the Confederate States Army is here to establish a mammoth hospital at this place." A month later, the first five hundred convalescing soldiers from the Army of Mississippi arrived. Within less than six months, Atlanta, the center of manufacturing and merchant trade, was also the "hospital city of the South." One by one, the army took over larger buildings in town, warehouses, schools, ballrooms, concert halls, and hotels among them, to house and care for the sick and wounded. The Empire and Heery hospitals, Gate City, City Hotel, Alexander, Concert Hall, Wilson's, Denny, Medical College, and Jane's and Hayden's hospitals were named for their previous uses or owners. Beds lined the rooms and halls, with just enough space for a nurse or doctor to move between, and a surgical room, where available, was set off away from the other spaces to dampen the cries of the men in their unanesthetized pain. Without drugs to halt infections, few survived in pain for long in any case.

The hospitals could not keep up with the growing river of wounded and sick coming off the trains. Mayor Calhoun was charged with identifying more structures to be commandeered for hospitals and sites where new ones could be built. The army pressed to convert the large council and courthouse rooms in the City Hall into hospital wards, but Calhoun refused, insisting that maintaining a civic and administrative center for "the County, State, and City is a matter of great public necessity." In the summer, plans were drawn up to construct forty buildings on the fairgrounds on the south side of Fair Street near the Georgia Railroad and the army's munitions laboratories.

Soon, even those facilities were not enough. Tent hospitals and a two-hundred-bed "wayside" hospital went up near the tracks to distribute the wounded and to handle overflow from the more permanent facilities. Specialized hospitals were also erected, including one devoted to contagious diseases such as pneumonia, venereal diseases, measles, and smallpox that covered 155 acres of what was called "Markham's Farm," property seized by the War Department from the known Unionist William Markham. As long trains of cattle cars returned from the Tennessee front with their cargo of sick and wounded soldiers—up to 10,000 wounded men after a single battle—the passenger depot became a scene of crowding, odors, flies, and moans. The overfull hospitals could not handle the waves of new patients, and many were carried off the train and laid out on the depot floor or beneath the trees shading the neighboring City Park to await a physician's attention or triage. The stretchers became a maze through which departing and arriving passengers, often bewildered and exhausted refugees, needed to work their way. Townspeople crossing the city would walk blocks out of their way to avoid the terrible sights.

SALLIE AND GUSSIE CLAYTON helped darn socks with the older women and pulled lint together to make bandages for the wounded. Each morning they prepared bundles of food, clothing, and supplies to take to the hospitals. Now considered a woman, though, Sallie was frequently turned away from visiting the convalescing men. Only the younger Gussie was permitted to attend to their needs. For Gussie, this chance to help would one day prove tragic.

The girls had to leave their beloved Female Institute schoolhouse overlooking the city when the army took that as a hospital as well. They now met their classmates and teachers for school at the Neal house across Washington Street from their home. The inseparable Clayton sisters were drawn to their old schoolhouse when, out for a stroll one afternoon, they found themselves nearby. They decided to pay a visit. They entered quietly through the doors they had opened countless times. The girls looked about in stunned horror. The chapel, music room, and classrooms where they and their friends had once filled pews, chairs, and desks were now lined with rows of groaning, bandaged, and mutilated men. The odor was overwhelming. They ventured to look downstairs into the raised basement but quickly turned away from the sight of stacked corpses. Piles of amputated arms and legs lay there as well. It was now the "Dead House," where the remains of the dead and debris of surgeries awaited burial or shipment home.

Sallie could not comprehend such a transformation of a place she formerly thought of as filled only with the ringing laughter and playful voices of young girls dancing, singing, and reciting their lessons. "The change was so like a play," she recalled. "First, the ringing down the curtain on a picture of Life, and Joy, and Mirth, and raising it again to present one of Gloom and Sorrow, Suffering and Death."

THE TENS OF THOUSANDS of sick soldiers and the crowds of refugees, many exhausted from their long journeys, carried contagious illness with them. It didn't take long to spread to the wider population. Scarlet fever and smallpox swept the city starting in the fall of 1862 and continuing on into winter, despite a largely ignored, mandatory vaccination program for whites. Red quarantine flags marked out houses with smallpox cases within. Mayor Calhoun established a quarantine hospital with armed guards. Patients with mild cases still wandered off from quarantine, spreading the disease and setting off epidemic outbreaks in the city. Finding people to nurse the sick was nearly impossible. Few whites would work the low-paying contagious-ward jobs; nor did many owners want their costly slaves exposed to smallpox, typhus, and other virulent diseases. Soon, however, Confederate seizures of hundreds of bondsmen and women led to their comprising almost half the hospital workforce, including 80 percent of the attendants caring for the sick and wounded.

Their health care ignored, blacks, crowded in slave quarters, fell ill in large numbers. In December, the city ordered the complete isolation of infected blacks on a farm a few hundred yards from the army's Markham's Farm quarantine hospital. Christmastime 1862 was a somber one in Atlanta as people had little to celebrate and feared visiting friends and neighbors, whose homes might harbor smallpox, scarlet fever, tuberculosis, and other terrible diseases. A few weeks after his infant daughter Alice's death, Samuel Richards was "quite anxious lest [contagious illnesses] come into our *fold*." To keep any contagion at bay, he placed bags of herbs around his remaining children's necks "as haply it may do some good." Such protection could not prevent illness entering the Richards brothers' shared household, though. Jabez's young wife died of consumption in the early days of 1863.

# CHAPTER 13

# ENEMIES WITHIN

T HE FIRST CONFEDERATE DRAFT in April 1862 included men up to age thirty-five. By October, the upper limit had reached forty-five. It eventually included all able-bodied men from ages sixteen to fifty, and Georgia men up to age sixty faced state militia service. The effects of the draft transformed Atlanta, forcing every man to choose: Was he for the Confederacy or not? And if he was for it, was he prepared to die for it? On an afternoon in 1862, not long after Col. George W. Lee's installation as provost marshal, Samuel Richards and his brother, Jabez, were working in their Decatur Street store when two young army officers barged in. The men, whom the brothers knew because one of them owed on an account at the store, were not looking for books or paper. The two bookstore proprietors, the soldiers said, had been "watched for some time." Their support for the war was "unreliable." As they left, the officers warned the merchants to watch their step. They were now considered, a shaken Samuel Richards shuddered, "unsound."

"Insulted," Richards protested his loyalty to the rebellion, declaring, "I pray God that we may not have to submit to the rule of the hated Yankees again," but his warlike statements and the Confederate flag hanging in the store window were literally window dressing. The officers were right: He and his brother were entirely "unsound" when it came to making war on the northern people Richards referred to as "atrocious vandals." Despite his righteous words, he had "not the slightest intention" of joining the fight. "My whole nature revolts at the thought of going into this war," he wrote. The church deacon and bookman was no fighter. He felt nothing but "loathing and horror" at the thought of witnessing "scenes of blood and carnage." He also disdained the foulmouthed, illiterate soldiers he saw on drunken binges in the Five Points. He would never willingly condescend to spending "months or years perhaps in . . . the company of such men as form the greater part of our army—to be ordered about by incompetent, drunken officers."

When the draft's upper age limit included him, Richards "stuck to his room and the back streets, afraid to go about town now or to the store as I hear that the officers are about, taking up the conscripts vigorously." He frantically cast about for a draft-exempt profession, trying his hand at shoe making, a skilled and muscular craft about which he knew nothing except that he had spent $1,000 to open a soon-failed cobbler's shop over the bookstore. When that didn't work out, he was elated upon landing his part-time job as a proofreader and typesetter in a printing house—in return for an investment in the business. Seeing both a business opportunity and a draft exemption, he and Jabez bought out the house's religious periodical, the *Soldier's Friend*, which was distributed among the troops. They could work for it as editor and proofreader, exempted trades.

Still nervous in March 1863, Richards decided to take out an added "insurance" policy by paying $2,500 for a substitute to fill his place in the army. By the following summer, the combined fear of inevitable combat service and inflation drove the price of substitutes to levels beyond the reach of even the very wealthy. Jabez risked conscription when he couldn't find a replacement for less than $8,000 to $10,000. Desperate to stay out of the fighting military, Samuel paid $500 for one of many shares in another publishing business that provided him an excuse to join a home-defense company comprising exempt pressmen. At the first muster, he idly chatted with another man who summed up their new mission: "Our object," he said, "is to have as little to do as possible."

SUSPICION AND ANGER AGAINST men like Richards, who "dodge round corners when the enrolling officer comes along," now spread with the virulence of smallpox. Everyone could see plainly who was conniving, wrote the *Southern Confederacy*, "to fix up some plan to keep out of the army." The newspaper condemned men "opening up shoe shops, tanyards, turning blacksmith . . . scrambl[ing] for every little office—Militia Captain, Justice of the Peace, Judge of the Inferior Court . . . rush[ing] into the ranks of companies that are called for to mind some public building where liquor is convenient and Yankees scarce." It decried the "skulkers, shirkers, and home staying grumblers" and suggested that authorities do what was necessary "to make this class of men do their duty." If they didn't, defeat would not come in the field but at the hands of "the people at home."

Atlanta was estimated to contain as many as 10,000 draft dodgers, men on extended furlough and out-and-out deserters. Few could fault them after even the city government gave itself a Christmas present on December 25, when Mayor James Calhoun petitioned that he as mayor, the city council, and all employees, plus the officers and forty members, of each volunteer fire company be declared exempt from military duty. One dismayed observer counted around 3,000 firemen who were otherwise healthy and eligible to enlist now placed beyond the reach of a desperate army.

THE ATLANTA GOVERNMENT'S self-recusal from taking part in the war was another salvo in an increasingly open conflict with Col. George W. Lee. Mayor Calhoun insisted publicly that "no clash or difficulty has ever arisen between the military and civil authority here," but since his collision with army officials over the declaration of martial law and his short-lived, spurious appointment as "civil governor," relations between the city and Lee's nearly 700-man personal army continued to deteriorate.

Though not a slaveholder, Lee was an ardent Confederate. He had been one of the city's earliest backers of secession, a fire-eating minuteman, and although ravaged by tubercular fits that left him debilitated and ultimately unable to continue in the field, he immediately volunteered as an infantry officer at the head of a company when the first fighting broke out. He had strong backers in Richmond, politically influential friends in his hometown, and far more firepower at his disposal than did city officials. A millwright by trade and saloon keeper on the side, he had struggled before the war to sustain his middle-class status in a town where so many country and working people had managed to become wealthy practically overnight. Atlanta's high society, which included disproportionate numbers of educated former Yankees, may have resented a consumptive saloon keeper and possibly illiterate mechanic holding a position of near-absolute authority over *their* city. He regularly sent out what one businessman harassed by his guards called his "second class set of cow bred Confederate officers" to intimidate, arrest, and even beat opponents among the local citizenry. Lee, for his part, thought ill enough of his Atlanta neighbors to describe the town "since the commencement of the revolution [as] a point of rendezvous of traitors, swindlers, extortioners, and counterfeiters." The Five Points teemed with, he colorfully snarled, "a mixture of Jews, New England Yankees, and of refugees shirking military duties."

Gen. Braxton Bragg, commander of the Army of Tennessee and, as such, chief of the Atlanta military post's many hospitals and other installations, could not bring Colonel Lee to heel. He complained about Lee to Gen. Joseph Johnston, the commander of the army's western department and his superior, shuddering at the thought of Lee at the head of a personal army "of nearly 500 men in Atlanta, more than half conscripts, 'home guards,'" whom he had assembled "by misrepresentation and downright falsehood, and by evading and misconstruing orders." The situation in Atlanta had become "disgraceful." The provost marshal kept prisoners "confined for months, even without charges," made "expenditures most lavish," and used his command to employ men "by the dozen, able-bodied and without occupation," loyal to him and nobody else.

John Steele's *Daily Intelligencer* rarely criticized wartime officials outside Mayor Calhoun's City Hall office, but he found enough fault with Lee's men to warn, "We will very soon have nothing but a rabble, instead of a body of organized men to protect us." Lee himself had trouble controlling those among his men who were drunken looters and arbitrary lawmen. When one of Lee's patrols heard reports that a farmhouse close to town harbored robbers, the officers approached through the nighttime darkness and, without announcing their identity, smashed the windows and burst into the house. The startled farmer grabbed his shotgun and fired on the intruders, mortally wounding the first officer who came after him. In their fright, the other guardsmen began shooting wildly around the house, barely missing the farmer's cowering children and wife. Retreating, the officers then attempted to burn down the house with all its occupants still inside. The farmer and his family managed to escape the flames, but he was soon arrested and charged with murder. The state supreme court threw out the case, holding instead that the lower court should have found the guardsmen guilty of "aggravated riot."

Such rebukes did little to slow Lee's drive to control the town and bring in what he regarded as criminals, draft dodgers, and suspected traitors. And he was encouraged by the War Department in Richmond, which ignored Bragg and applauded his aggressiveness. In January 1863, the army placed him in command of its conscript bureau covering a vast swath of northern Georgia and southwestern North Carolina and gave him command of a combined cavalry and infantry regiment charged with filling out the necessary manpower quota for the army—and punishing those who refused to do their duty. Little matter that Lee himself was eventually charged with selling draft exemptions. He was also expected to stamp out the anti-Confederate insurrectionist wildfires spreading through the up-country region. Lee set to it, promising Gov. Joseph Brown that "those who violate[d] the laws of the State or Confederacy [would suffer] retribution due the crimes of which they [were] guilty." He posted and published stern broadsides around town to "all malcontents," including "deserters, tories, and conscripts resisting the laws," warning, "I will pursue them into their fastnesses, and use all the power and means at my control, to arrest and *bring them to condign punishment.*" His men would "fire upon them, and, at all hazard . . . capture the last man."

Composed in part of his provost marshal forces, Colonel Lee's conscript bureau army was even more high-handed and violent when it struck out into the countryside to enforce the draft laws and suppress resistance. Antidraft and Unionist guerilla bands operating in the northern parts of the state attacked conscription agents and militia units. Lee's men were soon embroiled in an anti-insurgency war. Twice in 1863, they invaded Lumpkin County, the center of up-country resistance. Lee's soldiers traveled through the hollows and remote backwoods, beating the bushes for "Tories" hiding in the Blue Ridge foothills. They rounded up as many as a thousand deserters, whom they forced to return to their commands, and, in the course of the two campaigns, brought another four hundred men in chains back to Atlanta. Critics charged that many of those prisoners were severely beaten and that some of those in chains were too old for conscription but had been held by Lee until they agreed to join the army.

Those who refused to surrender faced swifter justice. Lee's army and local vigilante backers summarily shot or hanged many of the men they caught. By 1864, they were dispatching as many as fifteen in just two months, often leaving the bodies where they fell as warnings to other would-be resisters.

LEE KEPT A CLOSE EYE on people moving through Atlanta. He considered his hometown a crossroad for the worst sorts to be found anywhere in the Confederacy: Tories and speculative extortionists, draft dodgers, and actual traitors and spies. He set out to hunt down the members of what he called the "Jacobin Club"—even men like Richards who proudly and loudly sung out their support for the Confederacy. Lee assigned men from the provost marshal guard to trail suspects and goaded his officers to "arrest them if they did anything to be arrested for." Before leaving on his blockade-running expedition, attorney Amherst Stone described Lee's pursuit of dissenters as a "perfect reign of terror." He employed his martial law powers to detain without charges several suspected Unionists, particularly people from the North, nearly all of whom were among the city's upper class. His men brought six men and three women in shackles from their homes and businesses and locked them into the barracks jail, according to one of the jailed men, "in a room with all the rebel 'roughscuff,' the dirtiest, filthiest set I ever saw." Foundry owner James Dunning was among the jailed; so were the successful dry goods store owner Michael Myers and Stone's wife, Cyrena. Even Mayor Calhoun's closest aid, James Crew, a prominent railroad official, was detained for a period. They were put through long and intimidating interrogations about rumors of "a Union organization, of three hundred white men, and of a plot for the negroes to rise, the prisoners to emerge from their confinement, and all to unite in rebellion against the Southern Confederacy."

When Mayor Calhoun learned of the detentions, he immediately intervened, though at first he could only get his friends and colleagues moved out of the filthy, stifling, and overcrowded jailhouse barracks, which they shared with common criminals and Confederate army deserters, to more comfortable accommodations. Several of the detainees were eventually brought before a specially convened Mayor's Court, which handled civilian cases, to be tried for treason. Although he was aware of how dangerous Lee's men could be, Calhoun nonetheless quickly dismissed all charges.

His action came too late for Michael Myers, whose loyalty was considered suspect since an earlier refusal to accept Confederate money in his store. Lee's force of club-wielding young teens took him up in the late-summer sweep of suspected Unionists and, when they got him alone in a cell, beat him to death. An autopsy supervised by Colonel Lee found no foul play involved in Myers's death. The coroners determined he had fractured his skull in "a fall upon the floor of the room in which he was confined," but the fatal fall "resulted from the peculiar condition of his system at the time, consequent upon his habits." The Irish immigrant, Lee insisted in a letter to the Confederate secretary of war after questions had been raised, was "a decided victim of inebriety." A loyal friend of Myers refused to accept the findings. After he protested to Richmond, Lee had him arrested too.

LEE NOT ONLY WORRIED about draft dodgers and white Unionists but also shared the fears of many whites that the war would spark a black uprising. Reports circulated widely about an insurrectionary army of 10,000 East Georgia slaves led by infiltrating Yankee officers moving toward Atlanta. Would the rapacious black army descend upon Atlanta, where more and more blacks lived? White citizens had long sought to limit the place of slavery and the presence of all blacks within their town's bounds. The army's needs and the demands of the furiously busy factories and hospitals, though, had made slaves essential. By November 1863, slaves resident in town had increased by 30 percent over the census of 1860, to 2,534, more than half women. However, with many refugee households no longer able to support their slave families and rural slaves impressed for city projects for short periods before returning to their masters, far more blacks lived in Atlanta without ever being counted by tax collectors. Many bondsmen, including increasing numbers of runaways, lived unsupervised in camps on the outskirts of town. "We had never seen so many dark skinned people in all our lives," recalled Sarah Huff, a young girl growing up on the Marietta road at the edges of town.

The needs of the Confederate army that transformed Atlanta into an increasingly chaotic urban and industrial metropolis also made it a hub for black life—and set off a slow-fuse mine that would blow apart the slave foundation of the Southern rebellion from beneath. The high concentration of blacks formerly dispersed and isolated on plantations had, for the first time, exceptional access to outside news. Those few men and women who could read a newspaper discussed the war news at night in darkened slave quarters. Plantation slaves were impressed by Confederate authorities by the hundreds and thousands from the surrounding countryside for short periods to labor in military facilities. They learned from better-informed black Atlanta residents and in turn shared word about the war when returned to their rural homes. Throughout Georgia, men, women, and children caught in perpetual bondage could "hear" the tramping boots of the Union army coming nearer to the state borders. Only when Confederates were nowhere in sight, though, did they dare talk among themselves about what that meant.

Atlanta's teeming, transient, and often unsupervised black population knew almost instantly when President Abraham Lincoln signed his January 1, 1863, executive order known as the Emancipation Proclamation, declaring slaves in the rebellious states to be free. A war that started off as a battle of ideology, of unified national authority versus states' rights, flag versus flag, was at that point recast as a war to end, or keep, slavery. Whites in town, recorded Cyrena Stone in her secret diary, reacted with "great apprehension" to the announcement. They knew that every slave had heard of it "and understood its import." Remarking the slaves' apparently unchanged attitude and behavior, she believed, "The wild joy that thrilled their hearts, when they felt that their chains were at last broken," was not apparent to whites; their hallelujahs, she wrote, "*dared* not be spoken." Despite a war now being fought to free them, most slaves "submitted quietly" to the increasingly strict regulations imposed on their lives. However, when the question of arming blacks to fight on behalf of the Confederacy came up, an Atlanta friend's household servant told her, "Missus, they better keep them guns out of our folks hands—cause they dun 'no *which way we going to shoot!*"

BLACK HOPE WAS MATCHED by white paranoia, and few people were more militantly paranoid than Col. George Washington Lee. Racist vigilantism went unpunished and uncriticized. Blacks were not merely submissive; they were *made* aware of the consequences of any acts of defiance or hints of revolt they might be contemplating. Word got around quickly in 1862, when, during a matter of weeks, captors beat a runaway slave to death in Thomas County, a vigilante group in Washington County hanged a slave accused of stabbing his overseer, and another group near Columbus hanged and burned to death five blacks charged with murdering their master. Near Stone Mountain in sight of Atlanta in late 1863, a black man accused of attacking an eleven-year-old white girl was hung, "his body . . . left hanging on the gallows, there to rot, as a monument of warning to others," reported the *Columbus Daily Sun*. In Bibb County not long after that, two doctors castrated a slave named Melton accused of attempted rape, rendering Melton, according to the Macon *Daily Telegraph*, "much distressed, and [he] considered the sentence more dreadful than death itself." The paper hoped Melton's fate would deter other blacks as a "terrible warning and example."

Fearful about the swelling black population in the midst of their chaotic city, many residents organized and armed. A self-defense company of "old men" mustered, said one member, not so much out of fear of a Yankee invasion but "to keep order here at home. . . . We were really afraid of the darkies." Colonel Lee also tightened his grip on blacks, enforcing the dusk-to-dawn curfew. As slaves streamed into town with their refugee white families, they often had to curl up at night out in the open while their owners slept in churches or other makeshift shelters because of the lack of housing. Lee began rounding up the roaming black families and penning them in "Negro yards" and otherwise keeping them from moving about except with their owners' written permission or by his authority. Fearing a Trojan horse within the city, other ordinances ensured that blacks, slave and free, could not circulate freely or possess any "weapons" for insurrectionary purposes—which included many common tools. They could not play cards, ride in carriages, carry a cane or walking stick, or, of course, own or carry firearms or poisonous drugs. Livery stables were banned from letting a black man saddle a horse. A night curfew for blacks began fifteen minutes after the ringing of an evening bell and ended at sunrise.

Some sympathetic whites helped blacks circumvent the rules. Mayor Calhoun's young son Patrick, taking pity on young slave men in his household, wrote passes under his father's name for those wishing to visit their sweethearts after curfew.

But the mood of most of the city was bitter and afraid.


TIGHT RESTRICTIONS ON BLACK movement and activities could not stop some forms of slave resistance from being overlooked in plain sight. Whites simply could not see the determined efforts Atlanta's slaves were making on their own behalf to undermine the Confederacy from within and loosen the bonds of slavery. At the Ponder estate on the edge of town, also out the Marietta road, with the preoccupied mistress of the house turning a blind eye, Joseph Quarles, a Ponder slave who possessed a rudimentary education, opened a night school in one of the workshops for the many children living there. In 1864,

Festus and Isabella Flipper's eldest son, Henry, now age eight, learned to read from the first book he had ever seen, a Confederate version of the *Blue Back Speller*. Slaves who once feared the loss of a finger for daring to pick up a newspaper were now making sure their children learned to read and write.

Other hidden acts of defiance took place right under Provost Marshal Lee's own nose. After the court-martialing and execution as spies of the first eight of the Union men captured following the spring 1862 attempted train hijacking at Big Shanty, the surviving men remained confined for months in Atlanta's barracks prison. Lee, though, could not see "why fourteen of the engine thieves were respited while the others were executed." Languishing in jail with only enough nourishment to keep them alive, the remaining men relied upon "two great friends," the prison's slave servants, John and Kate. Though unable to read or legally buy or borrow newspapers, whenever possible they pilfered a guard's copy after he set it aside. Passing through many hands, news from the outside world arrived at the bottom of the pan in which the prisoners' food came to their cell. The Union prisoners could keep up with war news and feel hopeful of eventual liberation as Union forces advanced. After the prisoners finished reading the paper, the servants returned it in the same manner, and then it would find its way back through the secretive slave network to the unsuspecting guard's post.

The grateful prisoners discovered that the kindly John and Kate knew far more about war matters than they let on. "They could not be misled by their rebel masters," recalled one of the incarcerated Yankees, William Pittenger, "for they had adopted the simple rule of disbelieving everything told, even while professing unbounded credulity." The black men understood well what the war meant. They whispered with the Northerners about the Union army's movements, emancipation, and Lincoln's plans. "I never talked with a negro yet," found Pittenger, "who seemed to have the slightest doubt of the victory of the Union troops, and in their freedom as the result of the war."

In that respect, the slaves were more percipient than the majority of Atlanta's residents. Even twelve months later, the war, however real its consequences, remained a remote event yet to puncture their state's borders, one that still produced enough moments of heroic Southern success to fan the delusion that all was not inevitably lost. War would not reach the Gate City.

IN THE FALL OF 1862, a few months after their comrades' execution, Provost Marshal Lee interviewed the remaining Union raiders in his custody, supposedly to communicate their statements to the War Department in Richmond. He implied that their statements might improve their chances for a reprieve and perhaps make a prisoner exchange possible. After interviewing them, he promised to let the men know what he heard. However, apparently not satisfied with what he learned, he never followed through. Soon, the Union prisoners saw that preparations were underway to build another gallows. They needed to act, or they would join their comrades in a shallow Atlanta grave.

On November 15, 1862, though weakened by months of confinement and malnourishment in a crowded, stifling cell, they overpowered a guard when he opened their cell door to collect an empty bread tray. "The negro waiters," watching the escape play out, "kept perfectly quiet." The men climbed up and over the surrounding prison wall, then fled through the streets and from there out into the countryside. Pittenger was blocked in his attempt to get out of the jailhouse and returned in despair to his upper-story cell. He watched out the barred window as soldiers charged up to the prison and alarmed and shouting men and women scurried in fright through the neighboring streets. As the city's church bells rang wildly, he felt the crackle of the rapid gunfire he heard as if the balls had struck his own gut.

He saw Colonel Lee ride up blustering and red-faced on horseback. He was "in a towering passion." Lee issued orders "in a very angry tone" to hunt down the escapees. He shouted to his men, "Don't take one of the villains alive. Shoot them down and let them lie in the woods." A deserter being held in the same jailhouse had tried to escape with the Union prisoners but fell from the wall and broke his ankle. Pittenger saw the guards drag him back to his cell "in a very rough manner." He died a short time later from his injuries.

Ten men, including eight of the raiders, managed to elude Lee's men. All the Union escapees eventually reached freedom. A few days after the mass breakout, the furious provost marshal wrote a bitterly recriminatory letter to his superior in Charleston, blaming the escape on having too few men at his disposal and "outside influences" that enabled the plot. He insisted "sympathizers outside" must have hid the men after they fled; otherwise, his men surely would have tracked them down.

WHILE JOHN AND KATE dared assist the Union men in their escape only with their silence, Bob Yancey, the barber and currency and gold trader, took an active role in helping another Yankee break out of the same jail. With owner Ben Yancey fighting in Virginia, his trusted bondsman, now a popular local figure, regularly walked in and out of the barracks prison, where the guards thought nothing of seeing him carry his barbering tools and towels to shave prisoners and cut their hair. Within his kit, though, he hid large amounts of Confederate currency to exchange for the prisoners' greenbacks.

Yancey came to know several of the prisoners well. He often gave the needy men money and clothing and spent, he said, "many many days and nights . . . watching over them in sickness from exposure and wounds." He even took off his own shirts and jackets to cover freezing and feverish prisoners.

One afternoon, he was shaving a man he mistakenly later called "Colonel Cliff." William Clift was a Union prisoner much prized by his Confederate captors. The seventy-year-old had been leader of the resistance in the Chattanooga region where he waged a guerilla war against Confederate forces. After the Union army took control of the area, he became a courier for Gen. William Rosencrans, then leader of the Army of the Cumberland chasing Braxton Bragg's Army of Tennessee across the state. Ironically, Clift's own son, a Confederate cavalry officer, stumbled upon him on a mission and brought him in. Clift was shipped to Atlanta for confinement in the barracks jail.

While Yancey's razor scratched at Clift's whiskers, he whispered, "Bob, I want to get out of this place."

"Captain," Bob replied, "you know I can do nothing for you."

Clift persisted. "Yes, you can."

Bob distrusted the older white man who, he suspected, might be trying to entrap him. "Now, you want to get me into a scrape and then tell Wash Lee [Colonel Lee] about it, and he will hang me."

"I will die before," Clift insisted. He told Yancey that a friend stood ready to help him once he got outside the prison walls. He pleaded with Yancey to bring him a rope. "This fellow here will pull me over the fences if you will bring me a line."

Yancey soon smuggled a rope into the jailhouse. He refused twenty Yankee dollars Clift offered him for his troubles.

With the aid of his unnamed friend, Clift was pulled over to the busy streets of Atlanta and soon slipped out of the city. Eventually, he made his escape back through the lines into Union-controlled Tennessee territory.

"Wash" Lee hauled Yancey in for questioning—but not for long. A man of means now, he had no trouble bribing his way back to working in his barbershops and trading money between the warring sides for big profits.

UNION TROOPS PUSHED DEEPER into Tennessee and up from the Gulf coast throughout the first half of 1863. Fighting approached closer and closer to Georgia's borders. The death toll reported daily in the newspapers grew larger. The bodies returning, together with the thousands of sick and wounded soldiers recuperating and, when they could, walking the streets, made the realities of war clearer to Atlantans. While few advocated surrender or a restoration of the Union as it had been, many longed for a negotiated settlement to the conflict.

Calhoun's city was prosperous but in turmoil and under the thumb of Lee's ruthless and frequently lawless men. The mayor had worked to prevent war. After so much bloodshed and carnage, and with his son deep in the fight, he hoped a peace treaty might bring an end to the fighting. In the fall's state race for governor, "a friend and advocate of peace from the day the war commenced," Calhoun openly supported his fellow Constitutional Unionist and friend Joshua Hill in his race against Gov. Joe Brown. Brown wanted to fight on for independence. Hill advocated a negotiated end to the war.

Hill swayed few voters outside the strongly Unionist mountain region. Governor Brown swept Fulton County by a three-to-one vote and the rest of the state by large margins. Georgia voted to fight on.

HILL WAS A RESPECTED POLITICAL leader and wealthy slaveholder, a Confederate now by necessity and home loyalty. Still, some questioned his patriotism. In wartime, Steele in the *Intelligencer* insisted there could be no shade of gray in a person's loyalty to the Confederacy. "We have heard one or two names mentioned in connection with disloyalty," he wrote, "and, could we prove it, or give reliable authority for it, would certainly advocate a little hanging. This is no time for 'palavering.' A man must be either friend or foe; and if he is the latter, there is a proper way to get rid of him."

That was true even for candidates for governor. Not long after the 1863 gubernatorial race, a soldier walked into a Whitehall Street store and asked where Hill lived, wrongly assuming him to be an Atlanta man. He was told the antebellum congressman lived some sixty miles away in Madison.

"That lets me out," said the disappointed soldier. "Our company from Mississippi is here for a day, and we thought we would hang old Josh. . . . For disloyalty—he's a Union man you know."

A few men in town might not have objected to seeing Mayor Calhoun hanged as well, but for most he remained a popular figure—or at least the city was reluctant to change administrations in the middle of a war. While he had lost a bid in the fall for a state senate seat, he easily won an unprecedented third City Hall term in December.

ON NEW YEAR'S DAY 1864, the temperature dropped to the point that pitchers of water froze even in heated rooms. Outside, the high reached only six degrees, and that night it fell below zero. The forests in and surrounding town had been denuded to meet the arsenal's demand for charcoal. Firewood now sold for $80 a cord, well beyond the reach of most Atlantans. Supplies of coal gas were exhausted, leaving the street lanterns and church sconces dark. During the coldest winter in thirty years, people fed small stove fires with broken furniture and skipped icy church services altogether. Livestock and poultry, always in danger of being stolen, were now threatened with freezing or starving to death, so they were moved from their pens into people homes.

The fifty-two-year-old Calhoun's hair remained thick but had given over to gray, and his hands shook while he read his third annual State of the City speech on New Year's Day. No traces of optimism from the previous year remained. Crime, he admitted, plagued the city. He couldn't hire enough good officers to contain the disorder. A few dishonest ones he had had to dismiss. Smallpox and other diseases kept the pesthouse at Markham's Farm full. He recognized the huge need for relief, resulting in an appropriation of about $40,000 for public assistance. "The drain upon the Treasury to supply the wants of the suffering poor and arising out of the increased salaries of the Officers has been unprecedented," he intoned. His own salary, which started at $600 in 1862, had grown to $2,500 (less than the city clerk's of $4,000 and the marshal's of $3,500). The rapid growth of the city also made food distribution a challenge; the city market near Whitehall and Alabama streets was "altogether inadiquit [sic]" to handle its traffic. He hoped to move and enlarge it before the end of the coming year. However, the "scarcity and high price of material and the difficulty of obtaining mechanics" made any near-term solution unlikely.

Troubled times, though, cleared the earth for planting new solutions. He knew intimately the value of an education; in his own life, the opportunity to learn had enabled a destitute country boy to rise to wealth and power. Public education might cure the problem of gangs of poor, unsupervised children who presently roamed Atlanta's streets and engaged in petty crime. He called for the establishment of a system of public elementary schools for the children of the poor and those whose fathers were in the service. He proposed that each ward employ a teacher for its resident children. He asserted that the city could bear the cost of five teachers at $1,000 per year each. "The expense to the City would be but a trifle," he contended, "and no one could estimate the good that would result from it." He promised, "As a taxpayer I would always be willing to pay my part." The notion never advanced far in the council's deliberations.

The day before the mayor spoke in City Hall, a depressed Samuel Richards noted that the miserable weather provided a "fit ending to a year of gloom and death." He was spitting mad. That day he had received a telegram announcing that Richmond had banned the widely reviled practice of paying for substitutes. After receiving word that his money had gone to waste, Richards moaned, "My $2500 Substitute becomes worthless to me." It was, he raged, a "grand Government Swindle." "What a blessed thing it is to live in *a free* country!" With the New Year's bells about to toll, he shivered in the winter night, "the fire nearly out." "God save us from evil in the year to come."

# CHAPTER 14

# RIVER OF
# DEATH

A S HE SPOKE IN A FRIGID City Hall about Atlanta's prospects, Mayor James Calhoun pointedly made no mention of the Union forces nibbling at the northwestern corner of Georgia just a day's train ride away from the Five Points. His thoughts, though, probably strayed there. William Lowndes Calhoun, his eldest child, was ninety miles away in the Army of Tennessee's winter camp among the snowy ridges and iced-over hollows around Dalton, Georgia.

Lowndes had already survived some of the fiercest and most sustained fighting of the war. He knew from direct experience what Generals Ulysses S. Grant and William Tecumseh Sherman would do to win. He had rejoined the Calhoun Guards, his Atlanta volunteer infantry company in the Forty-second Regiment of the Georgia Guards, at Vicksburg on December 31, 1862, just two days after their first victorious stand against the Sherman-led assault on the Chickasaw Bluffs overlooking the Mississippi River above the town. The celebration didn't last long. Calhoun's command shifted from the bluffs north of the lynchpin river port to the swamps below it, where from exposure, malaria, and short rations of "blue beef and sour cornbread," the men, he said, "became almost walking skeletons." When a springtime renewal of the Union assault on the riverfront was anticipated, his men were moved into the city and placed as a support for the lower water batteries. Calhoun's men were part of the rearguard against a massive, early-morning surprise attack by General Grant, then in command of the Army of the Tennessee. Surrounded Confederate forces fell behind Vicksburg's heavy fortifications. Unable to break through its defenses, Grant laid siege to the city.

By day, the Yankee artillery fire and mines blasted the earthworks, which the bone-weary rebels worked through the night to repair. With little ammunition, the Confederate soldiers snuck out to salvage cartridges and caps from the enemy dead and wounded lying in front of their defenses. The approaching Union lines drew within twenty-five yards of the Vicksburg works. For forty-seven days and nights, Calhoun and his men—except the dead—never left the trenches. They endured mining and countermining, the enemy approaching nearer and nearer and, when not assaulting, pummeling them with heavy sharpshooting all along the line and constant firing from their artillery and mortar fleet. Sometimes as many as two hundred guns fired at once into Vicksburg. In the meantime, meager rations kept growing smaller and were at last reduced to pea-meal bread and no meat, except mule meat carved out of animals struck down by shells. Even fouled water was scarce on the line, and many desperately thirsty men were shot down trying to obtain it. "Worn and weak as the troops were," recalled Calhoun, "if the order had been given" to break out of Vicksburg, "they would have succeeded, or died in the attempt; for the men who had gone through with so much fighting and hardships would have risked anything."

With "no hope of relief," on July 3, General John Pemberton offered to surrender. Calhoun regretted the decision. "I felt that a soldier's death was preferable," he said. Vicksburg and its 31,600 defenders surrendered on a monumental Fourth of July. The Forty-second Georgia was part of a brigade that lost 42 percent of its men. The surviving prisoners were paroled just two days later. Calhoun spent thirty days recuperating at his father's home, then reorganized survivors and new recruits for the Forty-second Georgia at Decatur. The company took the Western & Atlantic north through the old Cherokee country, whose former inhabitants his father had surveyed a quarter century before, and marched into the last corner of Tennessee still in Confederate hands. It wasn't long before Calhoun, now captain of his guard, and his men were back in the lines.

THE BRUTAL GRIND THAT led to the taking of Vicksburg, together with the much easier capture of New Orleans and the pushing out of Confederate forces from the Mississippi River's banks, had undammed the entire valley to the unimpeded flow of federal forces and completely severed the trans-Mississippi west from the rest of the South. On the same Fourth of July that Vicksburg surrendered, Gen. Robert E. Lee's invading Army of Northern Virginia was pushed back and finally smashed at the town of Gettysburg in Union territory and forced to retreat back across the Potomac River into Virginia. Word of the simultaneous victories elated a war-weary Northern people, disheartened by massive casualties, heavy taxes, draft riots, suspension of constitutional rights, and deep contention over Abraham Lincoln's emancipation of the slaves. Northern voters had swung heavily in the previous off-year election away from his Republican party. General Grant and many others in the North now believed that "the fate of the Confederacy was sealed when Vicksburg fell." But Richmond and Atlanta, the head and heart of the Confederacy, remained untouched.

General Sherman, whose Fifteenth Corps of Grant's army had been sent into the Mississippi countryside to hold off reinforcement of Vicksburg, was camped eighteen miles east of the invested city shortly after its surrender. Pleased with the state of affairs, if miffed that he did not personally get to march into Vicksburg, he wrote his wife Ellen's brother, Philomen B. Ewing, "All I ask is for the U.S. to give me 10,000 Recruits and I will have my corps ready for Mobile & Atlanta by October." Not long after, Grant would give him those men and more.

With the Mississippi River valley in undisputed Union possession, Atlantans began to fear that the Yankee army would gain complete control of Tennessee and Mississippi and soon come their way.

Meanwhile, the city council, taking stock of the meager turnout for the home guard drills outside City Hall, began to prepare for possible direct attack on the city. The members contracted for chests to be prepared "in which to pack up the City Records and papers for removal when necessary."

Even before the fall of Vicksburg, Brig. Gen. Marcus J. Wright, the Confederate officer in command of the Atlanta district, had ordered Col. Lemuel P. Grant, chief engineer of the Department of Georgia, to survey the surrounding area, draw up maps, and make plans for fortifications. Grant, like so many of his brethren in the leading circles of the city, was a self-made man grown wealthy off the railroads. Born in Maine, he had moved south to labor on the rail lines. He saw what lay ahead as he laid the ties and track and began buying land along the lines. Soon he was among the region's wealthiest men. The city now put his construction and engineering skills to use building its defenses. The fortifications would be massive, encircling the entire town over a mile from its center, perhaps the largest continuous defensive perimeter to that point in the history of the modern Western world. He planned a series of seventeen redoubts, Forts A to Q, forming a ten- to twelve-mile circle. In addition, a line of battlements would need to be constructed along the Chattahoochee River, which formed a natural northeast-southwest-running moat a few miles outside the city.

Digging out the miles of serpentine trenches and communications; building up the walls, redoubts, and palisades through the suburban fields, pastures, and woods, roads and rail cuts; chopping the trees and shaving the limbs; leveling the fields; bundling the branches into *facines* to reinforce the earthworks, then facing and flooring them with timber would amount to one of the largest public works projects in the history of the South—equal to, and perhaps exceeding, the building of the Western & Atlantic Railroad line itself. But who could build such an enormous great wall?

There were few strong white hands left to lift an axe or tote a bucket of heavy clay. With the shortage of civilian and military labor, Grant and Wright turned to slave owners for their bondsmen's muscle. Even then, there was not enough slave manpower to be had in Atlanta. Wright and Grant requisitioned a mandatory quota of slaves from the surrounding counties. Eventually, they sent an order through southern Georgia giving planters two days in which to fill the local quota and threatening that, if the call for slave labor fell short, "then . . . every male negro that can possibly be impressed will be sent to the front, regardless of past exemption." Atlanta would defend, and be defended by, slavery to the last.

Soon, thousands of slaves arrived in Atlanta. The laborers dug and sang while they worked, building up a ten-mile ring of fortifications, to form a nearly closed, shakily incised *C* with several points jutting out like small diamonds in the yawning ring around the city. The men moved millions of pounds of red clay, chopped down thousands of trees, and shaved and bound them into bristling, sharpened spike barriers before the fortifications. High earthworks linked the chain of redoubts, each holding five artillery pieces. The initial phase of the lines was completed by December 1863, but work resumed in the spring to clear the hills in front of the fortifications of trees. Up to half a mile of killing fields pocked with thousands of skirmish holes lay open to the artillery and troops within the earthworks should the enemy dare to approach them. A second line of defense behind this primary line was begun at the Confederate War Department's suggestion. When and if a federal force came to storm the city, it would encounter a man-made wall as impregnable as any titanic storm-tossed ocean waves ever broke upon.

AS THEY LABORED UNDER the broiling Georgia sun, hauling thousands of tons of earth and cutting and shaving foot after foot of lumber by hand, those slaves rarely ate more than a survival ration: half a pound of bacon or a full pound of beef and two pounds of cornmeal, substituted at times by rice or potatoes, on a good day. When supplies of food were exhausted and even the white soldiers were starving, the commissaries stopped issuing rations to the thousands of slaves at all, leaving Grant and Wright to figure out how to feed them. Even Confederate officials acknowledged that the little food the slaves shoring up Atlanta's fortifications lived on was "of the most inferior character."

To keep from starving, work teams very likely turned to the local slave families living in and around the fortifications. Among them were the scores of slaves on the Ponder place. The fortifications' northwest salient, known as Fort Hood, was probably the most formidable of all. Its trenches ran like a deep and rolling red cut and its palisades like a raised scar directly through the once handsomely maintained grounds. The elegantly colorful and copious gardens of flowers and vegetables had been trampled down, its fruit trees and boxwood hedges chopped out, and the facing of its many outbuildings stripped away to provide lumber for the palisades. Eventually, even the great stone, brick, and plaster house was converted into a home for convalescent soldiers. From its high vantage point, which first attracted Ephraim and Ellen Ponder, to buy the land, their briefly happy home's observatory and upper-floor windows overlooked the lines and provided a perfect sharpshooter's nest—or target for enemy artillery. The Ponders' most trusted bondsman and woman, Festus and Isabella Flipper, were doting parents who probably kept a close eye on their bright young son, Henry, when he ran through the freshly dug trenches and leaped down from the earthworks to the scraped-over field below. It was a child's red-clay playground while the soldiers remained distant. Standing atop the redoubts, he could watch the long lines of Confederates marching by on the Marietta road or standing in freight cars rolling up to Dalton. He probably took food and water to the black hands working under the hot sun in red clay.

A few of the impressed slaves would not build the defenses for the city against the army of their freedom. Cyrena Stone took in four escaped men she hid in her cotton house. Perhaps they had been sent to her by her neighbor Bob Yancey. They showed up and told her, "We don't want to make no fortifications to keep away the Yankees *our*selves. Let our folks build their own fortifications. The black'uns they *have* got, are dying up like any thing, for they works 'em so hard, and half starves 'em besides."

WITH THE INCREASING IMPRESSMENTS of slaves and more and more runaways in the face of an advancing Union army, many slave owners' confidence in the institution of slavery wavered. Two of Cyrena's slaves, knowing where her sympathies lay, while Union forces were gathering in Chattanooga, were busy turfing her yard near the northeastern fortifications. "Maybe we're fixing all this for nothing, for perhaps they'll fight right here," one said to her. The other piped up, "Oh hush such talk! I spect to wake up any of these mornins, and see this yer town just filled with Yankees." Another slave had overheard two white men talking about the need to flee the town before the Union army arrived. The slave recounted listening in when one of the men said, "The whole country round Chattanooga was just *blue*—and it was no use in trying to keep 'em back—for they'd got started, and would go whar they was a moun' to." Bleak tidings made some whites determine to sell out. Dextor Niles, who traded slaves wholesale on Marietta Street near the Ponder place, liquidated his large holdings of slaves "all at once," recalled Sarah Huff, who lived in the neighborhood. She went by one day, and "all the cabins were bare." She learned that they had been "rushed to a slave market beyond the shores to the south of us and sold before Confederate money entirely lost its value."

Other Confederate business investments also began to appear shaky. For Samuel Richards, it was "a time of perplexity" regarding Confederate paper. From one day to the next, it depreciated a third in value. In August 1863, the *Southern Confederacy*'s owner George W. Adair sold out his share in the fire-eater's favorite newspaper for $200,000 in Confederate currency. Rather than demonstrate his continued confidence in a Confederate future, he converted all his earnings from the sale to gold and had it sewn into the hems of his wife's skirts. Many feared their life savings would soon be worthless and went quietly to see Bob Yancey, Prince Ponder, and other slaves acting as moneychangers to convert whatever they could into gold and greenbacks. These men handled illegal transactions worth thousands of Confederate dollars daily, eventually taking three hundred Confederate dollars in exchange for a single Yankee dollar and then buying hard goods like tobacco, cotton, and whisky to have for when the Union army arrived. The grateful recipients of gold and U.S. dollars buried their treasure to keep it away from the bands of robbers moving through town.

Among those who had not lost confidence in his nation's future was Colonel Lee, who took up partial ownership in the *Southern Confederacy* after Adair sold out.

BY THE SUMMER OF 1863, the federal Army of the Cumberland's Maj. Gen. William Rosencrans had driven Gen. Braxton Bragg's Army of Tennessee out of western and much of central Tennessee, forcing the Southerners back to their main southeastern base at the railroad-crossing town of Chattanooga, just a few miles from Georgia's northwestern corner. The land around them was stripped to the point where even the horses could find nothing to graze on. The rebels were reduced to foraging for green corn and roasting rats. On September 9, Rosencrans's forces circled to the south of the town and severed the rebel supply lines from Atlanta into Chattanooga altogether. Without firing a shot, the Confederate army fell back to high ground and entrenched positions in the dark woods and tangles of vines covering the rolling landscape around Chickamauga Creek.

Perhaps encouraged by his easy triumphs, Rosencrans determined to drive the apparently badly weakened rebels out of Tennessee altogether and deep into Georgia. On September 19, he attacked them amid the virtually impenetrable woods and tall stands of corn, where each man could see only a few paces around him. Lines quickly became entangled and separated and entire regiments lost. The battle raged without a clear victor until the afternoon of the second day, when Rosencrans, believing he was filling a gap in his line, actually opened a mortal hole in it. The Confederates saw their chance.

A. J. Neal, the Floridian attorney and battalion officer whose parents now lived in Atlanta, commanded a battery that was part of a concentrated artillery fire on a portion of the Yankee line. Neal wrote his father in his mansion opposite City Hall Square that the half hour of continuous and deadly fire was "the most terrible bombardment I ever witnessed." The shattered enemy army broke and ran in panic, dropping guns, knapsacks, even boots and jackets, in its terror. Thousands of dead and wounded comrades remained behind. With terrified men sweeping past his headquarters, a distraught Rosencrans soon joined the rushing retreat. The Confederate infantry rushed into the field after them, capturing thousands more men and driving the remaining Northerners "back steadily several miles over breast works through field and wood," a proud Neal reported. The entire Yankee army would have fallen without the heroic stand made by the men who gathered around Maj. Gen. George H. Thomas. The phlegmatic Thomas, known as "Slow Trot Thomas" for his slow gait and methodical manner, steadied enough panicking men and broken units to organize a rearguard to hold off the furiously charging Confederates at Horseshoe Ridge. He earned a new nickname, "the Rock of Chickamauga," as he held on long enough to allow the army's survivors to crawl to shelter in Chattanooga. The slaughter at Antietam is known as America's bloodiest single day, but the bloodiest two days of the entire Civil War were those contesting Chickamauga. The Yankees left behind 16,179 killed, wounded, and captured men. However, the hooting rebel army, much less able to withstand heavy losses, sustained 18,454 of its own in victory.

The scene left behind on the field was terrible. Stunned by the hurricane of violence in which he had participated, A. J. Neal wrote his parents, "The dead and wounded [are] lying thick around me. . . . Their groans and suffering is [sic] awful." A rebel infantry private, Sam Watkins from Tennessee, surveyed the same gruesome field. "Men," he wrote, "were lying where they fell, shot in every conceivable part of the body. Some with their entrails torn out and still hanging to them and piled up on the ground beside them, and they still alive."

Ten days later, the Yankee dead still lay thick. Nobody was in any rush to bury them. An *Intelligencer* correspondent recounted his walk throughout the devastated Chickamauga area where the entire countryside "for miles" remained deserted, the corn fields flattened, and most trees shot to splinters—"no beasts, no birds, not even a buzzard, can be seen anywhere." At one Union artillery emplacement stormed by the rebels, he saw, "a hundred dead horses, broken caissons, dismounted cannon, broken ammunition, torn clothes, broken knapsacks, empty haversacks, bullet-torn canteens, broken gunstocks, hundreds of torn shoes and hats, bloody bayonets, broken sabre scabbards, broken cartridge boxes, dead Yankees in piles of four, five and a dozen; a cord of cannon rammers, ropes, torn harness [*sic*], numerous graves." He came upon what had been a corn field occupied by the Yankees until a Confederate corps had stormed from the neighboring woods, their rifle fire scything through man and cornstalk with equal effect. He surveyed the remains splayed out now on the red earth of "a large number of dead Yankees, whose black and swollen bodies glistening in the sunlight, are not either pleasant to the eyes, nor is the odor they omit a delightful perfume, except as an incense to our gratified soul that they are destroyed." He reminded his readers, who might take pity on the dead, "They are our mortal enemies. . . . They are all glossy and black as their own hearts or the gloomiest of ebony Ethiopian whom in life they pretended to love so well. It may be some consolation to know they turn to that color for which they are fighting, the blacks on earth, black in death, black in hell."

THE APPALLING BATTLE SENT a "River of Death," translation of the Indian name for Chickamauga Creek, on the rails back to Atlanta's hospitals. In September 1863 alone, 10,000 wounded men were admitted to the army hospitals in Atlanta, but there were only beds for 1,800. Thousands of horrifically wounded men arrived by freight car and were off-loaded in the depot to be triaged when beds became available in city hospitals. Many families opened their doors to the wounded. While out walking on a peaceful, late-September Sunday morning in 1863, Sallie Clayton, the teenage belle who lived across the street from the Neals' house, ran into two men carrying a wounded man in a litter on their shoulders. The man's arm hung down limp from the bouncing stretcher. She called the other men's attention to it. They lowered the litter. She recognized the wounded man. It was Daniel Pittman, her neighbors'—the Neals—son-in-law. He was too weak even to lift his own dangling arm.

"We have only to press them to reap the fruits of victory," wrote Pittman's brother-in-law A. J. Neal, hoping for a decisive endgame to the clash of the western armies. "The army is confident . . . we will be in Kentucky soon." Victorious on the field, but like a boxer who leaves the ring as bloody, bruised, and woozy as his defeated opponent, General Bragg instead chose to lay siege to the demoralized 50,000-man Union army isolated in Chattanooga. The Confederate Army of Tennessee established new positions three miles outside town.

From the valley in front and on top of Lookout Mountain and Missionary Ridge, highpoints above the town, the rebels partially encircled the Union forces. They lobbed shells and sent off raiding parties but never launched a full-scale assault on the federal troops. Bragg hoped to starve out the Yankees. The rebels, though, suffered just as badly—with poorer shelter and little food. The weather was constantly cold and rainy, and the valley full of standing water. The men in their butternut flannels, little better than wet matting on their bare skin, stood picket duty in ankle-deep mud and, without tents, slept partially submerged on the open ground. Rations fell short, and when the roads became impassable, as happened often, they got nothing to eat at all. Neal's men's mess was five miles away on the other side of Missionary Ridge. Deliveries of their small portions of cornbread and beef became sporadic. Neal conceded, "This service is rougher than any I have seen." Neal's men at least were sheltered behind rocks. Infantry private Watkins in the valley's cold swamp knew far worse. He recalled, "Never in all my whole life do I remember of ever experiencing so much oppression and humiliation. The soldiers were starved and almost naked, and covered all over with lice and camp itch and filth and dirt. The men looked sick, hollow-eyed, and heart-broken." They lived on parched corn, "which had been picked out of the mud and dirt under the feet of officers' horses. We thought of nothing but starvation."

Much of the time soldiers marched, and they marched barefoot by the thousands. In October 1863, General Bragg had seized all shoes and horses he could find in Atlanta, where shoes now cost as much as $500 a pair, but that still left many in his army with rags or nothing on their feet when they and slave teamsters pulled caissons and limbers over the rocky ridges.

IN ATLANTA, residents were disconcerted by the seizures but, like A. J. Neal, remained confident that the Army of Tennessee would keep the Union forces at bay. The *Intelligencer* called on all citizens to take heart at Chickamauga's stunning and sudden reversal of the summer's defeats:

> Viewed in any light, it must be apparent to all parties, both at home and abroad, that never has the South shown so much her ability to maintain her independence than the present time. Never has the fire of patriotism shone with a brighter light than since the first wearing off of the gloom that overcast our community after the disasters of June and July. . . . While our cause is

brightening in its aspect, that of our enemy is becoming daily more desperate.

In Atlanta, as throughout the South, people fed on hope. The significance of the victory at Chickamauga, wildly inflated in newspaper reports, renewed optimism that European nations would shortly recognize the Confederate government and that Lincoln would either be forced to negotiate peace or, in the next election, driven from office.

The same Atlanta newspaper, though, reprinted a *New York Herald* story for its readers to consider: "Atlanta is the last link which binds together the southwestern and northeastern sections of the rebel Confederacy. Break it and those sections fall asunder. . . . The present campaign . . . aims at nothing less than the military isolation of Mississippi, Alabama and Georgia, from the remaining States of South Carolina, North Carolina and Virginia." Any Gate City resident reading those words in his office or home had to swallow hard and wonder. Atlanta was the inevitable strategic target for the Union campaigns to come. If it fell, the South would be splintered. Who knew what a Union army, presently licking its wounds and still standing up to siege on the battlements of Chattanooga, was capable of accomplishing after weathering such a hellacious storm of exploding gunpowder, fragmenting iron, flashing bayonets, and whistling sheets of lead?

# A Day's
# Outing

I N MID-OCTOBER 1863 Ulysses S. Grant took command of the Military Division of Mississippi and fired Gen. William Rosencrans. He personally came to Chattanooga to assume overall command of the besieged Union army there. His arrival sent a shudder all the way down to Atlanta. The master of mass warfare surveyed the Confederate foe. The rebels were dug so deeply into the natural and man-made rises in the earth overlooking Chattanooga that anything short of a volcanic eruption would not shake them from their position. Grant was not a particularly imaginative strategist. He believed in increasing the weight of the army he brought to bear upon the enemy's defenses until they snapped like an overburdened shelf. He plotted the eruption of men he would need to overflow the landscape. He promoted his friend and protégé Gen. William Tecumseh Sherman to command of the Army of the Tennessee and brought his new force up to help the Army of the Cumberland's new commander, Gen. George Thomas, in breaking out of Chattanooga. While Grant amassed the armed weight he needed for almost two months, the warring sides engaged in artillery shooting matches, lines of men shifted, and sharpshooters took out any poor skirmisher who dared show his head. The picket lines were close enough for soldiers to converse about their shared misery as Confederate and Union soldiers mostly left off shooting and kept one another company.

A month later, at the front on November 20, A. J. Neal reassured his parents, "Prospects continue dull." With the armies likely to camp in position for the winter, he told his mother he hoped soon to receive a ten-day furlough and eagerly looked forward to a Christmastime reunion with his family in their big brick mansion on Washington Street. Delighted, the Neals shared their son's encouraging letters with their neighbors. That undoubtedly sparked an idea that quickly took root in the Clayton household. War still held a fascination for citizens; they recalled the glory and pageantry attending Atlanta companies each time they departed from the car shed. Their much-missed sons and brothers wrote of victories or, if pushed back, stable fronts and readiness for tomorrow's battles. The upbeat reporting in the newspapers and encouraging rumors in some circles heartened diehard Confederate supporters.

The Clayton family wanted to see for themselves what they imagined to be the romance of the battlefield. The impregnable Confederate heights outside Chattanooga seemed a perfect grandstand. In the crisp fall days of November, Missionary Ridge on the far side of Chickamauga offered "a beautiful view" of Chattanooga and the surrounding countryside. Sallie Clayton's mother's cousin, Anne Semmes, too, was visiting the Clayton family in Atlanta for a family wedding. She was the beautiful wife of Adm. Raphael Semmes, already legendary for the scores of Union vessels his CSS *Alabama* had captured and burned. Their son Spencer Semmes, a captain in the Confederate navy, was also on hand. Demonstrating an appalling naivety or a cat's ignorance of curiosity's dangers, Anne Semmes suggested they take a family outing. With Spencer and some other officers on leave on hand to serve as guides, they should know how to stay clear of any danger. Soon, a twenty-member party was made up, among them several children, including Sallie, now a young woman, and three of her little sisters and two brothers. They boarded a Western & Atlantic Railroad train at the car shed on the evening of November 21, 1863, and traveled overnight through the old Cherokee country.

ARRIVING ON A CLEAR, bright morning, they alighted at a stop four miles from Gen. Braxton Bragg's headquarters on Missionary Ridge. The festive party boarded ambulance wagons that carried them the length of the ridge. On this perfectly clear fall morning, they feasted on an autumn view of the entire seven-mile front, the Union camps and entrenchments across the valley, and the invested Chattanooga three miles distant. Reaching Bragg's headquarters in a small plank house on the crown of the ridge, they walked about and enjoyed a pleasant afternoon dinner. They could see the distant spark of the skirmish rifles and watch cannons flash along the ridge flanks. Smoke drifted up like quick cigar puffs.

The group planned to return home that evening, but the solicitous General Bragg convinced them to stay in the headquarters compound overnight with the promise of a musical serenade and a visit to Lookout Mountain, which stood directly opposite the town, the next day. There they would have the chance, for "those who wished to do so, [to] fire cannon." It would all be very entertaining.

The following morning, the group started out for Lookout Mountain in the ambulance wagons fitted out for a picnic. The artillery exchanges, though, seemed to be heating up. They watched as shells began falling and bursting about a wagon train heading up the road in front of them. When a shell landed near them, an officer accompanying them decided to turn back, which Sallie Clayton thought sensible. "I did not want to be one of the dead women to roll out of one of the ambulances when it was struck by a Yankee shell," she recalled. They traveled back along Missionary Ridge and, nearing Bragg's headquarters, saw him and several others looking anxiously through field glasses towards Chattanooga. They joined him to watch the "long rows of soldiers" marching outside the town. The general enjoyed parade reviews. Here, he thought the advancing blue masses, regimental banners flapping and bands playing, were marching in a display intended for Grant. The rebel lines had not been reinforced when the parade began to move forward en masse. A staff member near Bragg soon noticed a litter corps following behind. "That," he said, "is not done for dress parade." The soldiers were intending to fight. Grant's parade was camouflage for an attack.

Sallie's mother called for the visiting party to be on its way, but General Bragg still urged his guests to stay. There was time for dinner, he assured them, and asked the group to join him in his quarters. At the same moment they took their seats at the table under a big tent, Sallie heard "the sound of a volley of musketry from the valley below." Feeling like so many Cinderellas who "had overstayed [their] time at the ball," the visitors leaped up and hurried to their waiting wagons. As they took their seats, word came that the picket line had already been pushed in, and the hungry and weary men, with little confidence in their commander, were scrambling up the ridge for safety among the rocks. The Atlanta party raced down the rough and steep road toward the railroad station. They went without an escort. On the way, they passed through the main camp, where "wild confusion" had broken out. "The men," recalled Clayton, "were seizing their arms, and were almost running over one another, in their hurry to reach the front."

As the Atlanta party neared the station behind the ridge and out of artillery range, the sun was setting. They waited for their train back to Atlanta and "had a splendid view of the beautiful light above the trees caused by the cannonading which we employed ourselves by watching."

THE "BEAUTIFUL LIGHT" BROUGHT death to thousands. A. J. Neal was "amazed to see our troops steadily driven up the mountainside." His rapidly firing cannons were giving the advancing Yankees "fits," but the weight of the Union army's eruption out of Chattanooga and elsewhere across the Tennessee River drove in the Confederate front lines. Neal watched the panicking infantry retreat until they "rushed over us pell-mell & we could do nothing" to halt the enemy charge. "My men . . . would have stood with me to the guns until we were bayoneted," he insisted, but "valor was vain." His battery brought up the rear of the retreat. As he helped drag a munitions limber back, he grabbed at a sickening hot flash of pain in his shoulder. He was now doubly grateful for the heavy overcoat his parents had recently sent him. A minié ball had blown a "huge hole" through it, but the thick wool had muffled the bullet's impact enough that it only stung and bruised his flesh. Still, he could barely lift his arm enough even to write about its miraculous salvation.

The battle for Missionary Ridge and Lookout Mountain raged for two days until the routed Confederates finally fell back into Georgia. The federal forces tried to chase down the rebels, but they pulled back into the rugged ridgelines that sliced through the northwestern Georgia corner. The bluecoats were turned back at Ringgold Gap mountain pass, where under a withering fire from previously heavily fortified highpoints, the far-outnumbered Confederates mowed down Yankees charging up the slopes. After the battle, Pvt. Sam Watkins described a

scene unlike any battlefield I ever saw. From the foot to the top of the hill was covered with their slain, all lying on their faces. It had the appearance of the roof of a house shingled with dead Yankees. They were flushed with victory and success, and had determined to push forward and capture the whole of the Rebel army, and set up their triumphant standard at Atlanta—then exit the Southern Confederacy. But their dead were so piled in their path at Ringgold Gap that they could not pass them.

IN ATLANTA, the crushing implications of the defeat at Chattanooga and the retreat into Georgia by the Army of Tennessee were starting to sink in. The Army of Tennessee was now driven out of that state, and the Union pursuers had crossed Georgia's borders. "I am less hopeful for a speedy end of the war than I was a year ago—much less," Samuel Richards fretted. "The foe encroaches upon us so, holds on so constantly to whatever he does gain and seems so determined to subdue and exterminate us." In the *Intelligencer*, even John Steele could not escape the changed nature of his city. He recalled previous Sabbath days marked by "peace, happiness, contentment and prosperity . . . a few years ago." All had changed. "The Sabbath day comes enveloped in gloom and sadness. The Churches are filled with gentle women all clad in black." Their husbands and sons were no longer there to lean on. From the hospitals and houses filled with the wounded, "the wail of the dying breaks the solemn stillness of the Sabbath day. . . . Poverty walks abroad in her worst forms and the Sabbath day is broken upon by the starving widow and her children in an appeal for charity. All, all is changed."

He urged his readers, though, to fight on, not to believe the rumors about the "partial defeat" at Chattanooga. He called the accounts of Confederate losses "exaggerated" and was dismayed that "our people who, credulous as they are, eagerly swallowed every word of it, and half believed that our army has suffered an overwhelming defeat." He condemned those who now openly criticized General Bragg's leadership. "We detest such creatures who go about criticizing the actions of Gen. Bragg and his army, when they have never done a soldier's duty, for one day of their worthless lives.—Bragg wants more soldiers; which of those now censuring will go up to the front, and aid in keeping the enemy out of Georgia?" That very day, President Jefferson Davis accepted General Bragg's resignation. Not long after, he appointed Gen. Joseph Johnston, an officer far more popular with the troops, to command the Army of Tennessee.

Johnston worked swiftly to resurrect his broken command. He rid it of Bragg's fatuously rigid roll call, drills, and incessantly harsh discipline. He granted furloughs and released food, clothing, shoes, and other supplies to the desperate men. Desertions, which had been taking place by the hundreds every night, slowed. Johnston was the "very picture of a general," according to Sam Watkins, one who had driven back Union forces in Virginia and intended to do the same now. The men loved him. "The private soldier once more regarded himself a gentleman and a man of honor," Watkins recalled. "We were willing to do and die and dare anything for our loved South, and the Stars and Bars of the Confederacy."

On Christmas morning, the *Intelligencer* reported on the great revival of the Army of Tennessee under its new commander. The renewed army was no longer hemorrhaging men but still needed fighters. "The people's time has now come—every man is called upon to take up arms in his country's defense, if he would win Liberty and Independence." In the same issue, the paper published news that its demand for every man now to take up arms had become law. The state legislature's new Militia Act now authorized the enrollment of all white males not otherwise exempt, ages sixteen to sixty, in the district's militia. Anyone refusing enrollment would "be tried and punished as a deserter." Col. George W. Lee's Confederate Conscript Bureau army gathered young boys and old men alike. With Grant likely to move on Georgia sooner rather than later, Gov. Joseph Brown placed the colonel in command of a 6,550 state militia battalion Lee ordered into Atlanta to prepare for its defense.

TWO BATTERED ARMIES HUNKERED down for the winter. The Confederate army kept pickets on their new lines through to Ringgold, while the main body, William Lowndes Calhoun's Forty-second Regiment of the Georgia Guards among them, withdrew to its winter encampment at Dalton, Georgia. Grant pulled his army back to Chattanooga. Both sides knew what lay before them in the spring. The whole of Tennessee was now in federal hands, and Yankee troops had tasted the promising sweetness, if briefly, of Georgia's piney air. A few days after the Union army had pushed the Army of Tennessee down into Georgia, Col. Charles Fessenden Morse of the Second Massachusetts, now part of Gen. Joseph Hooker's Corps in the Army of the Cumberland, looked toward Atlanta, within four days' march. He had been fighting with the Union army since the early days of 1861 and knew victory and defeat with the Army of the Potomac at Antietam, Chancellorsville, and Gettysburg. Among the few northeasterners in the western Union army, the twenty-five-year-old

Boston architect recognized what the entire nation had come to understand: "Atlanta is our important point now. Get that, and we have again cut the Confederacy in two, and in a vital place."

A short march away from Morse's camp, the twenty-seven-year-old small-town Florida attorney turned artillery battery captain A. J. Neal sat down amid the lengthening shadows of early December. He dashed off a letter to his sister ninety miles south in Atlanta. The Yankees would not have an easy time of it, he wrote. When the fighting renewed in the spring, he was certain Confederate forces would redeem themselves. "This army will fight with all the desperation and valor displayed at Chickamauga for they are heartily ashamed of their conduct at Missionary Ridge. When we next meet the story of the conflict will be appalling." He gave up on the idea of coming home for Christmas. "I never want to leave this army till we have punished the Yankees who drove us from Missionary Ridge."

# IV

# THE HUNDRED DAYS' BATTLE

WILD AS A SWOLLEN RIVER hurling down on the flats,
down from the hills in winter spate, bursting its banks
with rain from storming Zeus, and stands of good dry oak,
whole forests of pine it whorls into itself and sweeps along
till it heaves a crashing mass of driftwood out to sea—
so glorious Ajax swept the field, routing Trojans,
shattering teams and spearmen in his onslaught.

—HOMER, THE ILIAD, 11:580–86,
TRANS. ROBERT FAGLES

→⊫ CHAPTER 16 ⊪←

# RAILROAD
# WAR

THE DEPLETED AND OFT-DEFEATED Army of Tennessee could muster around 40,000 ragtag soldiers in tatters by the end of 1863. Before Gen. Johnston's revitalization of the army, deserters slunk away from camp by the hundreds each day. Although the Confederates enjoyed the advantage of fighting for their home territory, the numerical odds looked so desperate that a once unthinkable idea was broached. In January 1864, Maj. Gen. Patrick R. Cleburne at Dalton sent off a proposal to enlist and train "a large reserve of the most courageous of our slaves," potentially a new 300,000-man army. Those who served would be guaranteed their freedom at war's end— along with other slaves who remained loyal to the Confederacy. A war fought to preserve slavery would, if the Confederacy emerged victorious, serve as the vehicle of black freedom.

Atlanta's *Southern Confederacy* newspaper came out strongly against any move to arm slaves, which would inevitably lead to their emancipation and "sacrifice . . . the principle which is the basis of our social system." The "cornerstone" was cracking under the weight of modern warfare. But the South was not ready for such a radical notion. The idea soon died.

MANY OF THE TROOPS who had deserted did so out of concern for the well-being of their wives and children. Letters from home told the men of their destitution. The heartsick soldiers felt powerless to help them. An Atlantan silenced the women in town. Their own pens, he told them, squeezed the firing squad triggers. "You had better let the last crumb of bread disappear from your table," he advised, "and then pray to God and trust Him for more, than to write anything to your relatives in the army that will make their lot harder to bear, and by your continual complaints at last lead him in very desperation, to desert from the army and bring upon themselves dishonor and a disgraceful death." He called upon the women to sacrifice their own lives before condemning their men to a worse fate. "If needs be, you had better die, even by starvation, than bring dishonor and an ignominious death upon those you love."

Such calls for silence were galling when the contrast was so great between the wealth of Atlanta's merchant and industrial aristocracy and the grinding poverty of its vast pool of poor laboring women and children. The letters continued.

Many of deserters from Dalton filtered down the Western & Atlantic line into Atlanta. Former U.S. secretary of the treasury and speaker of the U.S. House Howell Cobb now commanded the Georgia State troops from his headquarters on Whitehall Street. Walking out of his offices and traveling into the surrounding region, he could see "men enough at home able to be in the field to make another army." Col. George Washington Lee's men tried to round up as many deserters and shirkers as they could. Accusations that he and two other enrollment bureau chiefs were selling exemptions did little to encourage conscripts to report.

Many men facing conscription chose instead to form up brandnew companies. General Joseph Johnston complained that he never saw the new regiments. Often they were shams gotten up, he said, "ostensibly under authority of the War Department," but the apparently patriotic men "never complete their companies—having no other object than to keep themselves and a few friends out of service."

Samuel Richards mustered from time to time with his pressmen's home guard company gotten up with just such a purpose in view. He knew, like all people in town, that "the avowed intention of the enemy is to march upon Atlanta this spring." The paper goods merchant, though, did not want to be among those holding back that onslaught. "Somebody certainly must fight," he recognized, "but I never was a fighting boy or man and never want to be." In early January, however, it appeared he, too, would have to join the battle.

President Jefferson Davis and the Confederate Congress understood the terrible effect substitutes and other wealth-based exemptions produced on morale and reluctantly announced the end of the substitution policy. Not only was paying for a substitute no longer a permitted exemption, but a Conscription Bureau agent told Richards he was now under specific orders to "enroll all who had put in substitutes" as retribution for buying their way out of the war. Richards's earlier decision to take out an insurance policy against military service now put him in greater jeopardy of conscription. A few days later, though, much to his relief, he learned that his printer's exemption stood up. Money and connections continued to enable loyal Confederates to stay away from the army. The enrolling officers left him alone—for the moment.

AT ALMOST THE SAME TIME Richards learned he could depend on his tenuous exemption, an old farmer rolled up in his wagon to Cyrena Stone's house, where she greeted him from her porch. The gray-haired man stooped over as if he carried the weight of the world on his shoulders. He offered to sell her his wagonload of fodder. This, he said, would be "the last fodder or anything else I shall ever bring you. . . . They've got me in this war at last." No longer age exempt or permitted to continue raising desperately needed food crops on the farm, he sighed and said, "They've got me now, and I s'pose there's no getting away from them." He shared the view of many in the region: "*I* didn't vote for Secession—but them are the ones who have to go & fight now—and those who were so fast for war, stay out." The effectiveness of Lee's men in bringing in resisters and the insurrectionists' corpses hanging from trees made the futility of resistance clear. Although desertions plagued the army, it was increasingly a rich man's war and a poor man's fight.

Stone could do little more for the man than to buy his fodder. She had already bumped up against Colonel Lee and, like many Unionists, was kept under watch. So was her Houston Street neighbor, the slave barber and money trader Bob Yancey. Yancey, though, continued to employ the "invisibility" of his skin to move among the Union prisoners of war without suspicion. He often comforted the wounded men—and exchanged currency with them at rates very much in his favor. He must have told two Northern soldiers he met in the convalescent prison camp where to find his home. After the pair escaped, they worked their way through town and up the hill to his house on Houston Street. Despite risking a hangman's rope around his neck—and, as a black man, likely worse torture—Yancey did not turn them away. He secreted them in his cramped attic. He brought them food and news about the war, waiting for the time when it would be safe for them to return to the Union army.

Even some of Lee's own men assisted Union prisoners. When Stone felt courageous enough "to challenge watching eyes and bitter threats," she ventured into the prison barracks hospital to tend to wounded Union prisoners. During one of those visits, while another woman distracted the Confederate guard on duty, Cyrena whispered with a Union soldier working as a nurse in the prison. He told her that he and another nurse on duty there hoped soon to be exchanged and returned to their army. She was stunned when he told her that the night before, in anticipation of their return to Union lines, a Confederate guard had loaned a rebel uniform to the other nurse. Then, the real Confederate and the disguised Union prisoner had walked calmly out into the streets of Atlanta together. With the Confederate soldier as his guide, the Union spy spent the night exploring the city's perimeter defenses until returning to the prison barracks before dawn. "[I] saw every ditch, every fortification and preparation which has been made to meet our army," the prison nurse whispered to Stone. The soldier said if Grant and his army "had any idea how matters stand down here—I'm sure they wouldn't stay around Dalton much longer."


ATLANTA CARRIED ON ITS own secret internal civil war while the two warring armies were making preparations for the coming campaign. Gen. Ulysses Grant, now in his divisional headquarters in Nashville, learned soon after the new year's arrival that President Abraham Lincoln had decided to elevate him to overall command of the Union army. The forty-two-year-old Grant understood, as did few others, that he faced two great opposing armies and two prime targets for the spring: Virginia and the Army of Northern Virginia commanded by Robert E. Lee, and Georgia and the Army of Tennessee now under Joseph Johnston. To date, Northern military leaders had focused more on conquering and maintaining their hold on rebellious states than on crushing those two principle forces of resistance to federal authority. In doing so, they often ceded opportunities for aggressiveness to their foe and gave away their massive size and force advantages. The Confederates exploited the Yankees' lack of coordinated strategy by shuttling corps between zones to reinforce points under attack. Railroad lines made whole armies mobile. For the first time in history, masses of men and munitions could transfer quickly from a quiet front to an active one, even hundreds of miles distant, within a matter of days or just hours. Union advances simply placed rebel armies closer together, enabling them to shift and concentrate men yet more rapidly.

Confederate leaders exploited their troops' mobility to launch bold, if largely nuisance, raids back behind Union army lines into conquered territories of Louisiana, Arkansas, Kentucky, Missouri, and even Ohio. During the winter lull in fighting between the major armies, Southern forces had achieved several sensational, if strategically insignificant, battlefield victories. Those moves bolstered the South's popular hope that the Confederacy's losses on its borders were merely temporary setbacks. The enemy was in control only where he stood. All around him was hostile ground. The need to control and guard conquered but hostile territory, where guerilla bands cut rail lines, fired from banks on gunboats, and attacked outposts, further negated the federal army's overwhelming advantage in numbers and firepower.

Grant's Army of the Tennessee commander William Tecumseh Sherman was so frustrated by the difficulty of operating in Tennessee that he advocated removing the entire rebellious Southern population—or killing them. "Don't expect to overrun such a country or subdue such a people in our two or five years, it is the task of half a century," he warned his brother John Sherman in the U.S. Senate. "To attempt to hold all the South would demand an army too large even to think of. We must colonize & settle as we go south."

SHORT OF KILLING OR removing the entire rebellious population, the North needed to overcome its inept leadership and put its tremendous advantages into the fight against the Confederate army. Only simultaneous defeat of the two main Confederate forces, perceived Grant, would win the war. Slight and stooped, lacking the spit, polish, and charisma of several of his failed predecessors, Grant did not exude the brashness or killer instinct of a field commander ready to destroy an enemy in the field. But he could boast of having done it several times now. Lincoln called him in from his Nashville headquarters to Washington. He slipped into town with little fanfare on March 8 and met Lincoln in the executive mansion. Grant presented him with a plan to attack the Confederate head in Virginia and its heart in Georgia simultaneously, or as he wrote the following month, "to work all parts of the army together." This would turn the ponderous weight of the massive Union army to its greatest advantage. A war of attrition waged everywhere at once would descend upon the South like a rockslide down a mountainside. Lincoln believed he had found the man he could trust to finish the task. He promoted Grant to lieutenant general—he was the first to hold the title since George Washington—and named him general in chief of the Union army. The president fulfilled his ebullient declaration of faith made the day after Vicksburg fell to his fighting general: "Grant is my man, and I am his the rest of the war."

Grant wanted to return to his western headquarters. He believed the war would be won there. However, it could be lost in the North. Political conditions made it impossible for him to stray far from Washington or the Virginia battlefield. With the twin capital cities so near each other, the northern theater of operations captured public and media attention in a way the more remote western battlefields could not. Although the western armies could boast of multiple victories, Northerners perceived little beyond their own states' borders. The South's ill-clad, poorly equipped, and undernourished armies had invaded the North, carried out spectacular raids seemingly almost at will, threatened Washington, D.C., itself, and held off and badly bloodied a huge Army of the Potomac that approached within eyeshot of Richmond's church spires.

Maintaining political support for the war required that its foremost general remain close by the president's power to deflect those who would inevitably question his strategic decisions. Those who were ready to criticize the army were now legion. The horrific, once inconceivable carnage tolled far worse in the North than the South. Confederate troops fired rifled guns that ripped apart attacking lines of Union men with astonishingly lethal effect. With the war entering its third year, the North had suffered 100,000 more deaths than the South to that point. Lincoln continued to increase the call for men to fill the holes in the line, and increasingly men at home were unwilling to go. Bounties helped attract new soldiers, but men so enticed very often took their money and departed into the night. For every five bounty men who enlisted in the army, grumbled Grant, "we don't get more than one effective soldier." Desertion plagued the Union army almost as much as the Confederate. High taxes, draft riots, resentment of the substitution exemption, harsh suppression of dissent resulting in the suspension of the writ of habeas corpus in several states, imprisonment and even exile of opposition figures, and other constitutional infringements had soured popular support for the war. When Lincoln issued the Emancipation Proclamation, many outside New England rebelled against fighting other white men to free black slaves.

Abraham Lincoln was acutely aware of these issues. In the previous off-year's election, the Republicans had suffered heavy losses. Some prophesized that without victory by the end of the coming summer, Lincoln would fall, and his Democratic successor would sue for peace with the Confederates. Radicals in his own party, concerned about his demonstrated willingness to "reconstruct" the rebellious states, set a movement afoot to replace him as their candidate in the fall of 1864 election. Lincoln himself issued a "blind memorandum" advising that "it seems exceedingly probable that this Administration will not be reelected." While the president's ingrained pessimism seemed to have gotten the better of him, the *New York Times* reported on "a manifest ebb in popular feeling through the whole country . . . a regular period of despondency" because of the seeming inability of the Northern armies, even when victorious, to subdue the rebellion.

"Upon the progress of our arms," Lincoln said, "all else chiefly depends." With so many pressures to prove that the three-year-old war could be won, Grant would take personal charge in Virginia. He entrusted his wider strategic plan for ending the war in the West to a man he knew he could coordinate with well and one who understood personally what challenges lay ahead. He appointed Sherman to succeed him in command of the Military Division of the Mississippi, vaulting him over several more senior generals.

The logic of the choice was the right hand knowing the left. Even Sherman described himself as Grant's "second self." The two planned for the first time a coordinated western and eastern campaign. Grant laid out simple goals for each: in Virginia to pin down and kill Lee's army and capture Richmond, in Georgia to chase down and crush the Army of Tennessee and take Atlanta. The two generals would launch their spring campaigns simultaneously.

NOW FORTY-FOUR YEARS OLD, "Uncle Billy," as his soldiers affectionately called Sherman, was, according to a staff officer who described him in Georgia that year, "tall and lank, not very erect, with hair like a thatch, which he rubs up with his hands, a rusty beard trimmed close, a wrinkled face, prominent red nose, small bright eyes, coarse red hands . . . he smokes constantly." He wore a brown field officer's coat with a high collar and no stripes, muddy trousers, and a single spur.

He walked awkwardly, keeping his hands in his pockets, and talked nonstop and so quickly that those around him could barely take in one sentence before the next was complete. The officer memorialized afterwards, "General Sherman is the most American man I ever saw."

On January 31, while still in command in the West, Grant had Sherman embark with the Army of the Tennessee then in Vicksburg on a flank move through the center of Mississippi with a goal of keeping Confederate bands from raiding Union river shipping and bases by inflicting as much damage as possible around the countryside. Like the Lord of Hosts trumpeting the dominion of his god, the U.S. Constitution, Sherman issued a message to the people of the country he was about to invade. He wanted to "prepare them for my coming." He represented the U.S. government, which could exercise "any and all rights" against rebels—"to take their lives, their horses, their lands, their everything." He intended to make "war, pure and simple: to be applied directly to the civilians of the South," until they "submit."

The strategic lessons he had assimilated as a second lieutenant fresh out of West Point in the Second Seminole War in Florida could now be applied to another recalcitrant resistance force in the South. A force not unlike the natives—living off their homeland and fighting passionately for sovereign rights that they claimed as their own—continued to refuse to submit to his nation's authority. For Sherman, the time had come to fulfill what he knew needed to be done to put down the rebellion: convince the Confederates that they were a defeated people. "The army of the Confederacy is the South," he wrote his brother in late December, "and they still hope to worry us out. . . . We must hammer away and show strict persistence, such bottom that even that slender hope will fail them."

His army, he reported, "worked hard and with a will" through the Mississippi campaign of pillage without battle. After reducing Meridian, "with its depots, storehouses, arsenal, hospital, offices, hotels and cantonments," to rubble and ash, the army moved on from there. He concentrated less on seeking out and killing the enemy than on destroying his ability to make war. Encountering scant resistance, his army wrecked 115 miles of railroad lines and bridges previously able to move Confederate men and supplies. Teams of men ripped up iron rails and then roasted them red hot over intense fires made with railroad ties. They laced the softened glowing track into a bow about a tree or post. When the Confederates returned, they discovered thousands of deposited lengths of metal scrap. Confederate railroad crews could not relay the twisted lengths of track they nicknamed "Sherman neckties." His rapacious scavengers didn't stop there: Columns fanned out through the countryside plundering farms, plantations, and villages, eating what they needed, taking what they wanted, and destroying anything and everything that might serve to maintain Confederate resistance. They left behind a scraped-over landscape that could not support a grazing mule, let alone human life.

For Sherman, this was the cruel homecoming to the South that he had prophesized when secession came. He reminded his daughter Maria of his long sojourns in the South. Some of the boys his own troops now fought had once been students at the Pineville, Louisiana, military academy which he had superintended before the war. "In every battle I am fighting some of the very families in whose houses I used to spend some happy days," he told her with obvious regret. He preferred not to kill his enemy or place his own men in harm's way. "Of course I must fight when the time comes, whenever a result can be accomplished without battle I prefer it." His personal sentiment soon would become a strategic discipline that made war without battle a means to the nation's ends. Grant's orders to Sherman in planning for the Atlanta campaign left him complete freedom "to move against Johnston's army, to break it up, and to get into the interior of the country as far as you can, inflicting all the damage you can against their war resources." He answered Grant a month before the 1864 campaign commenced that he intended to reach Atlanta without the need to engage Johnston in a major battle.

SHERMAN HAD A GREAT advantage over the Confederate general Johnston. He knew the land they would fight over better than its defending army's leader. The geographical and engineering surveys he had made while living and traveling through up-country Georgia twenty years earlier could now providentially be brought back to mind in planning his invasion. His forces would move in a southeasterly direction, heading through a heavily forested region netted underfoot with junglelike tangles of vines and cut diagonally by steep ridges, the southwestern-most fingers of the Appalachian Mountains, and barred by rivers. It would be hard to imagine a terrain better suited for a defending army. Those ridges and rivers provided the Confederates with a successive series of natural palisades, barriers, and shelters. They required that the invaders attempt to advance through narrow gaps where they could easily be bottled up and forced to face impenetrable fire from three sides. Johnston, a temperamentally conservative military tactician, need not advance, merely defend, to emerge victorious. In Dalton, Johnston's men spent the winter constructing fortifications and artillery emplacements. They even dammed up streams to flood out the valley before Dalton. "A better drilled, better disciplined or more contented army is not in the Confederacy," proclaimed A. J. Neal to his brother. He was convinced that the Army of the Tennessee would soon reverse the fall's losses and return northwards.

Moreover, the Yankee course of invasion would follow in the main the route of the Western & Atlantic Railroad—and the bluecoats' advance would depend on holding that rail line. "The great question of the campaign," Sherman recalled a decade later, "was one of supplies." Supplies for his advancing army would need to roll down it. Like Grant (and Johnston), he was a former supply officer. In contemplating a campaign deep into hostile territory, keeping his army supplied would be crucial to victory. As the railroad was conquered, though, and he advanced ever deeper into enemy territory, its single track would become his huge army's sole supply artery. "Railroads," knew Sherman, "are the weakest things in war, a single man with a match can destroy and cut off communications." He would be invading into enemy territory, fighting along a broad front and leaving, as his army advanced, an ever more extended and tenuous lifeline behind, requiring guards along its difficult-to-defend length to protect it. When his army advanced, like a swimmer through water "the war closed in behind and [left] the same enemy behind."

He surveyed the work of war that lay ahead and the enemy army he faced. "The Devils," he wrote his wife, Ellen, "seem to have a determination that cannot but be admired—No amount of poverty or adversity seems to shake their faith—niggers gone—wealth & luxury gone, money worthless, starvation in view within a period of two or three years, are causes enough to make the bravest tremble, yet I see no signs of let up—Some few deserters—plenty tired of war, but the masses determined to fight it out." He considered Grant's great command to him to conquer the West and concluded, "All that has gone before is mere skirmishing—The War now begins."

# CHAPTER 17

# CANDLE
# ENDS

W HILE GEN. JOSEPH E. JOHNSTON was on his way to Dalton and
his new command, President Jefferson Davis wrote him to
convey his expectation that the Army of Tennessee would not delay
its move back into East Tennessee. He wanted "vigorous action."
Braxton Bragg, the Army of Tennessee's former commander and the
president's new military affairs advisor, assured Davis that the army he
left behind was "still full of zeal and burning to redeem its lost character." Corps commander William Hardee told Davis the troops were
"in good spirits" and "ready to fight." Once in Dalton, though, Johnston surveyed his rebel army and saw things very differently. He did
not wait long to rebuff Davis's request that he attack.

With Bragg at his elbow, Davis fumed at ceding first-strike advantage to the Yankees and at enduring the political costs his Southern nation was paying for letting the whole of Tennessee linger so
long in the invader's hands.

Davis had no choice. He knew from experience that if he ordered
his newly installed general to move before he was ready, the easily affronted Johnston would, in all likelihood, submit a hasty resignation—
something the Army of Tennessee and the Confederate president
could afford even less than leaving the Yankees in control of East
Tennessee for now. The differences between the general's and the
president's views were not surprising. They involved more than their
perspectives on the way things stood in North Georgia. Davis and
Johnston had a long history already and not a successful one. Both

men were West Pointers and had served in Indian Removal conflicts, but the reserved and genteel Johnston, with his imperial beard, melancholy and penetrating dark brown eyes, and aristocratic Virginia plantation manners, loathed the often prickly Davis, a self-confident and at times arrogant Westerner, smooth politician, and former U.S. secretary of war who trusted his own military generalship more than he did his general's. The touchy Johnston had felt slighted by Davis, believing the president should have made him the ranking general in the Confederate army at the war's outset. Instead Davis had designated four other generals higher. The two men had also disagreed over the defense of Richmond, which led Davis to place the more aggressive Robert E. Lee in command of the Army of Northern Virginia, the South's foremost army, which Johnston considered rightfully to be his. Now, fearing he was being set up to fail by Bragg and Davis, Johnston sized up the odds he faced and the dug-in strength of his fortifiable positions along the ridges. With his army hunkering down for the winter in what the Atlanta *Southern Confederacy* called "the Valley Forge of the Western Campaign," Johnston wrote back to Davis that the only strategy he could see was "to beat the enemy when he advances and then to move forward." He insisted, "I can see no other mode of taking the offensive here." He hoped, of course, soon to recover the lost territories, but a quick offensive to drive out the invaders was out of the question. "Difficulties," he explained, "are in the way," including a badly depleted and demoralized army. The Union forces had 130 freight cars of supplies rolling into Chattanooga each day, 193 at its peak. The single overtaxed Western & Atlantic Railroad track posed severe logistical challenges for the troops at Dalton; taking the offensive would require knocking the Yankees out of a heavily fortified base and grabbing their stockpiles. Confederate raiders had enjoyed such successes before, but never against a force not only double their number but also energized by recent victories. Johnston intended to stay put. He even considered making a retrograde movement back to the sturdier barrier of the Etowah River, with its slave-built fortifications.

Lt. Gen. John Bell Hood, one of the Army of Tennessee's three corps commanders, was much the opposite of Johnston. Also a West Pointer, he was twenty-four years younger, brash, combative, and certain that in battle the bolder leader reaped the rewards. With "the face of an old Crusader," he was all lion. He had a killer's impassive blue eyes and a readiness to send men charging headlong into the Yankee lines. His body showed his own fearlessness. Little below the apron of his massive light brown beard remained whole. It took three aides to strap him into the saddle. His left arm, turned to a limp pulp by shrapnel at Gettysburg, hung useless within its sleeve. His right leg ended a hand's width below the hip; a surgeon's bone saw had removed the rest after a minié ball shattered his thighbone at Chickamauga. As offensive-minded as Johnston was conservative, Hood grew impatient for a fight as Johnston worked to restore his army and dug in to face the coming invasion. In March, he went behind his commander's back. He wrote a series of letters directly to Davis, Bragg, and Secretary of War James Seddon calling for a "march to the front as soon as possible, so as not to allow the enemy to concentrate and advance upon us." All the Confederate president could do was warn Johnston against even considering any further retreat, which "would be so detrimental both from military and political considerations"; otherwise, he kept his peace.

The table for the spring campaign was set, but set for a campaign unlike any before in history. The invading army was led by a general who preferred to avoid battle whenever possible, and the defending army's general intended to fight only when the aggressor carried the war to him. It was as if the same poles of two magnets were preparing to meet, each constitutionally predisposed to veer away from the other. A Georgia up-country reel was in the offing in which the partners would approach like courting mates, touch briefly and tellingly, and then deflect across and away until they met again, around ridges and rivers, repeating their steps until, like lovers, they fell into a deep embrace. But here the embrace was that of war.

BY THE END OF APRIL, William Tecumseh Sherman had gathered 110,000 troops, 99,000 available for the fight, though every step they might take forward would require leaving more men behind as a rearguard to defend the army's supply line through hostile territory. Not counting officers' slaves and the thousands of others impressed to build fortifications, the Army of Tennessee started the defense of its Georgia bastion with almost 55,000 men, most of them hardened and not easily cowed by a charging enemy's force advantage. They were dug into the rocky palisades and had channeled the approaches through the ravines and mountain passes. A. J. Neal shared the general upsurge in confidence after Johnston's grand review of the entire army showed the assembled men they were "stronger than [we] had supposed." He undoubtedly warmed his mother's heart when he wrote that he and his artillery battalion were "having an easier time than ever" and "getting better and more abundant rations" than at any time since before Bragg took command of the army. He was certain, he wrote his sister, of "brilliant successes this spring and after a few hard fights a glorious peace."

He also shared in the spiritual preparation for the fight ahead. God, the Confederates increasingly believed by the thousands, stood by them at their posts. The hardened men sang "the sweet songs of Zion" by night; by day, preachers baptized men by the hundreds. Near Neal's battalion in Dalton, awaiting Sherman's army, Tom Stokes of the Tenth Texas Infantry exalted over the religious revival sweeping the army. "I have never seen such a spirit as there is now in the army," he rejoiced in a letter to his sister, Mary Gay, now living with her family and slaves in Decatur. "This revival spirit is not confined to a part only, but pervades the whole army." The rising religious fervor bolstered the warriors' courage. The Army of Tennessee was fast becoming "an army of believers." Stokes felt certain that when the Yankees stormed forward, "God will fight our battles for us, and the boastful foe be scattered and severely rebuked."


AS THE LAST DAYS OF APRIL ARRIVED, Pvt. Charles E. Benton reached Chattanooga with the 150th New York Infantry, one of the few eastern outfits in Sherman's army. Despite the western army's regular soldier's disdain for the "paper collar" and "white glove" easterners, the added troops knew combat. Benton had fought at Gettysburg and in Virginia. He felt, nonetheless, unnerved as he marched the twenty miles from Chattanooga toward the gathering front. Along the way, his regiment passed through the previous September's Chickamauga battlefield. More than half a year had passed. The stench of decaying flesh still hung in the air. Whitening skeletal remains lay scattered throughout the miles of battlefield. The hastily dug shallow graves of the dead showed protruding shoes with foot bones visible inside. Here and there, granite-color mummified hands reached from the ground. He noted one with its index finger pointing skywards. He picked up a skull by the roadside. A smooth, round hole peeked through it. "Small it was," he noted, "but yet large enough to let a life pass out."

On the night of May 6, orders went out that the advance was to begin the next day. An Indiana soldier looked around his knapsack and tent to eat, use up, or toss away whatever he wouldn't need. He pulled out his remaining candles. They would be of no further use. In a whimsical mood, he cut them into pieces and placed and lit each piece around his white tent. Others saw him and followed suit. No breeze stirred, and someone climbed a tree where he placed lighted candle ends in the branches. Before long, Sgt. George Puntenney of the Thirty-seventh Indiana looked around at "a most beautiful sight." Men by the hundreds from the division had placed their last candles up in other trees. Ten thousand candles glowed in the treetops. They cast a warmly flickering white light over the faces of thousands of silent men looking up at the ethereal display from below. That would be the last quiet night any of them would know for the next hundred days until they reached their destiny. Puntenney reflected later, "Hundreds of those poor fellows never saw another candle after that night."

Soon after dawn the next morning, Union skirmishers encountered Confederate scouts. The first shots of the spring campaign rang out.

# CHAPTER 18

# FIGHTING, FIGHTING, FIGHTING

T HE LAND TO THE SOUTH of Dalton was emptying out. A. J. Neal watched "nearly the entire population . . . moving off taking their Negroes south," even before the real battle began. Already chaotic and choked with soldiers and supplies heading toward the front, Atlanta was now jammed with refugees moving away from it. Proud Confederate Mary Gay left from the car shed to carry a last basket of food to her brother, Tom Stokes, at the front. She managed to get a seat on a train to Dalton packed with sad-faced young wives, children, and grandmothers going to see their men "for, perhaps, the last time on earth." Gay, too, thought "another fond embrace . . . would palliate the sting of final separation." As the train chugged at a crawl through the former Cherokee country where Gay had spent her early childhood, she looked out at an endless line of refugees in wagons heading south that "literally blockaded" the roads. Most made their way into Atlanta.

Increasingly nervous, the city held a rally of sorts for the army— and to fortify its own outlook—in early February. Young socialite Sallie Clayton called it "about the greatest day ever seen in Atlanta" when Gen. John Hunt Morgan came to town. Morgan had won fame for the cavalry raids he led for a thousand miles into Tennessee, Kentucky, Indiana, and Ohio. While the Great Raid of July 1863 (labeled derisively in the North the Calico Raid for its plundering of dry goods stores) had violated Gen. Braxton Bragg's express orders not to cross the Ohio River, it caused extensive damage, set off panic in the towns and countryside where Morgan operated, and showed the North's vulnerability to guerilla operations. Just as importantly, Southerners depressed after Vicksburg's fall and Gen. Robert E. Lee's defeat at Gettysburg were cheered by the show of bravado. Morgan's laurels, though, came at a high price. On July 26, 1863, federal troops captured him and nearly all his men—experienced cavalry the Confederacy could ill afford to lose—near New Lisbon, Ohio. In November, Morgan managed to escape. Atlanta was able to enjoy his company, but they had much greater need of his cavalry.

Morgan spent the night of February 6 at Mayor James Calhoun's house, sharing a grand meal with the town's fathers and local Confederate leaders. The following morning, he made the few-block ride to deliver a short speech and attend a reception in his honor at the Trout House. His carriage was born along by stout men through a crowd too thick for horses not to trample people. Sallie Clayton joined a throng dense enough for "a boy to walk on the heads and shoulders of men" from one end of the city's central district to the other. Samuel Richards also stood amid the "large concourse of citizens" to hear the general.

Mayor Calhoun introduced General Morgan to the vast crush of people before him. The mayor invoked the memory of Stonewall Jackson, the greatest Confederate cavalry hero, killed in battle in Virginia. Calhoun intoned,

> While we mourn the loss of a Jackson, we have great cause to rejoice that we still have many noble leaders left, and amongst them a Morgan, and feel that the spirit of the South can never be subdued while we have such men to lead and encourage our gallant armies. . . . I know our brave soldiers have almost performed miracles; that they have fought as no soldiers have fought before; yet in view of the dangers which threaten us, may I not hope that they will take another step higher upon Fame's proud temple, and fill the world with the renown of their patriotism and bravery.

It was a wildly hyperbolic introduction for a man who had left most of his troops in a Union prison and who, a few months later, would be hunted down and killed in a farmhouse in Tennessee. But Atlanta enjoyed the rhetoric.

Calhoun sought to encourage the citizens, telling them that those at home, too, should be inspired to feed, clothe, and sustain the army, and should, "if they have an excess" of food, turn it over to the commissary, "and by every kind word and deed, and by a united, persevering and determined effort of the army and the people, we may expect a glorious termination of our troubles and sacrifices, and our efforts to be rewarded with independence and a promising future."

EVENTS HAD FORCED A change in Mayor Calhoun's sentiments. He had resisted secession and the coming of the war with all his might, he supported peace candidates in Confederate elections even while the war raged, and he seemed to use his authority on behalf of the Confederacy only to the degree necessary for the leader of its second most important city, but the Confederacy was now his nation. His entire family was caught up in the cause. His revered older brother, Ezekiel Calhoun, now nearly seventy years old, had already buried one son and another young man he regarded as a son. The doctor's oldest son, Edward, was still pulling in the wounded from the Virginia battlefields in his ambulance wagon. Finally, despite Ezekiel's opposition to a cause that had once led neighbors to threaten his life, he, too, had entered Confederate military service. He now served as a regimental surgeon with the Sixtieth Georgia Regiment on the Island of Skidaway, a heavily bombarded barrier island near the blockaded mouth to the Savannah River.

James Calhoun, too, had a blood investment in the war. His oldest son, Lowndes, now held his rifle in a forward skirmish line north of Dalton. He had reorganized the Forty-second Georgia after its virtual destruction in the Vicksburg siege. Back in the lines, in February, he and his men had already helped to knock down an attempt by Gen. William Tecumseh Sherman's troops to push in the Confederate lines in the foothills above Gen. Joseph Johnston's winter camp. Waiting now for the full force of the Yankee invasion to strike, the Atlanta men behind their breastworks could hear the first gunfire pops echoing through the North Georgia forests and off the ridges. As James Calhoun looked out at the hopeful thousands gathered before him at the Trout House, waiting expectantly to hear cheering words from their Confederate hero, one hundred miles to the north a Yankee storm was building the strength to sweep all of them away.

NEARLY ALL ATLANTANS were at least aware of the preparations for battle being made at Dalton and recognized that their city was at the center of Sherman's crosshairs. "No event could be more disastrous to the Confederacy" than losing Atlanta to the Yankees, the *Intelligencer* insisted. Hope remained widespread that Johnston's forces would hold off the invaders long enough to force a negotiated settlement. The longer the Confederates succeeded in enduring, the more likely the so-called Peace Democrats would be able to defeat Abraham Lincoln in the election due to be held in the fall of 1864. The country was tired of the indecisive war; if the South could forestall Sherman and Grant in their grand designs for the campaign, the Unionist president might be voted out. Besides, the people trusted their army and its new general in Dalton. "Of the capacity of General Johnston none could utter a word of doubt," the *Intelligencer* proclaimed. Most in the city seconded that vote of confidence. Mary Mallard, a coastal refugee living in Ezekiel Calhoun's place, had shared the "perfect ecstasies" people felt when catching a glimpse of the dashing General Morgan during his stay. She trusted that with such leaders, Atlanta would remain unchallenged. "No one seems to apprehend any danger for this place," she wrote her mother on May 5. However, she also noted that the town's thousands of hospital beds were being emptied of the sick to make room for the anticipated wounded. "We will be in a dreadful predicament should General Johnston be unsuccessful or be compelled to fall back, but no one seems to contemplate this. All have the utmost confidence in his skill."

Some were less certain. At the end of the day on May 7, when the first shots of the spring campaign were fired, Samuel Richards sat at his desk in a quiet house. "If we are defeated in these battles," he reflected, "I fear the bright and cheering hopes of peace that now animate all hearts in the South will be dissipated quickly." Even so, Richards gave no indication in his diary that he feared his own life might be at risk. The idea that Atlanta might be devastated by a distant force held off by the high ridges and the Confederate defenders within them was still, for most, beyond comprehension.

THE CONFEDERATE LINES Sherman's men marched into that day started above the 840-foot rise known as Tunnel Hill. Perhaps the Lower South's greatest antebellum engineering feat, a 1,477-foot Western & Atlantic Railroad tunnel pierced through the pine-covered granite ridge ten miles north of Dalton. Starting in the valley north of there, which Johnston had flooded by damming up Mill Creek, his men stood ready to fight from dug-out emplacements and behind breastworks and boulders along the tops and cliffs of the parallel ridges that raked like scars across the face of North Georgia. Rocky Face Ridge, named for its sheer western palisade wall, was chief among these, stretching from above Dalton south for nearly twenty-three miles to its southern end near a loop in the Oostanaula River. Sherman knew the terrain his men now moved into from his youthful tour through a land "to which I took such a fancy" twenty years earlier. The ridge formed a natural rock barrier, much like Lookout Mountain, which Grant had surmounted outside Chattanooga, but far more impregnable to assault. "The Georgian Gibraltar" fronted the invaders like a bulbous castle wall, every niche in its face bristling with men and their guns. The cliff walls would never yield to even the strongest artillery battering ram, and the valley in front of them left little cover, or hope, for a successful assault.

When the Yankees made their first try, Mayor Calhoun's neighbors' son, A. J. Neal, directed his battery, shelling the initial wave of the charge from three miles north of Dalton on the Tunnel Hill Road. Fighting went on all around him; "shell and bullets fell among us," though in the confusion of the battle, he could judge little about what was going on, except from the crescendo of battle noise. After two days of fighting, though, he was pleased. His battery in Gen. Benjamin F. Cheatham's Corps protected the vital Mill Creek Gap through the Rocky Face Ridge, despite there being at times as many as ten attackers for each defender. The gray coats succeeded in repulsing the initial advances and then "made a sortie and drove the Yankees from the field." After two days, however, Sherman's army seemed only to be probing the lines and had not attacked Confederate forward positions in force. Neal hoped the Yankees would be foolhardy enough to undertake a full frontal assault on their lines "for I want a victory here." Driving back and then crushing the enemy now, as had already happened at Shiloh and Chickamauga before, "would end this war speedily." The Yankees, he felt certain, could not pierce their lines "except by flanking."

But flanking was just what Sherman had in mind.


SHERMAN, PERHAPS BETTER THAN Johnston, knew there were three possible doors through the long sweep of the Rocky Face Ridge wall. Closest to the federals' main force moving down on the rebels and also closest to Dalton was Mill Creek Gap (known to locals as Buzzard's Roost), about three miles south of Tunnel Hill. The railroad tracks between Chattanooga and Atlanta that served as opposite-running lifelines for the two armies passed through the gap and then ran south. That railroad provided a ready shuttle behind the ridgeline for moving rebels and their supplies in response to Sherman's attacks. Another three miles south of Mill Creek Gap was Dug Gap, a pass notched into the ridge. Thirteen miles southwest of Dalton, the Snake Creek Gap ran between two mountains and opened beyond them into Sugar Valley, running five miles to the banks of the Oostanaula at the village of Resaca. Sherman thought his breakthrough would come at the southernmost opening. However, he sent three-fourths of his entire force, combining the Army of the Cumberland under Gen. George Thomas, the Rock of Chickamauga, and the Army of the Ohio led by Gen. John M. Schofield, against the Mill Creek and Dug gaps. He might knock the Confederates back through one or both of the heavily defended northern gaps, though that seemed unlikely. Sherman himself described the Mill Creek Gap, its walls filled with hidden men able to fire down on any heads daring to approach from below, as "the terrible door of death." At the least, his two armies would pin down the main body of Johnston's men. Meanwhile Sherman's own beloved Army of the Tennessee, now commanded by his favored general, the fast rising and brilliant young fellow Ohioan James B. McPherson, would sidestep the Rocky Face Ridge altogether before marching south and through Snake Creek Gap.

Scouts involved in earlier skirmishes along the ridge had reported finding almost no defenders or obstructions there. Johnston had spent the winter months fortifying Dalton and protecting its northern approaches closest to the enemy's camp. He had paid scant attention to his southern flank except well south at his supply depot in the railhead town of Rome at the confluence of the Etowah and Oostanaula rivers. He may not have even been aware of the gaping hole he'd left. If McPherson could surge through Snake Creek Gap into the valley, his army could cut the railroad line at Resaca, severing Johnston's lifeline and forcing him to fall back across the Oostanaula or risk encirclement, logistical strangulation, and the utter destruction of the only army between Sherman and Atlanta.

On May 9, McPherson's men encountered little opposition as they moved warily through Snake Creek Gap. They entered Sugar Valley and approached within a couple miles of Resaca. McPherson sent Sherman word at his headquarters about their advance. Reading McPherson's message, the excitable commander pounded on the table, sending dishes and cups flying. "I've got Joe Johnston dead!" he exclaimed.

THE SNAKE CREEK GAP surprise had worked. But at the moment of his potential triumph, McPherson was caught flat-footed. Gen. Leonidas Polk, the corpulent Episcopal "Fighting Bishop" of Louisiana, commanded a 15,000-man corps, the Army of Mississippi. With the invasion of Georgia under way, he raced from defending Alabama to reinforce Johnston's army. In Resaca, 3,000 advance men joined the small guard already in place just as McPherson's army of 23,000 passed through the gap. A mile outside Resaca, the Yankees, who believed they had broken through unnoticed, encountered fire from the hastily dug-in defenders around the town. McPherson did not know that he outnumbered the Confederates nearly six or more to one in an open plain. Instead, shocked by the sudden resistance, McPherson reconsidered his position, fearing that the roads he marched on through the valley were dangerously exposed. He assumed Johnston had gotten wind of his movement and was prepared for his arrival, perhaps had even set a trap. Cut loose from the army's main body and supplies and charged by Sherman's somewhat contradictory orders to cut the railroad at Resaca, then withdraw back into the fortifiable approaches to the gap, he entrenched his men within the defensible confines of the Snake Creek Gap.

The rest of Polk's Corps flooded into Resaca, holding the rail line. Johnston soon learned about the movement to his rear and realized the potentially lethal threat he faced. "The Yankees," remarked Pvt. Sam Watkins of the First Tennessee, "had got breeches hold on us." He and the rest of Johnston's men started disengaging from Dalton to reinforce Resaca and defend along the northern banks of the Oostanaula River. Realizing the enemy was slipping away, Sherman ordered nearly his entire army on a parallel march south to follow McPherson into the Snake Creek Gap. But it was too late. "He could have walked into Resaca," spat Sherman, livid with frustration. If McPherson's Army of the Tennessee had taken the town and the rail line there, Sherman was certain Johnston's pinched-off and hard-pressed army would have been forced to scatter into the mountains. Not a week into the most significant western campaign of the entire war, he would very likely have bagged half of the opposing force and demolished any significant further resistance to his advance on Atlanta. The war in Virginia and elsewhere would have continued, but with no chance of reinforcements or further food and supplies reaching other fronts from Georgia, the Civil War would effectively have been won.

Instead, the reinforced Army of Tennessee now had nearly 70,000 well-positioned men in and around Resaca ready to defend their lines against a charge from a force not much larger than itself. The first attempt at flanking Johnston had driven him to retreat, but the retreat had left him stronger than before. A set-piece battle was in the offing along the Oostanaula with the odds no longer in the Union army's favor.

"A little timid," Sherman later called McPherson's actions on that day outside Resaca. Though Sherman himself had told McPherson to advance cautiously into Sugar Valley and retreat to the safety of the gap, he ruefully said when the two met a couple days later while the forces gathered for battle, "Well, Mac, you have missed the opportunity of a lifetime."

THOUGH HE MAY HAVE preferred to avoid such a fight, Sherman would have to battle. He hoped to pin the Army of Tennessee against the river banks and destroy it there. Starting with skirmishing and probing by the Union forces on May 13, the first major battle of the campaign began. "We have been in hot and heavy ever since," A. J. Neal wrote home two days later. The battle moved across the valley as the two sides charged breastworks, only to be driven back. The Yankees pushed forward a strong skirmish line near Neal's trench on the third day of the fight, May 15, and had sharpshooters "behind every tree and shelter." Shells fell all around Neal. "To expose your head one second," he found, "is to draw a dozen bullets." But rebel bullets and shells tolled too. When, the night before, the Union men charged his position, Neal's comrades set a large building on fire to light up the field, putting the approaching Yankees into ghostly visibility, "and opened on them with a dozen pieces of artillery repulsing the attack."

The day before, Gen. John Bell Hood's Corps had nearly broken through the Union lines until reinforcements arrived to force the attackers back. The Yankees regained the lines, but their dead littered the field. That night, the infantry from behind their chest-high fortifications around Neal's Confederate cannons taunted the Yankee line across the field with the news of Hood's bloody work. Neal heard a Yankee shout back, "What is Confederate money worth?" What Neal called "a rich scene" quickly ensued as the two lines hurled insults back and forth. A rebel shouted, "What niggers command your brigade?" ignoring the fact that General Sherman shared many of the same racist views as his foes. Although he was fighting to impose Union authority, including the abolition of slavery, on the slave states, the Union commander refused to admit black soldiers into his army. He despised as a dangerous weight upon his army the cloud of former slaves who, having fled their Southern masters, now gathered around the camp of their liberators as it moved into Georgia.

While Neal recorded his impressions, somewhere in the fields and woods nearby William Lowndes Calhoun lay moaning in pain, his hip shattered. During the fighting that afternoon, the Forty-second Georgia as part of the Georgia Brigade had charged against the Union lines. Moving through what their commander called "a thicket almost impenetrable" to sight or sound, they met a fierce hail of bullets and were almost immediately driven back, leaving more than one hundred men dead and wounded behind. Calhoun fell when a minié ball ripped into him. His comrades carried him back. Not long after, he lay in a boxcar with the other wounded bound for Atlanta. He would never walk again without pain. For the mayor of Atlanta's son, the Civil War fighting was over.

ON THE NIGHT OF MAY 13, an ashen Johnston gathered his generals. He had learned that an entire Union division had crossed the Oostanaula at Lay's Ferry several miles to the south of Resaca. That deeper flanking move, steadily reinforced by Sherman, threatened to cut off the Western & Atlantic Railroad again. This time the entire army would have to withdraw from its lines and fall back across the river. Working through the night, the rebels evacuated their positions and, after crossing the river, burned the railroad bridge behind them.

That began a series of running encounters south of the river through the gently rolling hills beyond. Johnston kept hoping to find a position that would give him the advantages he wanted, and Sherman marched his men around. "It was fighting, fighting, every day," Tennessee rebel Private Watkins recalled. "When we awoke in the morning, the firing of guns was our reveille, and when the sun went down it was our 'retreat and our lights out.'" By day the men fought, and by night they built breastworks. "I am well nigh worn out," admitted A. J. Neal, "fighting all day and running or working all night." He was sure, though, if the Yankees would "only give us a fair fight we could sweep them from the face of the earth."

Sherman, though, had no intention of giving such a fight for now. For his part, General Johnston could not find a position where he felt it safe to turn around and attack his pursuers. He decided to fall back across the next great regional barrier, the southwest-running Etowah River, crossing what Sherman called "the Rubicon of Georgia." Sherman expected to follow close behind through the heavy wilderness ahead and, at the final river-rampart, "to swarm along the Chattahoochee in a few days." At some point, he believed "a terrific battle" near that river was inevitable.

Bone-weary, the soldiers of both armies fought and marched without let up, through summerlike dust and heat. They scratched at poison ivy rashes and cuts from brambles and sharp rocks, swatted at swarms of flies, slapped at biting mosquitoes, and wriggled and danced about incessantly like marionettes tugged on razor-wire strings held by the cruel lice crawling over their raw skin. The misery of the campaign equaled the dangers of flying lead and exploding iron. The Yankee army, though, was deep in Georgia. In two weeks of hard fighting, Sherman had covered half the distance to Atlanta. A little more than fifty miles separated his soldiers from the citadel of the Confederacy itself.

On May 22, an enthusiastic Col. Charles Morse, of the Second Massachusetts Infantry, wrote that the next day began the drive over the Etowah. "In the words of Sherman's general order, we start on another 'grand forward movement,' with rations and forage for twenty days." Sherman did not need to tell his men, but, reflected Morse, "Atlanta is evidently our destination; whether we shall reach it or not remains to be seen. One thing we are certain of—Johnston cannot stop us with his army; we can whip that wherever we can get at it."

# CHAPTER 19

# ROMAN RUNAGEES

THE YANKEES' FEARSOMELY SWIFT advance shocked thousands of regional residents and drove them in terror to abandon their towns, homes, and farms. In the predawn hours of May 17, a neighbor roused Charles H. Smith and his family in Rome, Georgia. He shouted that Gen. Joseph Johnston's army was evacuating the town, despite his assurance that Rome, with its numerous hospitals and important ironworks, "was to be held at every hazard." The soldiers were pulling out of their lines along the Etowah and Oostanaula rivers, which join at Rome to form the Coosa. "Then," wrote Smith finding himself on the bitter road towards Atlanta, "came the tug of war" dragging the people out of their homes and forcing them to become refugees.

Smith was famous to readers of the *Intelligencer* and other newspapers around the South for his comic commentaries, written under the pen name Bill Arp, which usually made light of even the direst aspects of life in the Confederacy. Now he was himself, ironically, a "Roman runagee," using a slang variation on a word more often applied to runaway slaves. He found dark humor even as his own family was driven from the "eternal sitty" in search of "a log in some vast wilderness . . . where the foul invaders cannot travel nor their pontoon bridges float." His flight from Rome began as "a dignified retreat," but he was soon "constrained to leave the dignity behind." Those who could find an open corner and had the stomach to travel in boxcars alongside litters filled with groaning soldiers with gaping gunshot and artillery wounds, their blood and viscera slopping over the car floor and spilling onto the track bed below, clambered aboard trains bound for Atlanta. Most tossed whatever household possessions they could into wagons and fled down the dusty country highways, "flying in every direction in ruinous confusion." No "past favors shown . . . Confederate currency, new issues, bank bills, black bottles" or any other form of payment proffered could secure Smith and his family even space to stand in a car. They joined the dawn race by civilians across the Etowah River bridge, which went up in flames behind them. That temporarily halted the chasing Yankee army. William Tecumseh Sherman's men moved into the town, where Confederate stragglers had already begun the work of pillaging, which the invaders completed. General Sherman knew well what was going on. He had watched during the January campaign into Mississippi and described the similarly wanton destruction to his brother: "Farms disappear, houses are burned and plundered, and every living animal killed and eaten." There was little he or anyone else could do to stop it. "General officers," he admitted, "make feeble efforts to stay the disorder, but it is idle." Once war was unleashed, he preached, it had a life of its own. Until the rebellious people of the South accepted their defeat, "you might as well reason with a thunderstorm."

With the raging storm pressing down on them, the exiled North Georgians now formed "a grand caravan" rolling and shuffling down "a highway crowded with wagons and teams, cattle and hogs, niggers and dogs, women and children, all moving in disheveled haste to parts unknown." Charles Smith noted with "regret, however, that some of our households of African scent [*sic*] have fallen back into the arms of the foul invaders." The supposedly faithful black people were voting with their feet for freedom.

SMITH AND THE OTHER countryside refugees arrived in an already crowded Atlanta swelling with disoriented, frightened, and destitute people. The car shed echoed with the shouts of pushing and shoving people holding their bags and trying not to lose their children's grips as they continued their refugee journey beyond the city. The crush grew so heavy at times that engineers stopped their trains short of the station to avoid running over people attempting to jump aboard the rolling cars. In the last days of May, Samuel Richards noted the passing of a week "of great excitement in our city." Refugees were now "constantly arriving." With boardinghouses and extra rooms in private homes already full with the elite of Nashville, Memphis, Chattanooga, and other long-occupied cities, with church pews staked out and dilapidated boxcars long-established homes to extended families, the Smiths and others took to tents or slept under wagons, on porches or in the open. Affording food or other necessities was a challenge. Even before the army began falling back, prices had spiked by as much as 30 percent in less than two weeks. Paper money bought gold at the rate of $20 for $1 in gold coin, but rumors of Sherman's movements drove exchange rates higher at the fastest pace in American history. For those with money, stores still had goods to sell, but even the well off felt the pinch. Feed became too expensive for residents to purchase for livestock, so townspeople like Richards who still possessed milk cows and other animals butchered them.

In the last days of May, many people walked out to the edges of town. The sharp-eared ones, recorded Richards, could now hear "the report of the artillery at *the front*," now twenty-five miles to the north and west of Atlanta. The booming echoes of cannon daily seemed to draw closer, like some monstrous, fire-breathing beast slouching toward the city, destroying all it encountered. On the march, even General Sherman was stunned by what he saw. "All the people retire before us, and desolation is behind," he confessed to his wife. "To realize what war is one should follow in our tracks."


The warring armies collided, or stumbled into each other, several times in the junglelike tangles, small railroad towns, and rolling wooded hills below the Etowah River. The fighting continued almost incessantly; men fell by the hundreds day after day. Sherman sent heavily reinforced skirmish lines forward, hoping to pin Johnston's men down and then bring the weight of Union forces to bear on Confederate breastworks. The Union commander expected Johnston to continue his retreat until the Army of Tennessee had reached the enormous fortifications built along the Chattahoochee River by Lemuel Grant's hordes of impressed slaves or even to pull back into Atlanta itself. But Johnston was not planning to freeze and starve out an overextended Northern army in the hell of Georgia; instead, he wanted to draw Sherman's armies far enough apart to destroy a portion and turn the weight of numbers more in his favor. Johnston's strategy, his chief of staff explained, was "to keep close up to the enemy," to probe for an opening where his forces could break through. But Johnston's was much the smaller army, and with the two sides grappling, the Confederates needed to cover their own flanks even as they probed the enemy lines for weakness. Johnston took up position within a seventeen-mile stretch of fortifications northwest of Atlanta. The two armies collided in a series of interconnected battles at the "slaughter-pen" of Pickett's Mill and the "hell hole" of New Hope Church and Dallas.

In the thickets and forests, both sides stumbled into the opposing lines and suffered terribly—though the Union army lost many more men. At Pickett's Mill 1,500 Northerners fell when "the rebel fire . . . swept the ground like a hailstorm," wrote one Union soldier. While he fired shells into the enemy, A. J. Neal watched the "fun" the rebel infantry had "to stand in the trenches and mow down their lines as they advance[d]." The dead littered the ground. An Alabama fighter looked over a nearby field: "Such piles of dead men were seldom or never seen before on such a small space of ground." Another counted fifty Union dead within thirty feet of him. Entire regiments disappeared, every man shot down, in their advance on the Confederates. Soldiers observed they could walk the field, body to body, afterwards and not touch ground for hundreds of yards. A Yankee stated, "This is surely not war; it is butchery."

But once again, the manic Sherman zigged or zagged to try to cut Johnston's railroad line. Johnston, unable to prevent the Northerners' sally against his rear and again made vulnerable, was forced to fall back further. While Sherman believed Johnston would not come out to fight him, a frustrated Johnston accused his opposing number of being "so cautious that I can find no opportunity to attack him except behind entrenchments."

In the densely wooded country through which they carried on their dance, the Confederates quickly threw up works and refused to be dislodged from their dug-out positions—until pried loose by Sherman's flanking moves. Tennessee private Sam Watkins marked off the days of the Hundred Days' Battle, with "the boom of cannon and the rattle of musketry . . . our reveille and retreat." Of one thing he was sure: "Sherman knew that it was no child's play."

Sherman was losing men at a fast clip, with nearly 2,000 dead and another 7,000 wounded or missing after four weeks. He was deep in enemy territory, where a single line of vulnerable railroad kept his army in the battle. He was running low on food, though his army was picking the countryside clean. All around him "sharpshooters, spies & scouts in the guise of peaceable farmers" were shooting down wagon drivers and couriers and reporting his ponderous army's movements to the enemy. He had been in such fights before, going back to his first war out of West Point. He understood, perhaps better than any general, how to defeat such an enemy, such a warring people. "It is," Sherman wrote his brother, "a Big Indian War."

Every step backwards, often after a day's hard, bloody fighting, demoralized Johnston's men. Nearly 8,000 of them were now dead, wounded, or missing, and scores of deserters slipped away from his camps into Union lines each night. By the end of the first week of June, the entire Confederate Army of Tennessee formed a defensive wedge that covered a range of three ridges and the connecting fields above Marietta. Kennesaw Mountain was the dominant feature in the landscape. Sherman did not expect Johnston to remain there long and observed with apparent indifference, he "is still at my front and can fight or fall back as he pleases." The hardened men of Johnston's army were building up their latest fortifications on the heights, together with slave labor impressed from the countryside. When the pouring rain of the past week let up, the troops and slaves could look behind them to see the spires of Atlanta's churches twenty miles away.

IN A TEMPESTUOUS ATLANTA, "the busiest people in town were speculators and rumor mongers working almost every downtown street and shop," observed a refugee daily newspaper, the former Memphis *Appeal*. The *Intelligencer* tried to keep spirits up and ridiculed the doubters. "On the street, every minute, the ravens are croaking. Do you hear them? There is a knot of them on the corner shaking their heads, with long faces and restless eyes. . . . But we have no fear of the results, for we keep it constantly and confidently before us that General Johnston and his great and invincible satellites are working out the problem of battle and victory at the great chess board at the front." The *Appeal* noted Johnston's assurances "that Atlanta will be defended to the last extremity."

Most people accepted Johnston's word and trusted that he was falling back "in order to gain good fighting ground," explained Mary Mallard, the coastal refugee living in Ezekiel Calhoun's place while her preacher husband ministered to the troops. Even as Johnston retreated, the series of running battles repulsed Sherman's men, Mallard crowed, "with great slaughter." However, the retreating army's casualties were all too apparent: Some 2,500 wounded had already reached the city even before the worst fighting of the last week of May. Mary Mallard worked with the relief women to comfort the wounded. The surgeons termed the wounds they were contending with "slight," but to Mallard's eyes, "they all seem terrible." At the car shed, she saw rows of men on stretchers "wounded in all portions of their body." One man who had lost a leg conversed with those around him "as cheerfully as though nothing had happened." She reported calmly on her search for old sheets to spread over the groaning, filthy wounded now spilling out into the open, unpaved streets around the car shed. Blankets wouldn't do, for "when limbs are amputated and the clothing cut off a foot or two above the place, something cooler and lighter" needed to be thrown over them.

In passing through the depot, the passionate, secret Unionist Cyrena Stone had a different, if still ghoulish, impression of the scene. The floor of the station was crowded with the wounded, and "rough boxes with somebody's loved [ones] in them—were scattered around." A black man with a fiddle sat on top of one of the pine coffins and began to tune up. The "living" soldiers begged him play "a good lively chune." They blithely shoved the heavy wooden boxes aside to make room for dancing. Stone watched as "'the light fantastic toe' was tipped, until the cars came along, which was to take them to the front—& death."

Stone read through the daily news reports from the front. She quoted one: "Johnston is only falling back to get a better position; and when he *does* make a stand—dead Yankees will be piled up higher than Stone Mountain." She remarked on the style of the reporting. "The vandals," she mocked, "were mowed down without number. No loss on our side. One man killed, and three slightly wounded. Retreats invariably—We fell back in good order. No straggling, and no loss of artillery." The truth would eventually come out, she trusted. To keep up her faith in the face of what she believed—hoped—to be falsely optimistic reports, she visited a fellow Unionist. The two women shared a laugh. "Sherman is falling back," the woman said to Cyrena, "but he is falling this way." Even Cyrena's driver, Dan, a slave, told her, "It stands to reason that our folks ain't whipping as they say they be, when they're coming this way all the time."

Something else also demonstrated to her that her prayers would soon be fulfilled. The news of federal advances, she noticed, went hand in hand with a seeming change of heart among those who formerly were among the most ardent Confederates. People who had snubbed her for so long now sought her out and welcomed her into their homes, where they had long rebuffed her. "I shall look to you for protection," one woman beseeched her. "Others," Cyrena observed, "have attempted to make friends with those they have abused & persecuted untiringly for being suspected of Union sentiments, & showing kindness to prisoners." The Confederate grip on Atlanta, where loyalties were always suspect, began to slip.

THE TUBERCULAR COL. GEORGE Washington Lee's health forced him to resign his Confederate commission and disband his provost guard battalion. Secret Yankees like Stone could begin to breathe easier. Despite Lee's ill health, he went to Macon as Georgia governor Joseph Brown's aide-de-camp organizing his state militia hurriedly being assembled for Atlanta's defense. Atlanta's secret, inner Civil War was a more violent and complicated front in a long-running and more open dispute between Governor Brown and Confederate president Jefferson Davis. Many among the state's political elite disdained Brown as a "mountain boy," a largely self-made lawyer from Cherokee Georgia who had leaped over the entrenched powers in Milledgeville to win and retain the governorship for the past seven years. Known to his admirers as "Young Hickory," Brown resembled the Old Hickory, Andrew Jackson, only in his humble origins and populism. He despised federal power while in the Union and remained the most zealous states' rights militant in any Confederate capital. When Richmond passed its first conscription act in April 1862 to bolster the flagging army, Governor Brown declared it an unconstitutional usurpation of state power. He similarly attacked the national government's suspension of habeas corpus rights.

Rumors flew that Georgia's foremost political men, including Brown, Robert Toombs, and even the Confederate vice president Alexander Stephens, were seeking a separately negotiated settlement with Washington. The arch-Confederate John Steele at the *Intelligencer*, declared, "We want no 'peace parties' or 'State action' in the South. All that we desire are men who have determined to achieve independence or perish in the attempt, while of those who hesitate or act the traitor in this hour of peril, we need only say, that the hour which sees their vile carcasses swinging from the branches of a tree, should be hailed by the South as a sign of approaching success and the herald of deliverance." The governor might not swing from a tree, but any who failed to heed the call to step into the defense forces would.

Brown urgently appealed to the president to devote more men to the city's defense. "Atlanta is to the Confederacy almost as important as the heart is to the human body," he wrote Richmond. But the dual

Union army campaigns left Davis with few options or men to spare. Brown, for his part, had embraced the historic Georgia militia, the same citizen-soldier force that had mustered from across the state for each of the previous Indian wars. He created new regiments and placed all conscription-age men, aged sixteen to sixty, on their enrollment lists without exemption. Much to Davis's chagrin, he shielded the militia's officers from the army draft. The anti-Brown faction derisively called the Georgia militia "Joe Brown's Pets."

In May Brown issued an urgent call-up for the entire militia and commanded all eligible men to report to Atlanta. Whether or not he was forced, as before, by order of Col. Marcus J. Wright, the arsenal head who also commanded the defense of the city, and Brig. Gen. Henry C. Wayne, Governor Brown's inspector general, Mayor James Calhoun issued an urgent call of his own, requiring "all male citizens of Atlanta . . . without regard to occupation" to report for duty. Any "not willing to defend their homes and families" he requested to "leave the city." Their continued presence "only embarrasses the authorities and tends to the demoralization of others." Calhoun was at least polite toward those who refused; Governor Brown issued a broadside authorizing local marshals to "use all force necessary," even "to take life . . . to overcome resistance" by "those who attempt to skulk . . . and to hide under exemptions, or details not known to the laws," rather than report to Atlanta. Though still defending himself against charges of selling exemptions, Colonel Lee drew together a several-thousand-man militia force destined for his hometown.

The Georgia militia remained a safer place than the Confederate front line, as Toombs, now a militia general, remarked, for "all the shirks and skulks in Georgia trying to get from under bullets." As the militiamen came into town, a reporter joked about the "gray beards" arriving with bulging valises holding "clothes sufficient for two or three men . . . [toting] a gun in one hand and a walking stick in the other." Many had no guns at all but drilled with ten-foot pikes. Having no gun suited Samuel Richards just fine. He and his brother Jabez were now officially members of the printer's company enrolled in the militia for the city's defense. "I trust," prayed the pious and very unwarlike Samuel, "we may never be called into action. I hate the sight of a musket. May God deliver us from our blood-thirsty foe." God had no such plans.

≁➩ CHAPTER 20 ➪≁

# PRAYERS

WHILE SAMUEL RICHARDS "bunked" in his feather bed at home, the main body of Joe Brown's 1,500-man militia that came into Atlanta from the rest of the state slept in tents and on the ground. They camped within sight of Cyrena Stone's house. At night, from her porch, she watched the flickering light of the campfires play against the bushes and trees. By day, the men, mostly "past the conscript age," drilled. Few carried more than a shotgun. Many came by regularly to drink from her well. "I see only sad & dejected faces," she observed. One told her he wanted to cross the lines but feared state troops would hang his two sons and burn his house down. After a week she heard the cry go out: "To the front!" Joe Brown's Pets, "many of them actually in tears," broke camp to take up positions in the fall-back lines beyond the Chattahoochee River. A few came by to say goodbye. "I don't want to go and fight the Yankees," one told her. "I'd much rather fight the people who have brought this war upon our country, and forced us to leave our homes to murder & be murdered." By May 26, Allen T. Holliday, a thirty-five-year-old militiaman who had camped under a bush near Stone's house, lay in his tent near the Chattahoochee writing to his wife, Lizzie, at their plantation home in Wilkes County. "The roar of cannon is distinctly heard," he penned anxiously. "We are here without a gun and a Yankee raid is at every moment expected."

The next morning, Cyrena, now thirty-four, stood on her porch in the quiet of the evening. With the flowers that survived the record cold winter blossoming by her house and the early vegetables and oats ready to harvest in the garden, she breathed in the springtime fresh-ness. Her ears perked up to an unfamiliar sound. She heard low, deep hammering she could barely make out; then she was sure she heard the distant collisions, now relentlessly. "O that music!" Cyrena re-joiced. She was among the first in town to make out "distinctly" the echoing boom of the big guns firing twenty-five miles to the north-west. It was not long before most people in Atlanta heard the rolling cannon thunder and blanched with dread. For Stone, after three years, the cannons were, she secretly jotted, "the first notes of our redemp-tion anthem. Never fell upon my ear any sound half so sweet—so grand; nor on earth, will any sound so thrill my soul again."

The next day, a friend, a fellow Yankee loyalist, came by to listen with her. "Come, boys!" the woman cried out, beckoning toward the unseen source of the booms. "Come on! We're waiting for you!"

IN HIS HEADQUARTERS AT ACWORTH, a rail-stop town about ten miles north of Marietta, in early June, Gen. William Tecumseh Sher-man was infused with fierce optimism. He was as impatient to get to Atlanta as Cyrena's friend was for him to arrive. Nonetheless, he gave his men a few days to recover from the constant fight while waiting for his engineers to rebuild the railroad bridge another ten miles to the north over the Etowah River, which the retreating Confederates had destroyed. He would soon be resupplied and expected the arrival of more reinforcements. He rode down to survey his next hurdle. Once again, his army faced an enemy embedded along a ridgeline ris-ing as much as eight hundred feet above them in the plains. He looked up at the heights of Lost Mountain, a Confederate salient on his right, and, next to it, Pine Mountain, closer to Marietta. Gen. Joseph Johnston's men on Brush Mountain at the eastern flank of his line overlooked the Western & Atlantic Railroad tracks before they swept in an *s*, first to Brush Mountain's west and then back to the east around Kennesaw Mountain. The two-mile Kennesaw Mountain ridge loomed in the distant haze before Sherman now like a sleeping giant lying directly in front of Marietta. Deep in their fortified trenches, fewer than 65,000 rebel warriors, many of them now in the fight for the entire three years, ranged over those commanding heights and in the lines stretching down into the plains.

Even as Sherman studied the enemy lines, they were being steadily strengthened. General Johnston had ordered "every able-bodied negro man that can be found" to work on both Atlanta's outer defenses and the Kennesaw line. Union scouts could see gangs of black men digging and building up trenches and gun emplacements. They overheard engineers order the work crews, "This way with your axes. This way with your spades," while the entrenching parties sang.

Within the Confederate ramparts, artillery captain A.J. Neal mailed his letters home. Had the army been able to furlough him, he might have carried a letter to his family's big house on Mitchell Street in a day's march. His battery fired on federal emplacements from the western side of the line close to Lost Mountain. He wondered what Johnston planned to do. The enemy, he was sure, "cannot stay where he is long and to drive us from our entrenchments he is not able." Sherman, though, did not think it would be necessary. "I will not run head on his fortifications ... an immense line of works," he informed Washington on June 6, though he also knew more hard fighting was in the offing. He felt certain that Johnston intended to pull back toward the wide Chattahoochee River, crossing where "T." Holliday and his raw fellow militia recruits filled the lines. On June 9, Sherman assured his wife that he would "dislodge" Johnston from the hills and ridges within a day or two. He wanted to get into Marietta by the following day and then "feel down to the Chattahoochee."

The "great battle" he long anticipated with Johnston would take place soon after that on the Chattahoochee River, "the passage of which he must dispute." He expected to destroy the Confederate army there. Some Union soldiers felt so confident of Uncle Billy's strategic genius—and his ability to move forward without the massively cataclysmic battles which Civil War armies had grown used to—that they counted on drinking corn whisky on Peachtree Street by July 4. They were wrong on all counts.

THE DAY BEFORE SHERMAN wrote Ellen so confidently, the Republican Party nominated President Abraham Lincoln for a second term at its convention in Baltimore. As the war entered its fourth year, the North remained badly split over Lincoln. The Democratic *New York World* called him an "ignorant, boorish, third-rate backwoods lawyer" unequal to "a crisis of the most appalling magnitude." His one-time chief supporter, Horace Greeley's radical *New York Tribune*, "accepted" Lincoln's nomination but made clear that other candidates would have been preferable for concluding the fight and imposing the Union's authority on the former slave states. At home, the *Intelligencer* spared no venom for a man spawned "from foul and putrid stock . . . low, vulgar and unprincipled."

Atlantans shared the convictions of many in the South, a view even Lincoln in the executive mansion held, that what happened on the horizon to their north would determine the ultimate success or failure of their cause—in the court of Northern public opinion. The *Appeal* in Atlanta reported on the Democratic Party's postponement of its nominating convention until the end of August, apparently awaiting the outcome of Sherman's drive on Atlanta and Ulysses S. Grant's presently stalled move to reach Richmond. If the present Union army campaign, it stated, "is not positively or apparently successful, they may adopt straight-out peace resolutions, and make the fight on a candidate who has consistently opposed the war." That appeared likely to be Gen. George McClellan, Lincoln's ousted former general in chief, who favored a truce and discussions with Richmond—almost certainly prelude to a negotiated breakup of the warring sections.

Most Atlantans, hearing the cannon fire that now sounded above the street noise in the Five Points, expected that McClellan, if elected, would immediately propose "an armistice, with a view to final separation" of the South from the Union. The longer Yankee footsteps were kept off Atlanta's streets, the likelier the city's survival grew—as did the Confederacy's. Samuel Richards took heart in the common view that if Sherman's efforts "prove[d] abortive," "a peace candidate" was in the offing, and slave state independence would be won.


IN THE FIRST DAYS OF JUNE, Richards and his fellow Atlantans strained their ears to hear the sharp, spiteful crackle of musket fire. The "tug of war" dragged them down, too. War, so long a source of prosperity, took over the life of Atlanta and began to sap it dry. Deserters and stragglers fleeing south overwhelmed the city. "They respected the property rights of no one," recalled Sarah Huff, who as a young girl watched them raid farmyards around her family's Marietta Street home. Households and stores, left unprotected by men now in the field, were "at the mercy of robbers who claimed to have a right to whatever would aid maintenance or supply individual craving." Samuel Richards's Decatur Street store windows were smashed. A cash box stuffed with $2,500 disappeared. Huff's mother tried to keep "army scalawags" and others "calling themselves soldiers" from making off with the family's last two hogs. The men replied that if they "didn't take them, the Yankees would." They killed and skinned the pigs in front of her. To protect their honeybees from thieves, the family moved them into the attic. A wounded soldier convalescing in the home stole the honeycombs before he went off into the night.

Thieves spirited away nearly every single hen, turkey, and duck in the coops in the City Hall neighborhood where Mary Mallard lived with her children while her husband, a preacher, ministered to the Army of Tennessee near the front. Feeling "besieged by robbers," a growing fear consumed her. "Things are coming to a fearful pass in this city," she worried to her mother in a letter. "The exceptions are those who have not been robbed." Nothing was safe, not even a man's shoes. The nervous young mother stayed inside at night after she learned a man walking nearby on a previous evening had been knocked unconscious. "When he came to himself he was in his stocking feet." With shoes selling for a year's salary and many of the soldiers barefoot and in rags, even "gentlemen," she shuddered, "consider it unsafe to be much out at night."

On June 10, a city councilman put up a toothless resolution "in disapprobation of outrages on citizens by stragglers not worthy the protection of such a noble army." His motion was defeated.

THE CONFEDERATE ARMY EMPTIED its depots and hospitals nearest the lines. Long wagon trains of munitions and supplies lined the Marietta road and jammed into the center of Atlanta. Many Atlanta residents—mostly women, children, and old men—gathered their belongings while refugees took to the road once again. The *Intelligencer* practically begged the women in particular not to leave. "Lay aside your fears," editor John Steele wrote, "forget your panic, dismiss all thoughts of running." Instead of departing town in fear, consider the needs of the fighting men, he urged, and the shortage of people willing to help. "Can you, in this hour of peril, hesitate to come forward and render what assistance you can to your brave defenders?" However, his appeal also pointed to what might befall those who remained behind: "Look at the desolated fields, ruined homes and insulted women of those sections where the enemy has passed, and learn what your fate will be if we are defeated."

The refugee daily the *Appeal* painted a far more sinister picture of what awaited. Although there was almost no evidence of rape or civilian murders committed by Union army soldiers, the newspaper conjured up horrifying images of berserkers attacking local women. The writer claimed that women, young and old, were "subjected to outrages, by the bare recital of which humanity is appalled." Everywhere the Union army overran, local woman were "made to minister to the hell-born passions of . . . fiends." After such violations, by blacks and their fellow "madmen" out of the battlefield, "insanity, in some instances, came to the relief of sufferings such as never before were inflicted upon human creatures by remorseless fiends in human shape." Rather than stay to make a stand against such a hideous foe, most ran.

Many people claimed that they intended to remain in town to help but packed in secret and snuck away. Others, particularly Union loyalists, determined to remain. Neighbors asked Cyrena Stone what she planned to do when the Yankees came. She wanted to greet her liberators. "My answer is invariably," she penned, "I have no other home to go to & shall stay in this one—if permitted to do so."

Mary Mallard knew of the "very great" panic going on in Marietta near the front, where the crowds in the smaller town were so large that families waited days on end at the depot to get a seat on a train to carry them away. A number of her acquaintances had already left Atlanta, but she did "not think there has been anything like a panic" here. She remained convinced "that General Johnston will be successful in driving them away from the city" but, just in case, set out things for a quick departure.

THE BRIEFLY GRACIOUS PONDER house on its once beautifully manicured hilltop now served as a convalescent center for the wounded. Construction of the fortifications around it, particularly the salient artillery emplacement known as Fort Hood, had torn the landscape apart and finally driven the residents away. Militiamen now manned the ramparts. The Marietta road running through the property served as the major highway to and from the front. The trains on the Western & Atlantic Railroad line ran past so continuously that they seemed to form one long line of cars stretching all the way to Marietta. Ellen Ponder, the dissolute mistress of the estate, left for Macon. Festus and Isabel Flipper, her most trusted slaves, went with her, along with their sons. Twice the Confederate authorities had tried to impress Festus Flipper into the fortifications, but his owners had succeeded in keeping him at home. They were desperate to have a trustworthy and capable man on hand. As with much else in the war, the refugee experience broke down the divisions between master and slave and especially, with most men at the front, between mistress and slave. In Macon, the Flippers moved into a spacious house where they stored away Mrs. Ponder's valuable dishes and furniture, which she left under their care while she fled further south. "Here," Flipper's young son Henry recalled of his family's new home, "all was safe."

When still living in Atlanta, their mistress had threatened to sell into worse servitude her costly bondsmen, which she otherwise left free to hire their time, menacing them frequently with her intention to "send you to Red River" or some other far-distant countryside hamlet. Henry's parents and the others could now laugh off her toothless threat. Her many slaves regarded her as "perfectly harmless, for all knew, as well as she did, that it was impossible to carry it into execution." A substantial portion of the Ponder slaves ignored the household's departure, choosing to see what the Yankees brought. Her wealthy slave Prince Ponder stayed at his profitable store and sent his wife and valuable goods acquired as a trader during the war to the farm of his friend, Unionist Julius Hayden.

Bob Yancey, the barber and trader grown rich during the war, was the slave of a man fighting for slavery's permanence, a man whose brother had laid the foundations for secession. In his forty-four years, he had known five owners and never had a proper surname except that of the men who claimed him as human property. More and more often, he now insisted that he be called by his full name, Robert Webster, the name he proudly carried from the man he claimed as his father, Daniel Webster, the senator. Robert Webster kept two escaped Union soldiers hidden in his attic and moved about uneasily under the wary eye of the provost guards. The guards would have stopped him immediately had he attempted to leave town. He, too, had stored up so many valuables and other property in his house that leaving seemed impractical in any case. He took it upon himself to begin organizing blacks in town and some of the more daring Unionists to aid the Yankee wounded.

Even with the fate of the Confederacy far from determined, emancipation had begun.

DESERTION AGAIN PLAGUED THE Army of Tennessee, increasingly demoralized by fighting constantly on the defensive and, even after bleeding the enemy by the thousands, withdrawing deeper into home territory. Men threw their guns aside and hid themselves, waiting to fall into Yankee hands. "The men is all out of heart," a Georgia soldier wrote home, "and say that Georgia will soon have to go under and they are going to the Yankees by the tens and twenties and hundreds a most [*sic*] every night. Johnson's [*sic*] army is very much demoralized as much as a [*sic*] army ever gets to be."

If personally popular with his soldiers, who trusted that the general valued their lives, Johnston's defensive strategy did little to encourage their faith in ultimate victory. Wary of his critics and mistrustful of his corps' commanders, who continued to deal with Richmond behind his back, he shared little of his strategy with others, even President Jefferson Davis. Fear spread in Richmond that he would abandon Atlanta rather than risk his army. In the capital, criticism grew that his retreat from Dalton to the horizons of Atlanta put the Confederacy itself at risk. Many in the War Department clamored for Johnston to take the offensive, to move a force around Sherman's flank to get upon his vital railroad artery. Sherman's army in the field now totaled around 112,000 men. Nearly everyone believed that such a huge force could not survive long without freight cars running all day and night down from Chattanooga. Rations in the Union camp were now limited; Sherman ordered that ammunition be fired sparingly. The general termed the single track line "the delicate part of my game" and kept guards posted along its hundred-mile length and at his depot in Dalton, but he could not spare enough men to protect it adequately against frequent small-scale guerilla raids. A full-scale attack tearing up track, blowing up bridges, or destroying the long, irreplaceable passage through Tunnel Hill would deliver a serious, if not fatal, blow to Sherman's army swimming deep in a hostile Confederate sea.

Richmond urged Johnston to do just that. The ever-conservative commanding general insisted that he needed additional cavalry reinforcements to undertake such a raid or risk his army's being flanked to death. He pleaded with Richmond to send Nathan Bedford Forrest's freebooting cavalry, now causing havoc in Tennessee and Mississippi, down on Sherman's North Georgia lifeline. Davis, though, was unwilling to pull Forrest away from his brilliantly murderous work, which kept those states in play and drew federal troops away from other battlefields. Compared to the similarly beleaguered Confederate army in Virginia, he believed Johnston had sufficient force to turn to the offensive. Georgia senator Benjamin Hill, an emissary between the increasingly dyspeptic president and the equally dejected Johnston, telegraphed the general in desperation, "You must do the work with your present force. For God's sake do it."

NOT TRUSTING ENTIRELY IN JOHNSTON, Atlanta now asked for divine intervention. On the same day the city council offered up its disapproval of the army's stragglers, Mayor James Calhoun declared a citywide day of fasting and prayer, asking for God to spare them. "The voices of prayer are heard in every church in the city," Cyrena Stone noted. Richards listened to a chaplain visiting from the Army of Northern Virginia who preached from a pulpit in uniform and with a "pistol in his belt." The supplicant voices tried to rise above the distant metallic crash of the cannon. The following day Mary Mallard wrote, "I trust the prayers offered yesterday will be answered, and our city spared."

Rumors of victory and defeat swept back and forth through the town. It was said that "Johnston had turned upon the Yankees, and they were retreating as fast as they could." Newspapers assured, "Atlanta will never be taken by our ruthless invaders." In the absence of reliable information, prayers and such boasts raised the hopes of some among the thousands still in town that "all will yet be well."

Cyrena Stone was certain, though, that "the truth is kept from us." Watching the troops rushing through town, the stragglers, deserters, wounded, and dead arriving, and the despondent militiamen "dressed to kill" in their starched shirts and bowlers, carrying umbrellas and walking sticks, literally cannon fodder marching in wavering lines to the front, Cyrena Stone did not know what to believe. Like all in the city, no matter what their allegiance, she was tossed about like a boat awash on a stormy sea, its sails long blown out. Her spirits rose steadily with the news of Sherman's forward advance, but then "some terrible news will come to crush them." She feared that "this suspense and anxiety [will] take away our reason."

MANY CIVILIANS, ASTOUNDINGLY, had yet to lose their naivety about the dangers of war. Northern soldiers looked on in amazement as parties of women stood together on the tops of the ridges above Marietta from where they showered down curses upon the "vile Yankees." Sharpshooters would have no trouble dropping them, though one Union officer, feeling "a sort of admiration" for such brazen defiance, was sure nobody in his lines "would attempt deliberately to shoot" the women. Despite his faith in his men, battlefield tourists did die. Nonetheless, Sallie Clayton, who had breathed a sigh of relief when her viewing party had sped away from the Chattanooga battlefield, learned that from Kennesaw Mountain there was to be had "a finer view of [the armies] than at Missionary Ridge." She regretted that after "a party of us began to make preparations to go on another viewing expedition," orders went out banning civilian visits when "another civilian was added to the list of those who had been killed."

She was fortunate to have stayed away. On the morning of June 10, Sherman began his advance on the Kennesaw line. That day, the clouds again unleashed intense rain storms, which continued almost without let up through most of mid-June. Sherman sent his three armies "to develop the enemy's position and strength, and so draw artillery fire from his entrenched works." He expected it wouldn't take long before the works were evacuated. The outmanned Johnston would, he trusted, back away again.

Instead, in the rain, the Yankees managed a forward advance of only three miles over the next two weeks. Men who had during the previous month's fighting covered ground on some days as quickly as a soldier could charge ahead while firing his rifle now had to grind out each foot in the mud. A war of attrition began.

FOUR DAYS INTO THE drive on the Kennesaw Ridge line, the sun broke through the clouds. Sherman came out to make a personal reconnaissance of the field. In the late morning, he peered through his glass up at a group of Confederates standing indifferent to his artillery's prowess in the open on the top of the Pine Mountain salient in their line. "How saucy they are!" he spat. He told an officer in the battery nearest him to make the Pine Mountain party jump. He didn't know that gathering amounted to much of the Army of Tennessee's top brass, including Generals Johnston, William Hardee, and Leonidas Polk, the "Fighting Bishop." Polk had won many soldiers to his religious cause in the Army of Tennessee, even baptizing Generals Johnston and Hood in the field. Sherman closed his glass and turned away as the Union battery sent three successive, three-inch-solid shots screaming from a Parrott gun a third of a mile up toward the men on Pine Mountain. The first projectile scattered nearly all the men. General Polk, though, refused to take cover. Instead, he walked to the very edge of the hilltop and crossed his arms while gazing down on the valley below. A second shell flew up. Somebody shouted in horror, "General Polk is killed!" In Atlanta, the *Appeal* reported the following day that the direct hit had struck Polk's "right arm and passed through his body, severing the spinal column and almost tearing off both arms. He fell backwards and expired immediately."

His mangled body was brought back to Atlanta, where his death turned into an event of religious and patriotic grieving on a citywide scale. For hours mourners filed passed his bloodless, flower-encased body lying in state in Saint Luke's Church.

JAMES CALHOUN AND HIS FAMILY attended Polk's funeral and then returned home. He had seen enough. The mayor helped with the packing and then sent all of them, including his grievously wounded son Lowndes, to his wife's family plantation sixty-five miles south in Thomaston, Georgia. He gave his slaves a choice about their own future. About thirty went north toward freedom or disappeared into the growing shantytown on Atlanta's outskirts, while twenty traveled south with the family. Watching the cars depart from Atlanta with all those most dear to him, James Calhoun understood he was seeing the end of the world he had built up over the course of nearly forty years since riding out as a destitute teen from the Calhoun Settlement. He returned to City Hall to do what he could to save his dying city.

THE RAIN RESUMED AS THE Union forces moved on three fronts toward Marietta. Sherman's expectations for a quick sweep of the Confederates from the Kennesaw Ridge line proved wildly optimistic. The slog through the driving rain and mud went on for days and then weeks. During the fierce, close in fighting at the southwestern end of the lines, A. J. Neal waged an intense artillery duel from behind his lines and then leveled his guns against a charging Yankee line. His cannon fire drove back the enemy, who came close enough to leave their bodies in stacks on the outer walls of the breastworks. Bullets had flown so thickly and accurately that after the battle he counted thirty-one holes through the regimental flag still flying over the parapet. The flagstaff, though "not much larger than my thumb," was hit seven times. The horizontal storm of lead through the gun embrasures, as intense as the rain falling from above, riddled and splintered anything to the rear—wagons, canteens, tents. "To look one moment over the works," he penned in astonishment afterwards, "was to draw one hundred bullets around your head." Even his hat was pierced. Large trees were shattered by balls. He couldn't resist counting the lead in the remnants of one "little sapling." He picked out around eighty bullets.

Frustrated that retreats invariably followed "victories," Neal regretted he was not battling Grant in Virginia. All hammer, Grant rammed his huge army against Confederate fortifications relentlessly and head-on, losing men by the thousands, day after day, with almost no gain to show for the casualties. The foxlike "Sherman," Neal fumed, "will not give us a chance." The Yankees were "outgeneraling" the Georgia defenders and taking ground "by mere weight of numbers." The Confederates never broke, never gave up a line without determining of their own accord to retreat to a more defensible location. Neal hoped for a smash up collision between the two armies. "When [Sherman] marches his men up to the assault, God have mercy on the poor wretches." Neal and his comrades, "never more sanguine and confident of success," would show no such pity.

AFTER A WEEK AND A half of steady fighting, Johnston drew back from both his eastern and western salients at Brush and Lost mountains. The Union forces gained the heights and began firing down on the Confederate lines, forcing them to pull back further still to the Kennesaw Mountain line. There, Johnston could concentrate his troops' firepower within eight tight miles of heavily fortified trenches covering Kennesaw Mountain and extending to the south around Marietta and the Western & Atlantic tracks. As the first rays of the sun broke through the clouds on June 22, the men on both sides delighted in the return of sunshine that began drying out the mud they had lived in for nearly the entire month. The torrential rain and life lived continuously in muddy, blood-drenched trenches, where excrement fouled the water, had caused far more casualties from sickness than had flying lead and exploding shells. However, with the return of the sun, Sherman determined to challenge the heights of Johnston's Kennesaw stronghold. Despite his vow not to run directly against the Southerners' "immense line of works," by June 26, he had grown impatient with the slow grind of a war of attrition. So Sherman changed his mind. "We must attack direct or turn the position," he decided. The Union attack began at dawn the following day.

On the morning of June 27, "one of the hottest and longest days of the year," soon topping 110 degrees in the shade, at three different points along the ridgeline, after a blistering artillery barrage on the

Confederate defenses, blue-clad soldiers moved out of the cover of woods, rifle pits, and trenches and began their uphill charge. The lines broke apart as the men, by the tens of thousands, clambered over rocks and ran up the open slopes. The very air they moved through erupted, so full of bullets that they felt, remarked one soldier, as if they were "moving . . . against a heavy rain or sleet storm." Those who survived leaped into the rebel forward posts or took cover behind rocks and tree stumps or hugged the ground. A few squeezed through the abatis of sharpened trees and drove on toward the Confederate lines. They scrambled over and into the trenches, where they were shot down or killed, fighting gun butt to gun butt, or captured. The rebels threw everything they had at the Yankees, even rolling boulders down the hillsides. The result for Sherman's men was the type of carnage they had not known until that day.

The worst fighting took place during this endless day at the Dead Angle salient on Cheatham's Hill, as it was known forever after because of the stand made there by Gen. Benjamin Franklin Cheatham's division. In the thick of it, Tennessee private Sam Watkins and his mates killed, he was sure, between twenty and a hundred men each. To kill, "all that was necessary was to load and shoot." Yankees climbing the parapets were shot down, and those who followed behind climbed on the fallen bodies and were shot down in turn. The ground in front of Watkins was "piled up with one solid mass of dead and wounded Yankees . . . in some places . . . like cord wood, twelve deep." The two sides stalemated, but the firing continued so hot gun barrels glowed red, keeping men hugging the ground or at their gun embrasures for three days of continuous fighting. The woods where many dead and wounded lay caught fire. Watkins could hear the screams of the men when they saw the approaching flames—until the fire silenced their pleas for help. In the sun-baked, fire-scorched air, "a stench, so sickening as to nauseate the whole of both armies, arose from the decaying bodies of the dead left lying on the field."

Two of the Union attacks left hundreds of men to be buried, yet did not dislodge the defenders. A brigade under Gen. John M. Schofield's Army of the Ohio, though, broke through against minor opposition at the left fringes of the rebel line. They swiftly crossed around Johnston's flank and to the south, where they secured a position closer to the Chattahoochee than the drawn-in left side of Johnston's army. With his rail line and back door threatened once more, the Confederate general again had no choice. By July 2, the Army of

Tennessee had left its ridgeline redoubt and withdrawn back toward the Chattahoochee.

Four days later, T. Holliday, the Wilkes County militiaman, was in the fight for the first time. The militia moved forward to help fortify and hold the lines while Johnston's main army drew back. The barely trained men were learning in the unforgiving school of war to hunker down as the minié balls from sharpshooters raked the earthworks, and cannon balls flew overhead. "To have to gain honor by facing bullets and cannon balls doesn't pay very well," Holliday protested. "Some of the boys think we will all be at home soon but I will believe it when I get" there. On July 8, the Union army had a bridgehead on the far side of the Chattahoochee. The last major barrier before Atlanta had fallen.

SHERMAN HAD FLANKED Johnston's lines again. The price his men paid was terrible and perhaps unnecessary: The Northerners suffered 3,000 casualties in the June 27 Kennesaw battles; Johnston counted only 750 men killed, wounded, or captured. Entire Union brigades were wiped out, often with few corresponding casualties on the Southern side of the lines. After reviewing the condition of his badly mauled Army of the Cumberland, Gen. George Thomas warned Sherman that "one or two more such assaults would use up this army."

Sherman wrote his wife on the last day of June to tell her the news that he would shortly be across the Chattahoochee, an unprecedentedly swift and deep advance through enemy territory. But he, too, was appalled by the violence he herded over the landscape before him. He feared "the whole world [might] start at the awful amount of death and destruction that now stalks abroad." Killing and death had become as much a part of the North Georgia landscape as wood ticks and loblolly pine. He confessed that a certain callousness had taken hold of him. "I begin to regard the death and mangling of a couple thousand men as a small affair, a kind of morning dash." What truly appalled him was that even now "the worst of the war is not yet begun." Nonetheless, "the work [has] progressed and I see no signs of a remission till one or both of the armies are destroyed."

ATLANTA ITSELF, THE GREAT GOAL, was now within eyeshot. Lt. Henry D. Stanley, a quartermaster from Farmington, Connecticut,

drove his wagons behind the Yankee army's advance. In a free moment, he scrambled up two hills and climbed three trees before having
"the satisfaction of . . . seeing what I had so long been looking for. In
the distance and directly in front I saw the eastern portion of the coveted city for which 130,000 men are fighting; part to capture and part
to protect." He was surprised to see "a great many trees in the city
which of course hid most of the buildings from view." From his tree-
top perch, he could "distinguish a brick from a wooden house. I also
saw what I suppose to be the Arsenal. . . . I could also see the church
steeples." He sat in the gnarled tree "looking as hard as possible toward
A[tlanta] and wondering what the inhabitants were thinking of."

IT WAS NO SECRET: The people were thinking about Sherman's army.
On July 5, the *Southern Confederacy* insisted, "Atlanta will not and
cannot be abandoned." Confederate officials made clear, however, that
the city would likely fall. That day, they removed the arsenal's machinery, as well as the Confederate Quartermaster Department and
most of the fair grounds hospital complex's supplies and patients, to
more secure locations in Macon, Columbus, and Augusta. When the
"order came to remove all hospitals," Mary Mallard no longer hesitated. It was time to go. She threw her things together and ran to the
car shed. A few days later took up a new residence in Augusta.

The scramble to get out was now on. The city, recorded Richards
on July 10, had been "in a complete swarm" for days now. He and his
wife decided "to stay at home, Yankees or no Yankees." Despite the "terrible tales of them," he did not feel threatened or even have the same
hatred of all things Northern that had inflamed him for so long. "I
don't think they are as bad as they are said to be." He noted that many
others concurred and intended "to remain in the city if the enemy gets
possession."

The teen socialite Sallie Clayton's family wanted to leave. They
packed up whatever valuables they could, but then tragedy struck. The
entire family would have moved out of their big house opposite City
Hall, but Sallie's four sisters fell gravely ill. Gussie, the youngest and her
closest companion, had typhoid fever. Her "worn-out" parents needed
to stay home with their sick children, "happen what may." Sallie left
for the tranquility of an uncle's Alabama plantation.

At her home across the Five Points on Houston Street, Cyrena
Stone looked around her. All her white neighbors were gone. With

artillery crashing just a few miles away, she took a moment to note, I "am alone on the hill." Friends came to her and urged her to join the exodus. But, she insisted, "this is my home, & I wish to protect it if possible." She understood, however, that "there may be no battle here. If not I am safe; if there is one, where is any safety?"

# THE THIEF IN
# THE GLOAMING

By night there is fear in the City,
Through the darkness a star soareth on;
There's a scream that screams up to the zenith,
Then the poise of a meteor lone—
Lighting far the pale fright of the faces,
And downward the coming is seen;
Then the rush, and the burst, and the havoc,
And wails and shrieks between.

It comes like the thief in the gloaming;
It comes, and none may foretell
The place of the coming—the glaring;
They live in a sleepless spell
That wizens, and withers, and whitens;
It ages the young, and the bloom
Of the maiden is ashes of roses—

The Swamp Angel broods in his gloom.
    —Herman Melville, "The Swamp Angel"

# CHAPTER 21

# A PERFECT
# SHELL

THE MINERAL-GREEN WATER of the Chattahoochee River flowed sluggish and silty beneath the mid-July sun, still running about waist high from the heavy June rains. The longest river through the largest eastern state, the Chattahoochee spills cold water off the Appalachian Mountains in the northeast in a slanting course past Atlanta before making a beeline south along the Alabama border to join the Flint River at the Florida border and flow out to the Gulf of Mexico via the Apalachicola. With stone outcroppings and sandbars around Atlanta, it was not navigable except for small craft such as the native populations once used for their local commerce over thousands of years prior to their removal. Its many creek tributaries powered mills along their banks, and bountiful crops grew out of the river's bottomlands, that is, until the local millers and farmers fled before the approaching war. Seven vacant granite spires pointed skyward out of the riverbed in a line, bank to bank. The voids between the towering piers marked where the Western & Atlantic Railroad bridge, its ruins now lying tangled below on the river bottom, once perched. The rearguard Confederates had torched the bridge on July 9 before joining the rest of the army in its present position along the high southeastern banks and the outer works of Atlanta itself. At the back of the rebel fortifications, trainloads of munitions smoked up from Atlanta and then chugged backwards with the wounded over the six miles through the cuts and rises to the downtown rail yards. Along the northwestern riverbank stretched the Yankee lines. For the most part, William

Tecumseh Sherman's 106,000 veteran soldiers, perhaps 90,000 of them ready to fight, breathed easy while keeping their heads below the parapets and out of sharpshooters' sights. As a token of war, though, an occasional cannon crash or the crack of a sharpshooter's rifle from behind each army's red clay ramparts sent a chunk of metal whistling across the river, raising smoke, red dust, and sometimes a death cry within the enemy's fortifications.

Although Sherman's men had crossed the river fifteen miles above here near the town of Roswell and a raiding party was on its way to cut the rail line southwest of Atlanta at the Alabama border, for now he had decided not to push further against the main body of the 44,000 or so hardened rebel soldiers plus another 5,000 militiamen on the opposite bank. He had surveyed the works he'd need to assault— and that after fording the river, which ran anywhere from fifty to three hundred yards wide—and judged them "the best line of field intrenchments I have ever seen." After the debacle at Kennesaw Mountain, he preferred a return to his effective, if inglorious, flanking operations. He wasn't idle. Shortly he would begin wheeling his armies over the river, he telegraphed Washington, "to make a circuit [of Atlanta], destroying all its railroads," severing it from the Confederacy and rendering it an untenable base for the army within.

Ignoring his terrible casualties—already more than 15,000 men to date—and multiple failed assaults on impregnable rebel defenses, he took time to write a long letter to his friend, the commanding general in Virginia, Ulysses Grant, concluding that his strategy to date had "been rather cautious than bold." Unlike Grant, though, he had tangible successes to show. He was ninety-eight miles from his starting point in Dalton; for every man he had lost, he had taken one in return from an army far less able to sustain such attrition; most importantly, he had kept the Confederates opposite him pinned down and unable to send reinforcements to Virginia. But the war was far from won. Atlanta was still "a hard nut to handle," he admitted. The enemy, he knew, could still dart out and bloody him at any moment. "These fellows fight like Devils & Indians combined," he wrote his wife in grudging admiration, "and it calls for all my cunning & strength."

Within the shelter of the Confederate fortifications, T. Holliday was now a hardened militiaman after a month's baptism under fire. The slight, blond-haired, and squinty-eyed plantation owner was no longer without a gun; he now carried a repeating rifle and ammunition recovered from dead Yankees. He wrote his wife, Lizzie, at home in Wilkes County near the South Carolina border to tell her he had grown accustomed to the strangeness of battlefield life. Nothing about war shocked or even disturbed him any longer. He marched with indifference past blasted heaps that once were men, farms, and wagons and curled up on the ground to a metallic lullaby. "I can lie down under the mouth of a cannon and go fast asleep," he boasted. On duty beside the river, he would have preferred a hook and bait in place "of gun and my Yankee physic box hung to my side." Within it, though, he had "40 blue pills to administer to some patient of the Yank tribe. I hope that they may have the effect of rendering him unhealthy."

His enthusiasm for the cause remained strong. He hoped only "to get the Yanks out of Georgia and then come home in peace, yes, lasting peace; peace that my children can say that my father helped to obtain. I want it said by them in years yet to come that my father fought for my liberty." Many of his comrades in arms no longer shared his conviction. After battling to hold their lines all day beneath the torrid sun, only to fall back sleepless through the night to entrench new positions, day after day, Holliday admitted, "Hundreds are deserting every day and a great many declare that they will not go beyond Atlanta." He waited for the "fool" Gen. Joseph Johnston to go on the offensive while the Southerners still had a fighting chance. His army, Holliday contended, "is stronger to-day than it will be to-morrow." Despite the attrition, the cotton farmer believed his army could win. "The soldiers all seem to be of one mind and that is that we can whip the Yanks if Johnston would fight them."

Together with the "ditching and bullets and shells," he had but one complaint to share about his newfound life as a soldier: there was not enough to eat. He must have laughed when he wrote, "There seems to be some property in the water that has a tendency to give a man a good appetite. One that is sufficient to eat maggots and meal without sifting and no complaint laid only in one respect and that is that there is not enough of it."


NOT FAR FROM THAT SPOT, thoughts about food also gnawed at Confederate artillery captain A. J. Neal. He was exhausted like all the men after sixty-eight straight days of "continuous marching, fighting and entrenching." The men around him looked hangdog. They were losing teeth to scurvy and had taken to cooking up "polk, potato tops, May pop vines, kurlip weed, lambs quarter, thistle, and a hundred kinds of weeds I always thought poison." His boys called it "long forage," and in a note to his sister, he had to agree, "It beats nothing."

The current lull in fighting made him witness to one of war's more extraordinary sights. He eyed his opponents across the way in Gen. Joseph Hooker's Union army division. "Any of us would do anything to destroy the other," none would deny, but there before him were soldiers from both sides scrambling down the pine-shrouded banks to emerge at the river's edge, where they bathed without fear across from each other in the refreshing mountain water. Even General Sherman stripped bare and waded into the Chattahoochee in plain sight at one point.

The enemies, most of them not much older than boys, frolicked along the banks, ridding themselves of months of filth and cooling off bug bites. They called out to each other, taunted one another, and even serenaded the opposing camp with derisive songs. It wasn't long before many had laid aside their guns and waded out into the river. There they bartered canteens, hats, whisky, Northern supplies of coffee, and Southern tobacco. Boyish fraternity and commerce temporarily trumped the sectional rancor and stopped the violence of fratricidal war. Neal watched men in blue and butternut uniforms who "walk[ed] together] along the river banks talking as friendly and courteously as if to old acquaintances." Nobody dared break up the signs of enduring American fraternity by shooting. When officers came around and ordered the men back to their posts, they ducked away into the brush along the banks but left promising to shoot over their opponents' heads if forced to skirmish.

The easygoing meetings among the warring enemies did not surprise Charles F. Morse, in Hooker's Corps opposite Neal's battery. The Harvard-educated Second Massachusetts Infantry lieutenant colonel felt no hatred for the Southern men he had come to drive from the field and kill, if need be. "When we fight," he wrote his family in Cambridge on July 15, "we fight to crush the rebellion and break the power of the rebel armies, not against these men as individuals."

THUS IT WAS THAT THREE DAYS LATER, as Sam Watkins stood picket next to Neal's battery near the riverside, he wasn't surprised to hear a Yankee sing out from the other bank. "Johnny, O Johnny, O Johnny Reb," came a voice from Hooker's Corps.

A man near the Tennessee private in Gen. George Maney's brigade of Gen. Benjamin Franklin Cheatham's division answered, "What do you want?"

The Union soldier proceeded to tell him that their general, Joseph Johnston, "is relieved and Hood appointed in his place." He taunted, "You are whipped, aren't you?"

The Southern soldier refused to believe him. "You are a liar," he shouted and threatened to shoot the "lying Yankee galloot."

The affronted Northerner called back, "That's more than I will stand." He challenged the Southerner, "if the others will hands off," to fight a duel right there. The two men stepped out onto the banks across the river from each other. Watkins watched as each fired off seven rounds until the Confederate fell, "pierced through the heart."

THE YANK HAD NOT only shot straight; he spoke the truth. On the previous night, General Johnston had been in his new headquarters, a Marietta road house where the young girl Sarah Huff had watched a neighbor run a wholesale slave yard before he fled. A quarter mile back toward Atlanta, her mother sat out on her porch with some soldiers while others strolled in her gardens. The moon hung silver and near full in the hazy night sky, illuminating all around them in a magical, melancholy white light. A dance was on outside the headquarters house; the officers and their ladies had come out from the city to enjoy the evening. Sarah's mother listened in the distance as a military band played "Dixie" and other tunes. She thought the music on that night "the sweetest she ever heard." Sarah wondered why several soldiers at her house seemed to be crying.

Those men, like many in the Army of Tennessee, loved their commanding officer. They knew that while outside headquarters up the road all was gaiety, inside Gen. Joe Johnston was being relieved of his command. He had received a telegraph from Confederate president Jefferson Davis condemning his failure "to arrest the advance of the enemy to the vicinity of Atlanta" and relaying his lack of "confidence that you can defeat or repel him."

The downcast Johnston was stunned by the transfer of command. He should not have been. A short while later, Gen. John Bell Hood, just thirty-three years old, a veteran field officer little experienced in handling a large army, got his wish: Davis had chosen him to replace Johnston as commander of the Army of Tennessee.

FOUR DAYS EARLIER, Braxton Bragg had returned from Richmond to visit the army he had left in disgrace six months earlier. He came this time as Davis's chief of staff. The president had dispatched him to confer with Johnston to see if he could be made to go on the offensive and save Atlanta—and with it the Confederacy. Bragg's mission was largely predetermined. Johnston had telegraphed Davis on the evening of July 16 that as long as he was so vastly outnumbered, he was intent on continuing his strategy of waiting out the enemy, preserving his army while "watch[ing] for an opportunity to fight to advantage." Bragg's charge became helping select Johnston's successor.

General Hood met with Bragg shortly after he arrived and provided him with a memorandum for President Davis. The fighting West Pointer, his eyes ablaze for battle and perhaps with the searing pain of his amputation, declared that the only way to stop Sherman was to "attack him, even if we should have to recross the river to do so." Hood told Bragg to tell the president that he had "so often urged that we should force the enemy to give us battle as to almost be regarded as reckless" by his fellow officers. He viewed the failure to fight it out "many miles north of our present position" as "a great misfortune to our country." The crusader Hood might be reckless, but Davis concurred wholeheartedly with his assessment. In telegraphing word of his elevation on the night of July 17, the president urged the new leader of his army, which had been driven back deep into the heart of Dixie, "Be wary no less than bold," but the time for caution had passed. He expected Hood to move promptly to the attack.

A. J. Neal knew something was afoot with General Bragg's visit, even before the "woefully outgeneraled" Johnston's removal had been announced to the army. "I do pray," Neal wrote that day while awaiting word, "we may never move with our faces turned southward again."

THAT VERY DAY, five hundred miles to the north, two peace advocates from the Union side passed through the battle lines between the armies of Generals Ulysses S. Grant and Robert E. Lee in Virginia, traveling with President Abraham Lincoln's permission though not his official support. They reached Richmond where, in the evening, they met an irascible Jefferson Davis and his secretary of state, Judah Benjamin, in Benjamin's office. The pair of peace emissaries carried the same reconstruction terms Lincoln had offered the seceding states six months before. Except for the abolition of slavery, Lincoln's terms would forgive and forget the previous years of secession and bloodshed, providing for reunification of the states in a renewed federal union, emancipation throughout the United States and its territories, and amnesty for the rebels.

Davis's anger boiled up as he listened. He finally exploded. They were not criminals, he informed the visitors, but patriots battling for their freedom. "We are fighting for INDEPENDENCE," he declared, "and that, or extermination, we will have. . . . You may 'emancipate' every negro in the Confederacy, but *we will be free*." He must have been thinking about Johnston and Hood absorbing the news of the transfer of command on the very outskirts of Atlanta when he vowed, "We will govern ourselves . . . if we have to see every Southern plantation sacked, and every Southern city in flames."

WORD THAT JOHNSTON WAS GONE—he departed town with his wife by train soon after losing his command—and "Old Peg Leg," as the soldiers styled Hood, had taken his place reached Atlanta immediately. The storekeeper Samuel Richards had managed to remain with his pressman's home defense company and free of orders to report to the lines. With the ferocious former provost marshal Col. George Washington Lee now at Georgia state militia headquarters in Macon, in the present crisis few men in Atlanta not already in the service felt compelled to report for duty. Thousands of soldiers, militiamen, and stragglers moved about town, making it easy to get lost in the crowd. That seemed likely to change. Richards understood what lay ahead the night Johnston was relieved. He knew, he penned, there would be "a fight before Atlanta is given up, as Hood is said to be a fighting man, if he *has* only one leg."

The news ran like electricity through the remaining residents. The streets, reported a newspaper correspondent, were "crowded with wagons piled high with household effects, and every train of cars, freight or otherwise, was loaded to capacity with refugees struggling to leave the city." The editor of the *Southern Confederacy* had already packed his bags but didn't hesitate to urge readers to "exercise . . . a little philosophy and reason. . . . The chances are in many instances that removal may not be necessary at all."

The city council exercised itself a little as advised and quickly decided it was time to go. The members met for the last time the next day and asked Mayor James Calhoun to prepare to send city records, mules, and fire engines out of the city. The city police force, never able to bring order to the streets in any case, effectively ceased to exist. The courts halted all proceedings. Even churches, except Trinity Methodist, kept open by army chaplain Henry Lay, and the Roman Catholic Church of the Immaculate Conception under Father Thomas O'Reilly, shuttered their doors. Mayor Calhoun still had men who remained in his fire departments, exempted by his orders from military service, and he organized any other home guards he could find to patrol the streets. He had little else at his command with which to manage a much diminished and nearly unrecognizable city of women, children, old men, bondsmen, and former slaves, as well as the wounded thousands, supply corps, sutlers, and increasing numbers of deserters and stragglers of a battered army on its outskirts.

Calhoun visited neighboring families to offer them what assistance he could. His brother Ezekiel lay in bed at home, recovering from the army's most common, debilitating, and sometimes deadly ailment, the bloody flux, or dysentery, a parasitic infection acquired during his stint as a regimental surgeon with the Sixtieth Georgia outside Savannah. He was too weak to leave town even if he wanted to. In fact, he intended to remain with his brother.

James Calhoun also looked in on the Claytons at their big house across from City Hall. The situation there was alarming. The first floor served as a hospital for four of the Clayton girls, Julia, Mary, Kate, and Gussie, gravely sick with typhoid fever. (Sallie and her sister Caro were now safely in the Alabama countryside.) They likely contracted the bacterial infection drinking the fouled Atlanta water. Their worried parents dosed the patients with quinine and pepper tea, hoping they'd sweat the infection out. Three of the girls, after several days and nights of tremors and delirium, were now well enough to sit up. Not fifteen-year-old Gussie. She may have contracted the disease during her frequent visits to bring food and drink to the army hospital sick wards. Severe fever and stomach cramps tortured the fifteen-year-old. A Confederate army surgeon broke away from his around-the-clock duties to the wounded being off-loaded at the car shed to check in on her. After his examination, he told her stricken parents that "all was being done that could be."

CALHOUN'S FEVERISH CITY HAD its own brand of infection. People rose before dawn after barely sleeping, eager for news from the previous night. They remained jumpy all day, easily startled by the roll of carriage wheels or the clatter of wagons over the stones of the street. The slap of a fallen bale or a box hitting the floor sent passersby scurrying in panic. People wondered whether any sudden noise was a shell falling on some part of town. And, always, there were the rumors: "The news," according to an Augusta newspaper's frontline correspondent, "comes in shoals of falsehood, barely sprinkled with fact." Atlanta, he witnessed, had become "a perfect shell." The booming of the guns on the horizon hollowed it out, though thousands remained hidden within. "Houses are deserted. Gardens are left to their fate." The city had become an armed camp, even as the arsenal, factories, commissaries, and hospitals moved to Macon and the railroads ceased to run for anybody outside the military. "No place," wrote the reporter, "is quiet or uninvaded by the stir of war." Wagons lined the streets, soldiers slept in gardens and on the sidewalks, and the City Park and any available floor space became hospital wards, while surgeons operating on commandeered porches and makeshift tables sawed off the wounded soldiers' destroyed limbs, tossing the amputated leg or arm aside.

Fear of a rapacious enemy stalked the city, though the federals remained outside its boundaries. Atlanta's present invaders were the hundreds of men slinking away from the fighting. The uproar and chaos within the city provided easy cover for robbers who smashed open and looted houses, depots, and stores in the darkness. "Cavalry robbers" broke into nearly every shop in the Five Points on the night of July 21 and "stole everything that they took a fancy to," Samuel Richards discovered the next morning. His store was "stripped" of all its paper and cash on hand. A. J. Neal rode across the city from end to end that same night. He felt "sad to witness the ruin and destruction of the place." Army stragglers and hungry residents were smashing open and looting stores, leaving "scattered things over the streets promiscuously." He noted the crush of people and "the same noise and bustle on Whitehall, but instead of thrift and industry and prosperity it is hurried scramble to get away, fleeing from the wrath to come."

Neal looked over the riot in the Five Points and turned away from the shameful scene in disgust. He scorned Atlanta, the city where his parents, now fled to their Pike County plantation, had built their charming dream palace. He considered the Gate City's fate, in a measure, divine justice. "If Soddom [sic] deserved the fate that befell it," he proclaimed, "Atlanta will not be unjustly punished for since this war commenced it has grown to be the great capital place of corruption in official and private circles. While I regret the loss of Atlanta . . . I can scarcely regret that the nest of speculators, thieves, etc., is broken up."

Many others, of course, had long shared his disdain for the upstart cosmopolitan city; with "its detestable hotels, Jews and high prices," wrote the Augusta reporter at about the same time Neal surveyed Atlanta's collapse, "there has seemed little good in it." However, the correspondent felt only pity now for the expiring metropolis, a "city . . . growing in importance and population, that . . . has gradually become the theatre of events in this department, the reservoir of every species of enterprise, until it had reached a census of fifty thousand souls, and a versatility of society and interest which comprehended every class, from the wealthy refugee and native to the most squalid of outcasts, and every trade from the eminent journalist to the least consequential artisan of apple beer and peanuts." He called for open-mindedness in his readers: "Let any, I say, reflect upon these metropolitan features, and he will be ready to believe what I assure you is the truth, that no city has afforded so much health, pleasure and occupation as Atlanta." The great, growing, and all-welcoming Gate City, made by war, now belonged to the war.

The reporter declared boldly, though, that all was not yet lost. Reviewing the implications of Hood's replacement of Johnston, he wrote, "If it means anything it must mean this: Atlanta will not be given up without a fight."

ALONE IN HER HILLTOP HOUSE, Cyrena Stone could hear beneath the booming guns the commotion and falsetto shattering of glass in the Five Points down the hill from her. She now had the company of Robert (Yancey) Webster, the money-changing barber, and his wife, Bess. Stone sheltered the black couple in her barn, where they had taken refuge. They were no longer safe in their "cozy home . . . filled with many comforts" a few hundred feet from Stone's property. A few nights earlier, soldiers had burst through their door "pretending to search for runaway negroes." Clearly aware of Webster's wealth, they put pistols to the couple's throats, turned the house upside down, and took "everything of value they had—silk dresses—jewelry, watches & spoons." While the men walked away with their stolen booty, Webster raced to alert some cavalry who passed nearby. "They were negroes," a sympathetic Stone penned, so his appeals for help were "in vain."

She listened to the guns drawing closer to her house. "The clash of arms sounded so near" Stone thought Union army soldiers might reach her property at any moment. Confederate soldiers who moved by told her they did "not expect to make a stand here." Few defenders filled the earthworks in front of her house. The way seemed open to Sherman, or so she "hoped each day & night, until the last has come & gone," yet her prayers went unanswered. Instead, the cautious Sherman appeared sure to choose to "wait until breastworks are erected, over which brave men must march on to death—before victory." She grasped more clearly than most what lay ahead.

HOOD AWOKE ON THE morning of July 18 in command of an army in a desperate but well-fortified position. He seemed to have few options available to shift his army from its defensive posture to an aggressive fight. Sherman had begun his grand wheel to his left around Atlanta the day before. Gen. James B. McPherson had crossed most of his men in the Army of the Tennessee over the Chattahoochee at Roswell, and they now started to move eastward to strike the Georgia Railroad between Decatur and the distant hump of Stone Mountain. Hood would shortly learn the distressing news that a Union raiding party far to the southwest of Atlanta had already torn up the Montgomery & West Point Railroad at Opelika, cutting off hope for additional reinforcements from Alabama. With McPherson on the Georgia railroad, three of the four rail links that made Atlanta the transportation hub of the Lower South and the citadel of the Confederacy would be broken. The Macon & Western remained the last iron lifeline between Atlanta and the rest of the rebel world. Atlanta's Confederates defended an all but isolated island fortress.

Atlanta was now more an object of Confederate prayers than the living heart of the Confederate nation, but that symbolism mattered immensely to the nation's survival. So, too, did halting Sherman's army from tearing beyond Atlanta and further through Georgia. If unimpeded, his horde of 100,000 plus could turn south and west toward Mobile and Montgomery, en route freeing the 30,000 Union prisoners now held on a few acres under the broiling sun in Andersonville about one hundred miles south of Atlanta. That army unchecked could slice apart the Lower South, devastating its agricultural heartland and depriving the Confederacy of its few remaining military industrial resources. Sherman would deliver a lethal blow to the last, best hope for Southern freedom.

Despite Hood's numeric disadvantages, he had to attack and deliver a blow sufficient to drive Sherman back across the Chattahoochee River. Once there, Hood could move on Sherman's one rail line to cut his armies off from their supply bases. The fighting general was one to deliver slashing blows, and the ponderous and overstretched Yankee army, if struck in a vulnerable place, could bleed out its strength within the hostile rebel territory. A bold and effective attack might turn all those apparent federal victories into a historic, devastating defeat. An unexpected stroke of luck opened up the very opportunity Hood sought.

Scouts reported to Hood that in sending his forces sweeping out in a grand fiery wheel around the city's eastern flanks on July 18 and 19, Sherman had inadvertently allowed a gap to spread between his lines. The vanguard of McPherson's army swung far to the east toward Decatur, with Gen. John M. Schofield's Army of the Ohio following inside it to the east, while Gen. George Thomas crossed his Army of the Cumberland over the Chattahoochee at Paces Ferry and then marched in a more direct southern line via Buckhead toward Atlanta. Sherman had intended for his armies to move in concentric circles, their flanks overlapping and remaining in contact, leaving their wings protected and ready to move quickly to reinforce their neighboring armies if attacked. However, Atlanta's landscape deceived. Where its approaches appeared level except for a few small humps on the plateau, the country all around it remained rolling and thickly forested. The creeks cut deep and ran crooked. Despite the city's growth and the extension of its suburbs, roads were few, narrow, and enclosed by woods and dense undergrowth that could shelter an attacker. A commander could order an attack or prepare a defense, but neither attacker nor defender could anticipate precisely the place or the time of battle. And now the scouts informed Hood that a gaping hole had opened between Thomas's left and Schofield's right wings, leaving the Army of the Cumberland especially vulnerable as it felt its way south through the field. This was a strategic mistake on Sherman's part, which the younger general *had* to try to exploit.

Thomas's men, a force of nearly 60,000, were moving through Buckhead. With his far smaller numbers, Hood needed to surprise the Yankees. He intended to strike them immediately after they crossed the east-west-running Peachtree Creek, just three miles from Atlanta, before they had time to throw up breastworks. A. J. Neal's battery was one of those in Cheatham's Corps assigned to fire into the gap to the right of Thomas's army, keeping Schofield from rescuing it. Watkins was among Maney's men hiding in the woods while thousands of other rebel troops moved up Howell Mill and Peachtree roads to attack an isolated and vulnerable force. Hood wanted to drive the federals back into the angle formed by the creek, with its steep, deep, and densely overgrown banks, and the Chattahoochee, then smash them in place with enough violence to destroy a major wing in Sherman's army. The attack, designed by Hood overnight on July 19, was set to begin at 1 P.M. the next day.

MCPHERSON WAS THE FLY in the ointment. Unknown to Hood, his swift-traveling 25,000-man army had reached Decatur early that morning, where it met minimal resistance from a small cavalry force. A cautious McPherson began feeling his way tentatively west along the Georgia Railroad and the Decatur Road, soon threatening the approaches to Atlanta itself. Hood learned of the crisis at his Peachtree Road headquarters in mid-morning and ordered his army to shift to his right to hold McPherson back from the city. The clumsily executed movement confused the Confederate ranks. The resulting three-hour delay in assembling the line of attack allowed parts of the thinly spread Yankee lines time to dig in on the south bank of Peachtree Creek. After marching several miles in the sultry weather, though, most of the Northern soldiers relaxed in the open fields near the creek, their arms stacked, drinking coffee and smoking. Even their commanding general felt comfortably certain the rebels remained more than a mile away within their own defenses.

At 4 P.M. a Union soldier had wandered forward beyond his own skirmish line to pick blackberries along a ravine. He looked up to see the sun glinting off the bayonets of a six-deep line of rebels advancing steadily toward him through the woods. He raced past the federal skirmish line, which soon followed him back half a mile to the main line of lightly thrown up entrenchments. The alarm went through the startled Yankee army as Hood's men charged yelling and firing out of the woods. At one point, Neal recounted, the Confederate army approached within fifteen feet of the Yankee works and "could have taken them," but close-in artillery fire drove back the attackers. The fierce fighting beneath a broiling sun raged along Peachtree Creek into the evening.

THE RELENTLESS NOISE OF battle masked something extraordinary taking place on the other side of Atlanta. Moving down the Decatur Road, one of McPherson's batteries arrived within two and a half miles of the Five Points in the early afternoon. The battery commander,

Capt. Francis H. DeGress, stopped, raised his cannons, and fired off three quick rounds of twenty-pound exploding shells into the city, "the first ones of the war," DeGress proudly reported. A signal officer perched in a tree watched the shots explode against some buildings in the center of town.

Inside Atlanta, Henry Lay, the Episcopal bishop of Arkansas, was staying in a large house across from City Hall next to the Trinity Church, where he continued to lead services for troops. Lay was standing on the porch of the house where he was the guest of owner William Solomon. He heard an unearthly whistling coming across the sky, followed by a massive explosion in the square directly in front of City Hall. Other shots fell on the city. One burst near the car shed. Two struck Gussie and Sallie Clayton's old school, an easy target on its prominent hilltop. Flames, perhaps set off by an exploding shell or possibly looters, broke out in a store across from the Richards brothers' shop, gutting several buildings. Atlanta was under fire.

Hood had no choice. He abandoned the attack on Peachtree Creek to move more men into position to halt the Union drive from Decatur. He was not ready, however, to cease attacking.

IN THE FIELD BEFORE Peachtree Creek lay nearly 4,800 Confederates alongside the fewer than 2,000 fallen federals. The wonder, observed Union quartermaster officer Henry Stanley from the Twentieth Connecticut, was how anybody survived such a fight. He drove his wagon down through the Peachtree battlefield after the Confederates pulled back. Tree stumps and shattered limbs showed the fury of the fight that took place there. He saw a live oak, some three feet in diameter, pierced straight through by a three-inch shell "as though it had been a straw." He counted fifty or more balls deep in the bark of tree stumps. He could only shake his head. "It seems almost impossible that anyone could live through such a storm."

In his headquarters, General Sherman was disappointed that McPherson had once again not forged ahead after encountering such light opposition along the Decatur Road, but he was delighted with the day's accomplishments. He reported to Washington the next night that his armies were now "within easy cannon-range of the buildings in Atlanta. . . . Our shot passing over [the enemy's] lines will destroy the town." He instructed his batteries within range of the city to "open a careful artillery fire on the town of Atlanta, directing their shots so as to produce the best effect." Hundreds of rounds began falling on the city.

The following day, a shot struck next to Samuel Richards's house, tossing gravel through the windows. His wife and children spent the night bedded down on the floor behind the chimney as a shield against the shells falling throughout the city, while he completed digging a "pit" in his cellar as a bomb shelter. He was now a witness to war. "This," he reflected, "seems to me to be a very barbarous mode of carrying on war, throwing shells among women and children." He was not only witness, though; he was a participant. "City authorities," presumably Mayor Calhoun, put a gun in his hands. Richards stood guard on McDonough Street through much of the night, "carrying a musket for the first time in my life."

# CHAPTER 22

# THE BATTLE
# OF ATLANTA

AFTER THE FIRST SHELL fired by Capt. Francis DeGress's battery burst in City Hall Square, somebody ran into the empty Central Presbyterian Church, on Washington Street facing City Hall, to ring the great steeple bell in warning to the city inhabitants. Hearing other shells exploding nearby, he pulled the bell rope so violently that the clapper cracked the big bronze bell. It never sounded again. Soon, everyone in town knew the cause for the alarm.

A Kentucky cavalry officer coming back through town from the Peachtree Creek battlefield "found the city in a wild state of excitement. Citizens were running in every direction. Terror-stricken women and children went screaming about the streets seeking some avenue of escape from hissing, bursting shells. . . . Perfect pandemonium reigned near the union depot. Trunks, bed clothing and wearing apparel were scattered in every direction. People were striving in every conceivable way to get out of town with their effects."

War had come to town, but even now some people failed to recognize the dangers they faced. A block down Washington Street from Central Presbyterian at the house of Ezekiel Calhoun, one of the doctor's daughters stepped into the street to help a wounded Confederate soldier lying unattended in an ambulance outside her front door. While she aided the wounded man, she heard the report of cannons in the distance. A few seconds later, a shell exploded almost immediately over her head. She raced screaming back into her house. Not long after that, another shell slammed to earth in the yard, burrowing two feet into the ground. When opening fire, Union artillery batteries often launched a long-range projectile carrying a percussion fuse with their first shot. The shells exploded on contact and helped artillery men range their targets from up to two and a half miles off. They then followed up with timed or paper-fuse bombs that exploded overhead, showering lethal shrapnel on the men below. The ranging shells' mechanical percussion fuses, though, were often duds, and the shells plowed like thirty-pound meteorites into the earth, as had happened outside Ezekiel Calhoun's home.

Curious about the unknown object that had fallen in the garden, a young maid took a shovel and dug it up. She proudly carried her prize into the house to exhibit to the doctor's family. When they spied the detonator cap on its end and realized the shell was still live, they fled in terror. She was ordered to take the bomb back outside into the garden, where nobody dared touch it again for years afterwards.


FACING THE EASTERN BATTLEFIELDS, Cyrena Stone had grown increasingly accustomed to the relentless sounds and chaotic sights of life near the front lines. The skirmishing along the Decatur Road was less than two miles off. She could see more and more men filling the trenches behind the earthen fortifications that ran past her property just a couple hundred feet downhill from her house. Her yard, kitchen, and porch "swarmed" with soldiers and medics. They knocked down her fences and, she lamented, "dismantled" her home. Troops helped themselves to crops out of her garden; others came to her door begging for food or cooking utensils. "Overwhelmed" by the importuning men—and probably scared after so many robberies around town—she asked an invalided officer to protect her house in return for a bed within. The Confederate told her she had made the right decision in not "running from the Yankees." Unlike those who had fled their homes, he told her, she would prevent "immense losses & suffering" by staying.

At noontime on July 21, she was sitting in her house when "a horrid whizzing screaming thing came flying through the air." With a deafening blast, it exploded overhead. Bits of metal tattooed the trees and roof. The concussion shook the house timbers. She and the servants ran in fright to ask the officer, who was resting in bed, "What was *that*?"

Just an artillery shell, he responded without alarm. "There is no danger here." In fact, he said, they were safer here than downtown.

"The enemy are only trying the range of their guns," he reassured Cyrena. She left him to his rest. But a short time later, another shell followed, and then another came "screaming" overhead. One shell fell without exploding in her yard. Terrified now, she ran to the resting Confederate, who sat up and shrugged. There was nothing to be done. As more of the "murderous things" flew over the house, he told Stone to "put your trust in God. He alone can protect us." He returned to his nap. Having someone in the house who felt unruffled enough to sleep in the middle of a storm of artillery shells helped her to weather the cannonade, but the medical division seemed not to share his sense of security. That afternoon the order came to fall back.

An officer informed her that "the city would soon be evacuated by Confederate troops." She hoped to see Union forces march in tomorrow, but until they did, she and her servants were once more left alone next to the ramparts.

FROM HER HOUSE IN DECATUR, Mary Gay, whose brother Tom Stokes had fought with Gen. John Bell Hood's Corps until he fell sick, watched James B. McPherson's Union Army of the Tennessee in the village square. She observed what she could about the size, arms, and apparent movements of the force. She went among the Yankees and collected the latest Northern newspapers, which carried in-depth and up-to-date battlefield reports. She lined her petticoat under her skirt with the newspapers, making what she called a "very stylish bustle." Dressed as if she was heading out on a shopping stroll down Peachtree Street, she hiked through the sultry day some fourteen miles around the lines until she came to the McDonough Road. She advanced through the southern end of town, avoiding both armies' pickets. Once in Atlanta, she made her way to Confederate headquarters with her newspapers and her account of federal forces gathered around her home.

After that, she looked for what she called "our negroes." The family had hired them out in different parts of the city. She sought out Rachel, who had rented a room in a wealthy family's quarters on Marietta Street. Gay encountered the slave woman at the fence gate. Shells were falling about them, and cannon fire made "an unceasing sound." Speaking to her slave over the gate, Gay asked Rachel to come with her back home to safety in Decatur. Rachel refused. She told her all-but-former mistress she "preferred to await the coming of Sherman." Gay realized she "had no influence over her" any longer.

Slavery was coming to an end. As the women walked their separate ways, as if to symbolize the violent breakup of the mistress-slave relationship, a bombshell landed by the fence gate and tore it to pieces.

UNDAUNTED BY HIS LOSSES at Peachtree Creek, General Hood was determined to strike again quickly at the federals in hopes of slicing the ligaments tightening their stranglehold on the city. He drew in his forces from their outer defenses to the northern and eastern inner ramparts of Atlanta. At first Sherman thought Hood had abandoned the city, but the Northerners quickly fell back before the spiteful gunfire coming out of the fortresslike and virtually impregnable defenses. One of the generals leading the movement admired the earthworks—the labor of thousands of bondsmen over the course of many months—through a glass. They made, he recounted, Atlanta look "like a hill city defended by encircling well-fortified hills. Curtains, more or less regular, ran along connecting hill fort to hill fort. All the redoubts, or forts, and the curtains were well made under the direction of an excellent engineer. The slashings, abatis, *chevaux de frise*, fascines, gabions, and sand bags were all there and in use." He considered the potential cost of a frontal assault. "How could we run over those things when they had plenty of cannon, mortars, and rifles behind them?" It simply could not be done without catastrophic losses. In his headquarters, William Tecumseh Sherman was now convinced that Hood would fall back into a defensive fight like his predecessor, while perhaps more aggressively deploying his cavalry to get behind the Yankee line to break up his railroad supply line.

Sherman intended to beat Hood to the punch. Thinking he had more than sufficient force in place, Sherman detached the cavalry regiment protecting the Army of the Tennessee's left wing to tear up the Georgia Railroad to ensure it could not be used again to resupply Confederate Atlanta. He would so isolate the city that Hood would have nothing worthwhile left to fight for. The Union horsemen traveled well beyond Decatur and began pulling up miles of track and ties, methodically heating the rails into Sherman neckties. Hood's scouts, perhaps including Gay, informed him about the cavalry's departure on their railroad-breaking mission. Without cavalry ranging through the countryside, McPherson's left flank and rear now appeared vulnerable to attack. Hood saw a chance to flank the flanker.

While skirmishing continued all day on July 21, he dispatched an entire corps under Gen. William J. Hardee, as well as a major cavalry force, under cover of darkness that night. They were to move south across the city and then swing back around to the east. The following morning, they would strike McPherson's exposed flank by surprise, perhaps even getting on his rear.

THE DAY BEFORE THE MOVEMENT COMMENCED, the refugee daily the *Appeal* predicted that "the greatest battle of the war will probably be fought in the immediate vicinity of Atlanta." Nothing less than the entire Civil War hung in the balance. "Everything—life, liberty, property, and the independence of the South; the security of our homes, wives, mothers and children, all depend upon the endurance and heroism of the men whose toils may now be terminated with a brilliant victory." Not only would the battle determine the fate of the increasingly besieged city, but its outcome would likely decide "the pending Northern Presidential election. If we are victorious the Peace party will triumph: Lincoln's Administration is a failure, and peace and Southern independence are the immediate results." While some still believed the city would be abandoned, the *Appeal* insisted, "Atlanta and its connections are worth a battle. . . . Georgia will be redeemed."

Apparently, the *Appeal*'s editors did not trust their own prophetic powers. The following day, they printed their final issue, the last newspaper published in the embattled city. They packed their presses and departed town before the first shots of the coming battle were fired, heading for their fourth Confederate home since being driven out of Memphis two years earlier.

IN THE NIGHT, as part of Hood's movement in preparation for the assault on McPherson's army, A. J. Neal led his battery through town. He rested briefly along the Georgia Railroad's tracks near the city cemetery before moving with much of Hardee's Corps out of town on the McDonough Road. The force then planned to hike north through marshes and woods overgrown with thickets and around a large lake toward what they believed would be an exposed left flank of McPherson's line. As Hardee's train marched through town that night, Neal on horseback watched drunken stragglers breaking into the stores of Whitehall Street and elsewhere, leaving them, according to a reporter on hand from an Augusta newspaper, "literally gutted." The soldiers, the correspondent wrote, "entered the stores by force, robbing them of everything and wantonly destroying what they could not bear away."

A woman owner of a store tried to prevent some men from looting her shop. She pointed a pistol at them when they broke in. The soldiers snatched it from her hand and dragged her by the hair out into the street.

Hood finally ordered five cavalrymen caught looting executed and, perhaps worse, threatened to send others out of the cavalry into the infantry, but his measures amid the distractions of war did little to stem the spreading riot. Hearing the commotion, residents from the countryside came in to grab their share of the spoils.

THE NIGHT MARCH IN ROUGH COUNTRY—and the pillaging in the Five Points—confused and delayed Hardee's men. McPherson shared Army of the Ohio commander John Schofield's assessment that their West Point classmate Hood was a "brave, determined and rash man." McPherson disagreed with Sherman's conviction that Hood would not move to the offensive again. He saw defenses being strengthened to the south of his own lines. He was convinced that a major battle was in the offing and, trusting his instincts, placed infantry along his vulnerable southern flank. Hood's men, exhausted by their all-night march and what Tennessee private Sam Watkins called "one of the hottest days I ever felt," once again stumbled in coordinating their lines. Not until nearly 1 P.M. did the first of Hood's uneven lines shamble forward and finally charge. They met up with McPherson's protected, not exposed, flank. Hood shifted the attack more toward gaps at the center of McPherson's lines. The battle was close enough to the city that shells and even minié balls cracked into houses.

Through the afternoon, the rebels advanced several times against Yankees entrenched on and around a treeless knoll known as Bald Hill. Watkins was in a line that rushed forward into "seething fire from ten thousand muskets and small arms, and forty pieces of cannon hurled right into our faces, scorching and burning our clothes, and hands, and faces from their rapid discharges, and piling the ground with our dead and wounded almost in heaps."

The first charge was repulsed. Another charge followed, with "one long, loud cheer." Soon, Confederate and Union officers and men were tangled in hand-to-hand, -sword, and -bayonet combat. "Blood covered the ground" around Watkins, "and the dense smoke filled our eyes, and ears, and faces." He could hear the "groans of the wounded and dying . . . above the thunder of battle." McPherson rode out to rally his men at about the same moment Private Watkins fell, shot in the ankle and heel. Unable to continue, he watched the pitched, close-in battle from behind an embankment. Artillery and musket fire raked the field. A cannon ball shot out, decapitating a soldier in front of him, splattering viscera over the Tennessee soldier. He saw "cannon, caissons, and dead horses . . . piled pell-mell. . . . Blood had gathered in pools, and in some instances had made streams of blood."

Hunkered down, he watched a lone ambulance emerge from the Yankee line, pick up a single dead man on the edge of woods beside a road, and gallop back. He didn't know then that the wagon carried the body of General McPherson off the battlefield. The general had ridden along a road he thought safe directly into Confederate skir-mishers, who called for him to halt. He turned and started to ride away. The rebels fired. The commander of the Army of the Tennessee continued in the saddle a few feet and then slumped to the ground.

A. J. Neal's battery pulled back below the city cemetery not far from the rise from where General Hood observed the battle. Neal's artillery and nearby infantry were "having a hot fight." He was holding his horse by the bridle when a shell flew in between them. The explo-sion knocked him over, stunning him. When he regained conscious-ness, he saw his horse lying dead beside him.

The close-in fighting continued all afternoon and into the evening. Finally, at 7 P.M., the Confederates abandoned the attack.

GUSSIE CLAYTON, Sallie's typhoid-ravaged fifteen-year-old sister, had died in the predawn hours of July 22 while the wagons and troopers clattered through town toward the coming day's battle-grounds. Her devastated parents searched for a coffin in town but had trouble finding one. Then, the battle exploded near the city cemetery. With shells and balls flying, the Claytons could not bury her there. They hastily dug a grave in the garden of their Mitchell Street house opposite City Hall Square. Even there they found no respite from the war. Shells fell nearby while they held a graveside funeral forcing them to take cover.

The Clayton house was hit by the cannonade. One shell burst through a servant's quarters and exploded while two infant slave chil-dren slept, setting their bed on fire. Somehow, Sallie's father wrote her, the children "escaped unhurt almost miraculously." Another shell flew through her mother's bedroom window and slammed into a wall without exploding. With Gussie's three ill sisters now well enough to sit up, the family shut their house up and moved downtown to the

Georgia Railroad Bank building, where Mr. Clayton worked, on Whitehall Street, further away from the front. They set up mattresses on the floor of the stone building, hoping they were now safe against further artillery strikes.

Amid the family tragedy, Mr. Clayton felt heartened by the battle fought on the day his daughter expired. It proved "Atlanta will not be given up. This is general belief. It will be defended at all hazards."


MANY IN TOWN BELIEVED by the end of the day's fighting the Confederates could claim victory. A. J. Neal declared the bloodiest single day's combat in and around any American city in history, known ever after as the Battle of Atlanta, a "redemption" for the Southern cause. He believed the Yankee casualties "amounted to more than twice our own." Hood telegraphed Richmond to proclaim he had "routed the enemy in the neighborhood of Decatur" and claimed many thousand enemy prisoners taken along with scores of artillery pieces and stands of battalion colors. McPherson's death capped the triumphant announcement. Braxton Bragg, who visited Hood shortly after the battle, wrote President Jefferson Davis that Sherman was "badly defeated" and that victory produced an "admirable" "moral effect" on the troops. In fact, Hood lost an estimated 7,500 men or more that day, while Union casualties totaled a little over 3,700, including 1,700 prisoners. In four days under Hood the Army of Tennessee's offensive had already cost more men than Gen. Joseph Johnston had lost in the course of his entire command.

Militiaman T. Holliday held a position in the redoubt known as Fort Hood in front of the Ponder house. He was not as confident about morale among his fellow militiamen as Bragg. "A good many of the Regt. try to play out when they think a fight is on hand." He was not prepared to call it quits, he told his wife, for "who would not be a soldier and fight for his country?" But he had to admit, "I think we will soon disband and come home."


SAMUEL RICHARDS HAD, like many in town, expected the city to fall that night. Instead, he watched "dark crowds of prisoners" marched into town, "taken in a successful flank movement." He, too, understood now that General Hood "intended to hold the city."

A stricken Cyrena Stone also heard reports of a "glorious victory" at the end of the day's fighting. The Union partisan felt bereft of hope. "The heart-sickness that comes over us, when we hear *such* tidings, none can know," she confessed. The day's fighting had finally forced her to abandon her home. Soldiers had rushed about her property before the battle. Dark cannon were drawn into her gardens, pointing out toward the distant Yankee emplacements. A slave ran to her and insisted, "I tell you Miss Abby [the name she used for herself in her secret diary], we've got to git away from here now, for the men are falling back to the breastworks, & they're going to fight *right away!*"

She cried and rushed about from room to room, "not knowing what to do, or where to go, or what to save," before finally gathering things to move with her to a friend's house away from the front lines. "With this horrible pall of battlesmoke hanging over us" and the "minié balls . . . whizzing by so fast, & the shells screaming over the house," she told her remaining slaves they, too, should go. Their enslavement was at an end. She did not look back at the house and gardens, "for I felt as if leaving those pleasant scenes forever," and she did not want to mar her happier memories. The fighting that day very likely destroyed her property, to which she would never return.

BENEATH THE TUMBLING, screaming, whizzing, and sparkling shells, Robert Webster made his way down the hill from Stone's barn to the Five Points. The scene he came upon at the car shed was horrifying. Thousands of wounded men lay on the floor within the vaulted station, under surrounding tents, or out in the open. Surgeons operated without anesthesia; amputated limbs were piled on the ground. Physicians, medics, and women relief workers moved among the sea of bloody, perforated, and torn bodies, offering food and water in the intense summer heat and directing litter bearers and ambulance drivers to deliver those who could be moved to the various hospitals and many houses with beds and cots around town.

Sarah Huff, the young woman who had seen so much of the workings of the war from her Marietta Street home, was now forced by fighting near there to move into a Decatur Street house in town. She watched endless processions of "ominous black covered ambulances" with swarms of flies hovering over them carry the wounded past. She could see "the blood trickling down" to the dusty street after spilling out of the wounded men who lay suffering within those wagons.

Large numbers of other grievously wounded soldiers in blue were carried separately to the City Park neighboring the car shed. They were the wounded Union prisoners. Orderlies left them out on the dusty ground, where they moaned and shifted about in agony, without water and unprotected from the intense summer sun and stifling heat. The living sprawled alongside the stiff and bloated corpses of the dead. With "no one to attend them," said one witness, the wounded men suffered "intolerable" pain and appeared "in a dreadful condition." Many lay there for two days, some even longer, without water or assistance. Men were missing legs; others had arms blown off. The stench of gangrene rot hung in the air. Nobody dared come to their aid. One man admitted, "People feared to go among them" because of what he called "the excitement in the city"—the heavily armed Confederates clattering past on horseback, foot, and wagon.

Ignoring the obvious danger to anyone, particularly a black man, Webster waded in among the wounded Yankees. He got water, gathered whatever cloth he could find, and began washing and dressing their wounds. There were too many men in need. According to a witness, he "took charge of the whole matter himself." He called to other black people looking on. Many hesitated. Webster pulled out his wallet and offered to pay them to help. He gave other men money to purchase food to feed the starving men. Prince Ponder heard about the suffering federal prisoners. The Ponder slave, who like Ben Yancey's slave Robert Webster had grown wealthy through his currency trading during the war, ran down to the City Park. He brought water to the parched men and tried to see to their needs and comfort them in their misery as best he could. It was not long, he said, before "all the colored people did the same thing."

During that day, James Dunning, the foundry owner and Unionist once arrested by Provost Marshal George Washington Lee's men, looked on, perhaps fearing the consequences if he ventured to help the Union wounded. He watched Webster kneel down alongside one young man clearly in terrible pain. The soldier scratched furiously at his mangled hand, which was wrapped in bloody bandages, as if he wanted to tear the hand off his arm. Webster cut the bandages away. Dunning blanched at the sight. "The maggots fell out as grains of wheat would fall from the hand," he said. He looked around the field of moaning, bloody, filthy, mauled Yankees. Suddenly he realized that their open wounds quivered with life. "There was hardly one wound that was not stirring with maggots," he said.

Ignoring the horror, Webster organized the men into companies to carry the wounded to the Roy Hospital, which was taking in Union prisoners. A white businessman watched the black teams carrying away the wounded on litters and on their shoulders to the hospital.

He knew that "many of the wounded would certainly have died if it had not been for the attention of these men." Through the rest of the afternoon under the broiling sun and on throughout the entire night, while bombs whistled in and occasionally burst in lethal fireworks in the dark sky overhead, Webster and his team of fellow former slaves worked on the wounded. By morning, they had dispatched all the wounded men to the hospital for treatment.

IN HIS HEADQUARTERS, Sherman was distraught over the death of his protégé general. He wrote his wife, "I lost my right bower [anchor] in McPherson." In McPherson's death, stumbling into an enemy outpost, Sherman saw his own, "for with all the natural advantages of bushes, cover of all kinds, we must all be killed."

He ignored his own misjudgment of Hood's intentions, which had contributed to his friend's death, and his even graver failure to make good McPherson's accomplishments that day. The Army of the Tennessee had held off an attack that sent the bulk of Hood's own army out beyond the protection of his impregnable earthworks. Rather than counterattack the army while it was exposed in the field, the ever-cautious Sherman had held back nearly 50,000 men idle in reserve, close enough to the battlefield to reach it in less than an hour's march. Had he sent them in, they very likely would have obliterated Hood's army. Instead, when his two other army commanders urged an advance, he had insisted, "Let the Army of the Tennessee fight it out!"

THE CONFEDERATES DREW BACK into Atlanta. Sherman decided to leave them there. "The forts," he wrote his wife, "are really unassailable." For those inside the city, it seemed as if Sherman intended to lay siege to the town. T. Holliday believed, "They can't take Atlanta unless they make a Vicksburg scrape of it." That seemed Sherman's intention. A reporter on hand estimated some five hundred shells fell into the city over the next few days. He noted many houses, churches, hotels, railroad installations, and other buildings "bear marks of recent visitations of round shot and shell." Remarkably, he knew of few casualties among the civilian population. "Several members of a family up town were wounded by fragments of an exploded shell," he reported, "and one little child was killed." The slight civilian death toll was surprising, given the continuous fighting. The newspaper correspondent heard "a constant clatter of muskets . . . night and day around the city circle of fortifications, with a running heavy bass accompaniment of twelve and twenty-four pounders." Nights were "singularly picturesque and startling in effect. The rockets' red glare and bombs bursting in the air, with the flash of guns, like heat-lightning on the horizon, presents a panorama at once exciting and wildly beautiful to the uninitiated in war."

In the federal lines along the abandoned Western & Atlanta tracks to the northwest of town, Massachusetts infantry captain Charles Morse also noted, "Operations now bear the character of a siege." He could not leave the protection of the trenches, with cannons firing back and forth day and night without halt. His company covered Marietta Street, from where he could see "a fine house in plain sight," the former home of Dexter Niles, the Bostonian slave wholesale dealer and the same house where Johnston had made his headquarters until he had been so recently relieved. Morse's men moved forward along Marietta Street, assaulting and taking a rebel picket line. That left them exposed to close-range artillery and musket fire from the fort next to the Ponder house, which was now a sharpshooter's nest and target of the Yankee guns. "I had a whole chapter of wonderful escapes" during the assault, Morse recounted. "One shell burst within ten feet of me, throwing me flat by its concussion and covering me with dirt." He took time to eat breakfast, but a sharpshooter thought he didn't need the meal. "A rifle bullet struck the board on which was my plate, and sent things flying," he penned, "but it seemed that my time to be hit had not come."

SHERMAN, TOO, WAS NOT yet resigned to any fated siege of the city. His strategy, he informed his wife, was to "gradually destroy the roads which make Atlanta a place worth having." Just one operating railroad line remained to supply the Confederate army. Trains ran continuously on the Macon & Western in and out of town to the southwest. The artillery batteries aimed to land their shells on the car shed, puncturing it and other nearby structures, but they did little to slow the arriving freight cars. Train engineers blew their locomotive whistles in defiance of Sherman. He, in turn, hoped to cut Atlanta's last lifeline to rebeldom, forcing its defenders to abandon their citadel.

Starting on July 26, he sent out his favored Army of the Tennessee, still flush and stinging from the fight four days earlier and the loss of their commander. They swept back around Atlanta, aiming to move to the west and then down to the southern outskirts of town, where they would break the railroad. Aware of Sherman's maneuver, Hood sent two corps out to meet the Yankee army. At around noon on July 28, the opposing forces encountered each other near a meeting-house known as Ezra Church, about two and a half miles west of Atlanta. The Confederates had the advantage again of moving to the attack through rough country that hid their advance against a force not fully entrenched. But again, the initial rebel assault was uneven and piecemeal. The federals threw up barricades of logs, planks, and church benches as the enemy lines approached.

Several times the rebel attackers reached within twenty feet of the Yankee lines, only to be repulsed. Soon the Yankees could see that many of the charging soldiers had lost their heart for the fight. Henry Stanley, the Connecticut quartermaster, heard afterwards that many entire regiments simply fired their muskets off "in the air," instead of at the enemy in front of them. Feckless, rebel soldiers stumbled forward. They were drunk, he recorded, and "many of the pensioners we captured were so under the influence of liquor that they had to be led off the battlefield."

The Confederate dead lay in piles where the fiercest fighting occurred, swept down in whole ranks at a time. Once again, Hood's bold moves devastated his already thinning army. Confederate losses totaled around 3,000 or more men; the federals' about 630.

SHERMAN MOVED HIS LINE around further in an attempt to reach the railroad, but Hood simply extended his entrenchments until Sherman dared not stretch his lines any further from his base at the Western & Atlantic's rebuilt Chattahoochee River crossing. He sent out two cavalry raids to break the railroad to Macon and reach the Andersonville prison; both failed badly. Now, he looked up at the Confederates' virtually impregnable, high ridge of fortifications encircling Atlanta and concluded that the nut was indeed too hard to crack. "To assault their position would cost more lives than we can spare," he told Ellen, and he was too deep in enemy territory, he presently feared, to move further around and away from the city, which would require him "to cut loose from our base, which is rather a risky business in a country devoid of all manner of supplies." He had to admit that, for now, the far smaller but relentless rebel forces, fighting like "Devils & Indians," had checked his advance.

On August 1, he issued explicit orders to his three army commanders to commence an orderly, sustained artillery fire from their twenty-pounder Parrott gun batteries, totaling more than one hundred rifled cannons, concentrated north and west of downtown: "You may fire from ten to fifteen shots from every gun you have in position into Atlanta that will reach any of its houses. Fire slowly and with deliberation between 4 P.M. and dark." Hundreds of shells fell into the city. On August 7, the impatient general ordered heavier rifled cannon freighted down from Chattanooga. Those four 4.5-inch naval siege guns would add thirty-three-pound projectiles to the barrage. He wired Washington that night. Using the more powerful guns, he explained, "we can pick almost any house in the town." He intended to "make the inside of Atlanta too hot to be endured. . . . One thing is certain, whether we get inside of Atlanta or not, it will be a used-up community by the time we are done with it."

*Frank Leslie's Illustrated* engraving of Union forces storming Lost Mountain
during the Battle of Kennesaw Mountain, June 16, 1864

General Joseph E. Johnston,
commander, Army of
Tennessee

General John B. Hood,
Johnston's replacement

General William T. Sherman,
Union forces commander

Tennessee private Sam Watkins

Colonel Charles F. Morse,
Union provost marshal in Atlanta

Militiaman and Wilkes County
plantation owner Allen T. Holliday

"Dearest Lizzie," Holliday's wife
remained on their plantation

Ponder house after the siege of Atlanta looked "like a huge coal screen" to Union troops

Ponder estate including house and other
buildings within fortifications around
Fort Hood

*Harper's Weekly* engraving of Union army's destruction of Atlanta's public and downtown buildings, an untouched City Hall at left

*Harper's Weekly* engraving of last Union troops leaving a burning Atlanta on November 16, 1864

Georgia Railroad Roundhouse ruins after the war

Fort Hood, abatis and other fortifications protecting Marietta Street on the city's outskirts

Huff family house on Marietta Street, where Sarah Huff spent her
Confederate childhood, stood between the lines but survived the fighting

Ruins of the Georgia Railroad, Atlanta Rolling Mill, and surroundings following detonation of munitions train by departing Confederate Army on September 1, 1864

Postwar Peachtree Street crossing tracks, with ruins of Georgia Railroad Bank at the corner, where the Clayton family sought refuge, with wagon turning on Marietta Street in distance

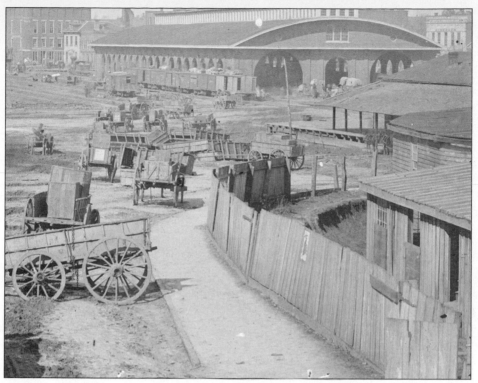

Car shed with wagons and freight cars loaded for civilian evacuation under Union Army orders in September 1864

Union railroad demolition crew making "Sherman neckties" out of Western & Atlantic Railroad track in November

*Frank Leslie's Illustrated* engraving of Battle of Bentonville, NC, where Confederate
James Neal, brother of Andrew J. Neal, made his last charge

The first black West Point cadet,
Henry O. Flipper

Ruins of the car shed after being knocked down
by Union demolition crews, November 15, 1864

# War Is Cruelty, and You Cannot Refine It

I AM AFEARD THERE ARE FEW DIE well that die in a battle, for how can they charitably dispose of anything when blood is their argument?

—WILLIAM SHAKESPEARE,
*KING HENRY V*, ACT 4, SCENE 1

# CHAPTER 23

# GOODBYE, JOHNNY

"WE HOVER AROUND ATLANTA, and can look square into the city, as did Moses into the land of Canaan," reported the *New York Times* war correspondent. "We are so close to the city in some places that our shells, destined for its center, oftentimes pass clean over." It seemed as the hot days of August unfolded that Gen. William Tecumseh Sherman, like Moses, might never enter Atlanta. The same reporter wrote, "As the rebels themselves say, Atlanta is safe." Despite the 30,000-man differential between the armies, the city's brilliantly laid-out lines and densely reinforced earthworks could not be breached without a monumental loss of life that would very likely destroy the army Sherman had so carefully conserved through four months of continuous battle deep in the Confederacy's heartland. "You may take this to heart—that Atlanta is beyond our reach, so far as fighting for it is concerned."

Settling into a siege mode, Union batteries lofted shell and shot that sailed over the Confederate ramparts and pelted the spread-out city like thousands of biting horseflies preying upon exposed flesh—unpredictable in their targets and, for most of the 4,000 or so civilians left in town, terrifying and sometimes painful yet rarely lethal. Marietta Street led out to some of the heaviest batteries firing on the city and drew especially heavy fire. Sitting on her family porch a mile from the Yankee lines at night, a young girl watched the cannon flash on the horizon, followed by a booming report. She then saw each shell flying "like a big ball of fire, making its way towards us." It passed overhead "with a shrieking and hissing that must be heard to appreciate its diabolical sound." That was followed soon after by the crash from a strike and then an explosion that echoed and rattled dishes and windows far into the countryside. The screams of terror—or sometimes of agony from wounds—could be heard in the lull between volleys.

Shell and shot chased people from pillar to post about town all day and night. The same girl recalled just sitting down at the breakfast table when a shell blew a three-foot hole through the brick wall, slammed through a door across the room, and careened down the hall into another room, where it exploded near a piano, tossing it upside down and blowing out all the windows. The explosion set the house ablaze. The family fled to a friend's house on Alabama Street that "had not been troubled with shells." Finally settled in, at 2 o'clock that afternoon the famished family had just sat down to their first meal of the day when, she recalled, "Bang! came a shell and buried itself in the ground near the gate." Shells, the residents had quickly learned from experience, fell in clumps. The family didn't wait for the next to fall on the house but instead dashed off in haste until they arrived atop the Peters Street hill about a mile from the center of town.

Relieved to be well away from the bull's eye at the center of town, they laid out a picnic on the exposed knoll. Just as they had started to eat, a man rode up to them fast and cried out, "For mercy's sake, get away from here. The Yanks will see this wagon and mule, think you are some soldiers camped here, and shell you." Gen. John Bell Hood had made his headquarters on the heights there and was shelled out two days earlier. "You must leave." They'd had enough running, though. They decided to risk more shelling and finished their picnic while enjoying the spectacle of shells streaking into town.

THAT YOUNG GIRL AND other children found the experience of running away from home under shell fire, racing around in a covered wagon, and watching the bombs burst in white puffs in the air "fun," but the adults soon conveyed their terror to the young ones. Ezekiel Calhoun's little grandson Noble Calhoun Williams and his young cousin became so used to the bombardment that they played outside and regularly climbed the grape arbor to gather baskets of grapes without worrying about the fiery balls and their showers of hot metal fragments. Noble often accompanied his grandfather, still weak but recovering from his bout of dysentery, to his pharmacy in the Five

Points. Each time they heard a distant cannon's report while they walked, they dropped down behind the nearest fence or stone wall, then rose and continued until startled by another report. As they neared the shop, they grew warier. Shells dropped frequently into the Five Points. Those projectiles scared them most. They came whistling and tumbling down and sparked off the hard paving stones. Nobody could calculate what course they would take as they skipped and rebounded along until they exploded or crashed into some wall or other object.

Oftentimes the shelling developed a predictable-enough regularity for people to get out, shop; if poor, receive distributions of free food from the Confederate commissary; or run other errands before returning to shelter. While moving about, they could hear and see projectiles coming and generally had time to seek cover. An unearthly spinning whine and, at night, a shining thread of sparkles strung across the dark sky warned those in their path to find shelter. Ezekiel Calhoun's grandson Noble recalled feeling "a strange fascination" at night. He couldn't resist looking up to see traveling meteor-like through the night air "at almost any time numbers of lighted shells, which brightly illuminated the sky with their fiery trails."

Many buildings in the Five Points took direct hits. Samuel and Jabez Richards's store building was shelled several times. One shot tore off a piece of cornice before flying on into the building across the street. Another crashed through the back door and exploded as it went through the floor. Yet another entered through the roof and bowled through five plaster partition walls in the top floor before finally striking the chimney flue. From there it dropped down to the ground floor, where it exploded, blowing the stove across the room. Samuel was not there for that, but he was checking in on the premises a few days later when another explosion from the floor above him coated him with plaster dust.

A WEEK AND A HALF after General Sherman ordered the siege shelling to begin, he mentioned to Gen. George Thomas that "the inhabitants have, of course, got out." He was being disingenuous. He almost certainly knew that thousands of civilians remained trapped within the city limits. Three days later, on August 13, a Union colonel sent a report saying that one of his officers "could distinctly hear loud cries from women and children, as if praying &c." Sherman considered the south side of the city "of little depth or importance." Many families, especially the poorer ones without other refuge, moved into an encampment there largely spared bombardment. However, Union gunners understood well that their charge was not only to target military installations. Posted at Fort Hood "about 100 yards from the Ponder Home on the State Road," Confederate battery captain A. J. Neal carried on a sporadic artillery duel with a facing Yankee battery. Both batteries were so well protected within their lines, though, that the exchanged shots did as much damage "as the sledge hammer makes out of the anvil," he penned. Whenever the Yankee batteries opened up, federal shells and solid shot first went "screaming just above our heads." They exploded around and pounded against the reinforced redoubt within which his guns nestled. After firing their fruitless, close-in shots, the Yankees, he remarked, "then elevate their guns and send the balance into the city."

Riding away from his battery in the hot first days of August, Neal had inspected much of the city. He found it "considerably marked by the enemy's shots. In some parts of town every house has been struck a dozen times." He rode to his family's big mansion opposite City Hall. What he saw must have depressed him and redoubled his hostility toward the federals if that were possible. "Two balls," he found, "have gone into our house," one destroying a room belonging to his older brother James, also a rebel soldier, while another blew into the parlor.

Increasingly intent on rendering Atlanta uninhabitable, Sherman wrote Gen. Oliver O. Howard, whom he had appointed to replace James B. McPherson in command of the Army of the Tennessee, to redouble the pace of the bombing. "Let us destroy Atlanta and make it a desolation," he declared. Neal could see Sherman's command was working. According to Neal, the Yankee bombardment had "ruined [Atlanta's] value to us in a great measure." Even as the siege shelling heated up, though, he believed the enemy would never drive them out. He was pleased to see more militia enter the line and also knew Hood intended to send cavalry out to break Sherman's crucial railroad supply line. Despite the Union pickets having dug their forward positions to within an easy shot of his works, Neal never lost the general conviction that "the enemy will [not] get any nearer Atlanta."

Andrew Jackson Neal would not live to see the battle's end. A few days later, while moving through the Fort Hood redoubt, he exposed himself to a Yankee sharpshooter. His men buried him in a shallow grave alongside dozens of others on August 10.

Within two weeks, word of A. J. Neal's death had reached his older brother James, a colonel at the head of the Nineteenth Georgia Infantry, also holding off a siege—Grant's against the Petersburg fortifications in Virginia. When James heard about Andrew's death, his "heart," he told his mother, was "too full to utter words of consolation." He thought of the happy days they had shared at the family's handsome Washington Street house and found it impossible to accept "that we will not all meet again at home after this war is over as I have so long anticipated, hoped and prayed for." James Neal would have his chance at revenge, eventually returning south to confront Sherman's armies.


THE CLOCKWORK SHELLING limited civilian casualties. Citizens dug their own or shared so-called bombproofs or gopher holes, deep pits extended out within existing cellars, such as Samuel Richards added to his house, or freshly constructed caverns beneath household gardens. The chambers were typically eight feet or more high. Some were opened up enough to accommodate large families and their servants, small cooking areas, and tables to eat at. Heavy beams supported the ceiling, which was lined with boards or tin to keep out seeping rain, then covered with three to five feet of earth. Even a direct hit could not blow in the subterranean shelters. A small, exposed entry to the ground led to a covered ditch that ran through a double right angle to the bombproof space, shielding the doorway to the shelter against a blast.

Prominent buildings and residential streets that stood high enough to be seen by Yankee signalmen perched in treetops drew especially close fire. Sited on high ground and topped by a handsome and very visible bell cupola, the Clayton girls' former school, the Female Institute, was a favorite target. Virtually every house—except, by luck, that belonging to Robert Webster and his wife—along the rise up Houston Street, including Cyrena Stone's, was destroyed during the bombardment or taken apart during the Battle of Atlanta or later on. Most houses along Marietta Street lay beneath the pathway shells took toward the center of town; they were torn to pieces. Church steeples provided inviting targets, and the concentration of churches around City Hall Square attracted heavy fire. Above all, Sherman wanted to "demolish the big engine-house," the car shed where the unabated arrival of trains announcing their presence with their whistles infuriated him. He directed that one of the four-and-a-half-inch navy siege guns concentrate its fire on the depot. Those four heavy guns alone fired more than 4,500 shells into the city—at least 75 tons of iron and gunpowder. The smaller guns, though, caused untold damage. On August 9, Sherman ordered all his cannon to open fire with fifty rounds each. A paroxysm of Union shells "burst immediately over all parts of town," some 5,000 solid shots and exploding artillery shells fell that day. Federal lookouts reported seeing "great commotion" by people under the hellacious bombardment.

To leave the city "used up," Sherman's army tried to inflict as much damage as possible by setting it on fire. Batteries kept furnaces stoked near their cannons to experiment with heating up shot enough to ignite fires when they struck. An officer deemed "the experiment . . . a perfect success." His lookouts reported, "Large fires were visible in the city every night hot shot was used." When flames were spotted within the city, the artillery concentrated their shelling on the area—to keep away the three remaining fire companies in town and to spread the conflagration. The Atlanta correspondent for the *Intelligencer*, now relocated to Macon, recounted their efforts, writing, "The shells were flying thick and fast around the burning buildings, but the firemen stood to their posts without flinching." Most nights, Mayor James Calhoun moved through the city with his fire companies. The *Intelligencer*'s editor John Steele had refugeed to Macon; however, he still had his knives out for the mayor, blasting him for being, he falsely claimed, "absent."

During one night's particularly fierce bombardment, a fire leaped through large parts of downtown. Against the flames licking up into the night sky, shells fell at a rate of about one every two minutes. It didn't help the companies battling the blazes under the shell fire that the summer heat had dried up all the city cisterns. The fierce fire grew into a holocaust fed by hidden stores of cotton warehoused illegally by many downtown merchants. The *Intelligencer*'s correspondent expressed surprise, either mock or true, to discover that so many "good loyal citizens . . . have cotton stored away in Atlanta." When the bales of cotton went up, small fires touched off by the hot shot flared into firestorms. "And," asked the newspaperman, "if the city is to fall who will be benefited by the cotton and tobacco left in the city? Certainly not the Confederacy!"

THUMBING THEIR COLLECTIVE REBEL noses at Sherman, amid the siege, Atlanta's party life went blithely on. Distillers sold corn whisky to soldiers, and prostitutes serviced the troops behind the lines. Officers went to festive balls, where bands played even while the fiery exploding shells passed overhead. On the night of August 12, the Medical College Hospital physicians took a break from their grim labors to attend a ball. Among those cavorting with the officers and surgeons was Sarah Collins, a beautiful young widow of "high position in the first circles of this city," noted a correspondent in town. She had come to Atlanta more than a year before as a refugee from her former Memphis home and quickly found her place among Atlanta's leading socialites. The Medical College ball was her last society outing.

The day after the festive gathering, in what the *Intelligencer* proclaimed "the most horrible crime that has ever been committed in this city," she was found strangled to death in her bed. The reporter breathlessly described, "Her throat was perfectly black where she had been choked, her arms were bruised, and her body terribly mutilated; her clothing was torn and muddy as though she had been dragged through the mud by some villain who had violated her person." An inquest supposed "that she came to her death at the hands of those who had her in charge at the ball." In the chaos of the siege and with no city marshals left to investigate Collins's rape and murder, nobody was arrested.


IN THE WAR'S TUMULT, crime was only one of the many dangers people faced. The federal artillery terrorized the population stranded within the city. Samuel Richards noted after a particularly severe shelling that commenced at midnight and lasted until dawn, "Our *humane* foes allowed us to get well to sleep before they began their work of destruction." The cannon fire mostly damaged property, but people died, too. In the first days of the siege, a shell came whizzing down at the corner of Whitehall and Alabama streets when the ironically named Solomon Luckie happened to walk out of his nearby barbershop. The popular barber was among the handful of free blacks in the city. The shell bounced off one of the long-extinguished cast iron gas lampposts on the corner and ricocheted off the street before exploding. Fragments shot out around the crowded corner. One ripped into the unfortunate Luckie's leg. Several passersby picked up the badly wounded man and took him to a hospital, where, despite a surgeon's cutting off the mangled leg, he soon bled to death.

John Warner, the superintendent of the defunct Atlanta Gas Works, had remained a Union loyalist, despite having briefly been forced into Confederate service. During a furlough home, he deserted. Now the widower hoped to hide out from the conscript officers looking for him until he could flee north with his eight-year-old daughter, Lizzie. A woman who helped take care of the girl recalled, "The officers were then threatening his life." To hide from them, the well-to-do industrialist installed a secret brick crypt entered through a trapdoor beneath his bed. The woman watched a conscript officer search the house until he stood almost directly over Warner in his hiding place. Storming away, the frustrated Confederate warned the woman that he would be back. "I will fix him when I get him," he said.

The fierce Union cannonade quickly drove the Warner household members underground, forty-eight feet down a ladder in the well to a nook Warner had carved into its side. Out of fear that conscript officers would come looking for him in the night, he descended at sunset into the underground space with his daughter while the servant members of the household slept in their own beds. In the first week of August, though, little Lizzie fell ill, and Warner, fearing the dampness of the well would further sicken the frail girl, decided to return to his own bed with his daughter beside him. In the middle of the night, the woman helper awoke with a start to the sound of groaning coming from Warner's room. She rushed in to find the room demolished and a still hot shell lying unexploded on the floor. The bomb had plunged down through the bed, killing the little girl instantly. Her father lay there with both his legs severed. He had a few minutes to write out his will before he died.

A heavy bombardment commenced shortly after that. With "the missiles of death . . . flying in every direction," the distraught servant left the pair lying in their blood-soaked deathbed. She grabbed her own young son sleeping soundly in bed and dragged him down the ladder to the shelter deep in the well. Once there, she fell apart. "I sat down and wept, crying at the top of my voice, but there was no one to come to my relief, or even to hear me."

THE TERROR FELT BY those under the siege fire came to have an existential cast to it. The shells dropping down from the sky destroyed property and snuffed out lives like an arbitrary hand of fate. "It is," observed Samuel Richards, "like living in the midst of a pestilence, no one can tell but he may be the next victim." By the last week of August, a correspondent speculated that Northern artillery had wounded 601 and killed 487, though he did not distinguish between civilian and military casualties. The numbers, particularly the proportion of wounded to dead, seem unlikely. More reliably, on August 21 Samuel Richards noted in his diary, "It is said that about twenty lives have been destroyed by these terrible missiles." A surgeon in town reported that 107 citizens required amputation of limbs. Even those relatively small numbers mark the highest civilian casualty toll of any siege bombardment in American history.

AFTER A QUICK RECOVERY from his Battle of Atlanta foot wound in a Montgomery, Alabama, hospital, Tennessee private Sam Watkins returned to the Army of Tennessee. He walked out Marietta Street to rejoin his regiment stationed near what he called "a fine concrete house," the Ponder place. From within the formerly much admired mansion, Watkins fired out the windows at the Union batteries half a mile off in the woods across the open field beyond the fortifications. His Ponder house post, though, proved an easy target for the Yankee gunners. When federal quartermaster Henry Stanley made his way forward, he could see it was "perfectly riddled with balls and shell." The whitewashed walls drew so much fire that more than a ton of shell fragments and spent bullets was later collected from within it. Stanley thought it "looked for all the world like a huge coal screen," but astonishingly, the stone, brick, and plaster house withstood the continuous fire like an aboveground bombproof blockhouse. Those nearby viewed the battered, but still standing, white structure as a symbol of diehard Confederate resistance.

Watkins fought alongside Gov. Joseph Brown's Georgia militiamen. He ridiculed what he called a "double-ringed circus" put on by Joe Brown's Pets, "dressed in citizen's clothes . . . the knock-kneed by the side of the bow-legged; the driven-in by the side of the drawn out," many still carrying their double-barreled shotguns. After he led a militia company on a charge that captured a Yankee squad, though, he commended "many a gallant and noble fellow among them." Militiaman A. T. Holliday from Wilkes County shared Watkins's mixed feelings about the motley company he fought alongside in the trenches.

"The old men looked sad and desponding; they looked as though they never intended to laugh again," he told his wife. "It was exactly to the contrary with the little boys or as we call them Joe's [Brown] babies. . . . They are as brave soldiers as we have in the field and if the Yanks want to save their bacon they best keep a good distance from them. They are not old enough to fear danger. . . . Some are nothing but babies."

CONFEDERATE BATTERIES AND PICKETS kept the federals from approaching. Massachusetts captain Charles Morse in the woods opposite Fort Hood admired "the very obstinate defense" his men faced. He shared the universal belief that the works "can never be taken by assault." He, too, saw long faces, but they were among the Union siege force. Rations were short. Most men had been in the fight for four months without relief. "Everyone looks thin and worn down," he observed; "large numbers of sick are sent to the rear every day." Even hunkered down, casualties mounted. He stood in front of his tent watching enemy shells burst, when he saw one come "through a tree in front, strike the ground and ricochet." He knew it would bounce through camp. "It was a twenty-pounder with a disagreeable whiz and end-over-end motion," he noted, "and it went into a squad of three men, breaking the thigh of one of them."

WITH MEN CONTINUING TO die or fall out every day and his progress halted, Sherman came to view the siege as a personal affront. He was losing his detachment and now wanted vengeance on the city. "This city has done and contributed more to carry on and sustain the war than any other, save perhaps Richmond," he raged. "We have been fighting Atlanta all the time, in the past: have been capturing guns, wagons, etc., etc., marked 'Atlanta' and made here all of the time: and now since they have done so much to destroy us and our government we have to destroy them." He understood as well that culmination of the siege—and the eventual conquest of Atlanta—had become a political imperative. He was about the business of convincing the rebel soldiers that the federal army could outlast them and that they faced utter destruction should resistance continue here. He shared his sentiments with Ulysses S. Grant, still besieging Petersberg: "Any sign of a let up on our part is sure to be falsely construed and for this reason I always remind them [Confederates] that the siege of Troy lasted six

years and Atlanta is a more valuable town than Troy." He would outlast them and outfight them down to the very last man.

DESPITE THE TONS OF shot and shell poured into the city day and
night, Confederate resistance did not falter—or at least the words in
its support continued to embolden. The *Intelligencer* declared,

> We are very certain that the Yankee forces will disappear from
> before Atlanta before the end of August, and that a tremen-
> dous movement against him [Sherman] will almost destroy his
> army. . . . The prospect to us has never been without the beauti-
> ful sunlight of prospective victory lighting our hearts through
> the gloom and the dark shade of defeat through which we have
> traveled these many weary months past. Our confidence in the
> prowess of General Hood and his invincible army of veterans is
> unabating and with such firm belief we wish to imbue the spirit
> of the people and the army. So long as the feeling that all will end
> well enthuses us, we are unconquerable and we will be successful.

Hope provided the fuel for the Confederate war engine. Every
day the siege continued pumped up those hopes.

A siege, too, was not Sherman's style of war. "I am too impatient
for a siege," he wrote Washington in frustration. He worried, too. The
longer his men remained in the trenches, the greater the risk his
forces faced, particularly for attacks on his supplies and the hard-
to-defend rail line down from Chattanooga. "We must act," he decided. "We cannot sit down and do nothing because it involves risk."
He also resented that Hood's inferior force held *his* army in place. "I
feel mortified that he holds us in check by the aid of his militia. . . .
It seems we are more besieged" than the Confederates.

National politics, too, weighed on the shoulders of the men fighting to conquer and defend Atlanta. The Democratic Party was set to
hold its nominating convention, postponed from the spring, starting
on August 29 in Chicago. Peace Democrats hoped to capture the
party there and, with the popular Gen. George McClellan as the party
nominee, take the presidency from Abraham Lincoln in November.
Two stalemated battlefronts poisoned national political sentiments,
already appalled by the costs of the war. Even with Union armies battering and besieging the rebels, many believed the war remained un-
winnable. The *Intelligencer* summarized the growing hopes that

Sherman could not hold out much longer. A victory by the Army of Tennessee here, declared Steele, "will end the summer's campaign . . . so disastrously to Lincoln that we shall look confidently to his defeat in the coming presidential election, and the triumph of the peace party in the North. Under such circumstances no more armies could be raised in the North to prosecute the war." The North would lose the war before the ramparts of the citadel of the Confederacy.

And then, amazingly, it seemed that Atlanta *had* won.


ON FRIDAY, AUGUST 26, Atlantans woke up startled. They listened intently to something they had not heard in months: silence. No gunfire. Not a single cannon report. "Everything is as still as death in our front this morning and has been since 3 o'clock this morning," a stunned T. Holliday penned in wonder. "The shelling ceased altogether," recorded Samuel Richards not long after. Rumors flew "that the enemy was retreating and . . . have deserted their camps around the city." Gray-coated scouts felt their way forward, expecting shots to ring out at any instant, until they scrambled into the empty Union lines. Finally, an ecstatic Holliday confirmed the rumors. "Sherman is compelled to fall back for the want of supplies for his army!" he elatedly reported. "The Yanks are gone now and they are not likely to return soon."

Baffled, stunned, delighted, Atlantans streamed out of their bombproofs and shelters and walked and rode to the lines. Thousands of tourists quickly ventured through the fields to inspect the Yankee camps and pick up souvenirs. Holliday scoffed when he saw them "riding in buggies with white linen coats on." "Where, where oh where," he asked, "were they in their holes in the city?" The fight apparently won, he began to dream of going home. "I am coming home," he mused, "and play with my wife and babies before a great while and sleep on a feather bed too. Now won't that be a great luxury after I get used to it? I am reminded of eating strawberries and cream with plenty of sugar mixed."

Over the next two days, the *Intelligencer*'s correspondent in Atlanta explored "all over the Yankee works . . . and I did not see a Yankee in all my rambles. It is said the enemy has massed his forces on our left, but I doubt that very much. I am of the opinion that the whole Yankee army is now on the western bank of the Chattahoochee River." Atlanta was reborn. "The city," he reported, "has already begun to fill up. Today the streets are crowded as they were of old. Officers, soldiers, citizens, women and children and negroes are crowding on the streets, and everybody wears a smile on their countenance." Walking through the desolate Union camp, he found a note written "in a large bold hand with coal on the headboard of one of the Yankee bunks." It read, "Goodbye, Johnny. We are going to see you soon, and when we come to Georgia we will remember Kennesaw." It was signed, "YANK."

# CHAPTER 24

# THE FIRST BONFIRE

MILITIAMAN T. HOLLIDAY now skipped about the lines and through town with a light and even joyous step. Yankee cavalry deserters told their Southern hosts that soldiers in the Union lines had "been living on one cracker a day for four days," explaining to Holliday why the invaders had been driven to backtrack across the river. The militiaman ignored those who returned from the abandoned federal camp carrying armfuls of hardtack and bacon. Some even found unheard of treats, according to one scout, "feasting on sardines and lobsters, canned fruit of every kind, candies, cakes and raisins, besides many other good things their stomachs had long been strangers to." Strange leavings for a starving army, yet Holliday shared the thrilling optimism infusing the city. "I feel more confident and hopeful this morning about the salvation of Atlanta than I have since I have been here," the militiaman cheerfully related. When relieved, but still unsure, citizens came to see the lines, several asked him, "Where are the Yanks gone?" He answered, "Gone up a spout." He was going home. "I think we will not be out but a short time now," he reassured his wife.

Gen. John Bell Hood kept part of his forces on alert, leery of trusting that Gen. William Tecumseh Sherman really had gone. On the evening after the Union men disappeared, though, he telegraphed the Confederate secretary of war in Richmond to tell him that the Northerners had indeed withdrawn from his eastern and northern fronts. "Last night," he conveyed, "the enemy abandoned the Augusta

railroad, and all the country between that and the Dalton railroad."
The sense of vindication and, indeed, rebirth for the cause could be
felt from Atlanta to Richmond. "The prevailing impression" in
Hood's headquarters, recorded a staff officer, is that Sherman is
"falling back across the Chattahoochee River." Added another, the
prospect of Sherman's "speedy destruction" infected Hood and his
staff with "high glee." Military bands played in the streets, while jubilant residents danced in step behind them.

Walking through the battered town three days after the Yankees'
withdrawal, a euphoric Holliday gushed, "Everything looks brighter
and brighter to me every day." He believed he had accomplished his
historic mission for his land, "one of the noblest acts of my whole life."


NOT EVERYONE WAS CONVINCED that Sherman was indeed falling
back. Soldiers around Holliday jumped about "in such high spirits,"
he reported, yet at the same time he had never "seen them so anxious
before." Even if the signs pointed to a hasty, forced evacuation under
the cover of darkness, the regular army knew Sherman too well by
now not to suspect some new flanking trick. The veterans he called
"the old soldiers . . . have a great anxiety to know where the Yanks
have gone and seem anxious to follow them."

Despite the rumors of Sherman's retreat that reanimated the
moribund city of Atlanta, even Samuel Richards, who never once entered the trenches—though he had shouldered a musket as part of the
toothless home guard—distrusted Yankee intentions. The issue
gnawed at him. They "are going somewhere," he fretted, "but what is
their design it is hard tell. I fear that we have not yet got rid of them
finally, but that they have some other plan in view to molest and in-
jure us."

His anxiety about the "blank book" of the future mounted: An-
gered once again at his restive bondsmen, who seemed less and less
willing to obey their masters' orders, he cursed the day he purchased
them. "I wish they were safe in my pocket in hard coin at old valuation, or near it," he declared. Secession, however, had made the old
valuation a dream.


IN MID-AUGUST GENERAL Sherman's commissary chief had issued a
serious warning, stating, "Our supplies will soon be exhausted." Feeding men and mules, however, was not the western armies' commander's

foremost concern. "My only apprehension," Sherman insisted when the alert about supplies came, was the draining away of fighting men. Bullets and shells, dysentery and typhus, even malnutrition, took their share of soldiers, but Congress and Northerners without the will to see the fight through were, he argued, the real enemy siphoning off his fighting force. The three-year enlistment terms for entire battalions would expire over the next two months. He fretted as "daily regiments are leaving for home," taking from him their veteran soldiers, his "best material." Replacement troops under current federal conscription acts came through state-based quotas and arrived fitfully, unpredictably, and poorly prepared; the only new men he could expect to join his ranks in the near term were what he called "niggers and the refuse of the South," men, the racist general believed, who could not be made into soldiers and would "never come to the front." Sherman forecast that before the siege reduced Atlanta, "my army on the offensive, so far from its base, will fall below my opponent's, who increases, as I lose." He looked over the fortifications and saw no diminution in the Southern enemy hunkered down there beneath the storm of shells he hurled over their heads into Atlanta. "I rather think," he muttered, "today Hood's army is larger than mine, and he is strongly fortified."

He was wrong about the size of General Hood's army, which remained far smaller than his, but the secessionists refused to be driven from their earthworks. Indeed, Hood wanted to turn the tables, laying siege to the invaders' railroad lifeline. Sherman could not remain in place forever. The ever-daring Army of Tennessee commander wanted to speed the uninvited Northern guests' departure. As President Jefferson Davis had long urged on the reluctant, now displaced Gen. Joseph Johnston, Hood sent the cream of his own cavalry across the Chattahoochee at Roswell on August 10 and set them loose in North Georgia. The 4,000 horsemen rode six hundred miles through Union-held territory over the next month, first tearing up three long stretches of Sherman's vital railroad line, then attacking the Dalton fort and capturing some 3,000 head of beef cattle destined to feed the Yankee army. The cavalry continued their raid deep into Tennessee, threatening Chattanooga and even causing panic in Nashville.

Where others panicked, though, Sherman saw opportunity. With the rebel cavalry "out of the way . . . when shall we use cavalry, if not now?" he had wired Gen. George Thomas. On August 18, 4,700 of their own cavalry under the command of Gen. Judson Kilpatrick set off with Sherman's orders to "ride right round Atlanta and smash the Macon road all to pieces." If Kilpatrick succeeded, Sherman's massive army would be spared the need to make "a long, hazardous flank march" of its own.

The Yankee raiders spent the next six days riding a circuit of plunder and destruction around the city. They succeeded in destroying a stretch of track at Jonesboro, an important station town fifteen miles south of Atlanta, as well as two locomotives. They captured enemy horses, wagons, and guns and took out plenty of time to pillage and burn houses, stores, and public buildings in a couple of crossroad villages where many of Kilpatrick's horsemen ended up drunk on the whisky stashes they found—all while keeping rebel skirmishers off their front and rear.

Weary but bursting with pride, Kilpatrick reported back to Sherman on the evening of August 22 and recounted tales of high adventure on horseback. He triumphantly declared that his men had so demolished the Macon & Western Railroad that no train would run over it for at least ten days and perhaps as long as a month. The cavalry officer was not aware that Confederate railroad mechanics needed less time to repair the breach he'd made in the line than it took his men to make it. Early the next morning, an eleven-car train of munitions and food chugged into Atlanta behind three locomotives.

AGAIN DISAPPOINTED BUT LITTLE surprised by his cavalry's ineptitude, Sherman now knew, as he telegraphed Washington, "I will have to swing across" the Macon railroad "in force to make the matter certain." With this likely eventuality in mind, he and his three army commanders had already devised a plan for such a risky movement. His entire force would have to disengage from its grappler's headlock on Atlanta—and feint away from the secessionists' counterpunches— along the entire siege line. And the evacuation needed to take place without alerting the Confederates and exposing the withdrawing troops to attack while their backs were turned. The plan called for a complex grand wheel right by three entire armies who would march counterclockwise around Atlanta. It would be necessary to interweave the movements of more than 60,000 men from three armies to set the clockwork in motion. And the entire evacuation would need to be accomplished in just a few hours in the blackness of two nights—and in silence.

It was a risky maneuver under any circumstance, made doubly dangerous by enemy scouts and spies roving the countryside. Kilpatrick's cavalry's short-lived triumph did provide Sherman with valuable intelligence about the roads and terrain he would need to march across to reach his goal of breaking the Macon & Western Railroad line for good above the village of Jonesboro. Getting there meant marching his troops from the easternmost trenches more than thirty miles through enemy territory.

BEGINNING AFTER SUNSET ON August 25 and continuing through the night, the Yankees crept out of their trenches and stealthily abandoned their camps north and east of the city. The siege guns were pulled back, their embrasures covered with brush. Surplus wagons, horses, men, and materiel went across the Chattahoochee, while the remaining wagons with rations for fifteen days for men and horses and a hundred rounds of ammunition per man rolled out—with batting tied to the wheels to muffle the wagons' rattling. Confederate scouts reported hearing "unusual train" movements north and noticed stacks of brush piled in front of the embrasures but did not realize the Yankees had evacuated their fortifications. A Union corps, including Lt. Col. Charles Morse's Second Massachusetts, took up a position at the Chattahoochee River bridgehead, left there by Sherman to protect the railroad. Should disaster befall the wider movement, that line also would provide a last refuge for a retreating army. A second corps moved behind the first, then marched west and south to form a line well beyond the July 28 Ezra Church battlefield but facing northwards to cover the advancing column's rear from surprise attack.

The silence of the morning of August 26 confounded the Confederates in their earthworks. Officers ordered an extended artillery barrage to pound the rear of the former enemy positions, hoping to draw return fire. The Yankees were gone, wrote Pvt. Sam Watkins, "no one knew whither—and our batteries were shelling the woods, feeling for them." The shells exploded in vacant copses and camps. Later that morning, nervous vedettes pushed out beyond the picket posts until they reached the empty Union camps. They found the torn-up earth cluttered with abandoned knapsacks, tents, coats, food, empty ammunition crates, and broken-down limbers, the light-industrial detritus and fouled landscape left behind by an army that had packed up and departed quickly, as if gone up into thin air.

AFTER SUNSET ON AUGUST 26, a second Union movement began. The main body of the three armies commenced swinging out to the west of Atlanta and then south in a successive and concentric wheel by column. A corps left in the trenches at East Point screened the 60,000 men and supporting wagons and artillery in movement. The federal ruse worked as well as Sherman might have hoped. Hood telegraphed Richmond, "The enemy have drawn back so that their left is now on the Chattahoochee at the railroad bridge, their right unchanged."

By noon on Sunday, August 28, the Army of the Tennessee had struck the Atlanta and West Point Railroad about sixteen miles southwest of the city, and the Army of the Cumberland had fallen upon the same line several miles northeast of there, closer to East Point. For the rest of that day and all the following, the troops worked steadily to demolish five miles of the line—though it was already effectively useless to the Confederates because of earlier operations near Alabama. Sherman, however, had grown to hate the Confederate trains running into Atlanta almost as much as the armies behind the city's earthworks. He declared, "Let the destruction be so thorough that not a rail or tie can be used again." The troops had a two-day-long Sherman necktie party. Sherman even had crews fill in railroad cuts with trees and dirt and loaded shells as vicious booby traps should an attempt be made to clear the cuts, "so we may rest perfectly satisfied as regards the use of this railroad during the remainder of the campaign."

Keeping the trains from rolling was foremost in Sherman's thinking. He would sever Hood's last railroad links to the rest of rebeldom and also complete part of his primary mission to ensure Army of Tennessee troops could not reinforce Robert E. Lee in Virginia. Atlanta should never again serve as a rail hub for Confederate troops on the move. But just as importantly, he wanted to blast Confederate communications—what today is termed "infrastructure"—beyond repair. That would render the Confederate heartland incapable of supporting a campaigning army or other large-scale insurrection forces. Atlanta to Sherman was only a battle, albeit a crucial one, in what he believed would be many more years of war to come. In the fighting ahead, he did not want to have to garrison a conquered Atlanta with a full division of troops, as Memphis, Vicksburg, and other occupied Confederate cities required—"so that," he explained, "success was actually crippling our armies in the field by detachments to guard and protect the interests of a hostile population." The railroads' destruction would ensure that Atlanta, even if no Union troops remained within it, could not support another Confederate army; thus, he would be able to continue his war on the Confederacy without leaving crucial men behind to keep a grip on another hostile city.

Sherman was thinking well beyond the war-making armies of the South. He wanted to destroy the South's will to continue waging war. Inflicting desolation upon the wellspring of the rebellion was as important as the destruction of the Army of Tennessee. Much as the homes and crops of the Florida Seminole resisters needed to be destroyed when they made clear they would never leave voluntarily, Sherman believed that most secessionists would never willingly give up their cause. Large numbers of rebel soldiers and their civilian supporters would need to be driven from their homes, their means of livelihood obliterated and many, perhaps all, killed before the rebellion would be ended. His "aim then," he admitted, "was to humble their pride, to follow them to their inmost recesses, and to make them fear and dread us." He was there to teach a hard lesson, he wrote, quoting one of his favorite proverbs: "Fear of the Lord is the beginning of wisdom." He believed, he told Washington as he cut a swath of desolation through Georgia, "we cannot change the hearts and minds of those people of the South, but we can make war so terrible . . . [and] make them so sick of war [that they will] sue for peace." Destruction of the railroad was another psychological weapon in his nation's arsenal against those who would otherwise continue to resist the will of the United States.

Not until the morning of August 30 was he satisfied the job at hand was done. The railroad left beyond repair, movement toward his ultimate destination, the Macon & Western Railroad, could now commence.

SHERMAN'S INSISTENCE ON THE utter destruction of the railroad gave Hood's scouts the chance to alert him before the full Yankee movement struck out on its last leg toward the Macon railroad. Not until August 29, forty-eight hours after the grand federal wheel began circling Atlanta, did Hood grasp Sherman's main objective: to cut his last rail and all-important line in and out of town. Sherman's three columns were feeling their way toward the crossroads village of Rough and Ready and the station town of Jonesboro. However, Hood still misjudged the gravity of his danger—or feared a Yankee deviation from their march in on his southern perimeter. At first he sent parts of just two corps to Jonesboro to intercept the six-mile-long federal columns.

By the afternoon of August 30, Sherman's leading divisions had reached within a mile and easy cannon range of Jonesboro. Skirmishing soon began there and five miles north near Rough and Ready.

Unruffled in Atlanta, Hood sent word at 1 P.M. that he didn't think "the necessity would arise to send any troops to Jonesboro today." Only as the sun began to set did he understand the dire threat developing against his communications. Hood called the two corps' commanders he had sent into the field, Generals William Hardee and Stephen D. Lee, back to his Atlanta headquarters that night. Unlike Johnston, who would almost certainly have withdrawn at this point to a more defensible location after a successful flanking movement by the enemy, Hood *had* to go on the attack.

Without enough cars to move his soldiers to the field by rail, he marched the remaining men from Lee's and Hardee's corps—about 20,000 troops—through the night out of Atlanta to head off the 60,000 federal forces, virtually Sherman's entire troop strength. Hood kept a corps in Atlanta, still unsure where Sherman was going. Private Watkins joined the "forced march" out of town. He and his fellow Confederates tramped through the night and much of the next hot day along a circuitous route to avoid stumbling into contact with entrenching Union forces. Hardee and Lee were still uncertain where Sherman's forces were concentrated. Watkins joked ruefully, "A small portion—about a hundred thousand—were nigh about there somewhere." Strung out along the road from Atlanta, the sleepless rebels needed most of the day to reach Jonesboro and then line up for a charge, which Hood insisted upon repeatedly. He commanded that the lines should "go at the enemy with bayonets fixed, determined to drive everything they may come against."

Not surprisingly, when the two worn out Southern corps, depressed to be facing the bulk of Sherman's armies after thinking for days they had won, advanced starting at 3 p.m. on August 31, their lines were badly disorganized, more like an "infuriated mob," remarked one witness, than a veteran army. They charged into well-entrenched positions rife with artillery. Some companies simply refused to advance. "We did our level best to get up a fight," recalled Watkins of the battle, "but it was no go, any way we could fix it up." The Confederates were used up, horribly outnumbered and outgunned. The battle was a "killing time" for the Yankees. When it was done, at least 2,000 rebels lay dead or wounded against a loss of just 172 Union soldiers.

STILL NOT SURE WHAT Sherman's next move might be, Hood ordered Lee's Corps above Jonesboro back into the city in the early morning hours of September 1. It was his final error—and should have been a fatal one for the Army of Tennessee. The men marched, recalled Watkins, "without any order, discipline, or spirit to do anything. . . . Everyone was taking his own course, and wishing and praying to be captured. Hard and senseless marching, with little sleep, half rations and lice, had made their lives a misery." Sherman's 60,000-man army interposed itself between Hardee's heavily damaged corps dug in above and to the west of Jonesboro and Lee's weak and exhausted force slinking toward Atlanta. Watkins thought the end of the war was upon the army. The Northerners attacked General Hardee's remaining forces at Jonesboro that afternoon. Sherman personally commanded the battle, attempting to use his superior numbers to hold Hardee's front while getting on his rear. However, he still insisted on keeping a large portion of his force well above the battlefield at work destroying the railroad. That left otherwise easily cut off routes of retreat open for Hardee—and the corps moving toward Atlanta.

Still, the trap at Jonesboro nearly slammed shut. The night prior, though, Southerners had thrown up entrenchments in the heavily wooded and bramble-tangled countryside. The stout defensive position allowed Hardee's men to slip out of the trap even as the jaws snapped down. The Northerners captured nearly an entire brigade, more than six hundred prisoners, but the rebels held off the attackers until nightfall. Hardee lost another 1,000 men in total; Sherman just as many. Under the cover of darkness the Confederates fell back seven miles to Lovejoy's Station. The Yankees advanced on them the next day but encountered strong earthworks with swamps and thick tangles of vines protecting the defenders' flanks. Sherman decided to leave the rebel remnant there.

At this juncture, the Northern general had the opportunity to crush and destroy at least one, and probably both, of the badly demoralized, exposed, and truncated components of the Georgia defense by driving on Atlanta or encircling Hardee's remaining men at Lovejoy's. Sherman's army commanders asked permission to do just that. With the maddening whistles of the trains still echoing in his head, Sherman again ordered his vast army to stop and concentrate on destroying the railroad. He gave instructions to wreck the railroad between Jonesboro and Rough and Ready, declaring to General Thomas, "I don't believe anybody recognizes how important it is now to destroy the railroad." That allowed Hood the time he needed to reorganize. This time, though, it was not for another attack.

BY NOON ON SEPTEMBER 1, Hood's forces were pulling out of the fortifications and assembling along the Atlanta roads. Some Atlantans, recalled one young man on hand, "could not believe that the city was to be given up." Many residents ran back to the bombproofs they'd believed they'd exited for good. Now they feared Confederate forces marching down the Decatur and McDonough roads were massing for another battle.

Soon it was readily apparent, though, that the Army of Tennessee was leaving, this time for good. "Then," recorded Samuel Richards, "began a scramble among the inhabitants . . . to get away." Anyone who still doubted Hood intended to abandon his base, their city, understood the truth when the commissary depots' stores of grain and food, which could not be loaded quickly enough into the bulging army wagons, were thrown open to hungry citizens. Hundreds descended upon the depots to carry off supplies of bacon and hardtack, grain and corn meal, recounted Richards, "by the sackful and the cartload."

THE UNION FORCES WERE expected to take possession of the city at any moment. The night was cool and starry. After what he described as "a day of terror," Richards needed to decide what to do. Orders came for his militia battalion "to be on hand to go out with the army." He did not want to go, "so," he recorded matter-of-factly that night, "I thought I would resign." In the middle of "a night of dread," with cavalry racing around the city streets and the tramp-tramp of soldiers marching in long columns out of town resounding near his house, he and another militia company member who "had backed out" went down to a commissary depot along the Macon & Western Railroad. Richards loaded three sacks of corn meal into his buckboard. As the men started off, a "terrific" blast "jarred the ground and broke the glass in the windows around."

Tongues of flame, visible nearly two miles off, erupted skyward. The "incessant discharge" of explosions large and small continued for the next four hours, shaking houses and shattering glass in every direction.

THAT NIGHT GENERAL SHERMAN was bivouacked in the field below Jonesboro. At the end of a day's fighting, he was "so restless and impatient" for the next step in the action that he couldn't sleep. He paced about his camp until, around midnight, he heard shells exploding and other sounds "like that of musketry" coming from the direction of Atlanta. The noises from twenty miles off were so intense he couldn't tell if they were the sounds of battle or of magazines going up—a sign that Hood was leaving the city. He walked to a farmhouse next to his camp. He called the farmer to come listen with him to the blasts still reverberating from the direction of Atlanta. Sherman asked the man if he had resided there long enough to be familiar with such sounds. The farmer said they sounded like battle noises to him. Sherman went back to his camp. At about 4 A.M., more explosions like the first shook the countryside.

He still remained in doubt whether Hood was engaged in blowing up his own munitions as part of an evacuation of Atlanta or the Union forces outside the city had felt their way forward and become engaged in a real battle. As late as the following evening, he was still not sure. He informed his army generals not to attack "until we hear from Atlanta the exact truth." He saw no reason to "push . . . your men against breastworks." Instead, he wanted them to "destroy the railroad well up to your lines." But General Hood's army was already long gone as the flames of Atlanta lit up the night's darkness throughout the region, and the explosions echoed as far off as Macon. Only a cavalry regiment remained behind as a rearguard to slow the Union army's entry into the wrecked city. ·

GENERAL HOOD HAD SENT word early on August 31 to empty out the army's remaining stores in Atlanta before the Macon railroad was cut off. He still had a plentiful supply of munitions and other materiel on hand for the fighting to come. Five locomotives and eighty-one boxcars stood lined up in a double row on the Georgia Railroad tracks running out along the eastern edge of the city. Most cars were loaded with food and medical supplies, but hundreds of gunpowder kegs, hand grenades and shells by the thousands, thirteen pieces of heavy artillery, 5,000 rifles, and 3 million cartridges filled twenty-eight of the cars. The trains idled next to many of the industrial shops and factories that had propelled Atlanta in its dizzying ascent to becoming the citadel of the Confederacy, including the Atlanta Rolling

Mill—the former Scofield and Markham Mill that the two Unionists had been forced to sell to Confederates—the Western & Atlantic Railroad roundhouse, arsenal shops, a cannon foundry, and the Atlanta Machine Company. Many homes and warehouses packed with cotton bales fronted the yard.

The chief quartermaster officer assigned to send the trains out of Atlanta failed to act, too drunk according to Hood to carry out his orders. The troops began their outbound march the following night. At that point, the precious military cargo sat stranded on the tracks, prevented from rolling out of town by the severing of the rail line. The munitions could not fall into Yankee hands. Home guardsmen alerted people living near the tracks to flee. Staff officers torched the boxcars and hurried off to join their departing troops. Sixteen-year-old Mary Rawson, asleep in her father's mansion on Pryor Street, was startled awake around midnight by "a most beautiful spectacle." The sky was "in a perfect glow," as "flaming rockets" burst overhead and "sparks filled the air with innumerable spangles." In another direction she saw "bright light" come from stores of cotton that went up in flames.

The exploding trains leveled every structure for hundreds of yards almost instantly. Only a few chimneys and the wheels of the obliterated rolling stock hinted at what once existed there. Bricks, shrapnel, shot, unexploded shells, fragments of machinery, chunks of track, and boilers, flywheels, and smokestacks from locomotives, along with millions of bullets, shot out, perforating buildings more than a quarter mile off. Even days later, nobody dared approach too close as hot shells strewn far and wide continued to explode. Four days after the blast, one sightseer came upon what he called a scene of "perfect destruction." He was stunned at the blast's power, seeing rails "twisted into the most curious shapes imaginable and the heavy timbers on which they rested . . . torn into splinters no larger than matches."

That night hundreds of people went to high ground to watch the display of munitions fireworks; hundreds more fled underground. "Language falls short," recorded Rawson, "in expressing the suspense and anxiety experienced by everyone." Atlanta was being consumed by the war-making weaponry left behind by its former defenders, who had deliberately touched off the city's first great bonfire.

ALLEN T. HOLLIDAY WAS in the column marching out of town when the first explosion went off. "I thought I had heard a noise before," he penned, "but never anything to equal that. The noise continued all night." He marched and marched, sleepless, never stopping to eat for twenty hours, one foot in front of the other without pause. "I thought I had been tired but I never knew what it was to be tired," he wrote when he finally stopped at 4 p.m. the next afternoon. "The bottoms of my feet are worn out to a blister."

As the morning light broke, more than ten miles out of town, marching with Atlanta's departed defenders on their way to meet up with the rest of Hood's army at Lovejoy's Station, Holliday could still see the light of the fires burning on the horizon. A last big blast went off shortly before dawn.

THE SUN ROSE THAT morning with an unearthly glow, looming red within the smoky sky. Not long after sun up, Mayor James M. Calhoun left his house. The city was deathly quiet. Only about seventy-five cavalrymen under Brig. Gen. Samuel Ferguson remained behind. Other than Ferguson's men, some soldiers too badly wounded to move, and hundreds of stragglers, for the first time in more than three years soldiers did not fill Atlanta. Also, for the first time in his four years as mayor, Calhoun was Atlanta's unchallenged leader. Now, he desperately wanted to save his ravaged city and its few thousand remaining inhabitants from total destruction. Around 7 o'clock that morning he went out Marietta Street to see General Ferguson. He found Ferguson's brigade formed up in a line of battle behind barricades they'd thrown up in the road. He went to the general and pleaded with him "to withdraw his brigade and make no further resistance." Even a token defense, he feared, would bring down a final fury of violence upon the badly wounded city from the Union invaders.

Hood's orders to Ferguson, though, were clear. He told Calhoun he was "to defend the City to the last, which he would do." Knowing what this meant, Calhoun returned home to await the worst.

OVER THE NEXT THREE HOURS, expecting the Union army to move forward at any instant, General Ferguson must have reflected on his grim situation. Late in the morning, he sent a courier to Calhoun asking him to meet. The last Confederate officer in Atlanta agreed now, the mayor recalled, to "comply with my request and withdraw his forces and have no battle in the city." The general assigned the civilian leader "to notify the United States forces" after his withdrawal that Atlanta was theirs.

Despite his personal loyalty to the Confederate cause, Calhoun still considered himself a Unionist. He had never abandoned his friends who remained committed Union loyalists over the past three years of war and came to their defense even at risk to his own life. He now turned to them. He invited all he could find among the city's leading citizens left in town, most of them Unionists in any case, to meet him in his City Hall office. They decided to ride out—at Calhoun's insistence unarmed—with a white flag to where the Union army remained entrenched along the Chattahoochee River. They figured they would find General Sherman there. A crowd of five hundred stunned people gathered quietly amid the perforated stores and buildings surrounding the Five Points. They watched the surrender party ride up to the artesian well. The men on horseback included Alfred Austell, Thomas G. W. Crussell, Julius Hayden, Thomas Kile, William Markham, E. E. Rawson, and J. E. Williams, all of them among the town's wealthiest and most established citizens and several among those hounded for their Union fealty over the past four years.

The crowd must have been shocked to see Mayor Calhoun welcome a black man into their midst. Atlanta's mayor requested Robert Webster to ride out with the group. Even if they were Union loyalists, most of the men were slaveholders. Now, all set off together. A black man, perhaps the son of Daniel Webster, a slave belonging to one of the foremost Confederate families who had both made a small fortune from the war and done all in his power to help break the Confederacy's back, rode alongside the white fathers of the city. They felt their way out up Marietta Street, past houses reduced in many cases to piles of splinters.

For Calhoun the journey marked the end of the world that he and the other Virginians of old had fought the Indians to carve out of the Georgia landscape. For Webster the ride felt like the beginning of a new world.


THEY ENTERED THE EMPTY fortifications near the blasted shell of the Ponder house, its walls pulverized by thousands of pounds of shell and shot. Spiked and abandoned artillery pieces sat mute in Fort Hood. The limbs of the dead in their shallow graves poked up through the ground nearby. Somewhere around the fields lay the body of A. J. Neal, beloved son of the mayor's dear friends, just one among the tens of thousands fallen in the fight for Atlanta.

About two miles past the ramparts, they encountered a few Union troops led by Indiana captain Henry M. Scott, along with a cavalry escort who came forward to meet the white flag. Calhoun explained their purpose, and Scott told them to wait there. He soon returned with Col. John Coburn. Mustering as much authority and dignity as he could, the exhausted, gray-haired Mayor Calhoun said, "Colonel Coburn, the fortune of war has placed Atlanta in your hands, as Mayor of the City I came to ask protection for non-combatants, and for private property." Coburn had Calhoun write out a surrender note to deliver to his commander, Brig. Gen. W. T. Ward.

The city now formally surrendered, Captain Scott's cavalry moved forward down Marietta Street. As they did, he heard "loud reports" from the explosions still bursting around the Georgia Railroad. Scott's men had not gotten far when shots rang out. A few Union men fell dead and wounded. Scott warned some people he saw that "if the Rebels continued to fire from behind houses they need expect no protection." Alerted to the firing, Calhoun rode ahead of the Yankees. He found a few drunken stragglers and demanded they stop. The last Confederate fighters in Atlanta threatened to shoot the mayor dead. Union infantry came forward and in quick order cleared the city, taking more than one hundred prisoners, including wounded men left behind by the Confederate army.

The very last fighting for Atlanta took place in front of Mayor Calhoun's own house on Washington Street. Soon the Union forces reached City Hall, where regimental flags from Pennsylvania and New York were hoisted atop its cupola. Not long after that, James Dunning, the Unionist once arrested by Col. George Washington Lee's provost marshal force, ran the first U.S. flag to fly in Atlanta since 1860 up a pole on Alabama Street.

AT ABOUT NOON, Samuel Richards glanced out his window. His mouth dropped. There, "sure enough," five or six Yankees rode by. They were among the advance Union men moving across the city. Once the stragglers were cleared and the city secured, Colonel Coburn led the first in a long line of soldiers marching down Marietta Street into Atlanta. As they went, some residents looked on "with apprehension"; a few jeered; others hid. According to Coburn, though, "Many of the citizens ran gladly out to meet us, welcoming us as deliverers from the despotism of the Confederacy." Cyrena Stone was among them. She stood for two hours on a downtown corner as the long line of her liberators marched by. She waved a silk American flag that she had secretly harbored for the entire war. According to a friend's postwar account, "She was a splendid looking woman about thirty years old, and the whole army cheered her and her flag as they went past."

# CHAPTER 25

# THE SECOND BONFIRE

A T MIDDAY ON SEPTEMBER 2, Noble Calhoun Williams, Ezekiel Calhoun's grandson, and two friends went out to collect hardtack from the abandoned Confederate commissary for animal feed. Dr. Calhoun's slaves had had a laugh at the young boys' expense by terrorizing them with colorful descriptions of the approaching Yankees "as beastly and bloodthirsty monsters, whose delight it was to catch men, women and innocent children for no other purpose than to murder them." As the trio gathered the biscuits hard as stone, Noble and his two friends spied the first bluecoats approaching. They let out a yelp of fright and raced home without stopping. The young Calhoun darted under his grandmother's bed and refused to come out. His grandparents finally coaxed the boy out from his hiding place. The family went out together onto the porch. Soon they saw a federal officer and his staff riding down the street in front of the house. An hour later, Noble recalled, came "the tramp, tramp, tramp" of thousands of soldiers marching down the street by the doctor's house. Even this small initial wing of Sherman's army—the first-arriving XX Corps— was so enormous, it took hours more for it to pass. Finally, the command went down the line to halt and rest.

No sooner had the bluecoats broken ranks than Noble saw scores of faces peering over the fence separating the street from the garden. They reminded the boy of a flock of hungry bluebirds. The Yankees looked longingly at the grape arbor, brimming with plump purple grapes. The soldiers' rations for the entire four months of campaigning had been nothing but hard bread, bacon, coffee, and sugar, plus the occasional slice of beef. For the past four months, none had seen even a piece of fruit except blackberries they picked in the ubiquitous brambles. Before long, they flew over the fence into the garden, fluttered about the arbor, and gobbled down every last grape.

SMALL GRAPES COMPARED TO the losses suffered by town shopkeepers. Samuel Richards heard that Gen. Henry W. Slocum, whose XX Corps troops led in the Union investment of the town, promised to respect private property. Richards was pleased to see that "private houses were not molested by the soldiers." He thought the same would be true for other property and, after visiting the store downtown earlier in the day, "left it all quiet." When he returned late that afternoon, though, his heart sank "to see armsful and baskets full of books and wallpaper going up the street in a continuous stream from our store." He entered the shop, and there saw something beyond his worst imagination: "Yankees, men, women, children and niggers were crowded into the store each one scrambling to get something to carry away." The looters took anything and everything, "regardless, apparently, whether it was anything they needed." The downtown streets were in an uproar. Doors were being smashed down, windows shattered, boxes and papers tossed out windows into the street. Throughout the Five Points, soldiers broke open stores and offices "in their mad hunt" for tobacco and whisky. "The rabble," lamented Richards, "had then 'pitched in' thinking it a 'free fight.'"

Overwhelmed, he looked on "almost resolved" to let them empty out his store, but then finally roused himself to shoo the mob out the door. He stood guard until nightfall. The next day, he went to get his mule to haul home whatever was left, but the mule was gone from the shed, probably stolen. Richards managed to borrow a friend's and went downtown to box his goods up. While he carried packages out of the store to the wagon, Union soldiers, "who *looked* like gentlemen," walked in and stole books "before our eyes." Several others, he did note, picked up books "and *paid* for them."

Even so, the Confederate Richards was much more fortunate than loyal Union man Robert Webster, as the former Bob Yancey now proudly called himself. The wealthy former slave's luck seemed at first remarkably good: The storm of shells from the Battle of Atlanta and the city's eventual occupation had demolished or heavily damaged every house on Houston Street; yet his came through largely unscathed. The Yankees even buried forty of their dead on Jared Whitaker's neighboring property—"to desecrate" the staunch Confederate former mayor's land, claimed the *Intelligencer*, the secessionist paper he once guided. Webster had done so much to undermine the Confederate cause and aid Union soldiers imprisoned in Atlanta throughout the war. He now watched in dismay as the Yankees went after the large cache of tobacco in his house as well as his livestock. Their victory rendered his remaining Confederate currency holdings from his arbitrage between the sides all but worthless. The boxes of tobacco he stored away represented a good portion of the wealth he had left from his enormous wartime earnings. Joseph Blood, another black man in town whose property Union soldiers had plundered, went to commiserate with his friend. Webster exclaimed to him, "My Lord, I thought they had come here to protect us, but they have taken everything I have got."

Prince Ponder, too, had done much to help prepare the way for the Union army, while hiring out his time as a slave from his owner, Ellen Ponder, to trade in currency and whatever else he could sell through his grocery store in Atlanta for the past three years. He had made around $100,000 in Confederate money and still possessed a storehouse of valuable goods. He hoped to profit from them after the war. Before the Battle of Atlanta, he moved his remaining goods and personal property a mile and a half out of town for safekeeping on the plantation of fellow Union loyalist, wealthy builder and industrialist Julius Hayden. The conquering Union army camped on the land. While there, the bluecoats confiscated nearly everything Ponder owned, among which he listed 175 bushels of corn and 60 of wheat, 600 pounds of flour, 425 pounds of bacon, 15 hogs, a cow and geese, two mules and a wagon, plus a dray and a bay horse, a buggy and harnesses, and 14,000 bundles of fodder. He was promised repayment for the requisitioned items he valued together at nearly US$3,700—enough to make him one of Atlanta's wealthier men after the war's devastation, no matter what his color. He believed, "If the government knew how much service I did for them they would pay me without a word." It would take more than a decade pursuing his claim, though, before he received barely fifteen cents compensation for each dollar he claimed to have lost.

AS BLUECOATS AND TOWNSPEOPLE alike went on their looting sprees in the first hours after Atlanta's fall, the Second Massachusetts Infantry from Slocum's XX Corps marched past the two Calhoun brothers' houses on Washington Street and into City Hall Square. Once they moved into their camp there, they set about taking charge of the city. Charles Morse, now lieutenant colonel of the Second Massachusetts, was named provost marshal. He appointed Capt. Henry Newton Comey officer of the day for the first twenty-four hours of the city's occupation. Comey's initial—happily performed—official duty was to pull the Confederate flag down from the City Hall pole and run up the Stars and Stripes. "Oh!" he exclaimed, looking up at his handiwork. "It has been a glorious victory."

He and Morse entered City Hall, which Mayor James Calhoun had locked behind him that morning. Their only "depredations" came when they broke the doors open into its main hall and courtroom, the scenes of so many events in the city's now ended Confederate life. As provost marshal, the twenty-five-year-old Morse was now the "'Mayor' and answerer of all questions to the citizens of a good-sized city." He was quickly "overrun with business," dealing with the distribution of provost guards, handling irate citizen complaints, getting the hundreds of Confederate prisoners under guard, and stopping the pillaging in town. He took the county courtroom as his office and assigned other rooms for guard functions. Comey moved about town the rest of his first day and night in Atlanta, returning order to the city and "trying to protect the citizens and their property from the depredations of the vandals of our army."

The provost guard seized and confiscated all tobacco for distribution to the troops and also every drop of wine and liquor that could be found. According to Morse, spirits of sufficiently good quality went to the medical department, while the "'benzene' variety of whiskey" went "into the gutters." By the following morning, the last looters had been driven off and Confederate prisoners taken in, and Samuel Richards grudgingly admitted that after the terrifying rampage of the first day, "The enemy behave themselves pretty well." He saw the "sad sight" of nearly 2,000 rebel prisoners lined up in the street under guard from his Baptist church all the way to Whitehall Street. After four years of graycoat rule, he found it "strange to go about Atlanta now and see only Yankee uniforms."

WHILE THE POINT OF all attention fell into Union hands, on September 2, Gen. William Tecumseh Sherman moved about a battlefield some twenty-five miles below the city. He did not yet know the fate of Atlanta and awaited clear pronouncements on the situation well to his north. General Slocum had already telegraphed Washington to announce, "General Sherman has taken Atlanta," but the man himself did not know that he had finally captured his prize. Willing prisoners fallen out of Gen. John Bell Hood's columns told of the city's evacuation and even detailed the route of march, but Sherman distrusted the reports and made no move to cut off the retreat when he could. Instead, he spent the day watching the repulse of his assaults by Gen. William Hardee's barely 10,000-man rebel corps outside Lovejoy's Station. That evening he decided to hold off further attack. Not "until we hear from Atlanta the exact truth . . . ," he explained, "will [I] determine what to do." Finally, early the next morning, a dispatch from Slocum confirmed the taking of Atlanta. Sherman called a halt to the destruction of the railroads, "our present task . . . well done."

From his headquarters half a day's ride south of Atlanta, he sent off a courier to carry his message to the city, from where it was telegraphed to Gen. Henry W. Halleck, the U.S. Army's chief of staff in Washington. It described the efforts of the past few days that had broken up Hood's last supply line and placed the Union army between the Confederate commander and "a considerable part of his army," compelling him to blow up his magazines stranded in Atlanta and leave the city for Yankee occupation. "So," he concluded, "Atlanta is ours & fairly won." Those few restrained words would be repeated and hailed again and again in reports about the fall of the Gate City throughout the North.

Sherman immediately dashed off a letter to his wife, Ellen, relaying the news. He was more boastful in telling her, "My movement has been perfectly successful."

He had already decided not to "push much further"—or complete the task of destroying the Army of Tennessee now struggling to regroup somewhere below and to the east of him. "Since the 5th of May we have been in one constant battle or skirmish & need rest," he informed Halleck. He would pull all his armies back into a fortified city. It was time to rest.

IN WASHINGTON, President Abraham Lincoln had hovered near the War Department telegraph office for days, anxiously waiting for reports to come in from Georgia. He breathed a profound sigh of relief when Slocum's first word clicked over the line. For the first time, he confidently knew that the war had not been fought in vain. He wrote to Sherman in gratitude, "The marches, battles, sieges, and other military operations that have signalized the campaign, must render it famous in the annals of war." He called for the firing off of a one-hundred-gun salute in Washington. Still stalemated in Virginia, Ulysses S. Grant ordered shots from "every battery bearing upon the enemy" fired "in honor of your great victory." The salutes echoed in towns large and small throughout the North, in Albany, Buffalo and Oswego, New York; Lynn, Massachusetts; Belfast, Maine; New Haven; New York City; Philadelphia; Cleveland; and hundreds of other places where the name of Atlanta had not existed until six months before, particularly in the West, home to most of the men campaigning with Sherman. By the hundreds ceremonial cannon went off in celebration, accidentally blowing off the hands of two men in Lewiston, Maine, and one in Boston; bells rang out, flags flew, and local infantry companies paraded before crowds of cheering townspeople. Rochester, New York, reportedly held some of the grander celebrations, firing two hundred guns and pealing every church and civic bell, while fireworks burst overhead, bonfires blazed, and "an immense throng" of citizens paraded rejoicing through the streets. A city now widely understood to stand second only to Richmond in the Confederacy—the heart to the brain—was in Union hands.

In Chicago, too, a hundred-gun salute went off, and bells rang all over the city on September 3. The delegates to the Democratic National Convention, gathered there for their final evening of deliberations, listened to the reverberations echo through the hall and understood their national hopes were now defeated, even if two months remained until the November elections. They completed their nomination of Gen. George McClellan as candidate for president and ratified their peace platform. The planks called, "after four years of failure to restore the Union," for "a cessation of hostilities" and negotiations among the states that "peace may be restored." A week earlier, their man McClellan had reportedly proclaimed, "If I am elected, I will recommend an immediate armistice and a call for a convention of all the states and insist upon exhausting all and every means to secure peace without further bloodshed."

A few days after leaving Chicago to start his half-hearted campaign for president, McClellan owned up to the implications of Atlanta's fall. The Democrats' candidate repudiated his own party's "four years of failure" platform plank. Peace would come only, he now declared, on the "one condition" of Union.

The blood spilled for Atlanta had indeed been appalling. Union forces had suffered 31,687 men killed, wounded, or missing during the campaign; the Confederates, 30,976. More than two-thirds of the rebel losses came after Hood took command from Gen. Joseph Johnston. After the greatest city siege in the nation's history, though, the surrender of Atlanta erased any doubt that the terrible war would be fought to its conclusion.

REVELING IN HIS CITY police chief duties some seven hundred miles south of Chicago, Officer of the Day Captain Comey of the Second Massachusetts understood precisely what his presence in Atlanta's City Hall meant for the future of the war and the nation. "A glorious victory," he exclaimed at the end of his first full day in the Gate City, "just at the correct time too. . . . It knocks McClellan into pie (as the soldiers say), and every soldier rejoices." He was shocked, however, that the Confederate city official he and Colonel Morse, the Yankee "mayor," dined with that day did not seem particularly dismayed by the turn of events. That man was Mayor James Calhoun.

According to Comey, the mayor of the city, whom he incorrectly believed "a nephew of John C. Calhoun," made known to the U.S. officers that he had "always been opposed to seceding." He told them about his service as a delegate "to the Bell and Everett Convention." With most diehard Confederates gone from the city—or dead—Comey realized that large numbers of those remaining, like the city's mayor himself, "represent a strong Union sentiment."

Now publishing in Macon, the *Intelligencer* got wind of Calhoun's dinner guests. The newspaper decided to publish a calumnious and false report that Calhoun and other Union sympathizers had attended an orgiastic ball at the Trout House with General Sherman and his staff on September 5, though the man and his officers remained more than twenty-five miles distant at the time. According to editor John Steele, though,

> About a dozen women of the town, not a decent lady amongst them, attended the thing. But what was wanting in white was made up in niggers. They mingled, oh! how they mingled. . . . Billy Markham brought two nigger women to the ball, and looked on the scene with grinning admiration. . . . The negro women were feted and toasted and monopolized the attention of

the entire crew of the Yankees; and in fact some of the sympathizers who have affiliated. They waltzed, schottisched, and polkaed and danced until everybody was tired and drunk and the stink became unendurable. . . . Mayor Jim Calhoun was present, toasting and congratulating the Yankees.

Calhoun refuted the story in a letter and even challenged the unnamed author "for the purpose of claiming personal satisfaction," but the paper stood by its reporting, even citing a Union newspaper's correspondent's report from the occupied city that Calhoun, "himself a professed Union man, avers that nine-tenths of the present inhabitants are loyal, and remained to welcome the entrance of the Federal army." More than a few Confederates thought the mayor deserved to be strung up with the rest of the Tories.

While the press besmirched Calhoun's Confederate reputation and endangered the lives of open loyalists like William Markham, the Yankee colonel Morse felt welcomed across the square from City Hall in the handsome home of William Solomon and his family, where he took quarters. It was the same house on Mitchell Street from which Bishop Henry Lay had witnessed the first Yankee shell burst across the street in the park nearly a month and a half before. Morse, trained as an architect, appreciated the gracious proportions of the large Italianate mansion. "The family," he believed, "were very glad to have us occupy the house for their own protection; they are very fine people, and I think have very little sympathy with the South."

Morse and others charged with ferreting out active Confederates and providing vouchers for federal government repayment for property seized from loyalists soon learned who the truly loyal people in town were, going in particular to William Markham, James Dunning, and Thomas Crussell to confirm their claims. When former Confederate provost marshal Col. George Washington Lee learned of their cooperation with the Yankees, he called Markham in particular "low and pusillanimous," describing him as a man with "no small quantity of the *canine* in his composition." He wished that others had not interfered with his earlier pursuit of the "traitors" of the "secretly organized . . . Union Circle." The same people were now "the identical ones who remained in the city and have resorted to every hellish design imaginable in securing the destruction of loyal Southern citizens' property." He hoped to have at them before the war was over.

With his architect's eye, Morse inspected *his* new town. "Atlanta is a very pretty place," he remarked, "and less Southern in its appearance than any I have seen." He was pleasantly surprised by what he found. "Quite a new town," he remarked, and its "depots are the best I ever saw for railroad accommodations." He noted the "large numbers of elegant residences . . . many deserted. Our shells destroyed a great deal of property." Upon reflection, he regretted the past month's largely indiscriminate shelling of the city. He was "sorry now that a single one was thrown into the city." He did not think "they [had] hastened surrender by a day. They did not harm the rebel army, the only casualties being twenty harmless old men, women and children, and two soldiers." Targeting a civilian population seemed wrong to him. "There are differences of opinion about this kind of warfare," he understood, "but I don't like it."

LIKE IT OR NOT, the man who ordered the siege was not finished with its residents. Without any martial fanfare, on September 7, five days after General Hood's departure, still wearing his dusty field jacket, General Sherman rode into the conquered city. He and his other officers chose their headquarters and residences from among the mansions and finer homes around City Hall and the square. Gen. John W. Geary, who commanded a division in Slocum's XX Corps, and his staff moved in with Mayor Calhoun on Washington Street. Gen. John M. Schofield took the house up the street at the Mitchell Street corner where the Clayton family had lived. Right across Washington Street, General Sherman chose the grandest and best-situated house of all for himself—the big, brick, white-columned mansion now abandoned to another owner by the family of artillery captain A. J. Neal, whose body lay in the ground somewhere near the ruins of the Ponder place a mile or so out Marietta Street.

Sherman wasted no time. He set in motion a shocking first and unprecedented step of what would become the most controversial military measure in American history.

He "had thought much and long" about what to do with Atlanta once he possessed it. The day after he learned of the city's fall, he proposed to General Halleck "to remove all inhabitants of Atlanta." He would send "those committed to our cause to the rear & the Rebel families to the front." He intended to empty the city of all civilians, turn it into a "pure Gibraltar," a fortified military camp, leaving the "entire use of the railroad" for military purposes. Not since the removal of the Indians—and never comprehending white inhabitants—had a major North American settlement been deliberately and systematically emptied by a conquering army. Now he proposed to re-move a large modern city's entire population. Atlanta was to cease to exist as a home for civilians.

Sherman saw many advantages to such a move. He would be freed of the need to police and feed the destitute thousands in Atlanta and for miles around. Poor white women and children, elderly men, and former black slaves had fled the desolation of the warred-over countryside and gathered into the city region, where they faced over-whelming hardships, even starvation. Three days after Atlanta's fall, James Comfort Patten marched into town with the Fifty-eighth Indi-ana Volunteers. While passing through the fortifications, the army surgeon was struck by "the most pitiful sight I have ever yet witnessed." Ignoring the troops marching along the road, a young mother skinned a dead cow at the roadside. Her daughter, "some six or seven years old," stood next to the carcass with "a piece of the raw bloody meat in both hands devouring it with the eagerness of a starving dog." It was nothing others had not seen repeated throughout the area.

In a city off-limits to civilians, Sherman and his men would not be troubled by such heartbreaking scenes or have to worry about pro-viding for the hungry and homeless. His men could carry out their occupation of the town without the tensions and occasional terrorist activities his investing armies had endured in every other hostile city taken so far. There was also important symbolism to his cruelty. He wanted the harshness of his actions to broadcast a message even louder than his artillery batteries' report. The South, he expected, would draw "two important conclusions" from his self-described "bar-barity and cruelty": First, if any doubted him before, his expulsion or-der made perfectly clear that he acted "in earnest"; second, if civilians and soldiers were alike "sincere in their common and popular clamor 'to die in the last ditch,' that opportunity would soon come."

His strategy for the war that lay ahead also figured in the decision to remove the civilian population. He wrote his wife, Ellen, ten days after reaching Atlanta that his work of crushing the rebellion throughout the South was not done. "Far from it," he confided. "We must *kill* these three hundred thousand I have told you of so often, and the further they run the harder for us to get them." Though badly mauled, demoralized, and disorganized, the enemy still lay armed in dug-in positions outside Atlanta. Other Confederate forces continued to fight in Tennessee, Mississippi, and even Kentucky. Their support-ers would provide for them. After the period of rest, Sherman would need to pursue the Army of Tennessee and other foes throughout his department. Emptied of civilians, Atlanta could be fortified and defended by a comparatively small force while serving as a base for the future operations he envisioned would be needed to kill the last Southern resisters.

He knew just what sort of reaction to expect. He was sure the people of the South would "raise a howl against my barbarity & cruelty." He had his response to their criticisms: "I will answer that war is war & not popularity seeking. If they want peace, they & their relations must stop war." For his part, he believed with "absolute certainty . . . [in my] policy's justness and . . . wisdom."

THE DAY SHERMAN ARRIVED IN TOWN, he called Mayor Calhoun to the Neal house on City Hall Square that the town leader knew so well. The red-haired Northern general handed the circumspect, gray-haired town official a letter addressed to General Hood and asked him to designate two men to pass through the lines to deliver it. Calhoun read the letter in shock. In it, the Northern general announced that the population left in Calhoun's city must go, choosing whether to head north for repatriation within Union-controlled areas or to travel by train or wagon to Rough and Ready, where, under flag of truce, Hood's Confederate army could transport them without interference through the lines and south.

When General Hood read the message, he was thunderstruck. He wrote back, not seeing "any alternative in this matter," that he would carry out the truce terms. In closing his letter, though, he protested that "the unprecedented measure you propose transcends, in studied and ingenious cruelty, all acts ever before brought to my attention in the dark history of war." He appealed to his opposite "in the name of God and humanity" not to expel "from their homes and firesides the wives and children of a brave people."

Sherman's policy hit its mark. Sherman wanted to make sure that others heard the message. He responded with deep scorn to Hood the following day by pointing to the blond general's own disregard for civilian lives during the warring in and around the city. He noted that the Confederate army had burned and otherwise destroyed scores of houses throughout their fighting—fifty in Atlanta he had seen just that day alone—"because they stood in the way of your forts and men." He further pointed to Hood's positioning his army's lines so close to town that inevitably Union cannon and musket fire "overshot their mark" and flew into civilian areas. Sherman ignored his express wish to employ his siege guns to "destroy the town." In any case, he scorned Hood's invocation of God in such an ugly business as war, telling him, "In the name of common sense, I ask you not to appeal to a just God in such a sacrilegious manner." He found it laughable that Hood should condemn him when, he wrote referring to the Confederacy, "You . . . in the midst of peace and prosperity, have plunged a nation into war—dark and cruel war." He concluded, "God will judge us in due time, and he will pronounce whether it be more humane to fight with a town full of women and the families of a brave people at our back, or to remove them in time to places of safety among their own friends and people."

It was Hood's turn to answer scorn with scorn. He wrote back a several-page letter in which he mocked Sherman's notion that his batteries "for several weeks unintentionally fired too high for my modest fieldworks, and slaughtered women and children by accident and want of skill." He proudly acknowledged that his independent nation had waged war on the "insolent intruders" from the Union who "came to our doors upon the mission of subjugation." He derided Sherman's claims that any Confederate actions, toward the United States and in the war, were less than legal and moral for a sovereign nation to undertake against its enemy's "hateful tyranny." He concluded, "You say, 'Let us fight it out like men.' To this my reply is—for myself, and I believe for all the true men, ay, and women and children, in my country—we will fight you to the death! Better die a thousand deaths than submit to live under you or your government and your negro allies!"

Wanting the last word, Sherman, who was probably as much a racist as his enemy, had no desire to see any black soldiers under his command, and noted in his brief reply, "We have no 'negro allies' in this army; not a single negro soldier left Chattanooga with this army, or is with it now." He also pointed out that he was "not bound by the laws of war to give notice of the shelling of Atlanta," since it was a fortified town replete with magazines and industrial centers of war.

As Sherman surely intended, their bitter exchange quickly became public, published within days in newspapers throughout both sections of the country. In the South, it confirmed Sherman's stature as "the brute." For those in the North, Sherman not only sealed his reputation as a military strategist of the first order but won fame as a political thinker who understood precisely the tragedy of civil war and the surest route to victory. And he could knock the hell out of his opponent on both the battlefield and the page. "What a 'buster' that

[Sherman] is!" wrote Charles Francis Adams Jr. to his brother Henry.
The Adams brothers were grandsons and great-grandsons of presidents. "No wonder they said in the early days of the war that he was
either a drunkard or a crazy man. How he does finish up poor Hood!"
Sherman was now widely touted as a future president, though he
scoffed at such notions, wanting nothing to do with politics. Comfortably situated in Atlanta, he wrote his foster brother, "The people
of the U.S. have too much sense to make me their President."

Charles Morse saw Sherman every day after that, often sitting
out with the general and other officers on the same balcony where the
Neal family watched the first Atlanta companies parade in the City
Hall Square. The new occupants listened to the Second Massachusetts band playing in the "pleasant shady" square in front of their
houses. Of Sherman's brilliance, Morse had no doubt. He found the
man's indifference to military order and chain of command confound-
ing at times but declared, "He is the most original character and the
greatest genius there is in the country, in my opinion."

MAYOR CALHOUN LOOKED ABOUT Atlanta and saw destitute people,
many of whom had no place to go and no means to get to safety. A
large portion of those left in the city remained because they were too
sick or too old to travel. Together with the last two city councilmen
left in Atlanta, Calhoun, as "the only legal organ of the people" of the
city, asked Sherman to reconsider the expulsion order. The genial
mayor penned a letter in which he appealed to the general's sympathies for the bereft population. The move would cause "consequences
appalling and heartrending." Calhoun asked Sherman to consider the
"many poor women [who] are in advanced state of pregnancy, others
now having young children, and whose husbands for the greater part
are either in the army, prisoners, or dead." People traveling through
the Southern army's lines would face terrible hardships because "the
country south of this is already crowded, and without houses enough
to accommodate the people, and we are informed that many are now
staying in churches and other out-buildings." Surely, after consideration of the "awful consequences" of such a measure, the likes of which
had never before been carried out against white people in the United
States, Sherman would allow the civilians to remain—for, the three
city burghers asked, "what has this helpless people done, that they
should be driven from their homes, to wander strangers and outcasts,
and exiles, and to subsist on charity?"

General Sherman read the Calhoun letter "carefully" and answered at length the next day. He drew on arguments he had previously made in letters to other Southerners but expanded and elaborated them in a way that would serve as a justification for his actions and for those of many future wars that swept up civilians in their destructive path. He understood "the distress that will be occasioned" by the expulsion order. But he had a far larger perspective than the "humanities of the case." The war needed to be pursued to its end as quickly and definitively as possible. "We must have peace," he insisted, "not only at Atlanta, but in all America. To secure this, we must stop the war. . . . To stop war, we must defeat the Rebel armies. . . . To defeat those armies, we must prepare the way to reach them in their recesses." Knowing "the vindictive nature of our enemy," he envisioned "many years of military operations from this quarter," which would make Atlanta unfit "as a home for families." What happened now in Atlanta affected the entire nation. He intended to "prepare for the future struggles in which millions of good people outside of Atlanta have a deep interest."

Sherman wanted to tell Calhoun and the people he represented that his actions were fully considered and not wantonly vindictive exercises in cruelty. He knew what he proposed would inflict pain of the worst sort on people who had not fired a weapon in the conflict. So be it. "You cannot qualify war in harsher terms than I will," he wrote. "War is cruelty, and you cannot refine it." He, though, was not the culprit. He pointed at "those who brought war into our country [who] deserve all the curses and maledictions a people can pour out." Should the United States accept "division now, it will not stop, but will go on until we reap the fate of Mexico, which is eternal war." The alternative to constitutional union for all Americans was endless chaos in his view. He wanted order, and once order was restored, its blessings would shine down on the Southern people. Only return to the Union, he admonished, "and, instead of devoting your houses and streets and roads to the dread uses of war, I and this army become at once your protectors and supporters, shielding you from danger, let it come from what quarter it may."

Once the South chose secession, what had happened to Atlanta became "inevitable." He preached fire and brimstone as if standing in the church pulpit that otherwise held no interest for him. He rode hard on an uncontainable, destructive force brought forth by others. "You might as well appeal against the thunderstorm as against these terrible hardships of war." For its hand in perpetuating the war, Atlanta had brought on its own demise. War and its desolation may once have taken place far off, but "now that war comes home to you, you feel very different." At this point, "the only way the people of Atlanta can hope once more to live in peace and quiet at home, is to stop the war."

He wished the city's inhabitants to understand that once *they* stopped the war, he would be their countryman and, more, their protector. "But my dear sirs," he closed, "when peace does come, you may call on me for anything. Then will I share with you my last cracker, and watch with you to shield your homes and families against danger from every quarter." Until the coming time when "the mad passions of men cool down, and allow the Union and peace once more to settle over your old homes at Atlanta," he was immovable: "Now you must go."

Passages from Sherman's letter to Mayor Calhoun would in time become nearly as recognized as those of President Lincoln's Gettysburg Address of a year ago. It was perhaps the greatest explanation for the causes and consequences of civil war ever written. The words became public and heartened the North for the hard fighting that remained. For Calhoun and his neighbors, they struck like a knife in the heart.

SHERMAN ASKED CALHOUN TO pull together a list of the remaining residents in Atlanta, indicating their direction of choice, north or south, together with their portable property. Over the next week, his office, reported a war correspondent, was "continually besieged with anxious faces enquiring for advice and instruction." Drawing on Dunning, Markham, and Crussell, Union officers drew up a list of the known loyal Unionists in town, Cyrena Stone among them, and about fifty families from the list received permission to stay. Sherman strongly advised them not to. He acknowledged their "service" "in the very highest degree" but urged them, "Do not judge from appearances at this instant of time, but rather with a knowledge that the future will make Atlanta an important battlefield." Any resident whose family members had already gone south seeking refuge, however, was required to head in that direction. As provost marshal, Lieutenant Colonel Morse was responsible for putting together the lists of people and their baggage destined for the North or the South.

Like many in town, Samuel Richards faced a dilemma. Although his brother Jabez waited for him and their boxes of books at Rough and Ready, he hoped to go to New York City, "want[ing] to get away from the war and the fighting if we can." He worried, however, that the Unionist citizen committee might blackball him. He met a Union officer come to purchase some of his furniture. The two men turned out to have mutual acquaintances. The sympathetic officer wrote a letter on Richards's behalf, and he received a passport to join the exodus north. He and thousands of others packed up their belongings and personal items, he moaned, "to start forth from our homes exiles and wanderers upon the earth with no certain dwelling places."

The slaveholders among the departing people packed without their bondsmen to shoulder their loads. They were no longer slaves. The former bondsmen, penned Richards, were "all free and the Yankee soldiers don't fail to assure them of that fact." On the streets and even at home, Richards and every other Atlanta slaveholder now confronted what he regarded as "the impudent airs the negroes put on, and their indifference to the wants of their former masters." They were "as independent as can be." He sold off furniture and only "wish[ed] I had the value of our city lots and negroes in gold at this juncture." His war gains were now of no value to him at all. "So," he acknowledged, "our negro property has all vanished into air."

Over the course of ten days, from September 12 to 22, an estimated 3,500 people departed Atlanta. Some 450 families—709 adults, mostly women, 867 children, and 79 willing "servants," along with 1,651 parcels of furniture and household items—went to Rough and Ready by rail and wagon, where they transferred to Confederate army wagons to continue their journey into the hospitable or unwelcoming arms of what remained of the Confederacy. Three hundred of the refugees ended up in a hastily erected log-cabin camp set up under Gov. Joseph Brown's orders 150 miles to the southwest in the village of Dawson, Georgia. Although the northern-bound refugee records disappeared, virtually as many people are believed to have headed north, traveling by rail with vouchers issued to them by Lieutenant Colonel Morse to their destinations.

After a month and a half hopscotching across the country, Richards and his family arrived in New York City. Living off his gold savings for a period, he soon found work as a low-paid clerk in a Broadway bookstore; they were now "sojourners," he wailed, "in the land of the enemy and invader so many hundred miles from our Southern home!" Not long after reaching New York, he reunited with his brother William, whom he had formerly reviled as an "alien enemy." On Christmas Day, Samuel reacted with wonder and gloom "that we should spend this day in the Yankee Gotham!"

BEFORE JAMES CALHOUN LEFT to rejoin his family at their plantation on September 17—with thirty pieces of luggage—he wrote General Sherman a letter thanking him for the civility shown during the civilian transport. Sherman felt touchy, yet proud of a process that sent thousands into exile—with few hitches. "Instead of robbing them not an article was taken away," he boasted to his wife, "not even their negro servants who were willing to go along, and we even brought their provisions which I know to have been Confederate stores distributed to the people at the last moment, and were really our captured property." Fulfilling Sherman's vision, Atlanta now became, he told his wife, "a real military town with no women boring me every order I give."

His men now enjoyed life within their fortified urban camp, free from fear of being shot at any instant, enjoying three regular and full meals a day and taking time to relax by the fireside and stroll through the town's blasted streets. Tens of thousands of Union troops built comfortable camp homes for themselves. They took planks off house and barn walls and pulled up fences to erect siding and lay floors; bricks removed from toppled factories went to build small chimneys for their cozy little residences, which filled all the open fields and meadows. Soon, remarked the provost marshal, Lieutenant Colonel Morse, the men were "living on the fat of the land." Every other day, the army sent a vast forage train of seven or eight hundred wagons out from the city to scour the countryside for twenty miles around. The "fattened" train returned after three or four days replete with corn, sweet potatoes, flour, chickens, hogs, cows, and whatever else the quartermasters confiscated.

In the cool fall evenings, Morse sat on his balcony with fellow officers, listening to the regimental bands playing in the square. "Isn't a soldier's life a queer one?" he wrote home. "One month ago, we were lying on the ground in a shelter tent, with nothing but pork and hard bread to eat; now we are in an elegant house, take our dinner at half-past five, and feel disposed to growl if we don't have a good soup and roast meat with dessert; after that, we smoke good cigars on the piazza and have a band play for us."

THAT SYBARITIC MALE EXISTENCE within the city walls was of course temporary. Sherman was already plotting "another still more decisive move in war." Even as the last trainload of civilians was pulling out of Atlanta's car shed, President Jefferson Davis, not one hundred miles away in Macon, exhorted an audience of refugees and soldiers to rekindle their fighting spirit after the "disgrace" their army had just experienced. "Our cause," he insisted to a packed church, "is not lost." He contended, "Sherman cannot keep up his long line of communications, and retreat, sooner or later, he must." When he did, the Confederate president proclaimed, the fate of the French empire's army retreating from conquered Moscow would be his. "Our cavalry and people will harass and destroy his army as did the Cossacks of Napoleon, and the Yankee General, like him, will escape with only a bodyguard."

Sherman heard about the speech the next day and wired President Lincoln about it. He wrote of the "bad effect" that would come should he be forced to guard his line back to Chattanooga and Nashville "to an extent that I could not act offensively." He seemed to be warning the president that what lay ahead might appear unorthodox while letting him know that strategic and political implications were being considered. Two days later, he offered Ulysses S. Grant a glimpse of his surprising intentions. He would "destroy Atlanta, and then march across Georgia to Savannah or Charleston, breaking roads and doing irreparable damage." Of one thing he was certain: "We cannot remain on the defensive." A week later, he was convinced that destroying Georgia's war-making ability was the best course of action as long as the South remained in rebellion, which he expected would continue, he told Grant, "until we can repopulate Georgia." Before then, it would be "useless to occupy it, but the utter destruction of its roads, houses, and people will cripple their military resources. . . . I can make the march and make Georgia howl."

Sherman's men wondered how long their respite might continue. The general spent the pleasant fall evenings together with his officers, who gathered about his headquarters. Lieutenant Colonel Morse and others were there in September when he said cryptically, Let's "wait until October, when the corn [will] be ripe, and then go down and gather it." They didn't know quite what he meant until preparations began. He sent all sick and disabled men to the rear. All superfluous supplies beyond those needed for a light marching army were also shipped north. Then, after the last train had departed, he stunned his men by ordering the total destruction of the railroad to their rear—

their lifeline to the rest of the federal army—almost all the way to Chattanooga. The 62,000 men still with Sherman were isolated, minimally supplied, in a hostile land. They would march through it, destroying anything that could support the rebel army, feeding themselves with whatever they could forage. Sherman had already practiced such a maneuver the previous January in Mississippi. Nonetheless, nothing quite like it—not in scale or distance, significance or risk—had ever been undertaken before.

IN THE VERY FIRST DAYS of November, Morse wrote home, "I am now going to let you into some of our mighty secrets. We are going to abandon Atlanta, first utterly destroying every railroad building, store, and everything else that can be of any use to the rebels. Then, cutting loose from everything and everybody, Sherman is going to launch his army into Georgia." The Second Massachusetts' officers were initially charged with surveying the city and preparing for its destruction, until the mission was placed under the more experienced Capt. O. M. Poe, the chief engineer of the army.

Sometime in the night of November 10, arsonists set fire to a cluster of private houses on the north side of town. According to Connecticut quartermaster Lt. Henry Stanley, the army made "every exertion . . . to extinguish the fire." Even Generals Geary and Slocum joined the fight to put out the flames. The next morning, Slocum offered a reward of $500 for the arrest of the arsonists or anyone who set fire to buildings after that.

Such attempts to thwart extracurricular destruction seemed pointless when four days later the work of pulling down the city began in earnest. On November 14, troops began systematically knocking down the stations, roundhouses, and other structures along the railroads. Poe directed teams of soldiers using iron rails suspended from a rigged chain, which they swung back and forth as a battering ram against building walls and supports. The men battered down alternate piers along one side of the massive vaulted car shed. With the collapse of the last pier, the enormous structure slid over under its own weight, and, said Morse, "the great roof carried the entire building to the ground, with a resounding crash." Tall brick industrial smokestacks, battered by the swinging rail below and pulled by rope tied above, toppled over and came crashing to the ground like great sequoias. Stanley watched the railroad "speedily transformed into *nothing* or a great quantity of small pieces." A roundhouse constructed from heavy granite blocks and able to store forty locomotives seemed impregnable, "but a few busy hands soon reduced it to nothing."

The night of November 15 provided a spectacle, Morse recorded not long after, "impossible . . . to imagine." Fire provided the coup de grâce for central Atlanta. He had stage seating for the conflagration. "We sat on top of our house for hours watching it. For miles around, the country was as light as day. The business portion of Atlanta, embracing perhaps twenty acres, covered with large storehouses and public buildings, situated in the highest part of the city, was all on fire at one time, the flames shooting up for hundreds of feet into the air. In one of the depots was a quantity of old rebel shells and other ammunition; the constant explosion of these heightened the effect." The spectacle went, he found, "from the sublime to the ridiculous" when, in the midst of this grand orgy of destruction, a Massachusetts regimental band "went up and serenaded General Sherman; it was like fiddling over the burning of Rome!"

He noted, though, that his forces "kept large patrols out to protect the dwellings and other private property of the few citizens remaining in the city; this was effectually done." Sherman would always insist that his army never torched a single private dwelling.


FINALLY, EARLY THE FOLLOWING morning, Morse could attest to the completion of the work. Sherman himself marched forth with his army out the Decatur Road to launch his march to the sea. "On the morning of the 16th," Morse witnessed, "nothing was left of Atlanta except its churches, the City Hall and private dwellings. You could hardly find a vestige of the splendid railroad depots, warehouses, etc. It was melancholy, but it was war prosecuted in deadly earnest." The last regular corps did not start off its march until about half past four that afternoon. The Massachusetts man wistfully recollected, "We followed after, being the last United States troops to leave Atlanta."

## ⭢⟹ CHAPTER 26 ⟸⭠

# THE NEW
# SOUTH

G EN. WILLIAM TECUMSEH SHERMAN'S army began its three-
hundred-mile furrow of destruction to the coast, pillaging and
destroying whatever might support a hostile army—the much-
reduced yet still determined Army of Tennessee, which had moved
behind Sherman's own advance and up into Tennessee—and seizing,
or stealing, whatever else served its purposes. Only light harassment
from a small Confederate force, much of it composed of the state
militia's old men and young boys, and cavalry skirmishers disturbed
the army's wide swath of devastation across Georgia's most fertile
lands. Sherman intended to prove "we can march a well appointed
army right through [Jefferson Davis's] territory." This action "may not
be war," he admitted, "but rather statesmanship," as he archly called it,
providing "proof positive" to any who still might think otherwise "that
the North can prevail in this contest." As Sherman's forces ploughed
remorselessly southeastwards, the Huff family, who had taken flight
to the countryside from their Marietta Street home, joined the
refugees returning—in a trickle at first and then in waves, like the re-
versing tide—to Atlanta.

The first returnees reached Atlanta in late November and early
December. What they found stunned and appalled them. They jour-
neyed back into "an ocean of ruins." The forests that once obstructed
the views all the way to Kennesaw Mountain to the north and Stone
Mountain to the south were gone. Any tree not cut down by the
armies or Confederate arsenal stood truncated and limbless, bleak

testaments to the storm of violence that had passed their way. The people traveling into town immediately noticed a peculiar absence: Silence engulfed a place famed, or reviled, for the constant caterwaul of its whistling, clanging, and puffing trains, pounding hammers, rasping saws, rushing carriages and jibbing horses, call-and-response barking between sellers and buyers, ringing church bells, and bustling sidewalks and passageways. That Atlanta was a city of the dead could not be doubted; the odor of death overwhelmed everything. "The putrid carcasses of dead horses and mules met the eye," reported one of the first people back in town, "while the stench that exhaled from them filled the air, producing a loathing on the part of all who ventured into the city, unutterably disgusting." There was no escaping the stench, for even "within its corporate limits lay the last remains of man and beast emitting the same disgusting odor."

Passing the city's battered ramparts, the Huff family took many detours to reach Marietta Street. Piles of toppled brick, once the walls of buildings, covered the streets and couldn't be crossed over. Their wagon had to be lightened and then pushed while the mule was cajoled to clop over frozen clay roads left nearly impassable by the heavy army wagons and artillery pieces that had cut them up. The pits of what had been cellars beneath charred buildings yawned open dangerously—many still held unexploded ordnance—as did cisterns and gopher holes, easy traps for the unwary, especially at night.

Miraculously, the Huff house, though atop a hill within the lines, had come through the fighting badly damaged but still standing. The family and their servants huddled together around their log kitchen house fire in the winter cold, while the big house underwent repair. In the unbroken darkness of their first night back, their ears perked up at an unsettling howling that rose and fell in the distance. "It seemed to start a long way off and come to us from the northeast or the direction of Peachtree Creek," recounted Sarah Huff. It sounded "like the moaning of doves" to her mother, but far louder and more piercing. Sarah was eight years old the first time she heard the mysterious howls echoing in the icy North Georgia night. "No," she realized, "it was not the sound of doves, but the distant baying of dogs, dangerous dogs." The farm families, and even many city dwellers, typically kept half a dozen or more hounds for hunting and other dogs to protect the barnyard animals. The owners had left their canines behind in their flight from Atlanta, and now, the eight-year-old Huff shivered, "the baying of these animals in unison was the only noise to break the profound stillness." The starving, half-feral dogs roamed in packs, snarling and snapping at anyone who dared approach, just part of a desolated landscape war had returned to an inhospitable, savage, and wild state of nature. "Ruin," cried one of the returnees, "universal ruin was the exclamation of all."

HUNGRY AND RAPACIOUS ex-Confederate soldiers wandering home and others from the countryside looking for easy plunder came into the largely abandoned city, where they broke into the vacant houses. They took what they wanted or moved in as squatters. Without protection, the fifty or so remaining families were easy targets for marauders. Georgia Gen. W. P. Howard surveyed conditions in Atlanta and wrote a December 7 report to Gov. Joseph Brown. He found,

> There are about 250 wagons in the city on my arrival load[ed] with pilfered plunder; pianos, mirrors, furniture of all kinds, iron, hides without number, and an incalculable amount of other things, very valuable at the present time. This exportation of stolen property has been going on ever since the place had been abandoned by the enemy. Bushwhackers, robbers and deserters, and citizens from the surrounding country for a distance of fifty miles have been engaged in this dirty work.

Among those who returned earliest to town, Ezekiel Calhoun and his daughters and grandchildren made their way back to their home off Washington Street. Dr. Calhoun's grandson Noble explored the warred-over landscape "of almost unequaled desolation." With Calhoun's brother not yet back, the few score men in town voted the elderly physician acting mayor. He appointed every man to serve as a police officer. The citizen police soon found robbers breaking into the Trinity Episcopal Church, where departing families had stored pianos and other valuable furniture, and at gunpoint the men forced them to return the stolen goods.

On December 10, John Steele and the *Intelligencer* staff, returned with their presses to town, brought out a single-sided issue on flimsy paper to distribute throughout the region. Given the "great scarcity of everything in the city," the editor invited "country friends" who read the paper and were "fortunate enough to escape the clutches of the Yankee hordes" to bring their produce to the city. The newspaper assured farmers that returning Confederate quartermasters would no longer seize their teams and provender.

That same day, weary and footsore, James M. Calhoun trudged into his devastated city. He had taken the train as far as Jonesboro and then walked the last twenty miles, carrying a heavy valise and overcoat in hand.

THE PROCESS OF REBUILDING the city was foremost on Calhoun's mind as he went back to work in the damaged but functional City Hall. Enormous piles of debris needed to be removed, roads resurfaced, holes that once were buildings filled in, walls and chimneys in danger of toppling knocked down, dead animals removed, and bodies buried; only then might reconstruction begin. The city was broke, the Confederate money it might raise for rebuilding essentially worthless, and any building supplies, other than old bricks, were many days' wagon ride away. The annual mayoral election was held amid the ruins, and the few men on hand returned Calhoun to office. He and the city council resumed their meetings on January 6, 1865, and immediately set about borrowing money to pay bills, issuing bonds and employing surveyors to review damage, to begin rebuilding and extending streets, and engaged the railroads in the removal or reconstruction of their depots.

The spirit of the old Virginians who had carved Atlanta out of a former native wilderness would rekindle. The *Intelligencer* invoked the city's still recent origins to remind those who now returned that the wreckage of Atlanta had just a few years earlier been "the abode of the red man who roamed over it in search of game. . . . The march of civilization—the rapid advance of the white man with his implements of agriculture—had imposed this necessity upon the poor Indian and soon after his removal, nay before it was fairly accomplished, the axe had felled the forest in many a locality and the ploughshare and the hoe had begun their work in fulfillment, as it were, of the decree of the Eternal." Atlanta, through its railroads, had become the most important interior city of the South and its commercial center. As far as the *Intelligencer* was concerned, the divine decree remained in force. Although returned to savage wilderness, Atlantans would, with the spirit of old, build a new and better Atlanta. The Gate City's strength lay in its people: "That which built Atlanta and made it a flourishing city, will again restore it, purified, we trust, in many particulars, by the fiery ordeal through which it has past.—Soon the whistle of the steam engine will again be heard in its limits. . . . Let no one despond as to the *future* of our city! . . . She will soon rise from her ashes."

EVEN IF THE ATLANTA OF old was dead, the Civil War, however, continued. Militiaman Allen T. Holliday marched on with the state guard. Falling back from Atlanta, he wrote his wife, Lizzie, in despair at his powerlessness to help or "advise you what to do should a Yankee raid get through Wilkes." He urged her, "Treat them as kind as you can under the circumstances. I know it is hard for us to love our enemies but we are taught to do so."

Union army cavalry on the eastern flanks of Sherman's march through Georgia did reach the 3,000-acre Wilkes County plantation outside the town of Washington near the South Carolina border in late November. In anticipation of the Yankees' arrival, Lizzie sealed the china and silver in secret lockers set inside the walls and moved the livestock into a forested river bottom. With her short brown hair tied back, she met the bluecoats on the front steps of the small plank house T. and the slaves had built for the couple and their five children a decade earlier. Many of the forty Holliday slaves joined the thousands of other freemen who now moved with the Yankee army like a vast, trailing cloud. Although T. still served, the officer leading the federals decided not to destroy the Holliday home after Lizzie told him that T. was a fellow Mason. Along with the rest of the militia, though, T. soon mustered out. He came home from the trenches a broken man, suffering from a severe respiratory ailment, probably tuberculosis, and died a year later, in November 1865 at age thirty-seven. However, 145 years later, his great-great-grandson farms the same land Holliday once did.

Sherman's columns swept from Wilkes south toward the coast. On December 22, a jubilant General Sherman telegraphed President Abraham Lincoln to present "as a Christmas gift the City of Savannah with 150 heavy guns & plenty of ammunition & also about 25,000 bales of cotton." Having completed their now world-famous march away from Atlanta virtually unimpeded across the entirety of Confederate Georgia, Sherman's proud army rested. The work of subduing the rebellion, Sherman lamented, would soon have to resume. "There seems no end but utter annihilation that will satisfy their [rebels'] hate of the 'sneaking Yankee' and 'ruthless invader'. . . . Although I have come right through the heart of Georgia, they talk as defiantly as ever."

ATLANTA'S INTERNAL CIVIL WAR also continued. Confederates returned to the city and resumed their battle against their Northern-leaning neighbors. The day Savannah fell, Steele published bitter recriminations: "Some months ago, aye, three years ago also, we predicted that if ever the enemy made his appearance in Atlanta, he would find among its citizens a number of them ready to bid him welcome and to take part in his behalf." He blamed "*traitors* who have fled to the enemy" for enabling the fall and destruction of Atlanta. The city, he contended, had "been cursed with the presence of men and women who were as spies in its midst, and did all in their power secretly to promote its downfall." He noted, though, that with their departure north, "our city [is] at least relieved from their presence, though no gallows is left standing to commemorate their exit from it."

The newspaper listed the names of forty-seven better-known among the men—the others "too numerous to mention"—including "a base traitor," William M. Markham, the wealthy former mayor who had built much of downtown Atlanta, now in ruins, and his rolling mill partner, Lewis Scofield, as well as James Dunning and Samuel P. Richards, who was presently in New York City. Richards might have protested, but their decision to immigrate to the Yankee land made their loyalties crystal clear. "Atlanta is better off in recognizing them as open enemies, than it was when they were recognized as citizens, being its secret enemies and enemies of the Confederacy and the cause of the South."

Among the most reviled of those now open enemies was Cyrena Stone's attorney husband Amherst. He had left town in 1863, with tens of thousands of dollars fleeced from fellow Atlanta citizens, Unionist and non-Unionist alike, in a half-baked scheme to employ his connections in official federal circles to set up a government-approved blockade-running outfit. Once in the North, he was quickly taken up by military police. He spent most of the remainder of the war in a U.S. prison on an island in New York City. Upon his release, he took a leading role in advocating on behalf of exiled Southern Unionists and agitating against the Confederacy. He eventually returned to Georgia to take up an official role in its reconstruction. His crooked plan to operate a blockade-running company, however, caused the U.S. government to deny his claims for restitution for the destruction of his Southern property. Cyrena had lived on her own, like so many women during the war, in her Houston Street home until she went north following Sherman's expulsion order. She and Amherst were probably never reunited. She died of cancer in 1868, aged thirty-eight, in Vermont, not far from where she was born. Her secret wartime diary and her personal accounts of her experiences provided her sister, Louisa M. Whitney, with the background for a loosely fictionalized 1903 retelling of Cyrena's experiences in Civil War Atlanta and her surreptitious resistance to the Confederates.


EARLY IN DECEMBER 1864, Lt. Col. Luther J. Glenn, another former mayor of Atlanta, returned with his Cobb's Georgia Legion infantry company from the fighting in Virginia to reestablish a Confederate military presence in Atlanta. He was joined by now Maj. George Washington Lee, the post's earlier provost marshal. Whatever previous animosity Lee felt toward the Yankees had redoubled because of the personal affront of having his entire extended family expelled by Sherman. The bluecoats had driven six Lee women and thirteen children, with their belongings packed in one wagon pulled by a single old horse, into exile from Lee's hometown. According to the *Intelligencer*, Lee earned a badge of honor in having Sherman single him and two other Atlanta officials—Alexander M. Wallace and E. T. Hunnicutt—out for arrest. Sherman may never have actually given the order. Nonetheless, the newspaper claimed the Northern commander, urged on by Markham, had said the trio should be "denied all privileges of captured soldiers and treated and punished as traitors and outlaws" for their mistreatment of "loyal persons" living in the city and Union prisoners held here.

Lee had faced charges of having sold Confederate service exemptions, but there was no doubting that he had personally fought to stave off the invasion. He had taken command of a four-hundred-man force that failed in its efforts to hold off the July federal army crossing of the Chattahoochee at Roswell. He had then gathered five hundred men, with arms but no ammunition, to protect the state capital at Milledgeville. After that, he formed a guard for federal prisoners held at Macon. In August, he had organized a home-guard defense against a Yankee cavalry raid on the town. Back in Atlanta, Glenn and Lee sought to reimpose their Confederate authority. They rounded up Atlanta's previously exempt railroad workers and anyone else they could conscript to serve in a Confederate army that, in fact, would exist only for a matter of weeks longer.

Glenn and Lee intended to bring to heel again any who might think that the Confederacy's days were at an end. Ever the instigator, Steele urged a thorough cleansing of Atlanta's population, for "all *our enemies* in this community did not go North. . . . Amid the ruins of our dwellings, and surrounded by the general desolation wrought by our accursed foes, there are persons who do not hesitate to say that they would rather have the 'Yankee army around them than the Rebs.' . . . We submit that people who feel thus should not be permitted to live among us. . . . It is the duty of our authorities to see that the country is rid of their presence, at least." But with a city mayor who in all likelihood agreed with such sentiments, the increasingly toothless Confederate officers in town, as desperately cold, ill-clad, and hungry as their neighbors in the midst of another biting winter, had little power left to enforce loyalty to their dying cause. Many simply used their power to enrich themselves.

They arrested a few of the men who had remained in the city during Sherman's occupation. Prior to the expulsion, James Calhoun had arranged with General Sherman for well-to-do townspeople to move their most valuable possessions into the Trinity Methodist Church on City Hall Square for safekeeping. Calhoun had left open Unionist James L. Dunning in charge of the property, but Dunning had moved north to the safety of New York City when Sherman's army moved out. He left John Silvey, who had provided "coffee and other refreshments" to the wounded Yankee prisoners during the fighting, responsible for the furniture. In early December, thirteen of Glenn and Lee's soldiers surrounded Silvey's house and arrested him, charging him with treason for cooperating with the Union occupiers. He and others taken in by the Confederates for disloyalty were held for a few days in town before being sent to Macon for trial. A bribe of $4,000 in Confederate money, however, won Silvey's release.

Lee's constant fight to bring to heel men he considered traitors to the Southern cause in Atlanta and throughout Georgia gained him plenty of enemies. A few months after he came back to town to reignite the city's dying Confederate embers, two men called him out of his house and blasted him with a slug shot. Though badly stung, Lee managed to draw his gun and shoot down one of his assailants. After the war reached its conclusion, Lee turned to managing the many properties, including a valuable rolling stock foundry, he had accumulated. He was a poor businessman. All his ventures failed, and when his decades-long battle with consumption ended with his death in 1879, the once fearsome Confederate enforcer was the operator of a third-rate boarding house.

THROUGHOUT THE FROSTY WINTER months at the beginning of 1865, people returned to their homes in small numbers day by day. Then, on March 3, the first train into Atlanta since Sherman's departure rolled in on the repaired Atlanta & West Point Railroad line from Alabama. The reception was much like that for the very first train into Terminus just twenty years earlier in 1845. "Upon hearing [the whistle of the locomotive], men, women and boys shouted with joy," a reporter wrote. "The old, familiar and inspiring sound was grateful [*sic*] to us all." The train whistle was a loud and clear signal that Atlanta would be rebuilt. "Soon," proclaimed the *Intelligencer*, "the other railroads will form their connection with our city, and then, from her ashes, Phoenix-like, Atlanta will rise to resume her former importance in Georgia and the South, never again, we trust, to be wrested from her by our savage foes." The railroad was the vehicle that once again brought people, goods, and cash washing into town.

By the first weeks of March, several businesses operating out of makeshift cabins in the downtown were up and running. More importantly, investors believed in Atlanta's future: "Building business lots are in great demand," reported the newspaper, "and are held at astonishingly high prices. This augers well for the future of Atlanta." With the spring, the previous trickle of returning and *new* residents became a torrent. Soon, 150 stores, most housed in shacks and lean-tos, were in operation. A new instant city was rising.


THE "GOOD GOVERNMENT" Whig politician of former days, Mayor James M. Calhoun devoted much of his time and the city's funds in his last term in office to making the roads passable. He concluded his political career prosaically by declaring, "We have removed incredible amounts of dirt and rubbish from the principal streets, filled up washes and low places in others, [and] done a great deal of heavy and expensive work in others." Even his old nemesis, Steele's *Intelligencer* could not help but approve the progress. "In every direction we notice that the rubbish is being removed, and preparations are making for the erection of new buildings. The sound of the trowel and the hammer is heard on every side, and everything betokens an earnest determination on the part of our people to restore Atlanta as rapidly as possible to its former commanding position in the commercial world."

Samuel Richards didn't see much progress when he stepped off a train car at a makeshift depot on August 10. He was met by "a dirty, dusty ruin." Three and a half months earlier, he had stood with the massive crowd in midtown Manhattan for three hours to watch President Lincoln's funeral cortege pass slowly by. That night, he spat, "Would to God that he had never been born." Despite the blasted state of Atlanta, he was pleased to see "busy life is resuming its sway over its desolate streets, and any number of stores of all kinds are springing up as if by magic in every part of the burnt district."

He and his brother resumed their trade. The revivified commercial magic touched them. Their sales grew rapidly, soon greatly outpacing those of the war years. Jabez and Samuel Richards expanded their store into one of the largest stationery firms in the South with customers throughout Georgia and beyond. Samuel Richards, however, did not willingly share the fruits of the business with his brother. In 1878, Jabez learned via an ad his brother had placed in the newspaper that the church deacon had dissolved their partnership, begun in 1848. Jabez battled debt for the rest of his life, while Samuel's new S. P. Richards Company thrived. Today it continues to operate and is one of the world's leading office-supply companies.


IN THE LAST DAYS OF the Confederacy, many of the new residents coming to Atlanta were black. Although slavery had ended legally, it nonetheless continued—in some cases by force and in others by necessity. War had impoverished bondsman and master alike. Families came back to town with slaves—or servants with nowhere else to turn for food or shelter—while former slaves who were turned out without provision for their survival from the devastated plantations in Sherman's path gathered in increasingly large numbers in the squatter camps sprawling about the outskirts of town. The *Intelligencer* eventually complained about the squalor

> in the suburbs of Atlanta . . . [where] a promiscuous assemblage of houseless and homeless creatures . . . [are] living in booths, arbors, tent-flies, and rude temporary structures of old cast-off plank. . . . Who these people are no one knows, and how they manage to subsist is equally mysterious. . . . There are many old and decrepit females and young children . . . utterly helpless. Poverty in its direct form reigns supreme among them. . . . [Black men and women], who have left their homes in pursuit of something they do not exactly know what, comprise the greater part of this unfortunate mass.

Not all of the former slaves suffered such miserable conditions. According to Mayor Calhoun's son Patrick, returning refugees found former slaves left behind by Sherman's departing army "well supplied with Yankee beans, coffee, canned goods, and cheese in great quantities, given to them by the Yankee soldiers when they left." Fortunately, most were willing to share with their former masters.

Robert Webster, despite the looting of his fortune and his active work with Union prisoners, remained in town after Sherman left. Although he insisted that the bluecoats had "ruined him"—leading him to lay claim in postwar years to US$10,000—he still remained among the town's wealthier men of any color. A white businessman G. C. Rogers said, "Bob was better off than any of us. [He] had money and had more money than his old master."

In fact, his former owner, Maj. Ben Yancey, had returned to Atlanta with his Fulton Dragoons to bolster the militia, but finally abandoned the Confederate fight and now lived in Athens, where the fey Sallie Clayton soon arrived to share the household's hospitality before returning to her family home in Atlanta. The Yankees had destroyed most of Yancey's numerous plantations and other properties and, of course, freed his many slaves. He was left with four horses and burnt-over land and otherwise penniless. His brother, William Lowndes Yancey, firebrand leader of the Alabama States' Rights faction who had worked so tirelessly to bring on secession, had died in 1863. Montgomery marked his funeral with a massive outpouring of grief. In his new state of poverty, Ben Yancey wrote to Webster and "asked him if he could loan me $150." Webster's reply came express in the form of "$100 in gold and $100 in silver." He also sent word, said Yancey, "I could get more if I wanted it."

Though the bondage of human chattel to owner was broken, master and slave remained intertwined even after slavery's demise. For years after, whites in town continued to call Webster by the name Yancey. He would correct them, "My name is and has always been Robert Webster." He was proud to claim Daniel Webster as his father. He insisted, however, he felt genuine fondness and respect for his former owner. "I love the noble name of Yancey," he proclaimed.


WHILE THE CONFEDERACY STILL ruled the land, changes in Atlanta raced ahead of the laws on the books. In the very last days of March, Steele reiterated his oft-issued call for Calhoun and the city council to forbid the "practice of allowing negroes to hire their own time," which was now much more widespread. The die-hard racist also pointed to "a case in our own city," very likely Prince Ponder or Robert Webster, "in which a slave has become the owner of a mule and dray, and has actually employed another slave to drive it for him. It is contrary to reason that that slave can be as valuable to his owner, when encumbered with his mule and dray and *hired man*, as he would be without it; much of his time is necessarily taken up to looking after his individual interests. There are other instances in our community of slaves living to themselves and carrying on business on their own account as though they were free." Steele and many other whites refused to accept that freedom for black people—or at least the end of their perpetual slavery—had truly come to the South.

The great equalizer was poverty. The abject conditions facing all city residents forced a blurring of the color divide, in which the previously inconceivable could now occur. Nine-year-old Henry Ossian Flipper had grown up on the Ponder place a slave until fleeing with his family to Macon. Although still slaves in theory, as far as any of them knew, without permission from Ellen Ponder or any other white authority, Henry, his cobbler father Festus, mother Isabella, and four brothers returned to Atlanta in the early spring of 1865.

Since their quarters at the Ponder place were an uninhabitable ruin, the Flipper family moved to a shack on Decatur Street where Festus opened a boot shop. Slave or free, he soon made good money. The family of an ex-rebel captain moved in next door to the Flippers. The wife of this soldier for a white man's empire offered to instruct Henry and his brothers "for a small remuneration." She needed the money, however little. The five Flipper brothers' education resumed. They soon moved to missionary schools and, eventually, into the first black colleges established in the Lower South. Each Flipper brother became a community leader: one a founder of Big Bethel, the leading African Methodist Episcopal church in Atlanta and a bishop of the Georgia church, another a professor at a black college in Savannah, another a physician in Florida, while a fourth carried on his father's shop and trade. Henry, who as a boy had watched soldiers marching past his slave quarters and owed his freedom from a life of slavery to the Union army, would overcome venomous racial hostility to become the first black man to graduate in 1877 from the U.S. Military Academy at West Point and one of the first black engineers in the nation, as well as an author and federal official.

AFTER THE WAR, institutions for improving the lot of former slaves grew more rapidly in Atlanta than any other city in the South. However, freedom in terms of full civil rights remained a far-off hope. When federal troops returned to the city, among their first acts was to impose another passport system to control the movement of freemen through town. Robert Webster, who had returned to the barbering business with renewed success, became a Republican Party leader during Reconstruction. He personally funded and housed many black officials from across the state who came to Atlanta to serve in the legislature but were unable to find hotels or boarding houses willing to take them in. Even after Webster's death in 1883, the legacy of his slavery continued to haunt his children. Ben Yancey's daughter held the deed to the former slave's Houston Street house, which as a slave Webster could not legally purchase. After Webster's death, the former slave's widow and his final owner's heirs each laid claim to the valuable property. The legal wrangling continued for seven years until the contending parties shared in proceeds from its auction.

Despite slavery's complex legacy, cruelly onerous race laws, and outright antiblack violence, Atlanta became a magnet for freedmen. By 1870, its black citizenry had grown to more than 10,000, not quite half of the city's population. The South's largest black middle class took root, many of its members drawing upon the wealth, skills, and education of the former slaves who had earned a measure of freedom and helped bring about the end of slavery during the war. Upon the ashes of Atlanta, African Americans erected the foundations their children and grandchildren would build upon in the next century to establish their full rights as American citizens.

THE FINAL CHAPTERS IN slavery's legacy remained many years off. In the winter and spring of 1864 and 1865, die-hard Confederates refused to give up their cause. After the crushing blow of losing Atlanta, the final defeat of the Army of Tennessee came not in Georgia but in its home state eight months later. Picking up recruits through the fall of 1864, John Bell Hood commanded as many as 30,000 troops. Promoted to corporal, Sam Watkins marched with Hood back into his native state. He and the remainder of Hood's force carried on despite their gnawing hunger, cut up and frozen feet, and deep demoralization. "We were a mere handful of devoted braves," he recalled, "who had stood by our colors when sometimes it seemed that God himself had forsaken us." Sherman dispatched 60,000 of his troops in Tennessee to chase down the gray coats. The Army of the Ohio split off to pursue Hood, while the Army of the Cumberland remained fortified within Nashville. On November 30, 1864, Hood, sensing a rare numeric advantage over the Yankee army, charged its lines at Franklin, Tennessee, fifteen miles south of Nashville. The charge was two miles across an open field toward, in Watkins' words, "the rampart of blood and death." Fighting raged all day and into the night until the Union forces pulled back to Nashville. Hood had forced them to withdraw, but at a terrible price. He had committed military suicide. When Watkins looked out over the battlefield beneath the red sunrise the next morning, he saw "a grand holocaust of death." Rebel dead—bodies in many cases riddled by dozens of bullets—lay piled upon one another before the emptied Yankee lines; horses shot down with their dead riders still atop them straddled the ramparts. In a single day's battle, the Army of Tennessee lost 7,000 men, threefold more than its enemy. Among the Confederate dead were a dozen generals and half Hood's remaining hundred regimental commanders.

Ever-confident of the reward for boldness in battle, the crusading Hood hoped for reinforcements—or if need be, martyrdom. He edged forward toward Nashville. Yankee general George "Slow-Trot" Thomas, behind the city's fortifications, took his time preparing to attack the last of the Army of Tennessee. Finally, on December 15, he sent his men out. Rebels outnumbered better than two to one held off the assault for nearly two full days. Watkins lived through "a hail storm of bullets" only because he was stationed in a flank skirmish line. Nonetheless, the war was over for him. He left the field perforated with eight bullet holes in his coat, two in one hand, a wound in his thigh, and a finger shot off. Blood from his many wounds sloshed about in his boots. The last Confederate stand in Tennessee turned into a rout. He watched as "nearly every man in the entire army [threw] away his guns and accoutrements" and gave up. Half awaited capture; more than 10,000 gray coats were taken prisoner. The rest ran to the rear and kept on going. Over the next weeks, thousands of soldiers filtered south into Mississippi, Alabama, and Georgia.

The battered and bloodied Watkins went to Hood's headquarters for a wounded furlough. He saw the long-haired general pulling at his blond locks with his one useable arm and crying at the shattering of his army. The Tennessee corporal bemoaned the fate of the Confederate army after four years of hard fighting. "The once proud Army of

Tennessee had degenerated to a mob." Out of Watkins's original 3,200-man regiment, just 65 were left to surrender.

THE LAST DAYS WERE UPON the Southern rebellion. Sherman's army started its march north from Savannah through the Carolinas, intent, if need be, upon reaching Virginia, where Ulysses S. Grant had yet to break through Robert E. Lee's defenses. President Jefferson Davis had enticed Joseph Johnston back to command an undermanned eastern army reorganized in late February in a last ditch effort to hold off Sherman's northward advance. In March, Col. James Neal, older brother of artilleryman A. J. Neal, now lying in a shallow Atlanta grave, commanded the Nineteenth Georgia regiment brought to North Carolina to reinforce Johnston's thin army. He must have hoped for a measure of revenge against the army that killed his beloved younger brother. At Averasboro, North Carolina, on March 16, Neal and the Nineteenth were caught up in heavy fighting with a portion of Sherman's forces, which included the Second Massachusetts Infantry, of which the promoted colonel Charles Morse, former Yankee provost marshal of Atlanta, had recently taken command. Johnston retreated, but the war ended that day for Morse. He caught a ball in the shoulder that forced him off the field.

That wound kept him out of the most severe resistance Sherman's army faced since it had taken Atlanta six months earlier. On March 19, the badly outnumbered Confederates managed to surprise a wing of Sherman's army near Bentonville, North Carolina. Fighting continued for two more days. When James Neal led his Georgia regiment racing and yelling forward into the Yankee lines, as part of the final full-on rebel charge of the war, a bullet pierced his eye killing him instantly. Sherman eventually brought his second wing into the fight, pitting a large component of his 60,000 men against Johnston's fewer than 20,000. Ever reluctant to risk losses in battle, Sherman let the rebels who did not lie wounded or dead in the field fall back in the night. He admitted afterwards, "I committed an error in not overwhelming Johnston's army" that day.

Little matter, though, as Johnston's army was now a largely toothless remnant. Sherman did not want to be delayed in his planned northern movement to where the last great Confederate army remained entrenched in Virginia. On April 1, however, Grant flanked Lee's army, and the next day Petersburg and Richmond fell. A week later, Lee surrendered at the Appomattox courthouse. Sherman personally accepted Johnston's formal surrender on April 26. Not long after that, John Bell Hood surrendered himself to federal forces in Natchez, Mississippi. Abraham Lincoln knew the Civil War had ended by the time he was assassinated on Good Friday, April 14.

AFTER THE SOUTH'S FORMAL surrender in April 1865, paroled or deserting former Confederate soldiers—hungry, destitute, defeated, embittered, and wounded—hobbled and hiked their way home through Georgia by the thousands, most traveling hundreds of miles barefoot and in the tattered remains of their uniforms, still carrying their guns. Many of these men came through Atlanta, a city they knew for its wealthy speculators and hired slaves, its complex loyalties and sometimes outright opposition to the Confederate cause, and its rich storehouses of food and other supplies. In early May, rioting and gunfights broke out as mobs of former troops smashed open the state and Confederate depots and looted private stores and houses throughout Atlanta. The new goods, food, and money coming into town went off into the countryside. The footsore men, according to the *Intelligencer*, also took "by force the horses and mules belonging to the Quartermaster's department, the only means for transporting supplies of meal, corn, &c, to provide for the brave men, the wounded and sick, who are daily arriving here and to furnish supplies to the sick now in the hospitals of the city."

On May 4, Union military forces moved back into Atlanta, taking its surrender from Luther Glenn. His cause crushed, *Intellligencer* editor John Steele quickly turned cheek and counseled reconciliation and an end to belligerence. Any "further resistance to our fate," he declared, "is both unwise and unpatriotic—*unpatriotic* because that which is *not directed to the public welfare* is not *patriotism*; and *unwise* because it is folly to resist. Hence it becomes our duty to conform to what now exists, and to our future *American citizenship.* . . . Let the sword return to its scabbard! LET THERE BE PEACE!"

The futility of further resistance was driven home when Jefferson Davis and the remaining members of his entourage, including his family, in their flight south were captured near Irwinsville, Georgia. On May 15, the prisoners were brought by train to Atlanta. With the Confederate president imprisoned in town, the American flag was raised on a large pole in the public square in front of the U.S. post commandant's headquarters. It was the same place where hundreds of horribly wounded Union prisoners had laid for days without relief after the Battle of Atlanta. The flag flew at half mast to mark President Abraham Lincoln's death. Resigned to his American fate, Steele looked at the flag out of his office window and ruefully declared, "We are reminded as we gaze upon the victorious banner that floats in the breeze of the return of Georgia to the national union, and of the duties consequent thereon."

QUICKLY ASKING FOR AND receiving a pardon from President Andrew Johnson, Mayor James Calhoun took the lead in ushering Atlanta back into the Union. He organized a public meeting for June 24 at City Hall "for the purpose of considering the great questions of the day and of expressing their honest and loyal sentiments towards the Government of the United States." Never the firebrand, always plainspoken, Calhoun nonetheless opened the meeting with a rare burst of eloquence. He told the gathering of men who had witnessed and participated in the rise of the Confederacy and its defeat,

> For one I can truthfully say, and am proud to say, that it was not my desire to destroy the old Union, the Union of our fathers; and I can say that it is the desire of my heart, honestly and in good faith, to return to it. On returning to the Union of our fathers, while it will be our right to claim the protection of the Flag of our Country, the Stars and Stripes, emblematic of the Union of the States, and of our nationality, it will be our solemn duty to protect and defend it, and that with our lives if necessary. Under it, in times which have past and gone, many of us have fought the enemy of our common country, and let us again resolve, should it ever become necessary, that we will do so again. And if, as a people, we have erred in the past, let us try to make compensation for it in the future, and let us not cherish, or keep alive, any unkind feelings for the people of any section of our common country, but let us rather cultivate feelings of kindness, friendship and confidence.

Calhoun's voice for reconstruction of the Union quelled many calls for violent resistance. He appointed a committee to draft a resolution for the meeting to approve. The committee members included both leading Union loyalists, such as Alfred Austell and James L. Dunning, and active Confederates, including Jared Whitaker and

George W. Adair. The resolution declared, "We . . . have thus convened to express our anxious solicitude for a speedy restoration and return to our original status in the Union, hopefully anticipating that the day is near at hand when the sun of our former prosperity and happiness may again shine upon us with undiminished and increased splendor; when each one may sit under his own vine and fig tree with no one to 'molest or make afraid.'"

The gathering counseled "a ready and hearty obedience to the laws of our country." It contended "in the assassination of Abraham Lincoln, we gaze upon a deed horrible and horrifying. We hold it up to universal execration." Those in attendance expressed "full confidence" in the administration of Andrew Johnson and "tender the President our firm attachment, fidelity and support, and trusting, that in all time to come, we shall be known, and *only known*, as one people, sharing one destiny, having one interest, one liberty, *one Constitution* and *one Flag*."

The resolution was adopted "unanimously and warmly."

# Sherman's Return

WHAT THOUGHTS AND FEELINGS coursed through William Lowndes Calhoun's mind as he stood in Atlanta's depot at midday on January 29, 1879, cannot be known. He surely must have felt nervous. He waited at the front of a large jostling crowd gathered in the ornate vastness of the still fresh-feeling Union Station. The vaulted brick and iron depot had been built eight years earlier on the site of the old car shed. It was far grander and more ornate than the one the very man he now came to greet had knocked down and burnt back in the fateful fall of 1864. Rumors rippled about the city that fifty-nine-year-old William Tecumseh Sherman's return to Atlanta, originally set for the day before, had been delayed as a security precaution. In fact, General Sherman took an extra day in North Georgia so he could tour with two of his daughters through the old Cherokee country he had first encountered as a tourist himself thirty-five years before.

As the 12:45 puffed slowly over the Western & Atlantic tracks into the station, Lowndes Calhoun probably felt some concern over how his city would receive its special guest. He still felt the hobbling effects and lasting ache of the bullet he took in the hip while fighting with Joe Johnston at the Battle of Resaca in May 1864 to keep Sherman out of Atlanta, but today he wanted the general to feel the warmth of his city's welcome. Nothing could better symbolize to the rest of the nation that a new Atlanta had risen out of the ashes of the old.

The recently elected first-term mayor of Atlanta did not need to worry. A friend had invited Sherman to town five years earlier. "No," replied the general then, "the time has not yet come for me to visit Atlanta." In the words of a reporter on hand this day, "We suppose the times have ripened now." They had. Few people in Atlanta remained ill disposed toward Sherman—or, at least, few bore him enough hatred to do much more than crack off-color jokes about the man's past behavior toward his "host" city. Somebody in the crowded station called out to Mayor Calhoun to ask if he intended to offer Sherman "the freedom of the city." A riposte came from the crowd: "He made too free with it when he was here before." The talkers carried on with their gallows humor. Somebody else proposed that in mock imitation of the days of war when the fair young women of Atlanta used to turn out all in white to send off the soldiers at the car shed, widows in black mourning clothes bearing bundles of kindling should form a procession preceding the general "to facilitate his work."

As the train sighed to a halt, somebody called out over the big W&A locomotive's steam release and clanging bell, "Ring the fire bells! The town will be gone in forty minutes!"

BUT THE FIRES OF WAR were out. Atlanta's phoenixlike rise from the literal ashes made it the regional center to which enterprising people, black and white, came to build a new future and gave the city a reputation as the center for those in the South ready to move beyond the defeated Confederate cause. The four original railroads returned; a new one to Charlotte planned since before secession went through. Atlanta's geographic destiny as a hub of transport and commerce forecast so long ago proved true—this time for good. Within months after the surrender, people again marveled at Atlanta's spark and lust for business, comparing it to northern and western cities on the move. In 1868, a visiting northern merchant repeated the frequent antebellum praise of his Atlanta counterparts for being "more like New York merchants than any he had met outside the metropolis."

Most Southern cities languished as moribund shells in their first postwar decades, but Atlanta (along with Richmond and Nashville) was one of the very few larger cities to grow significantly. In 1868, Atlanta got its wish for recognition as Georgia's premier city and became the new seat of the state capital and its government. Elected mayor a month earlier, the forty-one-year-old Lowndes Calhoun now stood at the head of a fast-growth city with a population of 37,409, marking a nearly fourfold increase since 1860. Between 1860 and 1870, real estate values had plummeted in once-prosperous Mobile, Savannah, and Charleston, while they had risen in Atlanta by 40 percent—and gone up since then.

Lowndes Calhoun, James's eldest son and law partner, had followed his family's century-long tradition of public service. His election as mayor came after four terms in the state legislature. He was the first Calhoun to occupy City Hall since his father's wartime tenure had ended in December 1865. James Calhoun had hoped his brother Ezekiel might succeed him, but the city, awash in fractious debate over the terms of its return to the national union, passed over the elderly physician. James himself had tried one more time for national office—a bid for a U.S. congressional seat from the district comprising Fulton County in 1866. In support of his candidacy, he recounted his long political and personal engagement with the politics and society of the South, beginning with his strong antebellum opposition to secession and his belief "that the South ought to exercise patience and forbearance and to trust the ballot box and the power of reason and justice for a redress of our grievances." When the state's voters determined otherwise, he felt "bound by the act of the State . . . to go with the people of the South . . . although I had so conscientiously differed with them in opinion." Once the permanence of the national union was decided for all time, he worked to win support for restoration of Georgia's full rights within the Union. Though "opposed" to what eventually became the Fourteenth Amendment to the Constitution, the right to equal protection under law for all races, if it were passed, he "would no longer oppose it, but would endeavor to give effect to [the General Assembly's] decision." He remained as he was from the first, a man committed to democratic and constitutional principles.

In Calhoun's accounting of his life—which spanned his boyhood departure from a distressed Abbeville plantation, his fighting leadership in the last frontier battles with Creek and Cherokee tribal remnants, his role in building Atlanta and managing a city through its unprecedented changes during a uniquely devastating war, one in which the city itself eventually became a great battlefield, and finally the foundations he laid for its rebuilding—he took justified pride. He had not asked for those challenges, but he had met them forthrightly and without flinching. "I find nothing . . . to regret or condemn," he concluded, "although I may have been in error, in some instances, in the judgment of others, and even in fact. At all times, and in every emergency, I did what my conscience dictated was right, and if I had the same trying ordeals to pass through again, I do not know that I could pursue a line of conduct more satisfactory to myself."

He lost. Moderate voices urging accommodation with the federal government's emerging reconstruction program lost their races for office throughout the South that year. The election's outcome radicalized Republicans in control of Congress. Over President Andrew Johnson's objections, they passed a reconstruction act imposing strenuous federal military authority over Southern civil life and governance, taking the vote away from ex-rebels and enfranchising the region's new black citizens. James Calhoun would have to content himself with the fact that his portrait would hang in City Hall, even if he had been ejected from it. After losing his last Congressional race, gray-haired and increasingly shaky-handed, he withdrew from politics and devoted himself to his legal practice as well as dabbled in real estate development. Ezekiel, too, left Atlanta politics to focus on his large medical practice's patients. Ezekiel died of pneumonia in March 1875 at age seventy-six. The brother whom he helped to educate and saw grow to fill a central role on the world's stage suffered a paralyzing stroke less than seven months later and died on October 1. He was sixty-four years old.

SHERMAN HAD BEEN GENERAL in chief of the U.S. Army since 1869. Ever convinced of the value of "statesmanship" in the actions of the military, he believed there would come a right time for him to make his first extended return visit to the South since the war. By 1879 President Rutherford B. Hayes was making good on his preelection pledge to end Reconstruction. Hayes accepted white Southern legislators' promises to protect the civil rights of their black citizens by upholding the Fourteenth Amendment and its companion Fifteenth Amendment's ban on race-based restriction of voting rights. Those promises proved empty. The president ignored the swift dissolution of black political power and the passage of state laws effectively ending African Americans' briefly held political rights.

General Sherman was fine with that turn. He had opposed the imposition of harsh reconstruction measures on the South in the first place; he thought that previous white Southern leaders should return to power and that blacks, though no longer enslaved, should play a lesser role in society. Sherman retained his love for the South where he had spent his first, and many of his most fulfilling, years in active duty service, as well as a treasured sojourn living and teaching in

Louisiana, and passed the test of the Civil War years, which won him enduring worldwide fame. Moreover, he had another brutal race war on his hands, again carrying out a fight against Indians tragically unwilling to accept their race's U.S.-determined removal from their ancient—and treaty-based—tribal lands in the far West. With fewer troops needed now to enforce Washington's authority in the South, he could devote the military's attention to "operations against the hostile Sioux."

STOUTER THAN HIS FATHER and sporting a thick brush mustache, Lowndes Calhoun, according to his admirers, followed his father "in form and character." A good government man, he created Atlanta's first street paving system. He was devoted to the needs of Confederate veterans, helping build a home for old soldiers and serving as a leader in several veterans' organizations. He looked down the train to the last car where he caught his first glimpse of General Sherman, his hair still a reddish brown but his beard gray. His squinty eyes darted about within his still-thin, deeply weathered face. He was as talkative and constantly in motion as ever. He bounded off the last car's platform to where a military delegation from the army's McPherson Barracks greeted him. A reporter on hand seemed almost surprised to note that "there was no excitement and no demonstration" made by those on hand. The crowd pressed forward "curious to see" the man, but much like during his previous march through Georgia, "a sort of pathway was opened for the party, and the people stood alongside looking on quietly and keeping up a subdued run of comment."

Sherman was traveling with his two grown daughters, an aide, and friend Gen. Stewart Van Vliet and his wife, and the rail trip had so far been, as the press reported, a "mixed tour of business and recreation." Starting in Tennessee, dipping into Alabama, and heading back to Chattanooga, he inspected some military posts and a factory. He climbed Lookout Mountain and surveyed the battlefields where he had fought in 1863. The tour would take the party from Atlanta to Savannah, where he had lived for a period in 1844, on to his Florida Second Seminole War haunts, then to New Orleans and finally up through Mississippi and western Tennessee—scenes of many of his most famous triumphs and his advancing army's most notorious acts. He never heard one insult during his stops and was most often greeted warmly. Atlanta, however, was the place into which he had etched his name most indelibly with fire. Still, though, the crowds that came out to see him as he went about town were "curious and respectful." He declared, "We have had nothing but the most courteous treatment everywhere." He bore a similar attitude toward his Atlanta hosts. He registered his party at the city's leading Kimball House hotel and, while he did, "expressed wonder at the magnitude of the hotel and the general thrifty look of the city."

In the afternoon, the Sherman party took a carriage tour around town. He passed by the former Neal house, where he had headquartered. He was interested to learn it now served as a girl's high school. The general's entourage rode through the streets to the principal battle sites around town. Along the way, he expressed his "great admiration" for Atlanta's "pluck and energy and the marvelous recuperation" it had made. "The growth of the city is wonderful," he remarked. He paid his respects at a memorial built on the site where his dearest friend in the war, Gen. James McPherson, had fallen during the Battle of Atlanta. Before dark he attended a dress parade at the army barracks and returned there later for a ball where he danced every dance and "seemed," recounted a reporter on hand, "to enjoy the fun hugely."

Chatting with visitors the next day, the voluble Sherman called to mind numerous vivid details about the sites over which his army had marched and fought, even asking about a paper mill and bucket factory that he remembered once stood along Peachtree Creek. He intended to take a stroll up Marietta Street, telling his company, "There are several localities which I wish to see again."

WHEN MAYOR CALHOUN MET with Sherman that evening, he told the general he had "fought him hard" at Resaca and reminded Sherman that he had "failed in his efforts" to defeat Johnston there. The general remembered the Mayor's father well and let the obviously proud son know he was "much attached" to him. "Duty," he told Calhoun, "compelled [me] to do many harsh things, yet [I] never failed to appreciate the oft-repeated appeals of the then Mayor Calhoun in behalf of the people of Atlanta. He was a noble-hearted, true man."

Sherman would only stay one night in Atlanta before his party continued on its way, leaving Atlanta on the same Macon railroad line he had finally destroyed in 1864, forcing the besieged Gate City to surrender. After his visit, he expressed his hope that his return symbolized a reunited America and had "done some good, something to make men feel more national, more disposed to labor with zeal and earnestness in the direction of national unity and national progress."

During the evening of his Atlanta visit, someone in the company expressed regret the war had ever taken place. Sherman disagreed. "Yes, it was terrible," he said, "and yet it had to come. It was inevitable. . . . Here we were claiming to be the freest people in all the world, and offering liberty to all mankind, and yet there was an abnormal state of things. There were 4,000,000 slaves in the United States, and we had in the heart of the country an institution antagonistic to the very principles of our government. So it had to be abolished."

# NOTES

## CHAPTER 1: FLAGS

6 **"I have never seen the city more quiet":** Kile quotes from *Webster v. U.S.*, CD 13502, folder 4, National Archives, Washington, D.C.

7 **The hoof clatter of Mayor James Montgomery Calhoun's horse:** Atlanta's Civil War mayor James Montgomery Calhoun should not be confused with his distant cousin James Martin Calhoun, a powerful Alabama legislator and secessionist, who was the nephew of John C. Calhoun. On James Martin Calhoun, see Thomas M. Owen and Marie B. Owen, *History of Alabama and Dictionary of Alabama Biography* (Chicago: S. J. Clarke, 1921), 3:285–86.

7 **"Our white flag will be our best protection":** Calhoun quote from Wallace Putnam Reed, *History of Atlanta, Georgia: With Illustrations and Biographical Sketches of Some of Its Prominent Men and Pioneers* (Atlanta: D. Mason & Co., 1889), 195.

## CHAPTER 2: VIRGINIANS

11 **The federal Tariff of 1824, which raised cotton import duties:** On economic conditions in the Calhoun Settlement and the impact of the Tariff of 1824, see William W. Freehling, *Prelude to Civil War: The Nullification Controversy in South Carolina, 1816–1836* (New York and London: Harper & Row, 1966), 106–8.

12 **While the Spanish, French, and British vied for control of the New World:** For a complete history of the relations between Cherokee and Colonial South Carolina settlers, see Tom Hatley, *The Dividing Paths: Cherokees and South Carolinians through the Era of Revolution* (New York: Oxford University Press, 1993).

13 **she hoped to find a permanent home:** On the early years of the Calhoun family, see W. Pinkney Starke, "Account of Calhoun's Early Life Abridged from the Manuscript of Col. W. Pinkney Starke," *Annual Report of the American Historical Association for the Year 1899* (Washington, D.C.: Smithsonian Institution Press, 1900), 2:65–9.

13 **As a sideshow to the far greater global war:** Edward J. Cashin, ed., *A Wilderness Still the Cradle of Nature: Frontier Georgia* (Savannah: Library of Georgia, 1994), viii–ix.

14 **With atrocities mounting on both sides:** On the Cherokee War of 1759–1761, see Hatley, *The Dividing Paths*, especially 119ff., and John Oliphant, *Peace and War on the Anglo-Cherokee Frontier, 1756–63* (Baton Rouge: Louisiana State University Press, 2001), 69ff.

15 **He finally found her:** Rebecca, cousin to John C. Calhoun, would live to marry the Revolutionary War hero Gen. Andrew Pickens of Abbeville, who went to the U.S. Congress from South Carolina. Their grandson, Francis W. Pickens, was governor of the state at the time of its secession and gave the order to fire upon Fort Sumter, marking the start of the Civil War. See Starke, "Account of Calhoun's Early Life," 68.

15 **So it was that the Calhouns first spilled their blood:** On the Long Cane Creek Massacre in the Cherokee War's context, see Hatley, *The Dividing Paths*, 127.

16 **In memory of Mrs. Catherine Calhoun:** From *South Carolina Gazette*, February 2–9 and 9–16, 1760, in A. S. Salley Jr., "Calhoun Family of South Carolina," *South Carolina Historical and Genealogical Magazine* (South Carolina Historical Society) 7, no. 1 (January 1906): 81–98.

16 **The surviving Calhoun brothers gradually built thriving farms:** On the rise of the Calhouns in and out of the Calhoun Settlement, see John Niven, *John C. Calhoun and the Price of Union: A Biography* (Baton Rouge and London: Louisiana State University Press, 1988), 7–12.

17 **"the patriarch of the upper country":** On the crucial role played by the South Carolina upstate in antebellum politics and the Calhoun family's regional and national leadership role, see Lacy K. Ford Jr., *Origins of Southern Radicalism: The South Carolina Upcountry, 1800–1860* (New York: Oxford University Press, 1988); for Patrick Calhoun's nickname, see 8.

17 **The teenaged James barely recalled his few meetings:** On the political rise of John C. Calhoun in South Carolina, see Niven, *John C. Calhoun*, 13–30.

18 **"The despotism founded on combined geographical interest":** Quoted in Freehling, *Prelude to Civil War*, 154.

19 **"There are thousands of her brave sons":** John C. Calhoun, "On the Revenue Collection Bill (Commonly Called the Force Bill), in Reference to the Ordinance of the South Carolina Convention, Delivered in the Senate, February 15th and 16th, 1833," in *The Works of John C. Calhoun* (New York: D. Appleton, 1888), 2:229.

19 **Calhoun, the plantation owner, saw little in the common man he liked:** On the differences between Calhoun and Jackson, see William W. Freehling, *The Road to Disunion*, Vol. 1, *Secessionists at Bay, 1776–1854* (New York and London: Oxford University Press, 1990), 263–66.

19 **Jackson mounted a military force and muttered a threat to "hang every leader":** On President Jackson's threat to impose federal will by force, see Freehling 278ff. On Calhoun's political evolution through the Nullification Crisis, see *The Road to Disunion*, 154–66.

19 **At a Washington Jefferson Day dinner:** The attempted reconciliation event is recounted in Robert V. Remini, *Daniel Webster: The Man and His Time* (New York: W. W. Norton & Co., 1997), 335.

19 **Another 140 years would pass:** Spiro Agnew's resignation in 1973 was the second by a vice president following Calhoun's in 1832.

21 **Among the men who owned one of the most productive mines:** On the Gold Rush of 1829, see David Williams, *The Georgia Gold Rush: Twenty-Niners, Cherokees, and Gold Fever* (Columbia: University of South Carolina Press, 1993); on Calhoun's mining interests, see 24.

21 **"To move was in the blood of everyone":** James S. Lamar, *Recollections of Pioneer Days in Georgia* (no publication data, 1900?), 4.

21 **"reared to a belief and faith"**: Gideon Lincecum, "Autobiography of Gideon Lincecum," excerpt, in Cashin, *A Wilderness*, 13.

21 **derisively calling them "crackers"**: On the derivation of the derogatory term *cracker*, the Oxford English Dictionary offers this passage of a letter from 1766: "I should explain to your Lordship what is meant by crackers; a name they have got from being great boasters; they are a lawless set of rascals on the frontiers of Virginia, Maryland, the Carolinas and Georgia, who often change their places of abode." See OED Online at http://dictionary.oed.com.

## CHAPTER 3: REMOVAL

24 **He had never dared to tell anyone**: Thomas H. Martin, *Atlanta and Its Builders: A Comprehensive History of the Gate City of the South* (Atlanta: Century Memorial, 1902), 2:639–41.

24 **Seven children would follow**: William Henry Dabney, *Sketch of the Dabneys of Virginia: With Some of Their Family Records* (Chicago: S. D. Childs & Co., 1888), 186; Lucian Lamar Knight, *A Standard History of Georgia and Georgians* (Atlanta: Lewis, 1917), 5:2291.

24 **As he traveled for the court circuit**: "He Sleeps," *Atlanta Constitution*, October, 5, 1875, 3; Dr. R. J. Massey, "Men Who Made Atlanta," *Atlanta Constitution*, October 22, 1905, D2.

24 **From the percentage of the payments he collected**: Legal earnings figure from Eric H. Walther, *William Lowndes Yancey and the Coming of the Civil War* (Chapel Hill: University of North Carolina Press, 2006), 146.

25 **his son Patrick would later insist**: "Reminiscences of Patrick H. Calhoun," *Atlanta Historical Bulletin* 1, no. 6 (February 1932): 42.

25 **A quarter of all slave families were separated by sales**: Slave family separation figure from James McPherson, *Battle Cry of Freedom* (New York and Oxford: Oxford University Press, 1988), 38.

25 **The U.S. Army manned a chain of forts**: For a general survey of Andrew Jackson's relations with the Indians of the Southeast, see Robert V. Remini, *Andrew Jackson and His Indian Wars* (New York: Viking, 2001); for the purposes of this book, I benefited from 226–72. Remini points out that Jackson took a paternalistic view toward the fate of the southeastern tribes, seeing their voluntary, if possible, and forced, if necessary, removal as the only way to stave off an extinction of the Indians like that which took place in New England following the encounter between natives and colonialists there. On the First Creek War, see James W. Holland, *Andrew Jackson and the Creek War: Victory at the Horseshoe* (Tuscaloosa: University of Alabama Press, 1968); Joel W. Martin, *Sacred Revolt: The Muskogees' Struggle for a New World* (Boston: Beacon Press, 1991), 1–3. On the impact of the Creek War and the Treaty of Fort Jackson on Andrew Jackson's later Indian removal policies, see Michael Paul Rogin, *Fathers and Children: Andrew Jackson and the Subjugation of the American Indian* (New York: Alfred K. Knopf, 1975), 169–78.

26 **Concluded in 1826, the Treaty of Indian Springs**: Grace M. Schwartzman and Susan K. Barnard, "A Trail of Broken Promises: Georgians and Muscogee Creek Treaties 1796–1826," *Georgia Historical Quarterly* 75 (Winter 1991): 704–5.

27 **"McIntosh . . . has sold the land of his fathers"**: Auguste Levasseur, *Lafayette in America in 1824 & 1825*, quoted in Edward J. Cashin, ed., *A Wilderness Still the Cradle of Nature: Frontier Georgia* (Savannah: Library of Georgia, 1994), 119.

NOTES TO CHAPTER 3

27    **Not long after Lafayette's visit:** Cashin, *A Wilderness*, xxv–xxvi.
27    **The Indians complained but had no right:** On the defrauding of the Creek
      land deeds, see Martin, *Sacred Revolt*, 2, and Kenneth L. Valliere, "The Creek
      War of 1836: A Military History," *Chronicles of Oklahoma* 57, no. 4 (1980): 464–
      66.
28    **"I have heard a great many talks from our great father":** Jackson in "Proceed-
      ings of the Indian Board in the City of New York," (n.p., n.d.), 5, quoted, along
      with Speckled Snake, in Sharyn Kane and Richard Keeton, *Fort Benning: The
      Land and the People* (Tallahassee: Southeast Archeological Center, National Park
      Service, 1998), ch. 11, n.p.
28    **He paid the price for opposing the immensely popular legislation:** David
      Crockett, *The Life of David Crockett: The Original Humorist and Irrepressible
      Backwoodsman; an Autobiography, to Which Is Added an Account of His Glorious
      Death at the Alamo While Fighting in Defence of Texas Independence* (New York:
      A. L. Burt, 1902), 160.
29    **By the time the wanderers reached Oklahoma:** Kane and Keeton, *Fort Benning*,
      ch. 11, n.p.
29    **war erupted between white Americans and Alabama and Georgia Creeks:** On
      the Second Seminole War and its relation to the Creek War of 1836, see John K.
      Mahon, *History of the Second Seminole War, 1835–1842* (Gainesville: University
      of Florida Press, 1967), 160–61, 190–91. For history and interpretation of the
      Second Seminole and Second Creek wars within a wider argument about Jack-
      sonian paternalistic justifications for Indian removal, see Rogin, *Fathers and
      Children*, 229–43. For the most complete history of the Second Creek War's mil-
      itary aspects, see Valliere, "The Creek War of 1836," 463–85. For a more suc-
      cinct overview of its causes, major events, and consequences, see Jacob R. Motte,
      *Journey into Wilderness: An Army Surgeon's Account of Life in Camp and Field dur-
      ing the Creek and Seminole Wars, 1836–1838*, ed. James F. Sunderman (Gaines-
      ville: University of Florida Press, 1953), notes, 247–55.
30    **"men, women and children murdered in every direction":** Quoted in Valliere,
      "The Creek War of 1836," 471.
30    **Most men came from nearby towns:** On the Georgia militia's role in the war,
      see Gordon Burns Smith, *History of the Georgia Militia, 1783–1861* (Mil-
      ledgeville, GA: Boyd Publishing, 2000), 198, 213–15; Helen Eliza Terrill, *His-
      tory of Stewart County* (Columbus, GA: Columbus Office Supply Co., 1958),
      43–63; on the major events of the war, including several contemporary letters
      from participating officers, see Terrill, *History*, 55–63. See also William Warren
      Rogers, *Ante-Bellum Thomas County 1825–1861* (Tallahassee: Florida State Uni-
      versity Press, 1963), 35–38, for discussion of a county that also saw heavy fighting.
30    **In addition, 4,300 Alabamans joined the effort:** "Hon. Charles Murphey Can-
      dler's Historical Address to the DeKalb County Centennial Celebration at De-
      catur, Georgia, on November 9, 1922." For the Second Creek War's troop levels,
      see Motte, *Journey into Wilderness*, 254n1.
31    **"It seemed as if every ragamuffin of Georgia":** Motte, *Journey into Wilderness*, 3.
31    **both Calhoun brothers' companies mustered into the army in Columbus:** See
      Smith, *History of the Georgia Militia*, on Georgia's state militia tradition and on
      its role in the Creek War of 1836, particularly 195–215, and on Alford, see
      207n48.

31 **The Fort McCreary blockhouse and stockade commanded a hilltop:** On Fort McCreary and surroundings, see Terrill, *History*, 48, 50–51. The fort's name is sometimes spelled "McCrary."

32 **"nothing but a continued series of black heaps of ashes":** Motte, *Journey into Wilderness*, 11.

33 **He took the horse's reins:** "James M. Calhoun," n.d., no source, Atlanta History Society Calhoun Papers.

33 **"The Indians must not escape":** "The War Not Yet Ended," *Columbus Sentinel*, August 2, 1836.

33 **"With them their country was life":** Motte, *Journey into Wilderness*, 19–20, 69–70.

34 **Just 13,573 Creeks remained alive in Oklahoma:** Kane and Keeton, *Fort Benning*, ch. 11, n.p.

34 **The next would not come for another thirty years:** Dr. R. J. Massey, "Men Who Made Atlanta," *Atlanta Constitution*, October 22, 1905, D2.

## CHAPTER 4: SHERMAN IN THE SWAMP

36 **"disgraceful . . . to the American character":** Quoted in Jacob R. Motte, *Journey into Wilderness: An Army Surgeon's Account of Life in Camp and Field during the Creek and Seminole Wars, 1836–1838*, ed. James F. Sunderman (Gainesville: University of Florida Press, 1953), 312.

36 **With a force that numbered between 4,000 and 9,000:** For troop and Indian force numbers and deaths, see John K. Mahon, *History of the Second Seminole War, 1835–1842* (Gainesville: University of Florida Press, 1967), 122, 225, 307, and 325.

36 **"In twenty months or so":** Quoted in Mahon, *History*, 303.

37 **the nineteen-year-old William Tecumseh Sherman:** On the events of Sherman's life in Florida, this chapter draws heavily on Mahon's war history; William Tecumseh Sherman, *Memoirs of General W. T. Sherman*, 2nd ed. (New York: Penguin Classics, 2001), 17–28; John F. Marszalek, *Sherman: A Soldier's Passion for Order* (New York: The Free Press, 1993), 33–47; Jane F. Lancaster, "William Tecumseh Sherman's Introduction to War, 1840–1842: Lesson for Action," *Florida Historical Quarterly* 72, no. 1 (July 1993): 56–72.

37 **"as bright as the burning bush":** Quoted in Marszalek, *Sherman*, 38.

38 **"the abode of man or beast":** Sherman, *Memoirs*, 19, 27.

38 **"threading through the intricate mazes":** Quoted in Marszalek, *Sherman*, 38.

38 **"Good for nothing" and a "pack of rascals":** Quoted in Lancaster, "William Tecumseh Sherman's Introduction to War," 65.

39 **While in Florida, he studied geography and geology:** Sherman, *Memoirs*, 26.

39 **"the best officer is selected":** Quoted in Lancaster, "William Tecumseh Sherman's Introduction to War," 65.

40 **"Regardless of food or the climate":** Mahon, *History*, 295–97.

41 **Even the most intransigent among them:** Sherman, *Memoirs*, 23–36; Mahon, *History*, 298–302.

41 **The Second Seminole War was over:** Sherman, *Memoirs*, 27.

41 **"had caught more Indians":** Quoted in Lancaster, "William Tecumseh Sherman's Introduction to War," 69.

42 **"many a rich scene":** This and following quotes, unless otherwise indicated, are from Russell S. Bonds, "Sherman's First March Through Georgia," *Civil War Times* 46, no. 6 (August 2007): 20–27.

43 **"must necessarily unite":** Calhoun quote in Walter G. Cooper, *Official History of Fulton County* (Atlanta: History Commission, 1934), 55.

43 **Marthasville in 1844 didn't amount to much:** Early settlement description, from Cooper, *Official History*, 58–59.

43 **A move was afoot to rename it "Atlanta":** The story of how Atlanta got its name is disputed. For a common version, see Cooper, *Official History*, 59–60.

43 **"every bit of knowledge then acquired [was] returned tenfold":** Letter to Ellen Ewing Sherman, January 5, 1865, *Sherman's Civil War: Selected Correspondence of William T. Sherman, 1860–1865*, ed. Brooks D. Simpson and Jean V. Berlin (Chapel Hill and London: University of North Carolina Press, 1999), 792.

## CHAPTER 5: ANOTHER PASSAGE

46 **Once beneath the soaring rotunda:** On the very different Capitol structure at the time, see William C. Allen, *History of the United States Capitol: A Chronicle of Design, Construction, and Politics* (Washington, D.C.: U.S. Government Printing Office, 2001), 146.

46 **People who reviled him:** Robert V. Remini, *Daniel Webster: The Man and His Time* (New York: W. W. Norton & Co., 1997), 27.

47 **"freekently came up to the Senate Chamber to see Senator Webster":** Quoted in Thomas G. Dyer, "Half Slave, Half Free: Unionist Robert Webster in Confederate Atlanta," in *Inside the Confederate Nation: Essays in Honor of Emory M. Thomas*, ed. Emory M. Thomas, Lesley Jill Gordon, and John C. Inscoe (Baton Rouge: Louisiana State University Press, 2005), 308. I rely extensively on Dyer's exhaustive research on Robert Webster's early life for this chapter.

47 **"Nature had not in our days":** Quoted in Remini, *Daniel Webster*, 29, 762.

47 **The "Demosthenes of America" swept away his audiences:** Remini, *Daniel Webster*, 219.

47 **"out of rant and out of declamation to history and good sense":** Remini, *Daniel Webster*, 762.

47 **"made for the people, made by the people, and answerable to the people":** Daniel Webster, "Second Speech on Foot's Resolution, Jan. 26, 1830," *The Works of Daniel Webster* (Boston: Little, Brown, & Co., 1890), 3:321.

47 **"the grandest specimen of American oratory":** Quoted in Garry Wills, *Lincoln at Gettysburg: The Words That Remade America* (New York: Simon & Schuster, 1992), 34.

48 **"our present day and nation the very greatest men":** James Henry Hammond, *Secret and Sacred: The Diaries of James Henry Hammond, a Southern Slaveholder*, ed. Carol K. Bleser (Columbia: University of South Carolina Press, 1988), 173.

48 **"slightly heathenish in private life":** Remini, *Daniel Webster*, 308.

49 **Swisshelm lost her *Tribune* job for publishing the stories:** Quoted in Remini, *Daniel Webster*, 307.

49 **But growing up, Bob always knew who his real father was:** Dyer, "Half Slave, Half Free," 308. Unlike Dyer, who insists that "not enough evidence exists to conclude even tentatively that Daniel Webster sired Robert Webster," I find the large amount of circumstantial evidence Dyer and Remini mount, drawn from

multiple contemporary sources, provides strong proof to accept Robert Webster's assertions about his parentage. The Swisshelm quote is found in Jane Grey Cannon Swisshelm, *Half a Century: The Memoirs of the First Woman Journalist in the Civil Rights Struggle*, ed. Paul Dennis Sporer (Chester, NY: Anza Publishing, 2005), 86; on Swisshelm's experience following publication of her article about Webster, see 88–91.

49   **"a mulatto of rare beauty":** Quoted in Dyer, "Half Slave, Half Free," 296.

50   **Gadsby's seventeen house slaves likely trafficked back and forth:** On the Decatur House's rich history, see www.decaturhouse.org.

50   **He went from the National Hotel to the boardinghouse:** William Tecumseh Sherman, *Memoirs of General W. T. Sherman*, 2nd ed. (New York: Penguin Classics, 2001), 12.

51   **he likely lived on Rosemont Plantation:** On the Cunningham's Rosemont Plantation, see Eric H. Walther, *William Lowndes Yancey and the Coming of the Civil War* (Chapel Hill: University of North Carolina Press, 2006), 26.

51   **Ben's first years of life:** On Ben's early life, see Walther, *William Lowndes Yancey*, 36ff. See also "Benjamin C. Yancey," in William Garrett, *Reminiscences of Public Men in Alabama: For Thirty Years, with an Appendix* (Atlanta: Plantation Publishing Co.'s Press, 1872), 626–27.

51   **he went to Upstate New York for prep school and then Yale Law School:** On Ben Yancey's education, see Walther, *William Lowndes Yancey*, 36–37.

51   **Each would come to the other's aid:** John Cunningham described Yancey in 1843 as "my friend" in a written challenge he delivered on Cunningham's behalf to another man to a duel, resulting in both Cunningham and Yancey being found guilty of breaking South Carolina's antidueling laws. See "State vs. Cunningham and Yancey" in R. H. Spears, *Cases at Law, Argued and Determined in the Court of Appeals of South Carolina* (Columbia, SC: A. S. Johnston, 1844), 2:246–56.

51   **W. L. in particular became an ardent states' rights advocate:** On W. L. Yancey's political career, see Walther, *William Lowndes Yancey*.

51   **He drafted what was known as the Alabama Platform:** Walther, *William Lowndes Yancey*, 47–49.

51   **Both avoided criminal charges and congressional censure:** On W. L. Yancey's duel with Thomas Clingman, see Walther, *William Lowndes Yancey*, 76–80.

52   **"is said to be a little more staid in temperament than I am":** Quoted in Walther, *William Lowndes Yancey*, 156.

52   **"I would have trusted him with anything":** Testimony of Ben Yancey, *Webster v. United States*, case file 13502, Court of Claims, RG 123, folders 2 and 4, National Archives, Washington, D.C.

52   **"I shipped him without a minute's warning":** Walther, *William Lowndes Yancey*, 153–54.

## Chapter 6: The Compromise

53   **The state assembly passed numerous reforms:** On James Calhoun's legislative record, see Dr. R. J. Massey, "Men Who Made Atlanta," *Atlanta Constitution*, October 22, 1905, D2, and James M. Russell, "Calhoun, James Montgomery," in Kenneth Coleman and Charles Stephen Gurr, *Dictionary of Georgia Biography* (Athens: University of Georgia Press, 1983), 148.

54 **an angry mob intent on lynching the prisoner:** On the attempted lynching incident, see Wallace P. Reed, *History of Atlanta, Georgia: With Illustrations and Biographical Sketches of Some of Its Prominent Men and Pioneers* (Atlanta: D. Mason & Co., 1889), 298.

54 **Calhoun seemed to be on course for a similar ascent:** "He Sleeps," *Atlanta Constitution*, October 5, 1875, 3.

56 **"Women were dragged from their homes":** John G. Burnett, "The Cherokee Removal Through the Eyes of a Private Soldier," *Journal of Cherokee Studies* 3, special issue (1978): 183.

56 **"the cruelest work I ever knew":** James Mooney, *Historical Sketch of the Cherokee* (1900, rpt. Chicago: Aldine Publishing, 1975), 124.

57 **"you may accomplish all you desire":** John C. Calhoun to James M. Calhoun, July 17, 1839, James M. Calhoun Papers, AHC, MSS 50, box 1, folder 2.

58 **Jacksonian Democrats outnumbered Whigs by nearly two to one:** For a table giving a breakdown of Georgian party voting patterns including the up-country region, see Anthony Gene Carey, *Parties, Slavery, and the Union in Antebellum Georgia* (Athens: University of Georgia Press, 1997), 108.

58 **Those assets were not enough to overcome:** There are numerous studies of the political crosscurrents whipsawing the antebellum nation. I found William W. Freehling's monumental *The Road to Disunion*, Vol. 1, *Secessionists at Bay, 1776–1854* (New York and London: Oxford University Press, 1990), most helpful; also see James M. McPherson, *Battle Cry of Freedom* (New York and Oxford: Oxford University Press, 1988), 6–46.

59 **Senator Calhoun sent James a copy:** "Speech on the Abrogation of the Joint Occupancy of Oregon (Revised Report)," in the Senate, March 16, 1846, *Papers of John C. Calhoun*, Vol. 22, *1845–1846*, ed. Clyde N. Wilson (Columbia: University of South Carolina Press, 1995), 704–29.

59 **He seemed to have set a course for himself:** On John C. Calhoun's decisive role in the Oregon question, see John Niven, *John C. Calhoun and the Price of Union: A Biography* (Baton Rouge and London: Louisiana State University Press, 1988), 295–97.

60 **"it has been a great misfortune to me":** James M. Calhoun to John C. Calhoun, Decatur, Georgia, May 7, 1846, *Papers of John C. Calhoun*, Vol. 23, *1846*, ed. Clyde N. Wilson and Shirley Bright Cook (Columbia: University of South Carolina Press, 1996), 80–81.

61 **"If we do not act now":** Quoted in McPherson, *Battle Cry of Freedom*, 57.

61 **"Many avow themselves disunionists":** McPherson, *Battle Cry of Freedom*, 69. On the impact of the Mexican cession on American politics, see Freehling, *The Road to Disunion*, 475–535, and McPherson, *Battle Cry of Freedom*, 47–88.

62 **"to respect our rights, we will promptly dissolve":** Quoted in Eric H. Walther, *William Lowndes Yancey and the Coming of the Civil War* (Chapel Hill: University of North Carolina Press, 2006), 112.

62 **"secession . . . resistance, open unqualified resistance":** Quoted in Walther, *William Lowndes Yancey*, 126.

62 **Cone pled guilty to attempted murder:** The two later reconciled with Stephens's move into the Democratic column in the following decade. On their fight, see Lucian Lamar Knight, *A Standard History of Georgia and Georgians* (Chicago: Lewis, 1917), 3:1353–54, and Richard Harrison Shryock, *Georgia and the Union in 1850* (Philadelphia: Duke University Press, 1926), 172–73.

63 **Together they came to be known as the Georgia Platform:** On the Georgia state convention's election, its debates, and the Georgia Platform, see Shryock, *Georgia and the Union*, 325–34.

64 **"Southerners . . . have a natural right to revolution":** Quoted in James L. Huston, "Southerners against Secession: The Arguments of the Constitutional Unionists in 1850–51," *Civil War History* 46, no. 4 (2000): 297. See also John T. Hubbell, "Three Georgia Unionists and the Compromise of 1850," *Georgia Historical Quarterly* 51 (1967): 307–23; McPherson, *Battle Cry of Freedom*, 87; Freehling, *The Road to Disunion*, 524.

64 **"She joined it in 1776 and she saved it in 1850":** Letter of February 20, 1851, quoted in Shryock, *Georgia and the Union*, 337.

64 **"You and others of your age will probably live to see it":** Quoted in Niven, *John C. Calhoun*, 1.

## CHAPTER 7: THE CORNERSTONE

69 **"The terminus of that railroad":** Calhoun's antirailroad comment and Powell's rejoinder came from the memory of Powell's daughter seventy-five years after the supposed conversation took place. See Franklin M. Garrett, *Atlanta and Environs: A Chronicle of Its People and Events* (New York: Lewis Historical Publishing Co., 1954), 1:168. On antebellum railroad politics in Georgia, see Anthony Gene Carey, *Parties, Slavery, and the Union in Antebellum Georgia* (Athens: University of Georgia Press, 1997), 134–38. In fact, it would not be until well into the 1850s that the Western & Atlantic Railroad operations turned a profit.

69 **Although Calhoun's Decatur neighbors vowed:** *Pioneer Citizens' Society of Atlanta, Pioneer Citizens' History of Atlanta, 1833–1902* (Atlanta: Pioneer Citizens' Society of Atlanta, 1902), 223–24.

69 **"It was said that no one was ever born in Atlanta":** Quoted in Robert S. Davis Jr., introduction to Sarah "Sallie" Conley Clayton, *Requiem for a Lost City: A Memoir of Civil War Atlanta and the Old South*, ed. Robert S. Davis Jr. (Macon, GA: Mercer University Press, 1999), 25.

70 **"very large rooms . . . handsomely finished and decorated":** Quotes from "Old Home Spared by Sherman's Torch Is Soon to Give Way for Improvement," *Constitution*, February 18, 1906, B8.

71 **"are social ties—nationalizing powers":** "Opportunities for Southern Travel," *New York Times*, May 18, 1854, n.p.

71 **for $5 more a passenger could continue:** "Railroad Guide," *Atlanta Daily Intelligencer*, January 1, 1861, and following, 1, Beinecke Rare Book and Manuscript Library, Yale University.

71 **Soon it trailed only Savannah and Augusta in size:** U.S. Bureau of the Census, *Seventh Census of the United States* (DeKalb County, Georgia, 1850), 3:305–11.

72 **"We had intimate relations with it":** Kate Massey, "A Picture of Atlanta in the Late Sixties," *Atlanta Historical Bulletin* 20 (January 1940): 32.

72 **The pedestrian unfamiliar with his surroundings:** February 19, 1852, quoted in Walter G. Cooper, *Official History of Fulton County* (Atlanta: History Commission, 1934), 82.

72 **"the most unattractive place":** Carlton H. Rogers, *Incidents of Travel in the Southern States and Cuba* (New York: R. Craighead, 1862), 269.

72 **a census of white residents' occupations:** Fulton County Census, June 4 to August 15, 1860, Occupation, quoted in Franklin M. Garrett, *Atlanta and Environs: A Chronicle of Its People and Events* (New York: Lewis Historical Publishing Co., 1954), 1:489–91.

73 **For the more family minded:** See City Council Minutes, July 23, 1858; Julian Harris, "Primitive Atlanta," *Atlanta Constitution*, August 12, 1894, 23; Elizabeth Hanleiter McCallie (Mrs. S. W.), "Atlanta in the 1850s," *Atlanta Historical Bulletin* 8, no. 33 (October 1948): 91–106; Garrett, *Atlanta and Environs*, 1:304ff.

73 **"A rougher village I never saw":** Quoted in James Russell, *Atlanta 1847–1890: City Building in the Old South and the New* (Baton Rouge: Louisiana State University Press, 1988), 72.

74 **the shanties and shacks that filled Snake Nation:** Wallace P. Reed, *History of Atlanta, Georgia: With Illustrations and Biographical Sketches of Some of Its Prominent Men and Pioneers* (Atlanta: D. Mason & Co., 1889), 48–50.

74 **The town also became the regional foodstuffs market:** Cited in Russell, *Atlanta 1847–1890*, 41.

74 **"Passing along Whitehall Street":** *Daily Intelligencer,* August 13, 1859, 3.

74 **Southern-born natives comprised more than 90 percent of the city's populace:** Cited in Russell, *Atlanta 1847–1890*, 69–70.

74 **"thousands of fine, substantial and costly houses":** Quotes from *Daily Intelligencer*, September 25, 1860, 3; May 28, 1859, 3.

75 **"rough and unpolished [the town] may be":** Mayor Luther J. Glenn, inaugural speech, City Council Minutes, January 28, 1859.

75 **"The Gate City: The only tribute she levies":** Quoted in Russell, *Atlanta 1847–1890*, 24.

75 **In Atlanta, only 44 slaveholders bothered to possess:** For regional population figures, see Carey, *Parties, Slavery, and the Union*, 3–4. For Atlanta slave ownership and population figures, see Russell, *Atlanta 1847–1890*, 71. Although Atlanta had a relatively small slave population and ownership, human chattel nonetheless represented the largest source of taxable property in the city. The 1859 state census for Fulton County, including Atlanta, tabulated the population as 11,572 free citizens and around 3,850 people in bondage. See Garrett, *Atlanta and Its Environs*, 1:488. The number of slave traders from city marshal's occupations list of 1860 is reprinted in Garrett, *Atlanta and Environs*, 1:489–91.

76 **Atlanta's urban bondsmen worked alongside whites:** For a discussion of the nonagricultural black population on the eve of the war, see Clarence H. Mohr, *On the Threshold of Freedom: Masters and Slaves in Civil War Georgia* (Athens: University of Georgia Press, 1987), 160–61, and Robert S. Starobin, *Industrial Slavery in the Old South* (New York: Oxford University Press, 1970), 11.

76 **Buchanan appointed W. L.'s brother:** Eric H. Walther, *William Lowndes Yancey and the Coming of the Civil War* (Chapel Hill: University of North Carolina Press, 2006), 204.

77 **"Owing to the existence of African slavery":** "Gentlemen of the Philomathic Societies," quoted in Walther, *William Lowndes Yancey*, 196–97.

77 **"I gave him practical freedom":** Ben Yancey quotes are from Deposition of Benjamin C. Yancey, *Webster v. U.S.*, CD 13502, folder 2, National Archives, Washington, D.C.

77 **He and his wife moved into a four-room house:** Bob (Webster) Yancey's ownership of the Houston Street house is mentioned in a report in the *Daily Intelligencer* on the properties spared by General Sherman's forces, December 23, 1864, 1. See also Thomas Dyer, *Secret Yankees: The Union Circle in Confederate Atlanta* (Baltimore: Johns Hopkins University Press, 1999), 17–19.

77 **Yancey, who could not write and probably could not read:** In his deposition of Robert Webster, *Webster v. U.S.*, CD 13502, folder 1, National Archives, Washington, D.C., Webster (Yancey) signed his statements with an *X*.

78 **"about a foolish bet":** *Daily Intelligencer*, March 8, 1864, 3.

78 **A slave became one of Atlanta's wealthier men:** Deposition of Robert Webster.

78 **His father could do little for him:** Henry S. Robinson, "Robert and Roderick Badger, Pioneer Georgia Dentists: Their Heritage and Descendants," typescript, Atlanta History Center, September 1987, 1–2.

78 **Joshua educated his slave sons:** "Reminiscences of Patrick H. Calhoun," *Atlanta Historical Bulletin* 1, no. 6 (February 1932): 42.

78 **anyone caught teaching a slave or freeman to read or write:** *Georgia Laws*, 1833, Vol. 1, 289, Sequential #133. William Henry Heard, *From Slavery to the Bishopric in the A. M. E. Church: An Autobiography* (Philadelphia: A. M. E. Book Concern, 1928), 31. On the punishment for learning to read and write, see also "Slavery as Seen through the Eyes of Henry Wright—Ex-Slave," in *Born in Slavery: Narratives from the Federal Writers' Project, 1936–1938, Georgia Narratives*, IV, Part 4, typescript, 8 (201).

79 **The skills greatly increased their market value:** For sale price of Festus Flipper, see William Warren Rogers, *Ante-Bellum Thomas County 1825–1861* (Tallahassee: Florida State University Press, 1963), 63; for value of land, see Clara Mildred Thompson, *Reconstruction in Georgia: Economic, Social, Political, 1865–1872* (1915; rpt. Manchester, NH: Ayer Publishing, 1971), 284, and author's telephone conversation, January 18, 2008, with Tom Hill, Thomas County Historical Museum.

79 **"the intolerant bigotry of New England hypocrites":** J. D. Ponder, "Rise of Lieut. Henry O. Flipper from Slavery to Be One of Most Respected Men, Reads Like Novel," *El Paso Morning Times*, September 13, 1917, 4. The 1855 lynching in Thomasville is cited in Jane Eppinga, *Henry Ossian Flipper: West Point's First Black Graduate* (Plano, TX: Wordware Publishing, 1996), 2.

80 **They purchased one hundred acres:** Garrett, *Atlanta and Environs*, 1:511.

80 **Flipper's wife and son would have to remain behind:** Rogers, *Ante-Bellum Thomas County*, 98–99.

81 **"The joy of the wife can be conceived":** Henry Ossian Flipper, *The Colored Cadet at West Point: Autobiography of Lieut. Henry Ossian Flipper* (1878; rpt. Whitefish, MT: Kessinger Publishing, 2004), 3.

81 **When in search of work:** Donald L. Grant, *The Way It Was in the South: The Black Experience in Georgia* (New York: Carol Publishing Group, 1993), 36.

81 **"but two other things to make them like other human beings":** Flipper, *The Colored Cadet*, 3.

81 **Some open-minded whites:** Jonathan D. Martin in his study of slave hiring, *Divided Mastery: Slave Hiring in the American South* (Cambridge: Harvard University Press, 2004), explores the contradictions both whites and blacks faced when slaves hired out their time. See, especially, 1–9.

82 **"proper authorities of the City of Atlanta":** Quoted in Garrett, *Atlanta and Environs*, 1:396.

82 **In 1858, two hundred white "regular citizen mechanics":** City Council Minutes, March 5, 1858. See also Grant, *The Way It Was in the South*, 35, and Reed, *History of Atlanta*, 78–79.

82 **The protestors appealed "for justice":** City Council Minutes, July 15, 1859.

82 **In 1861, another protest to the town fathers against Badger:** City Council Records, February 8, 1861, Vol. 3, April 9, 1859, to January 10, 1862, 515.

82 **A week later, the council backed down:** City Council Records, January 4, 1861.

83 **doled out summary judgment and punishment:** On the summary nature of racial law enforcement in the countryside, see "Slavery as Seen through the Eyes of Henry Wright—Ex-Slave," 8–9 (201–2).

83 **"fix . . . rings and poles on the calaboose":** Quoted in Alton Hornsby Jr., *A Short History of Black Atlanta, 1847–1990*, 2nd ed. (North Richland Hills, TX: Ivy Halls Academic Press, 2006), 2.

83 **"slave, free person of color or Indian":** Hornsby, *A Short History of Black Atlanta*, 5.

83 **In the face of such a risk:** City Council Minutes, May 20, 1859, cited in Reed, *History of Atlanta*, 81. In restricting freemen from moving into Atlanta, the city was little different from many municipalities, even in free states. For instance, Illinois voters overwhelmingly passed a state constitutional amendment in 1848 banning entry into the state by freemen. See Eugene H. Berwanger, *The Frontier against Slavery: Western Anti-Negro Prejudice and the Slavery Extension Controversy* (Chicago: University of Chicago Press, 1967), 48–51.

83 **"their selections just as they would have a horse or mule at a stockyard":** Quoted in Michael Rose, ed., *Atlanta: A Portrait of the Civil War* (Charleston, SC: Tempus Publishing, 1999), 100.

84 **"None of the slaves believed in the sermons":** "Slavery as Seen through the Eyes of Henry Wright—Ex-Slave," 8 (201).

## CHAPTER 8: EARTHQUAKE

85 **Among his many activities to better the growing community:** *Atlanta Medical and Surgical Journal* 1 (Atlanta: C. R. Hanleiter & Co., 1856), 56.

86 **"that opposition to the principles":** Quoted in Anthony Gene Carey, *Parties, Slavery, and the Union in Antebellum Georgia* (Athens: University of Georgia Press, 1997), 185.

87 **"We doubt not the[ir] success":** March 29, 1856, and April 4, 1856, quoted in Franklin M. Garrett, *Atlanta and Environs: A Chronicle of Its People and Events* (New York: Lewis Historical Publishing Co., 1954), 1:411. See also Wallace Putnam Reed, *History of Atlanta, Georgia: With Illustrations and Biographical Sketches of Some of Its Prominent Men and Pioneers* (Atlanta: D. Mason & Co., 1889), 84–86.

87 **It was not long before open guerilla warfare broke out:** On the Kansas-Nebraska Act of 1854 and its national consequences, see James McPherson, *Battle Cry of Freedom* (New York and Oxford: Oxford University Press, 1988), 121–30, and William W. Freehling, *The Road to Disunion*, Vol. 1, *Secessionists at Bay, 1776–1854* (New York and London: Oxford University Press, 1990), 536–65. On its impact in Georgia, see Carey, *Parties, Slavery, and the Union*, 184ff.

87 **But the effort put the rest of Georgia on notice:** Reed, *History of Atlanta*, 71–72.

88 **The voting patterns made clear:** On the election of 1856, see McPherson, *Battle Cry of Freedom*, 153–57.

89 **Whether the abolition Lincoln advocated came sooner or later:** "First Debate, Mr. Lincoln's Reply," August 21, 1858, in Abraham Lincoln, *Speeches and Writings, 1832–1858*, ed. Don E. Fehrenbacher (New York: Library of America, 1989), 1:512–13, 514. Alexander H. Stephens spoke in Savannah on March 21, 1861, declaring famously, "Our new government is founded upon exactly the opposite idea; its foundations are laid, its corner-stone rests, upon the great truth that the negro is not equal to the white man; that slavery—subordination to the superior race—is his natural and normal condition." Henry Cleveland, *Alexander H. Stephens, in Public and Private: With Letters and Speeches, before, during, and since the War* (Philadelphia: National Publishing Co., 1886), 717–29.

89 **A second conviction led to permanent reenslavement:** *Acts of Georgia 1859*, quoted in Clarence L. Mohr, *On the Threshold of Freedom: Masters and Slaves in Civil War Georgia* (Athens: University of Georgia Press, 1987), 14–15.

89 **"tremendous sway ... over the political arrangements of this State":** Printed in the *Daily Intelligencer*, April 30, 1864, 1.

89 **"no advocates of mob law":** *Daily Intelligencer*, January 4, 1860, 2.

90 **"well be chary of expressing such opinions":** *Daily Intelligencer*, January 5, 1860, 3.

90 **"The sooner he treads Northern soil the better it will be for him":** Quoted in Garrett, *Atlanta and Its Environs*, 1:471.

90 **Clayton's family soon moved into a large house:** Sarah Conley Clayton, *Requiem for a Lost City: A Memoir of Civil War Atlanta and the Old South*, ed. Robert Scott Davis Jr. (Macon, GA: Mercer University Press, 1999), 32.

91 **White citizens all along the Western & Atlantic armed themselves:** On the Dalton and other black insurrection panics, see Mohr, *On the Threshold of Freedom*, 33–35.

91 **"Every negro in Georgia should have a master":** *Daily Intelligencer*, January 9, 1860, 2.

92 **"slaves ... are much worse treated":** Harrison Berry, *Slavery and Abolitionism as Viewed by a Georgia Slave* (Atlanta: Franklin Printing House, 1861), 27 and 16. For my discussion of Harrison Berry, I am indebted to Clarence L. Mohr, "Harrison Berry: A Black Pamphleteer in Georgia during Slavery and Freedom," *Georgia Historical Quarterly* 67, no. 2 (summer 1983): 189–205.

92 **"Even now ... the oppression is commenced":** Berry, *Slavery and Abolitionism*, 13.

93 **"put manacles on every Slave":** Berry, *Slavery and Abolitionism*, 19.

94 **"perhaps even now, the pen of the historian is nibbed":** Quoted in Eric H. Walther, *William Lowndes Yancey and the Coming of the Civil War* (Chapel Hill: University of North Carolina Press, 2006), 241. On the Democratic Party's breakup, see McPherson, *Battle Cry of Freedom*, 213–16.

94 **Buchanan's vice president, Kentucky's John Breckinridge:** On Yancey's campaign for Breckinridge, see Walther, *William Lowndes Yancey*, 251–71.

94 **"that arch-enemy of true Democracy":** Quoted in Walther, *William Lowndes Yancey*, 250 and 257.

95 **"All branches of business are prospering":** *Daily Intelligencer*, January 5, 1860, 3.

95 **"strike, merchants of Georgia, at the black Republican":** Quoted in Garrett, *Atlanta and Environs*, 1:471–72.

95 **"the Atlanta ban . . . abjure all that is to be abjured":** "The Index Expurgatorius," *New York Times*, February 3, 1860, n.p.

96 **"Unless these people, therefore, want to go naked":** *Daily Intelligencer*, June 21, 1860, 2. Yancey quote in Walther, *William Lowndes Yancey*, 259.

96 **Still, he spoke out against those driving a wedge:** James M. Calhoun affidavit, *Timothy D. Lynes v. United States*, Southern Claims Commission, CD 12658, box 1452, National Archives, Washington, D.C.

96 **"the Union . . . cannot be preserved":** Quoted in Lucien E. Roberts, "The Political Career of Joshua Hill, Georgia Unionist," *Georgia Historical Quarterly* 21 (March 1937): 52.

97 **"to recognize no political principle":** Quoted in Horace Greeley and John Fitch Cleveland, eds., *A Political Text-book for 1860: Comprising a Brief View of Presidential Nominations and Elections, Including All the National Platforms Ever Yet Adopted . . .* (New York: Tribune Association, 1860), 29.

97 **"shifting, halting, ambiguous, Delphic":** Georgia newspaper editorial quoted in Carey, *Parties, Slavery, and the Union*, 224.

97 **"That issue must be met and settled":** *Kentucky Statesman*, May 8, 1860, in Dwight Lowell Dumond, ed., *Southern Editorials on Secession* (New York: Century Co., 1931), 76.

97 **His hands would be tied:** On Lincoln's nomination, see McPherson, *Battle Cry of Freedom*, 216–21.

97 **"Let the consequences be what they may":** Quoted in McPherson, *Battle Cry of Freedom*, 229–30.

98 **Few Northerners, Lincoln included, took the latest threats seriously:** "The Question of the Day," *New York Times*, October 29, 1860, n.p. On Lincoln's and other Northern politicians' discounting of secession warnings, see McPherson, *Battle Cry of Freedom*, 230–31.

98 **"take the banner of liberty":** Walther, *William Lowndes Yancey*, 245; *Atlanta National American*, August 21, 1860, quoted in Walther, *William Lowndes Yancey*, 255, 258.

98 **"secession doctrine is revolution":** Quote from Thomas Maguire, an Atlanta-area planter who attended the Douglas speech, in Garrett, *Atlanta and Environs*, 1:474.

98 **"upon the election of Abraham Lincoln":** McPherson, *Battle Cry of Freedom*, 231.

99 **"States' Rights men of Georgia":** Garrett, *Atlanta and Environs*, 1:474.

99 **"not as a partisan addressing partisans":** Quoted in Walter G. Cooper, *Official History of Fulton County* (Atlanta: History Commission, 1934), 95.

99 **The Unionist circle was almost an alternative:** For Union Association membership and quotes, see Thomas Dyer, *Secret Yankees: The Union Circle in Confederate Atlanta* (Baltimore: Johns Hopkins University Press, 1999), 36–37. I am grateful to Dyer for generously sharing portions of his exhaustive research findings on the Union Circle with me and for his correspondence responding to my queries.

100 **While many were Northern transplants:** Dyer, *Secret Yankees*, 12ff.

100 **Had Yancey wished to attend the nighttime gatherings:** Affidavit of William Markham, *Webster v. U.S.*, Southern Claims Commission, CD 13502, folder 1, National Archives, Washington, D.C.

100 **Most of the men meeting that summer:** On the Georgia Air Line Railroad, see Reed, *History of Atlanta*, 433.

101 **"Clip the telegraph wires":** *Daily Intelligencer*, June 7, 1860, 3.

101 **"All who are in favor of civil war":** Quoted in "The Question of the Day," *New York Times*, October 29, 1860, n.p. The *National American* did not survive secession.

102 **He failed to win a single slave-state electoral vote:** For Georgia vote breakdowns, see Carey, *Parties, Slavery, and the Union*, 228–29.

102 **"With the election of the Black Republican Lincoln":** *Daily Intelligencer*, November 15, 1860, 3.

102 **As he spoke, rumors flared of a slave insurrection:** *Special Message of Gov. Joseph E. Brown, to Legislature of Georgia, on our Federal Relations, Retaliatory State Legislation, the Right of Secession, etc., November 7th, 1860,* quoted in William W. Freehling and Craig M. Simpson, eds., *Secession Debated: Georgia's Showdown in 1860* (New York: Oxford University Press, 1992), xi–xii.

102 **Mobs in several communities responded by attacking blacks:** On the postelection racial backlash in Georgia, see Mohr, *On the Threshold of Freedom*, 46.

103 **Little imagination was needed to predict that worse lay ahead:** Berry, *Slavery and Abolitionism*, 3.

103 **"all suspected characters, with power to rid the community":** Quoted in Cooper, *Official History of Fulton County*, 99.

103 **Adair, a former lawyer and train conductor:** On Adair, see Thomas H. Martin, *Atlanta and Its Builders: A Comprehensive History of the Gate City of the South* (Atlanta: Century Memorial Publishing Co., 1902), 2:627–28.

103 **"dangerous for Union men to express themselves publicly":** Calhoun quotes from the affidavit of James M. Calhoun, *Timothy D. Lynes v. U.S.*, Southern Claims Commission, CD 12658, box 1452, National Archives, Washington, D.C.

103 **"war in every way":** Quoted in Ralph Benjamin Singer Jr., "Confederate Atlanta," PhD diss., University of Georgia, 1973, 54.

104 **flag came down, and a state flag flew:** Garrett, *Atlanta and Environs*, 1:476. The Georgia flag raising is noted in Samuel P. Richards, *Diary*, Vol. 9, October 1860–June 1864, typescript, December 19, 1860, 6, Atlanta History Center.

104 **"the shedding of a single drop of blood":** *Daily Intelligencer*, December 25, 1860, 3.

104 **"If you would hush this quadrennial struggle":** *Daily Constitutionalist* (Augusta, GA), January 1, 1861, 2.

104 **"no sufficient cause of war, or secession":** "James M. Calhoun, Atlanta, Ga, Rebellion, Filed July 19, 1865, Pardoned July 24, 1865," Case Files of Applications from Former Confederates for Presidential Pardons ("Amnesty Papers"), 1865–67, National Archives M1003, Washington, D.C.

105 **"There is, perhaps":** *Daily Intelligencer*, January 4, 1861, 3.

105 **On that historic day, Brown ordered Georgia militiamen:** On Gov. Joseph Brown's actions, see Freehling and Simpson, eds., *Secession Debated*, xx–xxi.

105 **On January 19, the convention delegates gathered:** On the statewide voting and the state convention decision, see Carey, *Parties, Slavery, and the Union*, 228–29, 249. On the Atlanta vote, see Singer, "Confederate Atlanta," 55–56.

105 **Little interested in life beyond his family:** On Richards's biographical background, see Frank J. Byrne, "Rebellion and Retail: A Tale of Two Merchants in

Confederate Atlanta," *Georgia Historical Quarterly* 79, no. 1 (spring 1995): 33. For the description of Richards, see Ella Mae Thornton, "Mr. S. P. Richards," *Atlanta Historical Bulletin* 3 (December 1937): 73–79.

107 **"form a Southern Republic, a 'White Man's Republic'":** Richards's emphasis (italics in typescript). Richards, *Diary* (typescript), Atlanta History Center, November 17, 1860, 5; December 8, 1860, 8; November 25, 1860, 6.

107 **"aid and comfort to the Abolitionists":** Richards, *Diary,* January 19, 1861, 13.

108 **Now, Sherman paced about and sputtered:** Exchange between W. T. Sherman and Prof. David F. Boyd, December 24, 1860. Lloyd Lewis, *Sherman: Fighting Prophet* (1932; rpt. Lincoln: University of Nebraska Press, 1993), 137–38, 143. On the psychology of irrational executive decision-making processes marked by excessive optimism, which closely parallels the excessive optimism in Southern views on the outcome of secession, see Dan Lovallo and Daniel Kahnemann, "Delusions of Success: How Optimism Undermines Executives' Decisions," *Harvard Business Review,* July 2003, rpt. R0307D.

108 **A minor earthquake lasting ten seconds:** *Daily Intelligencer,* January 4, 1861, 3. A much more powerful earthquake, the largest on record for the region, struck Atlanta, along with nearly the entire Southeast, early on the morning of August 31, 1861, startling sleeping soldiers to their feet, cracking walls, and toppling chimneys. Three years to the day after that quake shook the city, the Union army would launch its final assault on the Atlanta region's Confederate forces. See Gerald R. MacCarthy, "Three Forgotten Earthquakes," *Bulletin of the Seismological Society of America* 53, no. 3 (April 1963): 687–92. Additional information on southeastern earthquakes is based on e-mail correspondence with Timothy Long, Georgia Institute of Technology, and Jeffrey W. Munsey, Tennessee Valley Authority.

## Chapter 9: Never! Never!! Never!!!

111 **"could not express any opinion at all":** Deposition of Julius A. Hayden, March 10, 1869, *Hayden v. U.S.* (case file no. 2543), Court of Claims, RG 123, National Archives, Washington, D.C., quoted in Thomas Dyer, *Secret Yankees: The Union Circle in Confederate Atlanta* (Baltimore: Johns Hopkins University Press, 1999), 46.

111 **Whitaker won the office he had long had his eyes on:** Ralph Benjamin Singer Jr., "Confederate Atlanta," PhD diss., University of Georgia, 1973, 58–59. Whitaker resigned as mayor the following November 25 to accept an appointment from Governor Brown as commissary general of the Georgia army. He set up his headquarters in Atlanta, helping to consolidate its position as one of the manufacturing and supply centers for the Confederacy.

112 **"The man and the hour have met":** Quoted in Eric H. Walther, *William Lowndes Yancey and the Coming of the Civil War* (Chapel Hill: University of North Carolina Press, 2006), 295.

112 **"including . . . goobers, an indispensable article for a Southern Legislator":** Council Minutes, February 15, 1861, 519–20. *Gate City Guardian,* February 16, 1861, 1.

112 **"it was my duty to go with the South":** James M. Calhoun affidavit, *Timothy D. Lynes v. United States,* Southern Claims Commission, CD 12658, box 1452.

112 **"defining treason . . . to obey [to] which every citizen was bound":** "James M. Calhoun, Atlanta, Ga, Rebellion, Filed July 19, 1865, Pardoned July 24, 1865,"

Case Files of Applications from Former Confederates for Presidential Pardons ("Amnesty Papers"), 1865–67, National Archives M1003, Washington, D.C.

113 **The new government should wield its power to exile or punish:** *Southern Confederacy,* March 28, 1861, 3.

113 **"Every Union man they could find":** Quoted in Dyer, *Secret Yankees,* 46–47.

113 **"see him go off like he did to fight against the Union":** *Harrison Baswell vs. U.S.,* Southern Claims Commission, Affidavits of J. T. Baswell, Nancy Spinks (daughter), Jefferson Baswell (nephew), CD 12668, National Archives, Washington, D.C. One of Baswell's brothers fought for the Union and died in the war.

114 **Not long after that, his flour mill won a rich contract:** *Daily Intelligencer,* March 4, March 9, 11, 20, 1861, 3. See also Dyer, *Secret Yankees,* 47–50. On hardtack production by the Stewart and Austin flour mill, see Singer, "Confederate Atlanta," 101.

115 **Those who remained in Atlanta:** *Southern Confederacy,* March 28, 1861, 1.

115 **Little Alec had dropped his long-standing opposition:** On the selection of the Confederate States president, see Walther, *William Lowndes Yancey,* 293–95, and James McPherson, *Battle Cry of Freedom* (New York and Oxford: Oxford University Press, 1988), 258–59.

116 **"They were attempting to make things equal":** Henry Cleveland, *Alexander H. Stephens, in Public and Private: With Letters and Speeches, before, during, and since the War* (Philadelphia: National Publishing Co., 1886), 721–22.

116 **Alexander Stephens told his Atlanta listeners:** On description of Stephens, see "Letter of Georgia King to Henry Lord Page King," November 15, 1860, quoted in William W. Freehling and Craig M. Simpson, eds., *Secession Debated: Georgia's Showdown in 1860* (New York: Oxford University Press, 1992), xvi. Wallace Putnam Reed, *History of Atlanta, Georgia: With Illustrations and Biographical Sketches of Some of Its Prominent Men and Pioneers* (Atlanta: D. Mason & Co., 1889), 110–11. Walter G. Cooper, *Official History of Fulton County* (Atlanta: History Commission, 1934), 109–10.

117 **he placed Major Yancey in command of his famous legion:** On Ben Yancey's service, see Walther, *William Lowndes Yancey,* 429n58; see also 338 and 345.

117 **Fulton County had provided the Confederacy with 2,660 soldiers:** Reed, *History of Atlanta,* 114–17; Singer, "Confederate Atlanta," 70, 71, 73; Cooper, *Official History of Fulton County,* 110. Soldier total cited in James Michael Russell, *Atlanta 1847–1890: City Building in the Old South and the New* (Baton Rouge: Louisiana State University Press, 1988), 94.

117 **An Atlanta mother beamed with pride:** Memoirs of Mrs. R. M. Massey, Atlanta Pioneer Women's Society Papers Collection, Atlanta Historical Society.

118 **Soon, they and other women formed associations to make bandages:** Sarah Huff, "My Eighty Years in Atlanta" (no publication information, 1937), ch. 1, n.p.

118 **The Neal family had moved just the year before:** For the description of the Neal family, see "Dear Pa," May 18, 1861, Camp Magnolia, Andrew Jackson Neal Papers, Emory University Manuscript, Archives, and Rare Book Library, MSS218.

119 **"how affairs stand . . . and what are the prospects of war":** Sarah Conley Clayton, *Requiem for a Lost City: A Memoir of Civil War Atlanta and the Old South,* ed. Robert Scott Davis Jr. (Macon, GA: Mercer University Press, 1999), 35–36.

119 **"Everything seemed to be preparing for active service":** *Southern Confederacy,* June 29, 1861, 3. Clayton, *Requiem,* 44–45; Clayton quote is from 40.

119 **She and her more than two hundred fellow students from the Atlanta Female Institute:** On the Atlanta Female Institute, see Clayton, *Requiem*, ch. 2. Quotes are from 60 and 66.

119 **The Female Institute's dome atop what came to be known as College Hill:** Franklin M. Garrett, *Atlanta and Environs: A Chronicle of Its People and Events* (New York: Lewis Historical Publishing Co., 1954), 1:456–57.

120 **After many hours packed together on trains:** Clayton, *Requiem*, 80–81.

120 **"with the utmost difficulty":** Clayton, *Requiem*, 79–80.

121 **"the booming of cannon":** *Southern Confederacy*, April 1, 1861, 3.

121 **"too powerful to be suppressed":** McPherson, *Battle Cry of Freedom*, 250; Lincoln's proclamation quote is from 274.

121 **"be accommodated to a coat of tar and feathers":** Quoted in Russell, *Atlanta 1847–1890*, 94.

122 **"the house with stamping feet":** *Atlanta Commonwealth*, May 2, 1861, quoted in Dyer, *Secret Yankees*, 55.

122 **With many of Atlanta's leading citizens on hand:** On the founding of the Atlanta Female Institute, see Garrett, *Atlanta and Environs*, 1:456–57.

122 **"our country, so long the boast":** Holly, "The Spring of 1861," quoted in Dyer, *Secret Yankees*, 51.

122 **"nerv[ing] ourselves against despair":** Quoted in Dyer, *Secret Yankees*, appendix B, "Miss Abby's Diary," January 1, 1864, 284.

122 **"sad to think that our country":** Richards, *Diary*, April 14, 1861, 21–22.

123 **"Our family hitherto has been united":** Richards, *Diary*, October 1 and 7, 1861, 49 and 51.

123 **"a strong Union man":** Richards, *Diary*, May 10, 1861, 28.

123 **His longtime clerk Asa Sherwood:** Richards, *Diary*, April 20 and 25, 1861, 23, 24; May 31, 1861, 30.

123 **"We will teach Mr. Lincoln and his cohorts":** City Council Minutes, April 26, 1861, 550.

123 **"the people of the Slaves States":** City Council Minutes, May 31, 1861, 568.

124 **"We are now cut off from them":** *Southern Confederacy*, June 29, 1861, 3.

124 **"our cause is a just one in His sight":** Richards, *Diary*, June 23, 1861, 34; July 27, 1861, 42.

124 **"covered themselves with glory":** "Dear Ma," July 28, 1861, Camp Magnolia.

124 **The victory heartened the town:** Garrett, *Atlanta and Environs*, 1:516–17.

## Chapter 10: Speculation

125 **No place in the South was more prepared:** *War of the Rebellion: Official Records of the Union and Confederate Armies*, ser. 3, Vol. 4, 883.

126 **"Atlanta . . . is destined to be a great manufacturing city":** See James McPherson, *Battle Cry of Freedom* (New York and Oxford: Oxford University Press, 1988), 91, 94–95, 318, and Robert C. Black, *The Railroads of the Confederacy* (Chapel Hill: University of North Carolina Press, 1998), 4. Quote from *Daily Intelligencer*, January 25, 1863, 3.

126 **"Perpetual motion does exist in this city":** "A Trip to Atlanta," *Southern Confederacy*, May 23, 1863, 2.

126 **The Atlanta Sword Manufactory turned out 170 finished swords:** See Stephen Mitchell, "Atlanta, the Industrial Heart of the Confederacy," *Atlanta Historical*

*Bulletin* 3 (May 1930): 20–27; Ralph Benjamin Singer Jr., "Confederate Atlanta," PhD diss., University of Georgia, 1973, 101–3, 138, 141; Franklin M. Garrett, *Atlanta and Environs: A Chronicle of Its People and Events* (New York: Lewis Historical Publishing Co., 1954), 1:509, 532–33.

126 **Army of Tennessee:** Confederate armies, including Army of Tennessee, were typically named for their state of origin. They can easily be confused with similarly named Union armies which derived their names from rivers around which they operated, such as the Army of the Tennessee.

127 **One hundred cobblers in a government shoe factory:** Figures from Singer, "Confederate Atlanta," 159–61, 174, and Steven Davis, "Civil War: Atlanta Home Front," *The New Georgia Encyclopedia*, online at www.georgiaencyclopedia.org/nge/Article.jsp?id=h-824; Garrett, *Atlanta and Environs*, 1:532.

127 **"They are daily increasing":** "A Trip to Atlanta," 2.

127 **"wonderful sight" of powerful cutting machines:** Sarah Huff, "My Eighty Years in Atlanta" (no publication information, 1937), ch. 1, n.p.

128 **The Yankees would remember the name of the town:** See Henry Hitchcock, *Marching with Sherman* (New Haven, CT: Yale University Press, 1927), 58.

128 **"There was no better Confederate than he":** "Reminiscences of Patrick H. Calhoun," *Atlanta Historical Bulletin* 1, no. 6 (February 1932): 43. Compare Calhoun's statement in his request for amnesty shortly after the war: "James M. Calhoun, Atlanta, Ga, Rebellion, Filed July 19, 1865, Pardoned July 24, 1865," Case Files of Applications from Former Confederates for Presidential Pardons ("Amnesty Papers"), 1865–67, National Archives M1003, Washington, D.C.

129 **"The faces I had usually met":** "From Our Special Correspondent 'T. D. W.,'" *Southern Confederacy*, August 27, 1862, 2.

129 **"all day long and even during night":** "A Trip to Atlanta," 2.

129 **"scarcely a day or night":** Quoted in "Old Home Spared by Sherman's Torch Is Soon to Give Way for Improvement," *Constitution*, February 18, 1906.

130 **"want[ed] the freest possible trade with all the world":** Quotes from "A Voice of Southern Commerce," *New York Times*, October 20, 1861, n.p.

130 **"Almost everybody who had any money":** See the deposition of Amherst W. Stone, November 9, 1867, in *Lynch v. United States*, Court of Claims, quoted in Thomas Dyer, *Secret Yankees: The Union Circle in Confederate Atlanta* (Baltimore: Johns Hopkins University Press, 1999), 116.

130 **Root & Beach ships got through the blockade often enough:** Walter McElreath, "Sidney Root: Merchant Prince and Great Citizen," *Atlanta Historical Bulletin* 7, no. 29 (October 1944): 171–83.

130 **Traders overseas appeared eager:** On the blockade trade and the effectiveness of the Union naval blockade, see James Russell Soley, *The Blockade and the Cruisers* (New York: Charles Scribner's Sons, 1883), 44–45. See also McPherson, *Battle Cry of Freedom*, 378–82.

131 **"The blockade and the high price":** "The Blockade, from the Atlanta (Ga.) Confederacy," *New York Times*, July 27, 1862, n.p.

131 **"Atlanta to the South, is Chicago to the Northwest":** *New York Times*, November 15, 1863, n.p.

132 **"the value of property [was] advancing with railroad velocity":** "A Trip to Atlanta," 2.

132 **City council officials delegated to assist him:** Minutes of City Council, June 27, 1862, cited in Garrett, *Atlanta and Environs*, 1:525.

132 **"I am disappointed in Atlanta":** James H. Burton, Superintendent of Armories, CSA, to Colonel Josiah Gorgas, Confederate Chief of Ordnance, June 25, 1862, Record Group 109, ch. IV, Vol. 20, National Archives, Washington, D.C., and Richard W. Iobst, *Civil War Macon: The History of a Confederate City* (Macon, GA: Mercer University Press, 1999), 176–78.

133 **"I concluded that Atlanta, in point of business, was unchangeable":** "From Our Special Correspondent 'T. D. W.,'" 2.

133 **"dried up, the stores nearly all closed":** Samuel Richards, *Diary* (typescript), November 8, 1862, 136–37.

134 **"What I most regret in his case is that he is an alien enemy":** Richards, *Diary*, August 25 and 24, 1861, 49, 48; October 1, 1861, 57; September 7, 1861, 51; November 2, 1861, 61.

134 **"We could make a small fortune out of it":** Richards, *Diary*, December 31, 1861, 71; November 3, 1861, 62; January 9, 1862, 72.

134 **"Today Jabez sold a bill of pens":** Richards, *Diary*, March 21, 1863, 167.

134 **Jabez also bought several bondsmen:** Richards, *Diary*, August 8, 1862, 112; February 23, 1863, 162; May 24, 1862, 99; June 28, 1862, 106; October 22, 1862, 132; December 9, 1862, 145; April 12, 1862, 90; March 22, 1863, 168; August 21, 1863, 196.

135 **"when we come to a successful end to this war":** Richards, *Diary*, September 30, 1862, 115; May 5, 1862, 95; February 28, 1863, 163; May 2, 1863, 195.

135 **"put in healthy condition all privies":** Singer, "Confederate Atlanta," 117.

135 **The city government sold lime:** See James Russell, *Atlanta 1847–1890: City Building in the Old South and the New* (Baton Rouge: Louisiana State University Press, 1988), 111.

135 **"exempt me from conscription":** Richards, *Diary*, November 26, 1862, 141.

135 **"We live now in a state of feverish excitement":** Richards, *Diary*, September 6, 1862, 117.

136 **The Richmond government passed an impressment statute:** On impressments of supplies, see Rebecca Christian, "Georgia and the Confederate Policy of Impressing Supplies," *Georgia Historical Quarterly* 28 (March 1944): 2; Russell, *Atlanta 1847–1890*, 95–97.

136 **"high officials who set the example of lawlessness":** "Rioting Women," *Southern Confederacy*, April 16, 1863, 2.

136 **He offered to investigate unauthorized seizures:** Singer, "Confederate Atlanta," 196–97.

137 **Jabez Richards discovered that $1,000 in cash:** Richards, *Diary*, September 13, 1862, 119.

137 **"as thick as the frogs and lice of Egypt":** "Shinplasters," *Southern Confederacy*, August 27, 1862, 2.

137 **Eventually, inflation soared to ninety-two times prewar prices:** On inflation, see McPherson, *Battle Cry of Freedom*, 438–40; Russell, *Atlanta 1847–1890*, 98; Singer, "Confederate Atlanta," 193–94. Wholesale price rise figure cited in Teresa Crisp Williams and David Williams, "'The Women Rising': Cotton, Class, and Confederate Georgia's Rioting Women," *Georgia Historical Quarterly* 86, no. 1 (spring 2002): 3 (online version). "Markets and Other Matters," *Southern Confederacy*, January 27, 1863, 1.

137 **"No purse is large enough":** Dyer, *Secret Yankees*, appendix B, "Miss Abby's Diary," March 12, 1864, 289.

138 **Publishers themselves were forced to scramble:** On Civil War newspapers in Atlanta, see B. G. Ellis, *The Moving Appeal: Mr. McClanahan, Mrs. Dill, and the Civil War's Great Newspaper Run* (Macon, GA: Mercer University Press, 2003), ch. 11, 222ff. On Georgia newspapers during the Civil War, see Rabun Lee Brantley, *Georgia Journalism of the Civil War Period* (Nashville, TN: George Peabody College for Teachers, 1929).

138 **"Is it any marvel":** Dyer, *Secret Yankees*, appendix B, 294; January 20, 1864, 287.

138 **"There are a thousand little plans":** "How to Get the Very Best Coffee at About Ten Cents a Pound," *Southern Confederacy*, November 7, 1861, 3; "How to Get Coffee," *Southern Confederacy*, August 27, 1861, 1; "A Word to the Ladies," *Southern Confederacy*, September 28, 1861, 2.

139 **"Atlanta . . . is now made headquarters":** "Reason," *Daily Intelligencer*, April 4, 1862, 3. See rebuttal: "Speculation Again," *Southern Confederacy*, April 5, 1862, 3.

139 **"to get it out of reach of the city authorities":** Letter to Gov. Joseph Brown, November 16, 1862, quoted in Mark A. Weitz, *A Higher Duty: Desertion among Georgia Troops during the Civil War* (Lincoln and London: University of Nebraska Press, 2000), 114.

139 **"These men are greater enemies":** "Reason," 3.

139 **He came to regret his generosity:** State of Georgia, Thomas County Indenture, April 27, 1858, photocopy courtesy of Thomas County Historical Museum.

139 **"only thought or care was to remember when [her slaves'] wages became due":** Quotes from Henry Ossian Flipper, *The Colored Cadet at West Point: Autobiography of Lieut. Henry Ossian Flipper* (1878; rpt. Whitefish, MT: Kessinger Publishing, 2004), 4.

140 **With no white overseer on the estate:** See Garrett, *Atlanta and Its Environs*, 1:511–13.

140 **She had no idea how much money he was making:** Claim of Prince Ponder, December 20, 1875, box 34, Southern Claims Commission, Record Group 217, National Archives, Washington, D.C., 1, 13–15, 25.

141 **Few thought of the possibility that blacks:** *Daily Intelligencer*, February 3, 1863, 1. Deposition of William Markham, *Webster v. U.S.*, CD 13502, folder 3. Deposition of E. T. Hunnicut, *Webster v. U.S.*, CD 13502, folder 1.

141 **"about one of the biggest traders":** G. C. Rogers, quoted in Thomas G. Dyer, "Half Slave, Half Free: Unionist Robert Webster in Confederate Atlanta," in *Inside the Confederate Nation: Essays in Honor of Emory M. Thomas*, ed. Emory M. Thomas, Lesley Jill Gordon, and John C. Inscoe (Baton Rouge: Louisiana State University Press, 2005), 298.

142 **"He was put there to do it":** *Daily Intelligencer*, December 6, 1863, 3.

142 **"those capitalists who are using":** Minutes Superior Court, DeKalb County, 1861, Book D, quoted in Garrett, *Atlanta and Environs*, 1:513.

142 **"riding in their four-thousand-dollar carriages":** *Nashville Daily Times & Press*, June 28, 1864, quoted in Robert Scott Davis Jr., introduction to Sarah "Sallie" Conley Clayton, *Requiem for a Lost City: A Memoir of Civil War Atlanta and the Old South* (Macon, GA: Mercer University Press, 1999), 16.

142 **"regretting that her buggy wheels had not run over his neck":** *Rome Tri-Weekly Courier*, December 19, 1863, quoted in Williams and Williams, "'The Women Rising,'" 7.

142 **Citizens stopped bothering the city marshals with their troubles:** Singer, "Confederate Atlanta," 188–89.

142 **"A tall lady on whose countenance rested care and determination":** *Americus Sumter Republican*, March 27, 1863, quoted in Williams and Williams, "'The Women Rising,'" 9.

143 **Many people in town stood up for the "mob of ladies":** "A Mob of Ladies," *New York Times*, April 21, 1863, n.p.

143 **The *Intelligencer's* portly, fire-eating editor:** "Cousin Norma," a reporter for the *Chattanooga Rebel*, which printed in Atlanta following the fall of its hometown to the Union army, described Steele thus: "The Major (an honorific title from prior militia service) is a bold champion of States rights and as good a patriot as we have in the land. He is a large, heavy built man, about six feet in height." *Daily Intelligencer*, April 30, 1864, 1.

143 **"The tall female with determination in her eye":** "The Needy Women of Our City," *Southern Confederacy*, March 24, 1863, 1.

143 **But with inflation jumping manyfold faster:** On the budget for poor relief, see Singer "Confederate Atlanta," 135.

143 **"In view of the almost impossibility":** City Council Minutes, October 2, 1863, Vol. 4, January 17, 1862, to June 1, 1866, 196–97.

144 **Only a few sticks ever made it to the cold hearths of the needy:** *Daily Intelligencer*, October 22, 1863, 2.

## Chapter 11: Street Theater

145 **Convictions for bigamy and adultery rose sharply:** On the Mayor's Court caseload, see Paul D. Lack, "Law and Disorder in Confederate Atlanta," *Georgia Historical Quarterly* 60 (summer 1982): 178, table I. For Superior Court of Fulton County case figures, see Ralph Benjamin Singer Jr., "Confederate Atlanta," PhD diss., University of Georgia, 1973, 187.

145 **"I hope & believe":** Calhoun to George W. Randolph, October 3, 1862, quoted in Mark E. Neely, *Southern Rights: Political Prisoners and the Myth of Confederate Constitutionalism* (Charlottesville: University of Virginia Press, 1999), 34.

146 **Braxton Bragg made Atlanta a military post:** Quoted in Lack, "Law and Disorder," 182. See Franklin M. Garrett, *Atlanta and Environs: A Chronicle of Its People and Events* (New York: Lewis Historical Publishing Co., 1954), 1:525–28.

146 **The War Department turned to Col. George Washington Lee:** For quotes and information about Lee, see Thomas Dyer, *Secret Yankees: The Union Circle in Confederate Atlanta* (Baltimore: Johns Hopkins University Press, 1999), 98–99, and Singer, "Confederate Atlanta," 116–17. For Lee's saloon ownership, see Garrett, *Atlanta and Environs*, 1:543n12. Robert Scott Davis, "Guarding the Gate City from Itself: George W. Lee and Conflict in Civil War Atlanta," 33–35 (manuscript in progress), contends that Lee was never charged with stealing from his men and that General Bragg confused him with another officer with a similar name.

146 **"a great favorite" of General Bragg's:** *Daily Intelligencer*, July 24, 1861, 3.

147 **"untiringly . . . watch, direct and consign":** G. W. Lee to George W. Randolph, October 18, 1862, quoted in Neely, *Southern Rights*, 33.

147 **Lee's provost guard began shuttering offending barrooms:** Lee's General Order No. 1, May 14, 1862, published in the *Southern Confederacy*, May 16, 1862, 1. Samuel P. Richards, *Diary*, Vol. 9, October 1860–June 1864, typescript, May 24, 1862, 100, Atlanta History Center.

147 **General Bragg in his Chattanooga headquarters:** Special Order No. 14, August 11, 1862, quoted in Garrett, *Atlanta and Environs*, 1:527.

148 **Even in the midst of war, Atlanta remained a city of laws:** Quoted in Richard Malcolm Johnston and William Hand Browne, *Life of Alexander H. Stephens* (Philadelphia: J. B. Lippincott & Co., 1878), 421–23. For a summary of the principal documents of the Atlanta martial law controversy, see William A. Richards, "'We Live under a Constitution:' Confederate Martial Law in Atlanta," *Atlanta History* 33, no. 2 (summer 1989): 26–35.

148 **"'Governor Calhoun' is therefore defunct":** *Southern Confederacy*, September 20, 1862, 2; August 14, 1862, 2; September 18, 1862, 2. *Daily Intelligencer* quoted in Garrett, *Atlanta and Environs*, 1:528.

148 **"We do not know where the liquor comes from":** *Daily Intelligencer*, October 23, 1863, 3.

149 **"a fine looking, noble young man":** "More of the Fruits of Retailing Liquor," *Southern Confederacy*, October 23, 1862, 2.

149 **Calhoun placed a police officer in the hall:** *Daily Intelligencer*, November 1, 1863, 3.

150 **"seem[ed] to be the special champion of the theatre":** Quotes from *Daily Intelligencer*, October 18, 1863, 3; November 4, 1863, 3.

150 **"Ladies can now attend with perfect safety":** *Daily Intelligencer*, November 15, 1863, 3.

150 **Its stage was converted into a slave auction house:** *Daily Intelligencer*, March 10, 1864, 3.

150 **The crowd shaved, tarred, and feathered the woeful pair:** Lack, "Law and Disorder," 189; *Daily Intelligencer*, November 18, 1863, quoted in Singer, "Confederate Atlanta," 120–21.

151 **"We request the voters of Atlanta to make a small note":** *Daily Intelligencer*, November 29, 1863, 3.

151 **"go electioneering for their favorite candidate":** *Daily Intelligencer*, December 6, 1863, 3.

152 **Freed, Anderson became an Atlanta police officer and deputy sheriff:** See *Southern Confederacy*, February 3, 1863, 1; "Atlanta Police," *Atlanta Constitution*, July 22, 1894, 2; Garrett, *Atlanta and Environs*, 1:546–47.

## CHAPTER 12: THE DEAD HOUSE

155 **"We know not what another year may bring":** Samuel Richards, *Diary* (typescript), December 31, 1861, 71.

155 **More than 700,000 men had already enlisted:** James McPherson, *Battle Cry of Freedom* (New York and Oxford: Oxford University Press, 1988), 322, 328.

156 **"a general 'fall in to ranks'":** Stonewall, "Atlanta and the War," *Southern Confederacy*, February 9, 1862, 2.

156 **It was the first capital city of a Southern state:** On the capture of Forts Henry and Donelson and Nashville, see McPherson, *Battle Cry of Freedom*, 401–2.

157 **a group of twenty-two federal soldiers dressed as civilians:** For a complete history of the famous train chase and its aftermath, inspiration for at least two movies, see Russell S. Bonds, *Stealing the General: The Great Locomotive Chase and the First Medal of Honor* (Yardley, PA: Westholme Publishing, 2007).

157 **"the deepest laid scheme, and on the grandest scale"**: "The Great Railroad Chase," *Southern Confederacy*, April 15, 1862, 1.

157 **Sallie Clayton's eight- and ten-year-old younger brothers witnessed the hangings**: On the hanging, see Bonds, *Stealing the General*, 260–61.

157 **Atlantans' assurance of their immunity to the war's violence was no longer so easily sustained**: Sarah "Sallie" Conley Clayton, *Requiem for a Lost City: A Memoir of Civil War Atlanta and the Old South*, ed. Robert S. Davis Jr. (Macon, GA: Mercer University Press, 1999), 47–48.

158 **He felt glummer yet when walking through the car shed**: Richards, *Diary*, February 22, 1862, 79; February 27, 1862, 80.

158 **"Rather than affiliate with the North again"**: "Dear Emma," Camp of the Marion Light Artillery, Knoxville, Tenn., August 5, 1863. Neal quotes William Shakespeare, *Love's Labour's Lost*, act 1, scene 1: "'Tis won as towns with fire; so won, so lost."

158 **"Let any cruelties, any torments, any death"**: "The Way They Intend to Abolish Slavery," *Southern Confederacy*, March 11, 1862, 1.

159 **Named the Calhoun Guards in honor of his father**: See "Calhoun Guards," *Southern Confederacy*, February 27, 1862, 2.

159 **He would see plenty of action this time**: William Lowndes Calhoun, *History of the 42nd Regiment, Georgia Volunteers, Confederate States Army, Infantry* (n.p., 1900), 29.

159 **"The idol of the household"**: Noble C. Williams, *Echoes from the Battlefield; or, Southern Life During the War* (Atlanta: Franklin Printing and Publishing Co., 1902), 16.

160 **"without even receiving a scratch"**: Williams, *Echoes from the Battlefield*, 18–19.

161 **As Clingan stood, a Yankee sharpshooter put a minié ball**: Williams, *Echoes from the Battlefield*, 20–21, 27–28.

161 **"pure waters, salubrious air, and delightful climate"**: February (unspecified date) 1862, quoted in Richard Barksdale Harwell, "Civilian Life in Atlanta in 1862," *Atlanta Historical Bulletin* 7, no. 29 (October 1944): 214.

162 **"the County, State, and City is a matter of great public necessity"**: Quoted in Ralph Benjamin Singer Jr., "Confederate Atlanta," PhD diss., University of Georgia, 151.

162 **In the summer, plans were drawn up**: Franklin M. Garrett, *Atlanta and Environs: A Chronicle of Its People and Events* (New York: Lewis Historical Publishing Co., 1954), 1:530–31; Jack D. Welsh, MD, *Two Confederate Hospitals and Their Patients: Atlanta to Opelika* (Macon, GA: Mercer University Press, 2005), 12–13.

162 **Specialized hospitals were also erected**: Singer, "Confederate Atlanta," 150–51, 152–53.

162 **For Gussie, this chance to help would one day prove tragic**: On the women's relief work for the sick and wounded, see Clayton, *Requiem for a Lost City*, 81–82, 82n11–12, and 86–92.

163 **"First, the ringing down the curtain"**: Clayton, *Requiem for a Lost City*, 66.

163 **Soon, however, Confederate seizures of hundreds of bondsmen and women**: Clarence H. Mohr, *On the Threshold of Freedom: Masters and Slaves in Civil War Georgia* (Athens: University of Georgia Press, 1987), 129–33.

164 **Jabez's young wife died of consumption**: Richards, *Diary*, January 26, 1863, 156; February 15, 1863, 160.

## CHAPTER 13: ENEMIES WITHIN

165 **They were now considered . . . "unsound":** Samuel Richards, *Diary* (typescript), March 15, 1862, 85.

166 **"months or years perhaps":** Richards, *Diary*, March 5, 1862, 82.

166 **"stuck to his room and the back streets":** Richards, *Diary*, November 17, 1862, 140.

166 **"Our object . . . is to have as little to do as possible":** Richards, *Diary*, August 31, 1863, 196; March 4, 1863, 164; July 18, 1863, 194; December 31, 1863, 217; August 3, 1863, 192.

167 **defeat would not come in the field:** "Are We Whipped? Shall We Give Up?" *Southern Confederacy*, October 25, 1862, 2.

167 **Atlanta was estimated to contain as many as 10,000 draft dodgers:** Ralph Benjamin Singer Jr., "Confederate Atlanta," PhD diss., University of Georgia, 1973, 216–17.

167 **One dismayed observer counted around 3,000 firemen:** City Council Minutes, December 25, 1863, Vol. 4, January 17, 1862, to June 1, 1866, 215–16. On exempt firemen, see Robert Scott Davis, "Guarding the Gate City from Itself: George W. Lee and Conflict in Civil War Atlanta," 32.

167 **"no clash or difficulty has ever arisen":** *Southern Confederacy*, September 20, 1862, 2. On Lee's force's total, see Davis, "Guarding the Gate City from Itself," 16–17.

167 **Lee was an ardent Confederate:** For a description of Lee, see Louisa Maretta Whitney, *Goldie's Inheritance: A Story of the Siege of Atlanta (1903)* (Whitefish, MT: Kessinger Publishing, 2008), 165. For a description of Lee's officers, see the deposition of Thomas S. Garner, *Markham v. U. S.*, quoted in Thomas Dyer, *Secret Yankees: The Union Circle in Confederate Atlanta* (Baltimore: Johns Hopkins University Press, 1999), 99. Davis, in "Guarding the Gate City from Itself," offers much valuable detail on Lee's life and career and spotlights Lee's activities during the Civil War far more positively than does Dyer in *Secret Yankees*.

168 **"a mixture of Jews, New England Yankees, and of refugees shirking military duties":** From G. W. Lee to George W. Randolph, October 18, 1862, quoted in Mark E. Neely, *Southern Rights: Political Prisoners and the Myth of Confederate Constitutionalism* (Charlottesville: University of Virginia Press, 1999), 33.

168 **"confined for months, even without charges":** Braxton Bragg to Joseph E. Johnston, March 2, 1863, quoted in Dyer, *Secret Yankees*, 99.

168 **"We will very soon have nothing but a rabble":** *Daily Intelligencer*, October 25, 1863, 3.

168 **The state supreme court threw out the case:** Franklin M. Garrett, *Atlanta and Environs: A Chronicle of Its People and Events* (New York: Lewis Historical Publishing Co., 1954), 1:564–67. Regarding the other incidents, see Davis, "Guarding the Gate City from Itself," 17–20.

169 **Little matter that Lee himself was eventually charged with selling draft exemptions:** Lee was tried on the charge of selling draft exemptions in September 1864 and acquitted (Davis, "Guarding the Gate City from Itself," 45).

169 **"those who violate[d] the laws":** George W. Lee to Governor Brown, January 27, 1863, quoted in Jonathan D. Sarris, "'Shot for Being Bushwhackers': Guerilla

War and Extralegal Violence in a North Georgia Community, 1862–1865," in *Guerillas, Unionists, and Violence on the Confederate Home Front*, ed. Daniel E. Sutherland (Fayetteville: University of Arkansas Press, 1999), 39.

169 **"fire upon them, and, at all hazard . . . capture the last man":** Col. George W. Lee, "To the People of Northern and Northeastern Georgia and Southwestern N. Carolina," *Southern Confederacy*, January 30, 1863, 1.

169 **Critics charged that many of those prisoners were severely beaten:** Davis, "Guarding the Gate City from Itself," 24–26. William Harris Bragg, *Joe Brown's Army: The Georgia State Line, 1862–1865* (Macon, GA: Mercer University Press, 1987), 18–21.

169 **By 1864, they were dispatching as many as fifteen:** Sarris, "'Shot for Being Bushwhackers,'" 31–44.

170 **"perfect reign of terror":** Quoted in Dyer, *Secret Yankees*, 101.

170 **"in a room with all the rebel 'rough-scuff'":** Quoted in Dyer, *Secret Yankees*, 103.

170 **"a Union organization, of three hundred white men":** Whitney, *Goldie's Inheritance*, 164–65. On the detention of the Union Circle members, see Dyer, *Secret Yankees*, 100–114. For an opposing interpretation, see Davis, "Guarding the Gate City from Itself," 36–39.

170 **Although he was aware of how dangerous Lee's men could be:** James M. Calhoun affidavit, *Timothy D. Lynes v. United States*, Southern Claims Commission, CD 12658, box 1452, National Archives, Washington, D.C.

171 **"a fall upon the floor of the room in which he was confined":** *Daily Intelligencer*, September 3, 1862, 3.

171 **"a decided victim of inebriety":** G. W. Lee to G. W. Randolph, November 11, 1862, quoted in Dyer, *Secret Yankees*, 105.

171 **After he protested to Richmond, Lee had him arrested too:** Dyer, *Secret Yankees*, 103–5. Davis believes Lee's men were not responsible for Myers's death, though the newspaper report of the beating at the time of his arrest appears to substantiate the charges; see "Guarding the Gate City from Itself," 37.

171 **Reports circulated widely about an insurrectionary army:** Davis, "Guarding the Gate City from Itself," 27.

171 **By November 1863, slaves resident in town had increased:** See Clarence H. Mohr, *On the Threshold of Freedom: Masters and Slaves in Civil War Georgia* (Athens: University of Georgia Press, 1987), 194, and City Council Minutes, November 6, 1863, Vol. 4, January 17, 1862, to June 1, 1866. On slave seizures, see "Markets and Other Matters," *Southern Confederacy*, January 27, 1863, 2.

171 **Many bondsmen, including increasing numbers of runaways:** Alton Hornsby Jr., *A Short History of Black Atlanta, 1847–1990*, 2nd ed. (North Richland Hills, TX: Ivy Halls Academic Press, 2006), 1.

171 **"We had never seen so many dark skinned people":** Sarah Huff, "My Eighty Years in Atlanta" (n.p., 1937), ch. 1, n.p.

172 **Only when Confederates were nowhere in sight:** Mohr, *On the Threshold of Freedom*, 161–62. On the breakdown of slavery in urban life, see ch. 6, especially 196ff.

172 **"Missus, they better keep them guns out of our folks hands":** Dyer, *Secret Yankees*, Appendix B, "Miss Abby's Diary," March 20, 1864, 294; January 20, 1864, 286.

172 **Word got around quickly in 1862:** Mohr, *On the Threshold of Freedom*, 219.

173 **"terrible warning and example":** Quotes in Mohr, *On the Threshold of Freedom*, 220.

173 **A self-defense company of "old men":** Testimony of Ezra Andrews, *Ezra Andrews v. U.S.*, Southern Claims Commission, CD 12663, National Archives, Washington, D.C.

173 **Mayor Calhoun's young son Patrick:** "Reminiscences of Patrick H. Calhoun," *Atlanta Historical Bulletin* 1, no. 6 (February 1932): 42.

173 **Joseph Quarles, a Ponder slave who possessed a rudimentary education:** Quarles later became the first black lawyer to enter the Georgia judicial bar and, under President Rutherford B. Hayes, an American consul in Spain. See Henry Ossian Flipper, *The Colored Cadet at West Point: Autobiography of Lieut. Henry Ossian Flipper* (1878; rpt. Whitefish, MT: Kessinger Publishing, 2004), 11.

174 **"why fourteen of the engine thieves":** G. W. Lee to Hon. G. W. Randolph, September 16, 1862, quoted in William Pittenger, *Daring and Suffering: A History of the Andrews Railroad Raid into Georgia in 1862 . . .* , ed. Col. James G. Bogle, 3rd ed. (1887; rpt. Nashville, TN: Cumberland House Publishing, 1999), 310.

174 **"I never talked with a negro yet":** Pittenger, *Daring and Suffering*, 296–97. See also Russell S. Bonds, *Stealing the General: The Great Locomotive Chase and the First Medal of Honor* (Yardley, PA: Westholme Publishing, 2007), 276–77.

175 **Ten men, including eight of the raiders, managed to elude Lee's men:** On the Union, or Andrews, raiders' daring and ultimately successful escape, see Pittenger, *Daring and Suffering*, 316ff, for a participant's version, and Bonds, *Stealing the General*, 279ff, for a modern history. Quotes are from Pittenger, *Daring and Suffering*, 320, 323.

175 **He insisted "sympathizers outside" must have hid the men:** G. W. Lee to Clifton H. Smith, November 18, 1862, quoted in Pittenger, *Daring and Suffering*, 324.

177 **A man of means now, he had no trouble bribing his way back:** Deposition of Robert Webster, *Webster v. U.S.*, CD 13502, folders 1 and 3. See Dyer, *Secret Yankees*, 88–89.

177 **Hill advocated a negotiated end to the war:** "James M. Calhoun, Atlanta, Ga, Rebellion, Filed July 19, 1865, Pardoned July 24, 1865," Case Files of Applications from Former Confederates for Presidential Pardons ("Amnesty Papers"), 1865–1867, National Archives M1003, Washington, D.C.

177 **Georgia voted to fight on:** Joshua Hill to George W. Adair, J. J. Thrasher, and James M. Calhoun of Atlanta, Ga., in *Southern Recorder*, September 8, 1863, quoted in Lucien E. Roberts, "The Political Career of Joshua Hill, Georgia Unionist," *Georgia Historical Quarterly* 21 (March 1937): 58–59.

177 **"We have heard one or two names mentioned":** *Daily Intelligencer*, December 6, 1863, 3.

178 **"Our company from Mississippi is here":** Wallace Putnam Reed, "Atlanta's War Days Forty Years Ago," *Atlanta Constitution*, July 9, 1902, 6.

178 **Livestock and poultry, always in danger of being stolen:** See Singer, "Confederate Atlanta," 220–21; Mary Mallard to Mary Jones, January 6, 14, 1864, in Robert Manson Myers, *The Children of Pride: A True Story of Georgia and the Civil War*, abr. ed. (New Haven, CT: Yale University Press, 1984); Richards, *Diary*, January 2, 1864, 217–18.

179 **The notion never advanced far in the council's deliberations:** City Council Minutes, January 1, 1864, Vol. 4, January 17, 1862, to June 1, 1866, 230. For salaries, see City Council Minutes, April 1, 1864, Vol. 4, 263.

179 **"God save us from evil in the year to come":** Richards, *Diary*, December 31, 1863, 217.

## CHAPTER 14: RIVER OF DEATH

182 **The surviving prisoners were paroled just two days later:** Mike "Doc" Kinstler, "The Soldier's Handbook, 42nd Regiment—Georgia Volunteer Infantry," 42nd Georgia, www.42ndgeorgia.com/42nd_georgia_history.htm.

182 **It wasn't long before Calhoun:** For the description of Vicksburg battles and siege, quotes, etc., see William Lowndes Calhoun, *History of the 42nd Regiment, Georgia Volunteers, Confederate States Army, Infantry* (n.p., 1900), 29–36.

183 **"the fate of the Confederacy was sealed when Vicksburg fell":** Ulysses S. Grant, *Personal Memoirs* (New York: Modern Library, 1999), 303.

183 **Not long after, Grant would give him those men and more:** Letter to Philemon B. Ewing, July 28, 1863, *Sherman's Civil War: Selected Correspondence of William T. Sherman, 1860–1865*, ed. Brooks D. Simpson and Jean V. Berlin (Chapel Hill: University of North Carolina Press, 1999), 508.

183 **"in which to pack up the City Records":** City Council Minutes, August 28, 1863, Vol. 4, January 17, 1862, to June 1, 1866, 184.

184 **"every male negro that can possibly be impressed":** Quoted in Clarence H. Mohr, *On the Threshold of Freedom: Masters and Slaves in Civil War Georgia* (Athens: University of Georgia Press, 1987), 126.

185 **When and if a federal force came to storm the city:** On the planning and building of the fortifications, see Franklin M. Garrett, *Atlanta and Environs: A Chronicle of Its People and Events* (New York: Lewis Historical Publishing Co., 1954), 1:567–69.

185 **"of the most inferior character":** Quoted in Mohr, *On the Threshold of Freedom*, 177.

186 **"We don't want to make no fortifications":** Thomas Dyer, *Secret Yankees: The Union Circle in Confederate Atlanta* (Baltimore: Johns Hopkins University Press, 1999), Appendix B, "Miss Abby's Diary," Sabbath (date uncertain), 1864, 317.

186 **"The whole country round Chattanooga was just blue":** Dyer, *Secret Yankees*, Appendix B, "Miss Abby's Diary," March 24, 1864, 300–1.

186 **"rushed to a slave market":** Sarah Huff, "My Eighty Years in Atlanta" (n.p., 1937), ch. 1, n.p.

186 **From one day to the next, it depreciated a third in value:** Samuel Richards, *Diary* (typescript), March 22, 1864, 237.

187 **The grateful recipients of gold and U.S. dollars buried their treasure:** Ralph Benjamin Singer Jr., "Confederate Atlanta," PhD diss., University of Georgia, 181–82.

187 **Among those who had not lost confidence:** Robert Scott Davis, "Guarding the Gate City from Itself: George W. Lee and Conflict in Civil War Atlanta," article in progress (typescript), notes 72, 71.

188 **the hooting rebel army, much less able to withstand heavy losses:** On the Battle of Chickamauga, see James McPherson, *Battle Cry of Freedom* (New York and Oxford: Oxford University Press, 1988), 672–75.

188 **Stunned by the hurricane of violence:** A. J. Neal to Dear Pa, Williams Artillery Battalion, Battlefield Eight Miles South of Chattanooga, September 21, 1863, 10 A.M.

188 **"Men . . . were lying where they fell":** Sam Watkins, *Company Aytch, or a Side Show of the Big Show*, ed. M. Thomas Inge (1882; rpt. New York: Plume, 1999), 87.

189 **"They are our mortal enemies":** Cousin Norma, "The Battlefield of Chickamauga," "Ten Days After the Battle," *Daily Intelligencer*, October 6, 1863, 1.

189 **He was too weak even to lift his own dangling arm:** Sarah "Sallie" Conley Clayton, *Requiem for a Lost City: A Memoir of Civil War Atlanta and the Old South*, ed. Robert S. Davis Jr. (Macon, GA: Mercer University Press, 1999), 92–93.

189 **"The army is confident . . . we will be in Kentucky soon":** A. J. Neal to Dear Pa, September 21, 1863.

190 **"This service is rougher than any I have seen":** A. J. Neal to Dear Pa, Williams Artillery Battalion, Near Chattanooga, Tenn., November 1, 1863.

190 **They lived on parched corn:** Watkins, *Company Aytch*, 91.

190 **General Bragg had seized all shoes and horses:** For shoe price, see Singer, "Confederate Atlanta," 165–66.

190 **While our cause is brightening in its aspect:** *Daily Intelligencer*, October 18, 1863, 2.

191 **In Atlanta, as throughout the South, people fed on hope:** On Confederate optimism stoked through rumors and newspaper reporting on Chickamauga and during the Atlanta Campaign, see Jason Phillips, *Diehard Rebels: The Confederate Culture of Invincibility* (Athens: University of Georgia Press, 2007), 102–15.

191 **Who knew what a Union army, presently licking its wounds:** "The Importance of Atlanta," *Daily Intelligencer*, October 18, 1863, 1.

## CHAPTER 15: A DAY'S OUTING

193 **He personally came to Chattanooga to assume overall command:** For Grant's description of the preparation for, and fighting of, the Battle of Chattanooga, also known as Lookout Mountain or Missionary Ridge, see Ulysses S. Grant, *Personal Memoirs* (New York: Modern Library, 1999), 323–52.

193 **The picket lines were close enough for soldiers to converse:** On cordial relations across the picket lines, see Grant, *Personal Memoirs*, 325 and 329.

194 **he hoped soon to receive a ten-day furlough:** A. J. Neal to Dear Ma, Williams Artillery Battalion, Camp Before Chattanooga, Tenn., November 20, 1863.

194 **She was the beautiful wife of Adm. Raphael Semmes:** On the dashing and incredibly successful Confederate privateer Raphael Semmes, see Stephen Fox, *Wolf of the Deep: Raphael Semmes and the Notorious Confederate Raider CSS Alabama* (New York: Vintage, 2008).

196 **"had a splendid view of the beautiful light":** For the description of the trip to Missionary Ridge and all quotes, see Sarah "Sallie" Conley Clayton, *Requiem for a Lost City: A Memoir of Civil War Atlanta and the Old South*, ed. Robert S. Davis Jr. (Macon, GA: Mercer University Press, 1999), 101–9.

197 **"But their dead were so piled in their path":** Sam Watkins, *Company Aytch, or a Side Show of the Big Show*, ed. M. Thomas Inge (1882; rpt. New York: Plume, 1999), 99–100.

197 **"The foe encroaches upon us so":** Samuel Richards, *Diary*, December 5, 1863, 213.

197 **Not long after, he appointed Gen. Joseph Johnston:** *Daily Intelligencer,* November 29, 1863, 3.

198 **"We were willing to do and die":** Watkins, *Company Aytch,* 103.

198 **"The people's time has now come":** Quotes are from 290, *Daily Intelligencer,* December 25, 1863, 2, 3.

198 **Joseph Brown placed the colonel in command:** On Lee's state militia command, see Robert Scott Davis, "Guarding the Gate City from Itself: George W. Lee and Conflict in Civil War Atlanta," article in progress (typescript), 45.

199 **"Atlanta is our important point now":** Charles Fessenden Morse, *Letters Written During the Civil War, 1861–1865* (Boston: T. R. Marvin & Sons, Printers, 1898), 159.

199 **"I never want to leave this army":** "Dear Ella," December 6, 1863, Near Dalton, Ga.

## CHAPTER 16: RAILROAD WAR

203 **Those who served would be guaranteed their freedom:** Quoted in Clarence L. Mohr, *On the Threshold of Freedom: Masters and Slaves in Civil War Georgia* (Athens: University of Georgia Press, 1987), 275. For a frontline, eyewitness diary account of the debate, see Wirt Armstead Cate, ed., *Two Soldiers: The Campaign Diaries of Thomas J. Key, C. S. A., and Robert J. Campbell, U.S.A.* (Chapel Hill: University of North Carolina Press, 1938), December 28, 1863, 16–18.

203 **"sacrifice . . . the principle which is the basis of our social system":** *Southern Confederacy,* August 23, 1863, 2.

204 **"If needs be, you had better die":** M., "To the Mothers, Wives and Daughters of Soldiers," *Daily Intelligencer,* December 29, 1863, 2.

204 **"ostensibly under authority of the War Department":** David Williams, Teresa Williams, and R. David Carlson, *Plain Folk in a Rich Man's War: Class and Dissent in Confederate Georgia* (Gainesville: University Press of Florida, 2002), 178; on selling exemptions, see 107–9.

204 **"Somebody certainly must fight":** Samuel P. Richards, *Diary* (typescript), March 22, 1864, 227; December 9, 1863, 214.

205 **The enrolling officers left him alone:** Richards, *Diary,* January 16, 1864, 219–20.

205 **it was increasingly a rich man's war and a poor man's fight:** Thomas Dyer, *Secret Yankees: The Union Circle in Confederate Atlanta* (Baltimore: Johns Hopkins University Press, 1999) Appendix B, "Miss Abby's Diary," January 20, 1864, 284. For a useful study of the role of class in dissent and resistance to participation in the war in Georgia, see Williams, Williams, and Carlson, *Plain Folk in a Rich Man's War,* esp. 161ff.

206 **He brought them food and news about the war:** Affidavit of William Lewis, *Webster v. U.S.,* Southern Claims Commission, National Archives, CD 13502, folder 1.

206 **"had any idea how matters stand down here":** Dyer, *Secret Yankees,* Appendix B, "Miss Abby's Diary," April 9, 1864, 298–99.

207 **"Don't expect to overrun such a country":** To John Sherman, Memphis, August 13, 1862, in *Sherman's Civil War: Selected Correspondence of William T. Sherman, 1860–1865,* ed. Brooks D. Simpson and Jean V. Berlin (Chapel Hill: University of North Carolina Press, 1999), 272–73.

207 **Grant presented him with a plan to attack the Confederate head in Virginia:** On Grant's grand strategy for closing out the war starting in 1864, see Richard M. McMurry, *Atlanta 1864: Last Chance for the Confederacy* (Lincoln: University of Nebraska Press, 2000), 12–20.

207 **"to work all parts of the army together":** Quoted in McMurry, *Atlanta 1864*, 13.

208 **"Grant is my man, and I am his the rest of the war":** Quoted in James McPherson, *Battle Cry of Freedom* (New York and Oxford: Oxford University Press, 1988), 638.

208 **"we don't get more than one effective soldier":** McPherson, *Battle Cry of Freedom*, 720. On Northern conscription and enrollment policies, see 600–6.

209 **"it seems exceedingly probable that this Administration will not be re-elected":** August 23, 1864, quoted in McMurry, *Atlanta 1864*, 204. On Lincoln's political troubles, see McPherson, *Battle Cry of Freedom*, 698–717.

209 **"a manifest ebb in popular feeling":** "The Present Aspect of the War—Causes for Hope," *New York Times*, March 16, 1864, 4. Historians have long debated the likelihood of Lincoln's defeat in the November 1864 elections in the event Atlanta had not fallen. For a cogent summary of the issue and a military historian's refutation of the notion that the fall of Atlanta determined the election results, see McMurry, *Atlanta 1864*, appendix 4, "The Atlanta Campaign and the Election of 1864," 204–8.

209 **"Upon the progress of our arms":** Quoted in McPherson, *Battle Cry of Freedom*, 718.

209 **Even Sherman described himself as Grant's "second self":** Quoted in Albert Castel, *Decision in the West: The Atlanta Campaign of 1864* (Lawrence: University of Kansas Press, 1992), 43.

210 **"General Sherman is the most American man I ever saw":** Roland Gray, "Memoir of John Chipman Gray," *Proceedings of the Massachusetts Historical Society* 49 (October 1915–June 1916): 393–94.

210 **"war, pure and simple: to be applied directly to the civilians of the South":** Letter to Roswell M. Sawyer, January 31, 1864, in Simpson and Berlin, *Sherman's Civil War*, 601.

210 **"The army of the Confederacy is the South":** Letter to John Sherman, December 29, 1863, in Simpson and Berlin, *Sherman's Civil War*, 578.

211 **They left behind a scraped-over landscape:** Castel, *Decision in the West*, 52.

211 **"Of course I must fight":** To Maria Boyle Ewing Sherman, January 19, 1864, in Simpson and Berlin, *Sherman's Civil War*, 587.

211 **He answered Grant a month before the campaign commenced:** McMurry, *Atlanta 1864*, 49, 52.

212 **He was convinced that the Army of the Tennessee would soon reverse:** "Dear Brother," April 22, 1864, near Dalton.

212 **"the war closed in behind":** Quoted in McPherson, *Battle Cry of Freedom*, 515.

212 **"All that has gone before is mere skirmishing":** Letter to Ellen Ewing Sherman, March 12, 1864, in Simpson and Berlin, *Sherman's Civil War*, 609.

## Chapter 17: Candle Ends

213 **With Bragg at his elbow, Davis fumed:** Quoted in Richard M. McMurry, *Atlanta 1864: Last Chance for the Confederacy* (Lincoln, NE: University of Nebraska Press, 2000), 47–48.

214 **"I can see no other mode of taking the offensive here"**: Quoted in McMurry, *Atlanta 1864*, 22.
214 **"Difficulties . . . are in the way"**: Quoted in Albert Castel, *Decision in the West: The Atlanta Campaign of 1864* (Lawrence, KS: University of Kansas Press, 1992), 30–32.
215 **"march to the front as soon as possible"**: To Jefferson Davis, March 7, 1864, quoted in Castel, *Decision in the West*, 76.
215 **"stronger than [we] had supposed"**: "Dear Brother," April 22, 1864, near Dalton, Georgia.
216 **"having an easier time than ever"**: "Dear Ma," February 3, 1864, near Kingston, Georgia.
216 **"brilliant successes this spring"**: "Dear Emma," March 23, 1864, near Dalton.
216 **"God will fight our battles for us"**: Quoted in Mary A. H. Gay, *Life in Dixie During the War, 1861–1862–1863–1864–1865* (1892; rpt. Macon, GA: Mercer University Press, 2001), 80–83.
216 **"Small it was . . . but yet large enough"**: Charles E. Benton, *As Seen from the Ranks: A Boy in the Civil War* (New York: G. P. Putnam's Sons, 1902), 131–32.
217 **"Hundreds of those poor fellows"**: George H. Puntenney, *History of the Thirty-seventh Regiment of Indiana Infantry Volunteers: Its Organization, Campaigns, and Battles, Sept., '61–Oct., '64* (Rushville, IN: Jacksonian Book and Job Department, 1896), 79–80.

## CHAPTER 18: FIGHTING, FIGHTING, FIGHTING

219 **"nearly the entire population . . . moving off taking their Negroes south"**: "Dear Ma," February 3, 1864, near Kingston, Georgia.
219 **refugees in wagons heading south that "literally blockaded" the roads**: Mary A. H. Gay, *Life in Dixie During the War* (1892; rpt. Macon, GA: Mercer University Press, 2001), 95–96.
220 **"a boy to walk on the heads and shoulders of men"**: Sarah "Sallie" Conley Clayton, *Requiem for a Lost City: A Memoir of Civil War Atlanta and the Old South*, ed. Robert S. Davis Jr. (Macon, GA: Mercer University Press, 1999), 92–93.
220 **"large concourse of citizens"**: Samuel Richards, *Diary* (typescript), February 6, 1864, 222.
221 **"and by every kind word and deed"**: *Daily Intelligencer*, February 7, 1864, 2.
221 **Joseph Johnston's winter camp**: William Lowndes Calhoun, *History of the 42nd Regiment, Georgia Volunteers, Confederate States Army, Infantry* (n.p., 1900), 37–38.
222 **"No event could be more disastrous to the Confederacy"**: *Daily Intelligencer*, April 26, 1864, 2.
222 **"Of the capacity of General Johnston"**: *Daily Intelligencer*, April 26, 1864, 2.
222 **shared the "perfect ecstasies" people felt**: Mary Mallard to Mary Jones, February 22, 1864, in Robert Myers, *The Children of Pride: A True Story of Georgia and the Civil War*, abr. ed. (New Haven, CT: Yale University Press, 1984), 439.
222 **"We will be in a dreadful predicament"**: To Mary Jones, May 5 and 14, 1864, in Myers, *The Children of Pride*, 461, 462.
222 **"If we are defeated in these battles"**: Richards, *Diary*, May 7, 1864, 230.
223 **"to which I took such a fancy"**: To Ellen Ewing Sherman, Kingston, Ga., May 22, 1864, in *Sherman's Civil War: Selected Correspondence of William T. Sherman,*

*1860–1865*, ed. Brooks D. Simpson and Jean V. Berlin (Chapel Hill: University of North Carolina Press, 1999), 639.

223 **could not pierce their lines "except by flanking":** "Dear Pa," May 10, 1864, in the field above Dalton.

224 **"the terrible door of death":** To Ellen Ewing Sherman, Kingston, Ga., May 22, 1864, in Simpson and Berlin, *Sherman's Civil War*, 638.

225 **"I've got Joe Johnston dead":** Throughout I have drawn for my understanding of the battles of the Atlanta campaign on two extraordinary military histories: Albert Castel, *Decision in the West: The Atlanta Campaign of 1864* (Lawrence: University of Kansas Press, 1992), and Richard M. McMurry, *Atlanta 1864: Last Chance for the Confederacy* (Lincoln: University of Nebraska Press, 2000). For the Sherman quote, see Castel, *Decision in the West*, 141.

225 **"The Yankees . . . had got breeches hold on us":** Sam Watkins, *Company Aytch, or a Side Show of the Big Show*, ed. M. Thomas Inge (1882; rpt. New York: Plume, 1999), 120.

225 **"He could have walked into Resaca":** For quotes, see William Tecumseh Sherman, *Memoirs of General W. T. Sherman*, 2nd ed. (New York: Penguin Classics, 2001), 410 (see also back matter), and Castel, *Decision in the West*, 150. For a defense of McPherson's actions at Resaca by an officer in the field, see Henry Stone, "Opening of the Campaign," *The Atlanta Papers*, comp. Sydney C. Kerkis (Dayton, OH: Press of Morningside Bookshop, 1980), 357–70.

226 **What Neal called "a rich scene":** "Dear Pa," May 15, 1864, in the field near Resaca, GA.

227 **He despised as a dangerous weight upon his army:** On Sherman's attitude regarding the black camp followers in Georgia, see Clarence H. Mohr, *On the Threshold of Freedom: Masters and Slaves in Civil War Georgia* (Athens: University of Georgia Press, 1987), 191ff., and on their role as soldiers, see, for instance, his letter to Gen. Lorenzo Thomas, June 26, 1864, in Simpson and Berlin, *Sherman's Civil War*, 657–58.

227 **"a thicket almost impenetrable":** Castel, *Decision in the West*, 177.

227 **For the mayor of Atlanta's son, the Civil War fighting was over:** Calhoun, *History of the 42nd Regiment*, 38.

227 **"When we awoke in the morning":** Watkins, *Company Aytch*, 122.

227 **"only give us a fair fight":** "Dear Ma," May 20, 1864, in the field, Etowah River, GA.

228 **"a terrific battle" near that river was inevitable:** To Ellen Ewing Sherman, Kingston, Ga., May 22, 1864, in Simpson and Berlin, *Sherman's Civil War*, 639.

228 **"Atlanta is evidently our destination":** Charles Fessenden Morse, *Letters Written During the Civil War, 1861–1865* (Boston: T. R. Marvin & Sons, Printers, 1898), 167.

## CHAPTER 19: ROMAN RUNAGEES

230 **"flying in every direction in ruinous confusion":** B. G. Ellis, *The Moving Appeal: Mr. McClanahan, Mrs. Dill, and the Civil War's Great Newspaper Run* (Macon, GA: Mercer University Press, 2003), 283.

230 **"you might as well reason with a thunderstorm":** To John Sherman, January 25, 1864, quoted in Stephen E. Bower, "The Theology of the Battlefield: William Tecumseh Sherman and the U.S. Civil War," *Journal of Military History* 64, no. 4

(October 2000): 1020; to James Guthrie, August 14, 1864, in the field near Atlanta, in *Sherman's Civil War: Selected Correspondence of William T. Sherman, 1860–1865*, ed. Brooks D. Simpson and Jean V. Berlin (Chapel Hill: University of North Carolina Press, 1999), 694.

230 **The supposedly faithful black people were voting with their feet:** "Bill Arp, the Roman Runagee," Atlanta, Ga., May 22, 1864, in (Charles H. Smith) *Bill Arp, So Called: A Sideshow of the Southern Side of the War* (New York: Metropolitan Record Office, 1866), 84–92.

230 **Refugees were now "constantly arriving":** Samuel Richards, *Diary* (typescript), May 29, 1864, 231. See also Eliza Frances Andrews, *The War-Time Journal of a Georgia Girl, 1864–1865* (Atlanta: Cherokee Publishing Co., 1976), 149.

230 **With boardinghouses and extra rooms in private homes already full:** Mary Elizabeth Massey, *Refugee Life in the Confederacy* (Baton Rouge: Louisiana State University Press, 1964; new material 2001), 83–84.

231 **"the report of the artillery at the front":** Richards, *Diary*, May 29, 1864, 231.

231 **"To realize what war is one should follow in our tracks":** To Ellen Ewing Sherman, in the field near Marietta, Ga., June 26, 1864, in Simpson and Berlin, *Sherman's Civil War*, 657.

231 **"to keep close up to the enemy":** Quoted in Albert Castel, *Decision in the West: The Atlanta Campaign of 1864* (Lawrence: University of Kansas Press, 1992), 247.

232 **"to stand in the trenches and mow down their lines":** "Dear Emma," June 2, 1864, in the field near New Hope Church.

232 **"Such piles of dead men were seldom or never seen":** Quoted in Richard M. McMurry, *Atlanta 1864: Last Chance for the Confederacy* (Lincoln: University of Nebraska Press, 2000), 90.

232 **"This is surely not war; it is butchery":** Richard M. McMurry, *The Road Past Kennesaw: The Atlanta Campaign of 1864* (Washington, D.C.: Office of Publications, National Park Service, 1972), 21.

232 **"so cautious that I can find no opportunity to attack him":** See McMurry, *Atlanta 1864*, 95.

232 **"Sherman knew that it was no child's play":** Sam Watkins, *Company Aytch, or a Side Show of the Big Show*, ed. M. Thomas Inge (1882; rpt. New York: Plume, 1999), 122.

233 **"It is . . . a Big Indian War":** To John Sherman, Acworth, Ga., June 9, 1864, in Simpson and Berlin, *Sherman's Civil War*, 645–46.

233 **"is still at my front and can fight or fall back as he pleases":** To John Sherman, Acworth, Ga., June 9, 1864, in Simpson and Berlin, *Sherman's Civil War*, 646.

233 **"the busiest people in town were speculators and rumor mongers":** May 25, 1864; quoted in Ellis, *The Moving Appeal*, 293.

233 **"On the street, every minute":** Quoted in Franklin M. Garrett, *Atlanta and Environs: A Chronicle of Its People and Events* (New York: Lewis Historical Publishing Co., 1954), 1:585.

233 **"that Atlanta will be defended to the last extremity":** May 24, 1864, quoted in Ellis, *The Moving Appeal*, 294.

234 **"as cheerfully as though nothing had happened":** Mary Mallard to Mary Jones, May 19, 1864, in Robert Myers, *The Children of Pride: A True Story of Georgia and the Civil War*, abr. ed. (New Haven, CT: Yale University Press, 1984), 463–64.

234 **"when limbs are amputated and the clothing cut off":** To Susan M. Cumming, May 20, 1864, in Myers, *The Children of Pride*, 465.

234 **"'the light fantastic toe' was tipped":** Thomas Dyer, *Secret Yankees: The Union Circle in Confederate Atlanta* (Baltimore: Johns Hopkins University Press, 1999), Appendix B, "Miss Abby's Diary," May 6, 1864, 301.

234 **The truth would eventually come out, she trusted:** Dyer, *Secret Yankees*, Appendix B, "Miss Abby's Diary," May 9, 1864, 302–3.

234 **"It stands to reason that our folks ain't whipping":** Dyer, *Secret Yankees*, Appendix B, "Miss Abby's Diary," May 19, 1864, 306.

235 **The Confederate grip on Atlanta:** Dyer, *Secret Yankees*, Appendix B, "Miss Abby's Diary," May 21, 1864, 307.

235 **Despite Lee's ill health, he went to Macon:** Robert Scott Davis, "Guarding the Gate City from Itself: George W. Lee and the Conflict in Civil War Atlanta" (manuscript in progress), 43–44.

235 **The governor might not swing from a tree:** *Daily Intelligencer*, February 12, 1864, 2.

235 **"Atlanta is to the Confederacy":** Allen D. Candler, ed., *The Confederate Records of the State of Georgia* (Atlanta: Charles P. Byrd, State Printer, 1909), 3:582.

236 **The anti-Brown faction derisively called the Georgia militia "Joe Brown's Pets":** On Gov. Joseph Brown and the Georgia militia, see William R. Scaife and William Harris Bragg, *Joe Brown's Pets: The Georgia Militia, 1861–1865* (Macon, GA: Mercer University Press, 2004).

236 **"only embarrasses the authorities":** May 23, 1864, quoted in Franklin M. Garrett, *Atlanta and Environs: A Chronicle of Its People and Events* (New York: Lewis Historical Publishing Co., 1954), 1:589.

236 **"use all force necessary . . . to take life":** "Militia Broadside," in Garrett, *Atlanta and Environs*, 23.

236 **"all the shirks and skulks in Georgia":** For quote, see Garrett, *Atlanta and Environs*, 29.

236 **"clothes sufficient for two or three men":** Quoted in Ellis, *The Moving Appeal*, 294.

236 **"I trust . . . we may never be called into action":** Richards, *Diary*, May 29, 1864, 231.

CHAPTER 20: PRAYERS

237 **"I'd much rather fight the people":** Thomas Dyer, *Secret Yankees: The Union Circle in Confederate Atlanta* (Baltimore: Johns Hopkins University Press, 1999), Appendix B, "Miss Abby's Diary," June 1, 1864, 314.

237 **"We are here without a gun":** "To Dearest Lizzie," May 26, 1864, MSS 116, box 1, folder 1, Atlanta History Center.

238 **"Come on! We're waiting for you!":** Dyer, *Secret Yankees*, Appendix B, "Miss Abby's Diary," May 27, 28, June 1, 6, 1864, 311–16.

238 **"every able-bodied negro man that can be found":** Quoted in Clarence H. Mohr, *On the Threshold of Freedom: Masters and Slaves in Civil War Georgia* (Athens: University of Georgia Press, 1987), 126.

239 **"This way with your axes":** Lt. Col. L. B. Faulkner to Captain Speed, June 22, 1864, quoted in Clarence L. Mohr, "The Atlanta Campaign and the African American Experience in Civil War Georgia," in Lesley J. Gordon and John C.

Inscoe, eds., *Inside the Confederate Nation: Essays in Honor of Emory M. Thomas* (Baton Rouge: Louisiana State University Press, 2005), 280.

239 **"cannot stay where he is long":** "Dear Emma," June 2, 1864, in the field near New Hope Church.

239 **They were wrong on all counts:** Letter to Ellen Ewing Sherman, Acworth, Ga., June 9, 1864, in *Sherman's Civil War: Selected Correspondence of William T. Sherman, 1860–1865*, ed. Brooks D. Simpson and Jean V. Berlin (Chapel Hill: University of North Carolina Press, 1999), note 1, 644, and 643.

240 **"from foul and putrid stock":** Quoted in Albert Castel, *Decision in the West: The Atlanta Campaign of 1864* (Lawrence: University of Kansas Press, 1992), 268–69.

240 **"an armistice, with a view to final separation":** (Memphis) *Daily Appeal,* June 24, 1864, quoted in B. G. Ellis, *The Moving Appeal: Mr. McClanahan, Mrs. Dill, and the Civil War's Great Newspaper Run* (Macon, GA: Mercer University Press, 2003), 303.

240 **if Sherman's efforts "prove[d] abortive":** Samuel Richards, *Diary* (typescript), Vol. 10, July 3, 1864, 1.

240 **War, so long a source of prosperity, took over the life of Atlanta:** "Atlanta," *New York Times,* June 22, 1864, n.p.

241 **A wounded soldier convalescing in the home:** Sarah Huff, *My Eighty Years in Atlanta* (n.p., 1937), ch. 3.

241 **"gentlemen . . . consider it unsafe to be much out at night":** Mrs. Mary S. Mallard to Mrs. Mary Jones, Atlanta, Thursday, March 24 and 31, 1864, in Robert Myers, *The Children of Pride: A True Story of Georgia and the Civil War*, abr. ed. (New Haven, CT: Yale University Press, Abridged Edition, 1984), 448–49, 453.

241 **His motion was defeated:** City Council Minutes, June 10, 1864, Vol. 4, January 17, 1862, to June 1, 1866, 281.

241 **"Can you, in this hour of peril":** *Daily Intelligencer,* May 29, 1864, quoted in "From Atlanta," *New York Times,* June 14, 1864.

242 **"insanity, in some instances, came to the relief of sufferings":** (Memphis) *Daily Appeal,* June 23, 1864, quoted in Ellis, *The Moving Appeal,* 303.

242 **"My answer is invariably":** Dyer, *Secret Yankees,* Appendix B, "Miss Abby's Diary," June 1, 1864, 313.

242 **"General Johnston will be successful":** Mary Mallard to Mary Jones, May 27, 1864, in Myers, *The Children of Pride,* 467.

243 **Her wealthy slave Prince Ponder stayed:** Henry Ossian Flipper, *The Colored Cadet at West Point: Autobiography of Lieut. Henry Ossian Flipper* (1878; rpt. Whitefish, MT: Kessinger Publishing, 2004), 5.

243 **insisted that he be called by his full name:** On Bob Yancey's insistence that his name was Robert Webster, see, for instance, Robert Webster, "What Bob Says," *Daily Constitution,* July 18, 1879, 4.

243 **"The men is all out of heart":** Quoted in Richard M. McMurry, *Atlanta 1864: Last Chance for the Confederacy* (Lincoln: University of Nebraska Press, 2000), 130.

244 **"You must do the work with your present force":** Quoted in McMurry, *Atlanta 1864,* 135.

245 **On the same day the city council offered up its disapproval:** City Council Minutes, June 1, 1864, Vol. 4, January 17, 1862, to June 1, 1866, 279.

245 **"I trust the prayers offered yesterday will be answered":** To Mary Jones, June 11, 1864, in Myers, *The Children of Pride,* 474.

245 **"all will yet be well"**: (Memphis) *Daily Appeal*, May 24, 1864, quoted in Ellis, *The Moving Appeal*, 294.

245 **"this suspense and anxiety [will] take away our reason"**: Dyer, *Secret Yankees*, Appendix B, "Miss Abby's Diary," July 5, 1864, 319; June 10, 1864, 317–18.

245 **"would attempt deliberately to shoot"**: Quoted in Castel, *Decision in the West*, 306.

246 **"a party of us began to make preparations"**: Sarah "Sallie" Conley Clayton, *Requiem for a Lost City: A Memoir of Civil War Atlanta and the Old South*, ed. Robert S. Davis Jr. (Macon, GA: Mercer University Press, 1999), 113.

246 **"to develop the enemy's position and strength"**: Quoted in Henry Stone, "From the Oostanaula to the Chattahoochee," *The Atlanta Papers*, comp. Sydney C. Kerkis (Dayton, OH: Press of Morningside Bookshop, 1980), 418.

246 **"right arm and passed through his body"**: For an account of Polk's death, see Castel, *Decision in the West*, 275–76, and William M. Polk, *Leonidas Polk: Bishop and General* (London: Longman, Green and Co., 1893), 2:349.

247 **For hours mourners filed passed his bloodless, flower-encased body lying in state in Saint Luke's Church:** Clayton, *Requiem for a Lost City*, 114–15.

247 **He returned to City Hall to do what he could to save his dying city:** "Reminiscences of Patrick H. Calhoun," *Atlanta Historical Bulletin* 1, no. 6 (February 1932): 42.

248 **"never more sanguine and confident of success"**: "Dear Pa," June 20, 1864, in the field two miles above Marietta.

249 **"a stench, so sickening as to nauseate the whole of both armies"**: Sam Watkins, *Company Aytch, or a Side Show of the Big Show*, ed. M. Thomas Inge (1882; rpt. New York: Plume, 1999), 130–32.

250 **"Some of the boys think"**: "Dearest Lizzie," July 6, 1864, MSS 116, box 1, folder 2, Holliday Papers, Atlanta History Center.

250 **"one or two more such assaults would use up this army"**: Quoted in Castel, *Decision in the West*, 315.

250 **"the work [has] progressed and I see no signs of a remission"**: Quoted in Castel, *Decision in the West*, 325.

251 **"looking as hard as possible toward A[tlanta]"**: July 19, 1864, Civil War Diary, July 16, 1864–November 14, 1864, *The Siege & Capture of Atlanta Georgia*, Henry D. Stanley, 2nd Lieut., 20th Conn. Vol. Co. H, MSS645, box 2, folder 1, Atlanta History Center.

251 **"Atlanta will not and cannot be abandoned"**: *Southern Confederacy*, July 5, 1864, 2.

251 **"to remain in the city if the enemy gets possession"**: Richards, *Diary*, Vol. 10, July 10, 1864, 2–3.

251 **Sallie left for the tranquility of an uncle's Alabama plantation:** Clayton, *Requiem for a Lost City*, 118–19.

252 **"there may be no battle here"**: Dyer, *Secret Yankees*, Appendix B, "Miss Abby's Diary," July 19, 1864, 322.

## CHAPTER 21: A PERFECT SHELL

256 **"the best line of field intrenchments I have ever seen"**: Quoted in Richard M. McMurry, *Atlanta 1864: Last Chance for the Confederacy* (Lincoln, NE: University of Nebraska Press, 2000), 115.

256 **"to make a circuit [of Atlanta]"**: "To make a circuit," letter of July 6, 1864, quoted in McMurry, *Atlanta 1864*, 118.

256 **Ignoring his terrible casualties:** Force and casualty numbers drawn from Mc-Murry, *Atlanta 1864*, Appendix 2, "Numbers and Losses," 194–97.

256 **"been rather cautious than bold":** Letter of July 12, 1864, quoted in Albert Castel, *Decision in the West: The Atlanta Campaign of 1864* (Lawrence: University of Kansas Press, 1992), 343.

256 **"These fellows fight like Devils":** Letter to Ellen Ewing Sherman, July 26, 1864, *Sherman's Civil War: Selected Correspondence of William T. Sherman, 1860–1865*, ed. Brooks D. Simpson and Jean V. Berlin (Chapel Hill: University of North Carolina Press, 1999), 671.

257 **"There seems to be some property":** "Dearest Lizzie," Camp Grease Gut, July 7, 11, 12, 14, and 15, 1864, Allen T. Holliday Papers, MSS 116, box 1, folder 2, Atlanta History Center.

258 **"walk[ed together] along the river banks":** "Dear Emma," in the field, Chattahoochee River, July 13, 1864. Andrew Jackson Neal Papers, 1856–1881, MSS218, Emory University Manuscript, Archives, and Rare Book Library.

258 **When officers came around and ordered:** See Castel, *Decision in the West*, 351–52.

258 **"When we fight . . . we fight to crush":** July 15, 1864, near Vining's Station, Ga., in Charles Fessenden Morse, *Letters Written During the Civil War, 1861–1865* (Boston: T. R. Marvin & Sons, Printers, 1898), 177.

259 **"pierced through the heart":** Sam Watkins, *Company Aytch, or a Side Show of the Big Show*, ed. M. Thomas Inge (1882; rpt. New York: Plume, 1999), 142.

259 **Sarah wondered why several soldiers:** Sarah Huff, *My Eighty Years in Atlanta* (n.p., 1937), ch. 4.

259 **"to arrest the advance of the enemy to the vicinity of Atlanta":** Quoted in Castel, *Decision in the West*, 361.

260 **"watch[ing] for an opportunity to fight to advantage":** Quoted in Castel, *Decision in the West*, 358.

260 **He expected Hood to move promptly to the attack:** Quoted in Castel, *Decision in the West*, 356, 362.

260 **"I do pray . . . we may never move":** "Dear Ma," Chattahoochee River, July 17, 1864.

260 **two peace advocates from the Union side passed through the battle lines:** The peace mission is described in James McPherson, *Battle Cry of Freedom* (New York and Oxford: Oxford University Press, 1988), 767–68.

261 **"a fight before Atlanta is given up":** Samuel Richards, *Diary* (typescript), Vol. 10, July 17, 1864, 3.

261 **"exercise . . . a little philosophy and reason":** Quoted in B. G. Ellis, *The Moving Appeal: Mr. McClanahan, Mrs. Dill, and the Civil War's Great Newspaper Run* (Macon, GA: Mercer University Press, 2003), 309.

261 **The members met for the last time:** City Council Minutes, July 18, 1864, Vol. 4, January 17, 1862, to June 1, 1866, 291.

262 **He had little else at his command:** Ralph Benjamin Singer Jr., "Confederate Atlanta" (PhD diss., University of Georgia, 1973), 257.

262 **In fact, he intended to remain with his brother:** Noble C. Williams, *Echoes from the Battlefield; or, Southern Life During the War* (Atlanta: Franklin Printing and Publishing Co., 1902), 34.

262 **"all was being done that could be":** Sarah "Sallie" Conley Clayton, *Requiem for a Lost City: A Memoir of Civil War Atlanta and the Old South*, ed. Robert S. Davis Jr. (Macon, GA: Mercer University Press, 1999), 125, 175.

263 **"The news . . . comes in shoals of falsehood":** Grape, "Letters from the Front, July 17th and 19th, 1864," (Augusta) *Daily Constitutionalist*, July 22 and 20, 1864, 1.

263 **His store was "stripped" of all its paper and cash on hand:** Richards, *Diary*, Vol. 10, July 22, 1864, 4.

263 **"If Soddom [sic] deserved the fate that befell it":** "Dear Ma," in the field before Atlanta, July 23, 1864.

264 **"Atlanta will not be given up without a fight":** Grape, "Letters from the Front, July 17th and 19th, 1864," (Augusta) *Daily Constitutionalist*, July 22 and 20, 1864, 1.

264 **"They were negroes" . . . so his appeals for help:** Thomas Dyer, *Secret Yankees: The Union Circle in Confederate Atlanta* (Baltimore: Johns Hopkins University Press, 1999), Appendix B, "Miss Abby's Diary," July 21, 1864, Midnight, 324.

265 **"wait until breastworks are erected":** Dyer, *Secret Yankees*, Appendix B, "Miss Abby's Diary," July 19, 1864, 321.

267 **He raced past the federal skirmish line:** George A. Newton, "Battle of Peach Tree Creek," *G. A. R. War Papers, Papers Read Before Fred. C. Jones Post, No. 401, Department of Ohio G. A. R.*, Vol. 1 (Cincinnati: Fred. C. Jones Post, 1891), 153–54.

267 **"could have taken them":** "Dear Pa," in the field near Chattahoochee, July 20, 1864.

268 **Atlanta was under fire:** Stephen Davis, "How Many Civilians Died in Sherman's Bombardment of Atlanta?" *Atlanta History* 45, no. 4 (2003): 5–6. Stephen Davis, "'A Very Barbarous Mode of Carrying on War': Sherman's Artillery Bombardment of Atlanta, July 20–August 24, 1864," *Georgia Historical Quarterly* 89, no. 1 (spring 1995): 61–62. Richards, *Diary*, Vol. 10, July 20, 1864, 4.

268 **"It seems almost impossible":** July 22, 1864, Civil War Diary Henry D. Stanley, July 16, 1864–November 14, 1864, *The Siege & Capture of Atlanta Georgia*, Henry D. Stanley, 2nd Lieut., 20th Conn. Vol. Co. H, MSS645, box 2, folder 1, Atlanta History Center.

268 **"within easy cannon-range of the buildings in Atlanta":** Quoted in Davis, "'A Very Barbarous Mode of Carrying on War,'" 63.

269 **"carrying a musket for the first time in my life":** Richards, *Diary*, Vol. 10, July 23, 1864, 4–5.

## CHAPTER 22: THE BATTLE OF ATLANTA

271 **Soon, everyone in town knew the cause for the alarm:** Florence W. Brine, "Central Presbyterian Church," *Atlanta Historical Bulletin* 3, no. 14 (July 1938): 183.

271 **"found the city in a wild state of excitement":** J. P. Austin, *The Blue and the Gray: Sketches of a Portion of the Unwritten History of the Great American Civil War, a Truthful Narrative of Adventure, with Thrilling Reminiscences of the Great Struggle on Land and Sea* (Atlanta: Franklin Printing and Publishing Co., 1899), 131.

272 **She was ordered to take the bomb back outside:** Noble C. Williams, *Echoes from the Battlefield; or, Southern Life During the War* (Atlanta: Franklin Printing and Publishing Co., 1902), 32–33.

273 **She hoped to see Union forces march in tomorrow:** Thomas Dyer, *Secret Yankees: The Union Circle in Confederate Atlanta* (Baltimore: Johns Hopkins University Press, 1999), Appendix B, "Miss Abby's Diary," July 21, 1864, 322–23.

274 **As the women walked their separate ways:** Mary A. H. Gay, *Life in Dixie During the War* (1892; rpt. Macon, GA: Mercer University Press, 2001), 158–63.

274 **"How could we run over those things":** Oliver Otis Howard, *Autobiography of Oliver Otis Howard*, Vol. 2 (New York: Baker & Taylor Co., 1908), 3.

275 **"Atlanta and its connections are worth a battle":** (Atlanta) *Daily Appeal*, July 20, 1864, quoted in "The War in Georgia," *New York Times*, July 29, 1864, 2.

275 **"entered the stores by force, robbing them of everything":** Grape, "The Siege of Atlanta," (Augusta) *Daily Constitutionalist*, July 29, 1864, 3.

276 **residents from the countryside came in to grab their share:** Albert Castel, *Decision in the West: The Atlanta Campaign of 1864* (Lawrence: University of Kansas Press, 1992), 389.

277 **continued in the saddle a few feet and then slumped to the ground:** Sam Watkins, *Company Aytch, or a Side Show of the Big Show*, ed. M. Thomas Inge (1882; rpt. New York: Plume, 1999), 154–57. On the death of McPherson, see William E. Strong, "The Death of General James B. McPherson," *The Atlanta Papers*, comp. Sydney C. Kerkis (Dayton, OH: Press of Morningside Bookshop, 1980), 505–39.

277 **he saw his horse lying dead beside him:** "Dear Ma," in the field before Atlanta, July 23, 1864.

278 **"Atlanta will not be given up":** Sarah "Sallie" Conley Clayton, *Requiem for a Lost City: A Memoir of Civil War Atlanta and the Old South*, ed. Robert S. Davis Jr. (Macon, GA: Mercer University Press, 1999), 125–28; "My Dear Sallie & Caro," Atlanta, July 25, 1864, in Clayton, *Requiem for a Lost City*, 175–76.

278 **"amounted to more than twice our own":** "Dear Ma," in the field before Atlanta, July 23, 1864.

278 **Sherman was "badly defeated":** Castel, *Decision in the West*, 410. Quote on 423.

278 **"who would not be a soldier and fight for his country?":** "Dear Lizzie," Thursday, July 26, 1864, Sunday morning, July 31, 1864, Allen T. Holliday Papers, MSS 116, box 1, folder 1, Atlanta History Center.

278 **"intended to hold the city":** Samuel P. Richards, *Diary* (typescript), Vol. 10, July 22, 1864, 4.

279 **The fighting that day very likely destroyed her property:** Dyer, *Secret Yankees*, Appendix B, "Miss Abby's Diary," July 21, 1864, Midnight, 324–28.

279 **"the blood trickling down":** Sarah Huff, *My Eighty Years in Atlanta* (n.p., 1937), ch. 4.

281 **they had dispatched all the wounded men:** Affidavits of Thomas G. W. Crussell, William Lewis, John Silvey, James Dunning, *Webster v. U.S.*, Southern Claims Commission, National Archives, CD 13502, folder 1. Testimony of Prince Ponder, *Ponder v. U.S.*, December 20, 1875, box 34, Southern Claims Commission, Record Group 217, National Archives, 9–10.

281 **"for with all the natural advantages of bushes":** To Ellen Ewing Sherman, in the field near Atlanta, July 26, 1864, in *Sherman's Civil War: Selected Correspondence of William T. Sherman, 1860–1865*, ed. Brooks D. Simpson and Jean V. Berlin (Chapel Hill: University of North Carolina Press, 1999), 672.

281 **"Let the Army of the Tennessee fight it out!":** Quoted in Castel, *Decision in the West*, 414. Castel and many others have criticized Sherman's failure to counterattack on July 22. See, for instance, the bitter comments of Henry Stone, a staff officer with the Army of the Cumberland, "The Strategy of the Campaign," in Kerkis, *The Atlanta Papers*, 158–59.

281 **"They can't take Atlanta unless they make a Vicksburg scrape of it"**: "Dear Lizzie," 26 July 1864.

282 **"singularly picturesque and startling in effect"**: Grape, "The Siege of Atlanta," (Augusta) *Daily Constitutionalist*, July 29, 1864, 3.

282 **"a fine house in plain sight"**: July 25, 1864, in the trenches one and a half miles from Atlanta, in Charles Fessenden Morse, *Letters Written During the Civil War, 1861–1865* (Boston: T. R. Marvin & Sons, Printers, 1898), 181–82.

282 **"A rifle bullet struck the board"**: July 31, 1864, near Atlanta, in Morse, *Letters*, 185.

282 **"gradually destroy the roads which make Atlanta a place worth having"**: To Ellen Ewing Sherman, in the field near Atlanta, July 26, 1864, in Simpson and Berlin, *Sherman's Civil War*, 672.

283 **"many of the pensioners we captured"**: July 29, 1864, Civil War Diary Henry D. Stanley, July 16, 1864–November 14, 1864, *The Siege & Capture of Atlanta Georgia*, Henry D. Stanley, 2nd Lieut., 20th Conn. Vol. Co. H, MSS645, box 2, folder 1, Atlanta History Center.

283 **fighting like "Devils & Indians"**: To Ellen Ewing Sherman, in the field near Atlanta, August 9, 1864, in Simpson and Berlin, *Sherman's Civil War*, 685.

284 **"make the inside of Atlanta too hot to be endured"**: Quoted in Stephen Davis, "'A Very Barbarous Mode of Carrying on War': Sherman's Artillery Bombardment of Atlanta, July 20–August 24, 1864," *Georgia Historical Quarterly* 89, no. 1 (spring 1995), 68.

## CHAPTER 23: GOODBYE, JOHNNY

287 **"You may take this to heart"**: Epsilon, "Gen. Sherman's Division, Near Atlanta, Friday, August 19, 1864," *New York Times*, September 1, 1864, 1.

288 **They decided to risk more shelling**: Mollie Smith, "Dodging Shells in Atlanta," *Atlanta Constitution*, March 24, 1929, 13.

289 **Nobody could calculate what course they would take**: William C. Noble, *Echoes from the Battlefield, or Southern Life During the War* (Atlanta: Franklin Printing and Publishing Co., 1902), 32–33.

289 **"at almost any time numbers of lighted shells"**: Noble, *Echoes from the Battlefield*, 34.

289 **Samuel was not there for that**: Samuel Richards, *Diary* (typescript), Vol. 10, August 1, 7, 14, 21, 1864, 5–8, 10, Atlanta History Center.

289 **"could distinctly hear loud cries"**: Quoted in Stephen Davis, "'A Very Barbarous Mode of Carrying on War': Sherman's Artillery Bombardment of Atlanta, July 20–August 24, 1864," *Georgia Historical Quarterly* 89, no. 1 (spring 1995): 85.

289 **Many families, especially the poorer ones**: Quoted in Davis, "A Very Barbarous Mode of Carrying on War,'" 81.

290 **"Let us destroy Atlanta and make it a desolation"**: Quoted in Davis, "A Very Barbarous Mode of Carrying on War,'" 68.

290 **His men buried him in a shallow grave**: "Dear Ella," August 4, 1864, in the line before Atlanta, Ga., Andrew Jackson Neal Papers, 1856–1881, MSS218, Emory University Manuscript, Archives, and Rare Book Library, MSS218.

291 **James Neal would have his chance at revenge**: "Dear Ma," August 24, 1864, Hd. Qtrs. 19th Ga. Vol.

291 **Most houses along Marietta Street:** Pilgrim, (Macon) *Daily Intelligencer*, August 25, 1864, 1.

292 **He directed that one of the four-and-a-half-inch navy siege guns:** Quoted in Davis, "'A Very Barbarous Mode of Carrying on War,'" 68, 81.

292 **Federal lookouts reported seeing "great commotion":** Davis, "'A Very Barbarous Mode of Carrying on War,'" 68.

292 **"Large fires were visible in the city":** Quoted in Davis, "'A Very Barbarous Mode of Carrying on War,'" 81.

292 **blasting him for being, he falsely claimed, "absent":** Pilgrim, (Macon) *Daily Intelligencer*, August 26, 1864, 1; August 23, 1864, 2.

292 **"And . . . if the city is to fall":** B, August 24, 1864, *Daily Intelligencer*, August 27, 1864, 2.

293 **nobody was arrested:** Mirglip, *Daily Intelligencer*, August 18, 1864, 2.

293 **"Our humane foes allowed us to get well to sleep":** Richards, *Diary*, Vol. 10, August 14, 1864, 8.

293 **Several passersby picked up the badly wounded man:** Wallace Reed, *History of Atlanta* (Syracuse: D. Mason & Co., Publishers, 1889), 191–92. Reed wrote the first complete history of Atlanta and was present as a boy during the siege. He appears to have been the first to recount, at 175, the since oft-retold killing of an unnamed child in the company of her parents, also unidentified, at the corner of Ellis and Ivy streets by the first shell fired into the city on July 20. The child's death remains unconfirmed and appears likely not to have occurred. For a refutation of Reed's original story of the first civilian death, see Stephen Davis, "How Many Civilians Died in Sherman's Bombardment of Atlanta?" *Atlanta History* 45, no. 4 (2003): 6–8. The dented lamppost struck by the shell that did kill Solomon Luckie is now kept eternally lit as a memorial flame, presently in place not far from its original location in Underground Atlanta.

294 **"I sat down and wept":** Emily E. Molineaux, *Lifetime Recollections: An Interesting Narrative of Life in the Southern States Before and During the Civil War* (1902; rpt. Read Books, 2008), 31–36.

295 **"It is . . . like living in the midst of a pestilence":** Richards, *Diary*, Vol. 10, August 21, 1864, 10.

295 **"It is said that about twenty lives have been destroyed":** Richards, *Diary*, Vol. 10, August 21, 1864, 10.

295 **107 citizens required amputation of limbs:** See Pilgrim, (Macon) *Daily Intelligencer*, August 25, 1864, 1.

295 **Even those relatively small numbers:** Casualty figures are cited in Davis, "How Many Civilians Died?" 19.

295 **"a fine concrete house":** Sam Watkins, *Company Aytch, or a Side Show of the Big Show*, ed. M. Thomas Inge (1882; rpt. New York: Plume, 1999), 165.

295 **Those nearby viewed the battered:** September 5, 1864, Civil War Diary Henry D. Stanley, July 16, 1864–November 14, 1864, *The Siege & Capture of Atlanta Georgia*, Henry D. Stanley, 2nd Lieut., 20th Conn. Vol. Co. H, MSS645, box 2, folder 1, Atlanta History Center.

295 **"many a gallant and noble fellow among them":** Watkins, *Company Aytch*, 168–69.

296 **"The old men looked sad and desponding":** Letters to Dear Lizzie, Friday morning, July 29, 1864, Sunday morning, July 31, 1864, camp near Atlanta, Au-

gust 3, 1864. A. (Allen) T. Holliday Papers, MSS 116, box 1, folder 4, Atlanta History Center.

296 **"It was a twenty-pounder":** August 8, 1864, near Atlanta, in Charles Fessenden Morse, *Letters Written During the Civil War, 1861–1865* (Boston: T. R. Marvin & Sons, Printers, 1898), 185–86.

296 **"This city has done and contributed more":** Quoted in Henry Hitchcock, *Marching with Sherman* (New Haven, CT: Yale University Press, 1927), 58.

296 **"Any sign of a let up on our part":** Letter to Lieutenant General Grant, from near Atlanta, 8 p.m., August 7, 1864, in *Sherman's Civil War: Selected Correspondence of William T. Sherman, 1860–1865*, ed. Brooks D. Simpson and Jean V. Berlin (Chapel Hill: University of North Carolina Press, 1999), 684.

297 **"So long as the feeling that all will end well enthuses us":** (Macon) *Daily Intelligencer*, August 3, 1864, 2.

297 **"I feel mortified that he holds us in check":** Quoted in Albert Castel, *Decision in the West: The Atlanta Campaign of 1864* (Lawrence: University of Kansas Press, 1992), 467.

298 **"will end the summer's campaign":** "A Gleam of Hope," (Macon) *Daily Intelligencer*, August 11, 1864, 2.

298 **Holliday penned in wonder:** "Dearest Lizzie," Friday morning, 9 o'clock, August 26, 1864, Holliday Papers, box 1, folder 9.

298 **"the enemy was retreating":** Richards, *Diary*, Vol. 10, August 27, 1864, 10.

298 **"I am coming home":** "Dearest Lizzie," Midnight, August 26, 1864, Holliday Papers, box 1, folder 9.

299 **It was signed, "YANK":** Pilgrim, reports of August 27 and 28, (Macon) *Daily Intelligencer*, August 30, 1864, 1.

## CHAPTER 24: THE FIRST BONFIRE

301 **"I think we will not be out but a short time now":** For Holliday quotes, see "Dearest Lizzie," 9 o'clock, August 26, 1864, A. (Allen) T. Holliday Papers, MSS 116, box 1, folder 9, Atlanta History Center. For the Confederate's quote, see Albert Castel, *Decision in the West: The Atlanta Campaign of 1864* (Lawrence: University of Kansas Press, 1992), 485.

301 **"Last night ... the enemy abandoned the Augusta railroad":** Quoted in Henry Stone, "The Siege and Capture of Atlanta, July 9 to September 8, 1864," *The Atlanta Papers*, comp. Sydney C. Kerkis (Dayton, OH: Press of Morningside Bookshop, 1980), 123.

302 **Military bands played in the streets:** Castel, *Decision in the West*, 486. Stephen Davis defends Hood against the frequent charge of befuddlement at Sherman's movement in this last phase of the campaign in *Atlanta Will Fall: Sherman, Joe Johnston, and the Yankee Heavy Battalions* (Lanham, MD: Rowman & Littlefield, 2001), 190.

302 **"one of the noblest acts of my whole life":** "Dearest Lizzie," Monday morning, August 29, 1864, Friday morning, 9 o'clock, August 26, 1864.

302 **"the old soldiers ... have a great anxiety":** "Dearest Lizzie," Friday morning, 9 o'clock, August 26, 1864.

302 **They "are going somewhere":** Samuel Richards, *Diary* (typescript), Vol. 10, August 27, 1864, 10–11, Atlanta History Center.

302 **"I wish they were safe in my pocket":** Richards, *Diary*, Vol. 10, August 29, 1864, 11.

302 **"Our supplies will soon be exhausted":** Quoted in Castel, *Decision in the West*, 467.

303 **"I rather think . . . today Hood's army is larger":** To Thomas Ewing Sr., in the field near Atlanta, August 11, 1864, in *Sherman's Civil War: Selected Correspondence of William T. Sherman, 1860–1865*, ed. Brooks D. Simpson and Jean V. Berlin (Chapel Hill: University of North Carolina Press, 1999), 690.

303 **The cavalry continued their raid deep into Tennessee:** Stone, "The Siege and Capture of Atlanta," 121.

304 **"a long, hazardous flank march":** Quoted in Castel, *Decision in the West*, 469–70, 474. For a participant's account of the Kilpatrick raid, see W. L. Curry, "Raid of the Union Cavalry, Commanded by General Judson Kilpatrick, Around the Confederate Army in Atlanta, August, 1864," in Kerkis, *The Atlanta Papers*, 597–622.

304 **an eleven-car train of munitions and food chugged into Atlanta:** Henry Stone, "The Siege and Capture of Atlanta," 122. Castel, *Decision in the West*, 472–74.

304 **"I will have to swing across":** Quoted in Castel, *Decision in the West*, 474.

305 **They found the torn-up earth cluttered:** Sam Watkins, *Company Aytch, or a Side Show of the Big Show*, ed. M. Thomas Inge (1882; rpt. New York: Plume, 1999), 174.

306 **"The enemy have drawn back":** Quoted in Stone, "The Siege and Capture of Atlanta," 123.

306 **"so we may rest perfectly satisfied":** Quoted in Castel, *Decision in the West*, 489.

306 **"success was actually crippling our armies":** William Tecumseh Sherman, *Memoirs of General W. T. Sherman*, 2nd ed. (New York: Penguin Classics, 2001), 479.

307 **"Fear of the Lord is the beginning of wisdom":** Sherman, *Memoirs*, 608–9.

307 **Destruction of the railroad was another psychological weapon:** Many works analyze Sherman's total war strategy. For a succinct presentation of it in the Atlanta Campaign context, see James M. McPherson, "Two Strategies of Victory: William T. Sherman in the Civil War," *Atlanta History* 33, no. 4 (winter 1989–1990): 5–17. Quote from 16.

308 **"the necessity would arise to send any troops to Jonesboro today":** Quoted in Castel, *Decision in the West*, 495.

308 **"A small portion—about a hundred thousand—were nigh about":** Watkins, *Company Aytch*, 175.

308 **"go at the enemy with bayonets fixed":** Quoted in Castel, *Decision in the West*, 498.

308 **"We did our level best to get up a fight":** Watkins, *Company Aytch*, 178–79.

309 **The men marched . . . "without any order":** Watkins, *Company Aytch*, 181–82.

309 **"I don't believe anybody recognizes":** Quoted in Stone, "The Siege and Capture of Atlanta," 127.

310 **Now they feared Confederate forces marching down:** Wallace Putnam Reed, *History of Atlanta, Georgia: With Illustrations and Biographical Sketches of Some of Its Prominent Men and Pioneers* (Atlanta: D. Mason & Co., 1889), 194.

310 **"by the sackful and the cartload":** Richards, *Diary*, Vol. 10, September 1, 1864, 12.

310 **"jarred the ground and broke the glass":** Richards, *Diary*, Vol. 10, September 1, 1864, 12.

310 **The "incessant discharge" of explosions:** "The Anniversary of Atlanta's Fall," *Atlanta Constitution*, September 3, 1900, 4.

311 **Only a cavalry regiment remained behind:** Sherman, *Memoirs*, 476.

312 **"twisted into the most curious shapes imaginable":** September 5, 1864, Civil War Diary Henry D. Stanley, July 16, 1864–November 14, 1864, *The Siege & Capture of Atlanta Georgia*, Henry D. Stanley, 2nd Lieut., 20th Conn. Vol. Co. H, MSS645, box 2, folder 1, Atlanta History Center.

312 **Atlanta was being consumed:** Copy (typescript) of diary of Mary Rawson, Wife of Capt. John D. Ray, Capt. of 1st Ga. Vols. and daughter of E. E. Rawson of Atlanta, August 31, 1864, 1, Rawson-Collier-Harris Families, MSS 36, Atlanta History Center. Reed, *History of Atlanta*, 194.

313 **A last big blast went off shortly before dawn:** "Dear Lizzie," September 2, 1864, Holliday Papers, box 1, folder 10.

315 **Coburn had Calhoun write out a surrender note:** Affidavit of James M. Calhoun, Mayor of Atlanta, as to Facts in Regard to Surrender of Atlanta, September 2, 1864, Sworn to his Son W. L. C., on July 31, 1865, Calhoun Papers, MSS 50, box 2.4, oversized folder 1, Atlanta History Center. Affidavit of Thomas Kile, James Calhoun to Reuben Arnold, *Webster v. U.S.*, CD 13502, folder 4, National Archives, Washington, D.C.

316 **"She was a splendid looking woman":** Reports of Capt. H. M. Scott, Col. J. Coburn, and Gen. H. W. Slocum, September 3, 1864, in Thomas H. Martin, *Atlanta and Its Builders: A Comprehensive History of the Gate City of the South* (Atlanta: Century Memorial Publishing, 1902), 598–603. "Old Home Spared by Sherman's Torch Is Soon to Give Way for Improvement," *The Constitution*, February 18, 1906, B8. Richards, *Diary*, Vol. 10, September 2, 1864, 13. A. O. Brainerd, "Address to the Ladies—Wives of the Veterans in the G. A. R. Room, St. Albans (April 15, 1895)," quoted in Thomas Dyer, *Secret Yankees: The Union Circle in Confederate Atlanta* (Baltimore: Johns Hopkins University Press, 1999), 193–94.

## CHAPTER 25: THE SECOND BONFIRE

318 **they flew over the fence into the garden:** Noble C. Williams, *Echoes from the Battlefield; or, Southern Life During the War* (Atlanta: Franklin Printing and Publishing Co., 1902), 41–42.

318 **picked up books "and *paid* for them":** Samuel Richards, *Diary* (typescript), Vol. 10, September 2 (probably misdated from September 3), 1864, 13–14, Atlanta History Center.

319 **"My Lord, I thought they had come here to protect us":** *Daily Intelligencer*, December 23, 1864, 1. Deposition of Joseph A. Blood, *Webster v. U.S.*, Southern Claims Commission, CD 13502, folder 4, National Archives.

319 **It would take more than a decade pursuing his claim:** Claim of Prince Ponder, December 20, 1875, Southern Claims Commission, Record Group 217, box 34, National Archives, 1, 13–15, 24.

320 **Comey's initial—happily performed—official duty:** The Confederate flag Comey took down is now in Lexington, Massachusetts, at the Historical Society Museum.

320 **He took the county courtroom as his office:** Charles Fessenden Morse, *Letters Written During the Civil War, 1861–1865* (Boston: T. R. Marvin & Sons, Printers, 1898), 187.

320 **Comey moved about town the rest of his first day:** *A Legacy of Valor: The Memoirs and Letters of Captain Henry Newton Comey, 2nd Massachusetts Infantry*, ed. Lyman Richard Comey (Knoxville: University of Tennessee Press, 2004), 193–94.

320 **spirits of sufficiently good quality:** Charles F. Morse, "Personal Recollections of the Occupation of Atlanta and Sherman's March to the Sea 1864" (typescript). Houghton Library, Modern Books and Manuscripts, Harvard College Library, MS Am2058, item 12, 5.

320 **"strange to go about Atlanta now":** Richards, *Diary*, Vol. 10, September 4, 1864, 14–15.

321 **"General Sherman has taken Atlanta":** Quoted in Albert Castel, *Decision in the West: The Atlanta Campaign of 1864* (Lawrence: University of Kansas Press, 1992), 529.

321 **"our present task . . . well done":** Castel, *Decision in the West*, 532, 534.

321 **Those few words would be repeated:** To Henry W. Halleck, September 3, 1864, in the field near Lovejoy's Station, in *Sherman's Civil War: Selected Correspondence of William T. Sherman, 1860–1865*, ed. Brooks D. Simpson and Jean V. Berlin (Chapel Hill: University of North Carolina Press, 1999), 695–96.

321 **"My movement has been perfectly successful":** To Ellen Ewing Sherman, September 3, 1864, in the field 26 miles south of Atlanta, in Simpson and Berlin, *Sherman's Civil War*, 696.

321 **It was time to rest:** To Henry W. Halleck, September 3, 1864, in Simpson and Berlin, *Sherman's Civil War*, 696.

322 **"The marches, battles, sieges, and other military operations":** Quoted in William Tecumseh Sherman, *Memoirs of General W. T. Sherman*, 2nd ed. (New York: Penguin Classics, 2001), 478.

322 **"an immense throng" of citizens paraded:** "Rejoicings Over the Victory," *New York Times*, September 4, 1864, 1.

322 **Peace would come only, he now declared, on the "one condition" of Union:** Quoted in James M. McPherson, *Battle Cry of Freedom: The Civil War Era* (New York: Oxford University Press, 1988), 771, 776.

323 **"represent a strong Union sentiment":** Comey, *A Legacy of Valor*, 194–95.

324 **"for the purpose of claiming personal satisfaction":** *Chattanooga Gazette* report of September 11, 1864, reprinted in (Macon) *Daily Intelligencer*, September 18, 1864, 2.

324 **More than a few Confederates thought the mayor deserved to be strung up:** (Macon) *Daily Intelligencer*, September 10, 28, 1864, 2.

324 **"The family . . . were very glad":** Morse, *Letters*, 188–90.

324 **"the identical ones who remained in the city":** Thomas Dyer, *Secret Yankees: The Union Circle in Confederate Atlanta* (Baltimore: Johns Hopkins University Press, 1999), 196. For the Lee quote, see *Daily Intelligencer*, October 27, 1864, in Dyer, *Secret Yankees*, 201–2.

325 **"There are differences of opinion":** Morse, *Letters*, 188–90.

326 **It was nothing others had not seen repeated:** Robert G. Athearn, "An Indiana Doctor Marches with Sherman: The Diary of James Comfort Patten," *Indiana Magazine of History* 49, no. 4 (December 1953): 409.

326 **The South, he expected, would draw "two important conclusions":** Sherman states in his memoirs that he rode into the city on September 8, but official records of his correspondence place his arrival on September 7. See Castel, *Deci-*

*sion in the West*, 626n1. For the first and final Sherman quotes, see Sherman, *Memoirs*, 479.

326 **"We must kill these three hundred thousand":** To Ellen Ewing Sherman, September 17, 1864, Atlanta, Ga., in Simpson and Berlin, *Sherman's Civil War*, 717.

327 **"absolute certainty . . . [in my] policy's justness and . . . wisdom":** To Henry W. Halleck, September 4, 1864, in the field near Lovejoy's Station, Ga., in Simpson and Berlin, *Sherman's Civil War*, 697.

328 **"not bound by the laws of war":** The exchange of letters is reprinted in its entirety in Sherman, *Memoirs*, 487–92. On Sherman's decidedly racist attitudes toward blacks in his army, see Clarence L. Mohr, "The Atlanta Campaign and the African American Experience in Civil War Georgia," in Lesley J. Gordon and John C. Inscoe, eds., *Inside the Confederate Nation: Essays in Honor of Emory M. Thomas* (Baton Rouge: Louisiana State University Press, 2005), 272–94.

328 **In the South, it confirmed Sherman's stature as "the brute":** To Eugene Casserly, September 17, 1864, in Simpson and Berlin, *Sherman's Civil War*, 713.

328 **"What a 'buster' that [Sherman] is!":** Adams is quoted in Simpson and Berlin, *Sherman's Civil War*, 702–3.

329 **"The people of the U.S. have too much sense":** To Thomas Ewing Jr., Atlanta, September 17, 1864, in Simpson and Berlin, *Sherman's Civil War*, 715.

329 **"He is the most original character":** Morse, *Letters*, 192.

331 **"the mad passions of men cool down":** All of the letters exchanged among Sherman, Hood, and Calhoun, September 7–14, 1864, appear in Sherman, *Memoirs*, 486–96.

331 **"continually besieged with anxious faces":** *Chattanooga Gazette* report of September 11, 1864, reprinted (Macon) *Daily Intelligencer*, September 18, 1864, 2.

331 **"Do not judge from appearances":** Quoted in Dyer, *Secret Yankees*, 203–4.

332 **"So . . . our negro property has all vanished into air":** Richards, *Diary*, Vol. 10, September 9 and 21, 1864, 15–18.

333 **"that we should spend this day in the Yankee Gotham":** Richards, *Diary*, Vol. 10, December 25, 1864, January 1, 1865, 35–37. The number of people expelled south is well documented. The number who went north is based on scholarly estimates. On sources for the Atlanta exile numbers, see Dyer, *Secret Yankees*, 360n65.

333 **"Instead of robbing them not an article was taken away":** Calhoun's letter to Sherman does not appear to have survived, but he mentions it in the same letter quoted: To Ellen Ewing Sherman, Atlanta, October 1, 1864, in Simpson and Berlin, *Sherman's Civil War*, 728.

333 **"a real military town with no women boring me":** To Ellen Ewing Sherman, Atlanta, September 17, 1864, in Simpson and Berlin, *Sherman's Civil War*, 717.

333 **"One month ago, we were lying on the ground":** Morse, *Letters, 1861–1865*, 193.

334 **"another still more decisive move in war":** To Philemon E. Ewing, Atlanta, September 23, 1864, in Simpson and Berlin, *Sherman's Civil War*, 724.

334 **"Our cavalry and people will harass and destroy":** *The Papers of Jefferson Davis*, Vol. 11, *September 1864–May 1865*, ed., Lynda Lasswell Crist, Barbara J. Rozek, and Kenneth H. Williams (Baton Rouge: Louisiana State University Press, 2003), 61.

334 **He seemed to be warning the president:** To President Lincoln, September 28, 1864, Atlanta, in Simpson and Berlin, *Sherman's Civil War*, 726.

334 **"We cannot remain on the defensive":** To Ulysses S. Grant, October 1, 1864, Atlanta, in Simpson and Berlin, *Sherman's Civil War*, 727.

334 **"I can make the march and make Georgia howl":** To Ulysses S. Grant, October 9, 1864, Atlanta, in Simpson and Berlin, *Sherman's Civil War*, 731.

334 **"wait until October, when the corn [will] be ripe":** Morse, "Personal Recollections of the Occupation of Atlanta and Sherman's March to the Sea 1864," Harvard College Library, MS Am2058, item 12, 6.

335 **Tall brick industrial smokestacks:** Morse, "Personal Recollections," 9.

336 **"but a few busy hands soon reduced it to nothing":** November 14, 1864, Civil War Diary Henry D. Stanley, July 16, 1864–November 14, 1864, *The Siege & Capture of Atlanta Georgia*, Henry D. Stanley, 2nd Lieut., 20th Conn. Vol. Co. H, MSS645, box 2, folder 1.

336 **"We followed after, being the last United States troops to leave Atlanta":** Morse, *Letters*, 201–2.

## CHAPTER 26: THE NEW SOUTH

337 **"may not be war . . . but rather statesmanship":** To Ulysses S. Grant, in the field, Kingston, Ga., November 6, 1864, in *Sherman's Civil War: Selected Correspondence of William T. Sherman, 1860–1865*, ed. Brooks D. Simpson and Jean V. Berlin (Chapel Hill: University of North Carolina Press, 1999), 750. Many books tell the story of the March to the Sea; I found most useful to be Lee Kennett, *Marching Through Georgia: The Story of Soldiers and Civilians During Sherman's Campaign* (New York: HarperCollins Publishers, 1995).

338 **"within its corporate limits lay the last remains":** *Daily Intelligencer*, December 20, 1864, 2.

338 **"It seemed to start a long way off":** Sarah Huff, *My Eighty Years in Atlanta* (n.p., 1937), chs. 6 and 7.

339 **"Ruin . . . universal ruin was the exclamation of all":** *Daily Intelligencer*, December 23, 1864, 2.

339 **"Bushwhackers, robbers and deserters, and citizens from the surrounding country":** W. P. Howard to Joseph E. Brown, governor of Georgia, Atlanta, Ga., December 7, 1864, available at http://georgiainfo.galileo.usg.edu/atldestr.htm.

339 **The citizen police soon found robbers:** Noble C. Williams, *Echoes from the Battlefield; or, Southern Life During the War* (Atlanta: Franklin Printing and Publishing Co., 1902), 49.

340 **He had taken the train as far as Jonesboro:** "Reminiscences of Patrick H. Calhoun," *Atlanta Historical Bulletin* 1, no. 6 (February 1932): 45.

340 **He and the city council resumed their meetings:** City Council Minutes, January 6, 1865, Vol. 4, January 17, 1862, to June 1, 1866.

340 **"That which built Atlanta and made it a flourishing city":** *Daily Intelligencer*, December 23, 1864, 2, and December 20, 1864, 1.

341 **"Treat them as kind as you can":** To Dearest Lizzie, September 5, 1864, Allen T. Holliday Papers, MSS 116, box 1, folder 2, Atlanta History Center.

341 **his great-great-grandson farms the same land Holliday did:** Author's conversation and visit to family property with Holliday's great-granddaughter, Mary Ann Bentley, and great-great-grandson, Frank Bentley, on July 15, 2007.

341 **"as a Christmas gift the City of Savannah":** To Abraham Lincoln, Savannah Ga., December 22, 1864, in Simpson and Berlin, *Sherman's Civil War*, 772.

341 **"There seems no end but utter annihilation":** To Ellen Ewing Sherman, in the field, Savannah, December 25, 1864, in Simpson and Berlin, *Sherman's Civil War*, 778.

342 **"our city [is] at least relieved from their presence":** "What the Enemy Are Welcome to from Atlanta," *Daily Intelligencer*, December 22, 1864, 2.

342 **"Atlanta is better off in recognizing":** *Daily Intelligencer*, December 23 and 22, 1864, 1.

342 **a government-approved blockade-running outfit:** On Amherst Stone's blockade-running scheme, see Thomas Dyer, *Secret Yankees: The Union Circle in Confederate Atlanta* (Baltimore: Johns Hopkins University Press, 1999), 115ff.

342 **until she went North following Sherman's expulsion order:** On Cyrena Stone's postwar life, see Dyer, *Secret Yankees*, 263–64.

343 **provided her sister, Louisa M. Whitney, with the background:** Cyrena Stone's sister's book is Louisa M. Whitney, *Goldie's Inheritance: A Story of the Siege of Atlanta* (Burlington, VT: Free Press Association, 1903).

343 **"denied all privileges of captured soldiers":** Quoted in Dyer, *Secret Yankees*, 200–1.

344 **Many simply used their power to enrich themselves:** "Meeting of Loyal Georgians in New York," *Daily Intelligencer*, March 17, 1865, 2.

344 **A bribe of $4,000 in Confederate money:** Arthur Reed Taylor, "From the Ashes: Atlanta During Reconstruction, 1865–1876" (PhD diss., Emory University, 1970), 24, 42. Dyer, *Secret Yankees*, 214–16.

344 **All his ventures failed:** Robert Scott Davis, "Guarding the Gate City from Itself: George W. Lee and Conflict in Civil War Atlanta" (typescript), article in progress, 32, 45–48.

345 **"Soon . . . the other railroads":** "The Whistle of the Locomotive," *Daily Intelligencer*, March 5, 1865, 2.

345 **"Building business lots are in great demand":** *Daily Intelligencer*, March 5, 1865, 2.

345 **A new instant city was rising:** On the rebirth of postwar Atlanta, see James Michael Russell, *Atlanta 1847–1890: City Building in the Old South and the New* (Baton Rouge: Louisiana State University Press, 1988).

345 **"We have removed incredible amounts of dirt and rubbish":** *Daily Intelligencer*, January 10, 1866, quoted in Russell, *Atlanta 1847–1890*, 171.

345 **"In every direction we notice that the rubbish is being removed":** *Daily Intelligencer*, June 27, 1865, 2.

346 **"busy life is resuming its sway":** Samuel P. Richards, *Diary* (typescript), Vol. 10, August 10, 1865, April 25, 1865, 59–60.

346 **Today it continues to operate:** Frank J. Byrne, "Rebellion and Retail: A Tale of Two Merchants in Confederate Atlanta," *Georgia Historical Quarterly* 89, no. 1 (spring 1995): 33. For a description of Richards, see Ella Mae Thornton, "Mr. S. P. Richards," *Atlanta Historical Bulletin* 3 (December 1937): 51–53. On today's S. P. Richards Company, see www.sprichards.com/about/index.php.

346 **squalor "in the suburbs of Atlanta":** *Daily Intelligencer*, August 17, 1865, 2.

347 **Fortunately, most were willing to share:** "Reminiscences of Patrick H. Calhoun," *Atlanta Historical Bulletin* 1, no. 6 (February 1932): 45.

347 **"Bob was better off than any of us":** Quoted in Thomas G. Dyer, "Half Slave, Half Free: Unionist Robert Webster in Confederate Atlanta" in *Inside the*

*Confederate Nation: Essays in Honor of Emory M. Thomas*, ed. Emory M. Thomas, Lesley Jill Gordon, and John C. Inscoe (Baton Rouge: Louisiana State University Press, 2005), 303.

347 **the fey Sallie Clayton soon arrived:** Sarah Conley Clayton, *Requiem for a Lost City: A Memoir of Civil War Atlanta and the Old South*, ed. Robert S. Davis Jr. (Macon, GA: Mercer University Press, 1999), 154–57.

347 **"I could get more if I wanted it":** Quoted in Dyer, "Half Slave, Half Free," 303–4.

347 **"I love the noble name of Yancey":** "What Bob Says," (Atlanta) *Daily Constitution*, July 18, 1879, 4.

348 **Steele and many other whites refused to accept:** *Daily Intelligencer*, March 31, 1865, 2.

348 **Henry, his cobbler father Festus, mother Isabella, and four brothers returned:** Jane Eppinga, *Henry Ossian Flipper: West Point's First Black Graduate* (Plano, TX: Wordware Publishing, 1996), 11–12.

348 **Henry, who as a boy had watched soldiers marching past:** Henry Ossian Flipper, *The Colored Cadet at West Point: Autobiography of Lieut. Henry Ossian Flipper, U. S. A., First Graduate of Color from the U. S. Military Academy* (New York: Homer Lee & Co., 1878), 12. Henry Flipper was dishonorably discharged from the army after being falsely charged with—and found innocent of—embezzlement but having been found guilty of lying about his attempts to hide a deficiency in the base commissary accounts under his responsibility. He spent his life trying to disprove the accusation and have his discharge terms revoked. In 1999 President William Clinton issued a historic first posthumously granted presidential pardon of Flipper.

349 **The legal wrangling continued for seven years:** "A Queer Suit, This," *Atlanta Constitution*, May 29, 1895, 8.

349 **Upon the ashes of Atlanta, African Americans erected the foundations:** On the transition from slavery to freedom in Atlanta, see Jerry John Thornbery, "The Development of Black Atlanta, 1865–1885" (PhD diss., University of Maryland, 1977). For a particularly valuable study of the situation of black women throughout the South and in Atlanta in particular, see Tera W. Hunter, *To 'Joy My Freedom: Southern Black Women's Lives and Labors After the Civil War* (Cambridge, MA: Harvard University Press, 1997), 1–43.

349 **"We were a mere handful of devoted braves":** Sam Watkins, *Company Aytch, or a Side Show of the Big Show*, ed. M. Thomas Inge (1882; rpt. New York: Plume, 1999), 199.

351 **Out of Watkins's original 3,200-man regiment:** Watkins, *Company Aytch*, 207–9.

351 **He caught a ball in the shoulder that forced him off the field:** After the war, Morse moved from his Massachusetts home to Kansas City, where he was a successful stockyard manager. He was portrayed in the 1989 motion picture *Glory* about his closest friend from the 2nd Massachusetts, Robert Gould Shaw, who became the commander of the all-black 54th Massachusetts Infantry.

351 **When James Neal led his Georgia regiment:** *Daily Intelligencer*, April 26, 1865, 1.

351 **"I committed an error in not overwhelming Johnston's army":** William Tecumseh Sherman, *Memoirs of General W. T. Sherman*, 2nd ed. (New York: Penguin Classics, 2001), 661.

352 **"by force the horses and mules"**: "Mob Violence," *Daily Intelligencer*, May 5, 1865, 2.

352 **"further resistance to our fate"**: *Daily Intelligencer*, May 13, 1865, 2.

353 **"We are reminded as we gaze upon the victorious banner"**: *Daily Intelligencer*, May 18, 1864, 2.

353 **Quickly asking for and receiving a pardon**: "James M. Calhoun, Atlanta, Ga., Rebellion, Filed July 19, 1865, Pardoned July 24, 1865," Case Files of Applications from Former Confederates for Presidential Pardons ("Amnesty Papers"), 1865–67, M1003, National Archives.

354 **The resolution was adopted "unanimously and warmly"**: *Daily Intelligencer*, June 27, 1865, 1. Thomas H. Martin, *Atlanta and Its Builders, A Comprehensive History of the Gate City of the South* (Atlanta: Century Memorial Publishing Co., 1902), 1–5.

## EPILOGUE: SHERMAN'S RETURN

356 **"Ring the fire bells! The town will be gone in forty minutes!"**: "Gen. Sherman in Atlanta," *New York Times*, February 2, 1879, 2, reprint "From the Atlanta (Ga.) *Constitution*," January 30, 1879.

356 **"more like New York merchants"**: Quoted in James Michael Russell, *Atlanta 1847–1890: City Building in the Old South and the New* (Baton Rouge: Louisiana State University Press, 1988), 127.

357 **real estate values had plummeted**: Russell, *Atlanta 1847–1890*, 117.

357 **James Calhoun had hoped his brother Ezekiel might succeed him**: *Daily Intelligencer*, December 7, 1865, 3.

357 **Though "opposed" to what eventually became the Fourteenth Amendment**: On the debate over the Fourteenth Amendment and national and regional politics surrounding its passage, see Eric Foner, *Reconstruction: America's Unfinished Revolution, 1863–1877* (New York: Harper & Row, 1988), 251–71. On the debates within Atlanta, see Thomas H. Martin, *Atlanta and Its Builders: A Comprehensive History of the Gate City of the South*, Vol. 2 (Atlanta: Century Memorial Publishing Co., 1902), 27–38.

357 **"I find nothing . . . to regret or condemn"**: "Georgia," *New York Times*, November 11, 1866, 5.

358 **he believed there would come a right time**: On Sherman's 1879 tour of the South, see John F. Marszalek, "Celebrity in Dixie: Sherman Tours the South, 1879," *Georgia Historical Quarterly* 66, no. 3 (fall 1982): 368–83.

358 **Sherman had retained his love for the South**: On Sherman's continued fidelity to the South after the war, see John F. Marszalek, *Sherman: A Soldier's Passion for Order* (Carbondale: Southern Illinois University Press, 2007), 360–76.

359 **"operations against the hostile Sioux"**: Letter to Philip H. Sheridan, January 29, 1877, quoted in Foner, *Reconstruction*, 579.

359 **He was devoted to the needs of Confederate veterans**: "Sherman in Atlanta," no date, no source, newspaper clipping, Calhoun Papers, Atlanta History Center.

360 **"great admiration" for Atlanta's "pluck and energy"**: All quotes are from "Gen. Sherman in Atlanta," *New York Times*, February 2, 1879.

360 **"There are several localities which I wish to see again":** "Gen. Sherman," *New York Times*, February 3, 1879, 2, reprint "From the Atlanta (Ga.) *Constitution*," January 31, 1879.

360 **"He was a noble-hearted, true man":** "Sherman in Atlanta," no date, no source, newspaper clipping, Calhoun Papers, Atlanta History Center.

360 **"done some good, something to make men feel more national":** Sherman to Henry S. Turner, March 9, 1879, quoted in Marszalek, "Celebrity in Dixie," 381.

361 **"Yes, it was terrible":** "Gen. Sherman," *New York Times*, February 3, 1879.

# ACKNOWLEDGMENTS

B Y THEIR VERY NATURE Civil War histories are adjunctive and conversational, text to text over the years. Historians rely upon participant documents and contemporary reports. Further we depend upon—even when we disagree with—the vital present and past research and interpretation of events of such consequence that every American life, whether perceived as such or not, has since been shaped by them. I thank all the living and the dead with whom I conversed in the course of writing this book.

Many people very much still with us helped me in my research for this book. I made numerous research visits and spent many weeks in Atlanta and elsewhere in Georgia. I always encountered hospitality and helpfulness everywhere I went. The collections of the beautiful Atlanta History Center's Kenan Research Center were indispensible and the staff members were invariably welcoming and professional. In particular I thank the former research manager Beth McLean and reference manager Sue VerHoef. I also received valuable assistance from archivists at several other Atlanta-area and Georgia research centers: the Robert W. Woodruff Library of the Atlanta University Center; Emory University Manuscript, Archives, and Rare Book Library; the Auburn Avenue Research Library; and the University of Georgia Hargrett Rare Book and Manuscript Library. Other university libraries assisted me with many different phases of my work. In particular I am grateful to the magnificent Yale University Library, Beinecke Rare Book and Manuscript Library, the Cushing/Whitney Medical Library interlibrary loan services managed by Vermetha Polite, and the Wilson Library of the University of North Carolina at Chapel Hill. I also drew upon manuscript resources of Harvard College Library's Houghton Library and the University of Iowa Library. The staff at the Chickamauga and Chattanooga National Military and Kennesaw Mountain National Battlefield Parks led me to a better understanding of the vast and tragic events that took place there.

Many other individuals helped me in ways that were essential to the completion of this book. Mike Fillon, fellow freelancer, was a terrific friend and companion as we drove the byways of the Atlanta Campaign and visited the Funk Heritage Center and Southern Museum of Civil War and Locomotive History. His son Evan Fillon ably helped me with research. University of Georgia professor emeritus of history Thomas Dyer was unstintingly generous in guiding me to resources on the Unionist circle in Atlanta and sharing those already in his personal archives. His colleague Lee Kennett also responded to my queries, as did James M. Russell, history professor at the University of Tennessee at Chattanooga.

# ACKNOWLEDGMENTS

Robert Scott Davis, Jr., professor of history at Wallace State College in Hanceville, Alabama, shared work in progress on George Washington Lee and photographs of Lee in his possession. Sam Reed, Sexton of Oakland Cemetery, and Larry Upthegrove, member of its board of trustees, provided historical insights into that magnificent burial ground. In learning about Allen T. Holliday, I was ably assisted by Stephanie Macchia and Louise Denard of the Washington (Wilkes) Historical Museum, and owe a debt of gratitude to Mary Ann Bentley, Holliday's great-granddaughter, and Frank Bentley, his great-great-grandson, who shared family history and welcomed me into the original Holliday plantation home and grounds. Linda Chestnut enabled that access, and she and her daughter Caroline Chestnut Leslie provided me with historic images of A.T. and Lizzie Holliday.

Jack Hadley of the Jack Hadley Black History Museum of Thomasville guided me to information about Henry Ossian Flipper. Dr. William King shared Flipper family history with me. Independent historian Thomas Phillips knows much about Henry O. Flipper's life and shared his knowledge and insights freely with me. Thomas Hill of the Thomas County Museum of History provided very helpful information about the Ponder family. Mike Bunn of the Columbus Museum directed me to resources for the Creek War of 1835–1836. Timothy Long of the Georgia Institute of Technology and Jeffry W. Munsey of the Tennessee Valley Authority informed me about seismic activity in and around Atlanta during the period under study. Judith Johnson of the Connecticut Historical Society and Ann Arcari of the Farmington Public Library ably assisted me. Conversation, correspondence, sparkling drinks, and spirited wit—and often, at the same time, the reverse—shared with Debby Applegate, Stephen Fox, Mark Oppenheimer, Robert Farrell, Zach Morowitz, Michael Fitzsousa, Nathaniel Philbrick, Lee Branch, Walter Patten, Jr., Robert Harris, and others encouraged me and informed my work. I apologize to the many others whose assistance I failed to credit here.

My editor Clive Priddle commands my deepest respect for his ability to mold a long work into a coherent narrative whole. He was as patient and as eager as an editor should be in dealing with a tardy author. Other people at PublicAffairs have been true compatriots, including Whitney Peeling, Tessa Shanks, Laura Stine, Annie Lenth, and mapmaker Christen Erichsen. My agents, first and foremost Talia Rosenblatt Cohen and then Laura Dail of the Laura Dail Literary Agency, have shepherded this book along with warm and capable hands.

It need not be reiterated, but must: Though I benefited from the help of many, any errors of fact or interpretation are my own.

This project required the conversations, support, and laughter of friends and family members too numerous to name. You know who you are and my gratitude to you is abounding. Above all and through it all, I thank my wife, Jodi, my daughter, Rebecca, and son, Charlie, for your love and patience with a book that took far longer to complete than Sherman needed to conquer Atlanta. I dedicate this to you with love to the treetops, clouds and beyond.

*—Marc Wortman*
*March 2009*
*New Haven*

# PHOTOGRAPH CREDITS

## SECTION ONE

**Page 1**

Top left: Long Cane Creek Massacre Stone (Photo by Bob Edmonds)

Top right: Senator John C. Calhoun (Library of Congress, Prints & Photographs Division)

Bottom left: Senator Daniel Webster (Library of Congress, Prints & Photographs Division)

Bottom right: James M. Calhoun (Atlanta History Center Kenan Research Center)

**Pages 2–3**

Historical rendering by Wilbur G. Kurtz (Atlanta History Center Kenan Research Center)

**Page 4**

Top: Crawford, Frazer & Co. slave market (Library of Congress, Prints & Photographs Division)

Bottom: Looking north on Washington Street (Library of Congress, Prints & Photographs Division)

**Page 5**

Top: Train rolling into the car shed (Library of Congress, Prints & Photographs Division)

Bottom: Alabama Street (Library of Congress, Prints & Photographs Division)

**Page 6**

Top: Samuel P. Richards (Atlanta History Center Kenan Research Center)

Bottom left: Benjamin C. Yancey (University of North Carolina at Chapel Hill, Wilson Library Manuscripts Department)

Bottom center: Jared I. Whitaker (Atlanta History Center Kenan Research Center)

Bottom right: George W. Adair (Atlanta History Center Kenan Research Center)

**Page 7**

Top: *Intelligencer* offices (Library of Congress, Prints & Photographs Division)

Bottom: Atlanta City Hall and Fulton County Courthouse (Library of Congress, Prints & Photographs Division)

**Page 8**

Top left: Sarah "Sallie" Conley Clayton (Atlanta History Center, Courtesy Robert Scott Davis)

Top right: Clayton Family house (Atlanta History Center Kenan Research Center)

Bottom left: Colonel George W. Lee (Lee/Huss Family Papers, Georgia Archives, Courtesy Robert Scott Davis)

Bottom right: Captain William Lowndes Calhoun and Mary Jane Oliver (Atlanta History Center Kenan Research Center)

## SECTION TWO

**Page 1**

Top: Engraving of Union forces (*Frank Leslie's Illustrated, Famous Leaders and Battle Scenes of the Civil War*)

Bottom left: General Joseph E. Johnston (National Archives and Records Administration 111-B-1782 CW-144_2)

Bottom center: General John B. Hood (National Archives and Records Administration, 111-B-5274 CW-142_2)

Bottom right: General William T. Sherman (Library of Congress Prints & Photographs Division)

**Page 2**

Top left: Sam Watkins (Courtesy of Ruth Hill Fulton McAllister, Sam Watkins' great granddaughter)

Top right: Colonel Charles F. Morse (U.S. Army Military History Institute Civil War Photograph Collections, 2 SC469-RG98S-88.46)

Bottom left: Allen T. Holliday (Courtesy of Caroline Chesnut Leslie)

Bottom right: Lizzie Holliday (Courtesy of Caroline Chesnut Leslie)

**Page 3**

Top: Ponder house (Library of Congress Prints & Photographs Division)

Bottom: Ponder estate (Library of Congress Prints & Photographs Division)

**Page 4**

Top and middle: *Harper's Weekly* engravings (*Harper's* magazine)

Bottom: Georgia Railroad Roundhouse ruins (Library of Congress Prints & Photographs Division)

**Page 5**

Top: Fort Hood (Library of Congress Prints & Photographs Division)

Bottom: Huff family house (Atlanta History Center Kenan Research Center)

**Page 6**

Top: Ruins of the Georgia Railroad (National Archives and Records Administration, 111-B-4786 CW-083)

Bottom: Postwar Peachtree Street (Library of Congress Prints & Photographs Division)

**Page 7**

Top: Car shed (Library of Congress Prints & Photographs Division)

Bottom: Union railroad demolition crew (Library of Congress Prints & Photographs Division)

**Page 8**

Top: Engraving of Battle of Bentonville (*Frank Leslie's Illustrated, Famous Leaders and Battle Scenes of the Civil War*)

Bottom left: Henry O. Flipper (National Park Service: Fort Davis National Historic Site, Texas)

Bottom right: Ruins of the car shed (Library of Congress Prints & Photographs Division)

# INDEX

MARC WORTMAN is the author of *The Millionaires'
Unit: The Aristocratic Flyboys Who Fought the Great War
and Invented American Air Power*, now in development
as a feature film. An award-winning freelance writer,
his work has appeared in numerous national magazines. Born in St. Louis, MO, he grew up in Maryland. He now lives in New Haven with his wife,
daughter, and son.

PublicAffairs is a publishing house founded in 1997. It is a tribute to the standards, values, and flair of three persons who have served as mentors to countless reporters, writers, editors, and book people of all kinds, including me.

I. F. STONE, proprietor of *I. F. Stone's Weekly*, combined a commitment to the First Amendment with entrepreneurial zeal and reporting skill and became one of the great independent journalists in American history. At the age of eighty, Izzy published *The Trial of Socrates*, which was a national bestseller. He wrote the book after he taught himself ancient Greek.

BENJAMIN C. BRADLEE was for nearly thirty years the charismatic editorial leader of *The Washington Post*. It was Ben who gave the *Post* the range and courage to pursue such historic issues as Watergate. He supported his reporters with a tenacity that made them fearless and it is no accident that so many became authors of influential, best-selling books.

ROBERT L. BERNSTEIN, the chief executive of Random House for more than a quarter century, guided one of the nation's premier publishing houses. Bob was personally responsible for many books of political dissent and argument that challenged tyranny around the globe. He is also the founder and longtime chair of Human Rights Watch, one of the most respected human rights organizations in the world.

· · ·

For fifty years, the banner of Public Affairs Press was carried by its owner Morris B. Schnapper, who published Gandhi, Nasser, Toynbee, Truman, and about 1,500 other authors. In 1983, Schnapper was described by *The Washington Post* as "a redoubtable gadfly." His legacy will endure in the books to come.